Policing and Minority Communi

James F. Albrecht • Garth den Heyer
Perry Stanislas
Editors

Policing and Minority Communities

Contemporary Issues and Global Perspectives

 Springer

Editors
James F. Albrecht
Department of Criminal Justice
and Homeland Security
Pace University
New York, NY, USA

Garth den Heyer
School of Criminology and Criminal Justice
Arizona State University
Tempe, Arizona, USA

Perry Stanislas
Assistant Professor of Policing and Security
Rabdan Academy
Abu Dabi, UAE

ISBN 978-3-030-19184-9   ISBN 978-3-030-19182-5   (eBook)
https://doi.org/10.1007/978-3-030-19182-5

This Springer imprint is published by the registered company Springer Nature Switzerland AG
The registered company address is: Gewerbestrasse 11, 6330 Cham, Switzerland

This book is dedicated to my dear parents, James and Christa Albrecht (RIP), and to my two children, Jimmy and Kristiana, who through their curiosity and enthusiasm give me the energy and desire to stay committed to my research and who provide me with pleasant distraction from life's challenges.

–James F. Albrecht

This book is dedicated to my two grandsons, Liam and Joshua.

Garth Den Heyer

To my father, Horace Charles Stanislas, and cousin, Rosamund Stanislas.

Perry Stanislas

And this book is also dedicated to all of those who work in law enforcement across the globe. We understand and appreciate your commitment and sacrifices.
Blessed are the Peacemakers for they shall be called Children of God.

(Mathew 5:9 King James Bible)

Foreword

The police have power, and they use it. The precise dimensions of their authority certainly vary from country to country, according to legal systems and forms of government, but exercising the coercive power of the state is a defining characteristic of the police institution.

The question of who benefits when police exercise their power is a crucial one. In totalitarian states, the police role is mainly regime protection. In free societies, by contrast, police are expected to protect and serve all the people. These differences are a reflection of the fact that state power can be used to benefit just a few, or to benefit many.

The reality, of course, is much more complex. Totalitarian and free are two ends of a continuum, not a simple dichotomy. The degree to which political, economic, and coercive power are dispersed among competing interests varies widely among countries around the world. Furthermore, the distribution is not static but rather shifts over time, sometimes becoming more concentrated in the hands of a few, sometimes becoming more widely dispersed, and sometimes simply being redistributed among competing groups.

To the extent that states are totalitarian, there is not likely to be much concern about police-community relations or what we now call police legitimacy, as it is simply assumed that police will act in a repressive manner to protect those in power. At the other extreme, however, in democratic and free countries where police are expected to act in the interests of the people, any evidence of poor police-community relations is likely to be a concern, since it may indicate that police are not serving the public as well as they should. For states that are in the process of trying to become more free and democratic, which applies to many countries around the world, finding ways to improve police-community relations is typically a key focus of reform. If the public can be convinced that the police are paying more attention to their needs, that may be a big step toward building more confidence in the rest of the government.

So police-community relations are a concern in many countries. But why are those relations often poor? Some reasons are just inherent in the police function. Police are called upon to handle difficult situations – political protests, labor unrest, and family disputes – in which any actions taken, or not taken, can seem to favor some over others. Also, police are given impossible missions – handling people in mental health crisis, dealing with homeless people, and responding to epidemics of drug addiction – that are far outside their expertise, mainly because society has turned its back on such people. And even more fundamentally, police have the power to make us stop doing things we want to do, like driving too fast or having loud parties – power that we tend to resent when it is applied to us, even though we probably want the police to stop other people from doing the same things.

Besides the kinds of conflict that are just inherent in policing, the fact is that not all residents believe the police treat everyone fairly. It is a common belief that the well-to-do get treated better than average or poor citizens, for example. Since most police are men, it is often a perception, and may be a reality, that women victims do not get the level of service and protection they deserve. And frequently, young people bear the brunt of a lot of police attention – after all, police, their governing authorities, and the people who come to community meetings with complaints are all adults, while kids seem to be the cause of most crime and disorder problems (at least according to adults).

On top of these typical and perhaps endemic sources of police-community strains is one addressed throughout this book — police-minority relations. Racial, ethnic, religious, and other minority groups typically have less political and economic power than the majority groups, putting them at a disadvantage. People who are in the majority sometimes look down on minority groups, stereotype them, discriminate against them, fear them, and even hate them, making members of minority groups that much more powerless and vulnerable.

Where do police fit in this equation? Sometimes, police are openly and officially used to enforce discrimination. In other situations, the official role of police is to protect and serve all citizens, but social and economic discrimination puts minority group members in such a disadvantaged position that they become the focus of a large share of police intrusion and enforcement. This takes place in the name of public safety for all, including the poor who may need police protection even more than others, but one main result is disproportionate stops, arrests, and sanctions against people in marginalized communities. Also, of course, if actual prejudice toward minority group members is common in a society, it is likely that police themselves are affected, consciously or unconsciously.

In principle, at least, and hopefully in practice, it is equally possible that police are the main protectors of the rights and safety of minority group residents and other vulnerable persons. Police typically take an oath to protect the rights of all people, and there has been substantial emphasis on human rights in police training and policy-making in recent decades. This is especially true for countries that are in transition and receiving international assistance of one kind or another – police reform is often high on the agenda, and human rights protection is often a key component of that reform.

The contributions in this book address these kinds of situations across a wide range of countries, including Canada, Kosovo, New Zealand, Nigeria, South Africa, Turkey, and the United States. The details and the context of police-community relations and police-minority relations vary widely from country to country, yet there are similarities in the underlying challenge of providing effective policing that controls serious crime, protects innocent people, brings offenders to justice, and maintains public order while also treating all people fairly within the parameters of universal human rights. The editors and authors are to be congratulated for bringing attention to such an important topic and providing insights from around the world.

Kutztown, PA, USA   Gary Cordner

Contents

Contributors[1]

Magne V. Aarset received his education in Mathematics, Mathematical Statistics, Music, and Psychology at the University of Oslo, Norway. He has broad industrial experience from working in a number of different fields, including in European aerospace and in the Norwegian insurance industry. He now lectures and conducts research at the Norwegian University of Science and Technology (NTNU) and BI Norwegian Business School. His main field of research is within psychometrics.

James F. Albrecht served in the European Union Rule of Law (EULEX) Mission in Kosovo as police chief in charge of criminal investigations from 2007 through 2010. He is also a 22-year veteran of the NYPD who retired as commanding officer of NYPD Transit Bureau District 20. He was a first responder and incident command staff manager at the 11 September 2001 terrorist attack on the World Trade Center and possesses separate master's degrees in Criminal Justice, Human Physiology, and History and is currently a professor of Criminal Justice and Homeland Security at Pace University in New York. Moreover, he is editor and coauthor of a number of books and journal articles on policing, terrorism, criminology, and criminal justice, often from a global perspective.

Amos Oyesoji Aremu is a professor of Counseling and Criminal Justice at the Department of Guidance and Counseling at the University of Ibadan in Nigeria. His research interests cover police behaviors, police culture, and dynamics of police and public relationships in polity. He is one of the foremost police scholars in Africa.

Hasan Arslan is professor of Criminal Justice at Western Connecticut State University. He received his PhD in Criminal Justice from Sam Houston State University in Texas and is considered an international expert in police-involved shootings.

---

[1] The editors would like to extend their appreciation to all of the book's contributors.

Christiaan Bezuidenhout holds the following degrees: BA (Criminology), BA Honors (Criminology), MA (Criminology), DPhil (Criminology), and MSc in Criminology and Criminal Justice from the University of Oxford. He is currently a professor attached to the Department of Social Work and Criminology, University of Pretoria, where he teaches psychocriminology, criminal justice, and contemporary criminology at the undergraduate and postgraduate levels.

S. Hakan Can is a retired police chief in the Turkish National Police. He received his PhD in Criminal Justice at Sam Houston State University in Texas and is a professor of Criminal Justice at Penn State University.

Durant Frantzen is a professor of Criminal Justice at Texas A&M University. He received his PhD from Sam Houston State University in Texas.

Robert Hanser is a professor of Criminal Justice at the University of Louisiana at Monroe. He received his PhD at Sam Houston State University in Texas and is considered an authority on psychological issues impacting law enforcement and criminal justice officials.

Garth den Heyer is a professor at Arizona State University and Senior Research Fellow at the Police Foundation. He is also a contributing faculty member at Walden University and an associate professor at the Scottish Institute of Policing Research. He served with the New Zealand Police for 38 years, retiring as an inspector. His main research interests are policing, militarization, service delivery effectiveness, policy development, strategic thinking, and organizational reform.

Rune Glomseth received his education at the Norwegian Police Academy. He has a broad background in the police and now serves as associate professor in organization and management at the Norwegian Police University College in Oslo. He conducts research in management, organizational culture, and changes in police organizations.

Robert Jacobs is a large-scale change expert and was an instrumental part of the Charleston Illumination Project team. He has worked with countries, companies, and communities for the past 30 years in a wide variety of change efforts, always building partnerships between key stakeholders so they can formulate their collective future. It was his honor to serve the city of Charleston, its police department, and citizens in this exciting and very worthwhile project.

Kylon Middleton was a project leader in the Charleston Illumination Project. He serves as the pastor of Mount Zion African Methodist Episcopal Church in Charleston, South Carolina.

Nathan Moran is chairman of the Criminal Justice Department at Midwestern State University and senior distinguished professor of Criminology and Criminal

Justice. His research interests are in international organized crime, terrorism, law enforcement, and comparative systems analysis.

Colleen Morin is a professor of Criminal Justice at the University of Nevada in Reno. She received her Juris Doctorate from Gonzaga University.

Robert Morin is a professor of Political Science at Western Nevada College. He received his Juris Doctorate from Gonzaga University and a PhD in Political Science from the University of Nevada at Reno.

Gregory Mullen is the former chief of police for the City of Charleston, South Caroline. He is now the associate vice president for Public Safety and chief of police at Clemson University.

Catherine Parent has a Master in Education and is a registered nurse. She is presently a clinician promoting mental health for individuals, families, and communities in Vancouver area of British Columbia in Canada, who has conducted extensive research on mental health in policing.

Richard Parent is a retired police sergeant who worked in the Delta Police Department in British Columbia, Canada. He is now an associate professor in the School of Criminology at Simon Fraser University. He has written many books and articles on a variety of police-related topics and is considered an expert in police-involved shootings and suicide by police.

Kim Sadique is a senior lecturer in Community and Criminal Justice at De Montfort University in Leicester in the United Kingdom. She has published extensively on the impact of religion and hate crime on policing.

Michael R. Sanchez has 20 years of domestic police practitioner experience having served in positions from patrolman to deputy chief of police. He is a former director of personnel and administration for the UNMIK Police in Kosovo and is a former regional commander in the United Nations Mission in Haiti. He currently teaches criminal justice at the University of Texas Rio Grande Valley in Brownsville, Texas.

Margaret Seidler is the founding leader of the Illumination Project and is the polarity thinking master at Seidler & Associates in Charleston, South Carolina.

Perry Stanislas is an Assistant Professor of Policing and Security at Rabdan Security Academy in Abu Dabi, UAE. He has over 35 years policing starting his career as a security and intelligence officer for a Pan African political organization, before joining the Bedfordshire Police in the United Kingdom. He currently leads teaching and research on police and security leadership and related matters.

Theresa C. Tobin is a police chief within the New York City Police Department in charge of coordinating interorganizational collaboration. She received her PhD from the University at Albany, SUNY, and is a Professor of Criminal Justice at Molloy College in New York.

Fahredin Verbovci received his Master of Economics Sciences in Entrepreneurship and Local Development at the State University of Pristina in 2012. He is currently a police colonel in the Kosovo Police and serves as a professor in the Faculty of Public Safety.

Gregory Whitaker is a retired police captain in the Charleston Police Department. He is now an instructor at Trident Technical College in Charleston, South Carolina.

Part I
Policing and Minority Communities

Chapter 1
Evaluating Police-Community Relations Globally

James F. Albrecht

Introduction

At the inception of professional policing in the 1820s, Sir Robert Peel emphasized the relevance of the role that the community should play in assessing the efficacy of the police and in setting the priorities for professional public security. After highlighting the basic mission of the police in crime and disorder control, the second of Peel's nine principles of policing (Lee 1901) clearly delineates that *"(t)he ability of the police to perform their duties is dependent upon public approval of police actions,"* and continues in Principle five with the assertion that the *"(p)olice seek and preserve public favor not by catering to the public opinion but by constantly demonstrating absolute impartial service to the law."* And the most noteworthy point noted was that the police *"at all times, should maintain a relationship with the public that gives reality to the historic tradition that the police are the public and the public are the police."* It is obvious from the initial foundation of the law enforcement profession almost two centuries ago that the input and feedback of the public being served must be viewed as being paramount in assessing the effectiveness of police performance. Clearly the relevance of these perspectives applies to all members of the public, not only to those who have connections with the political leadership and the elite, but to all citizens, regardless of social class, ethnicity or other influential factor. More importantly, failing these vital principles will result in the loss of trust and confidence in the police, the criminal justice system, and likely the government as a whole.

J. F. Albrecht (✉)
Department of Criminal Justice and Homeland Security, Pace University,
New York, NY, USA

© Springer Nature Switzerland AG 2019
J. F. Albrecht et al. (eds.), *Policing and Minority Communities*,
https://doi.org/10.1007/978-3-030-19182-5_1

Examining Public Perceptions of Police Legitimacy

The actions and legitimacy of the police have been scrutinized since the profession's inception in the 1820s, however empirical analysis of citizen perceptions of the police did not take place until 100 years later in the United States (Bellman 1935; Parratt 1936). It was not until the 1960s that more concrete efforts were undertaken to examine police-community relations, normally following allegations that the police overstepped their authority or used force excessively (Roche and Oberwittler 2018). It was Weber (1947) who attempted to examine, through his theory of interpretive sociology, just how public perceptions of the police and other government actors are subjectively interpreted. This is supported by recent research which has indicated that the public will grant the police legitimacy if they feel they are being treated with fairness and respect, regardless of the outcome of the actions of the police (Donner et al. 2015; Jackson et al. 2013; Roche and Oberwittler 2018; Tyler 2011).

Understanding Public Perceptions of the Police

It was Bellman in 1935 who first attempted to gauge police performance by examining public perceptions of the police. Decades later, Decker (1981) examined the impact that individual and contextual variables play on citizen attitudes as it relates to the police. While Decker concluded that factors such as race, socioeconomic status, local crime rates, and victimization may influence personal perceptions of local law enforcement, a vast number of research studies concluded that recent 'negative' incidents that had raised distrust and doubt in the professionalism of the police, more so when sensationalized by the media, tend to dramatically and immediately reduce the generally positive image of the police (Jesilow and Meyer 2001; Kaminski and Jefferis 1998; Lasley 1994; Tuch and Weitzer 1997).

It has been proposed that the findings of public perception surveys evaluating police performance and attitudes could be utilized to influence the development of agency policies (Bordua and Tifft 1971; Klyman and Kruckenberg 1974) and organizational priorities (Peak et al. 1992; Thurman and Reisig 1996; Weisel 1999). While public perception surveys have not been found to be generally used by American police jurisdictions, even when they have been conducted, there is no strong evidence to indicate that their findings have influenced later decisions and policy reform measures of law enforcement administrators. However, since such critical factors as race, socioeconomic status, and age have been commonly found to influence public confidence and support, or lack there of, for the police (Brown and Benedict 2002), it is recommended that government officials and police executives strongly consider the incorporation of community policing strategies, which rely on the direct input of the public into police operational prioritization into their decision-making and policy revision processes.

A newer perspective advocates procedural justice theory (Tyler et al. 2015) as the contemporary method for assessing public perceptions of the police, particularly in western societies. This notion received further emphasis in the Final Report of the President's Task Force on twenty-first Century Policing (2015) that identified the need to strengthen the relationship between the police and the community in an effort to build trust and enhance legitimacy as the first as the first of six priorities for contemporary policing. Individuals perceive their interaction with the police to be positive or negative, not only based on that specific police-citizen contact, but also based on the influence of prior attitudes and their belief as to whether they were treated fairly. It is therefore proposed that individuals will view the police as being more legitimate when they believe that they have been given sufficient opportunity to directly participate in the identification of policing priorities and when they additionally believe that those policies will be being implemented fairly (Tyler and Sevier 2014; Tyler et al. 2010). And thus we return to Peel's nine principles of policing, which repeatedly advocate public input into local policing initiatives and practices, and which rely on citizen feedback as to how police agencies are perceived to be functioning.

Conceptualizing Public Perceptions of the Police: 'Trust' v. 'Confidence'

The terms 'trust' and 'confidence' have often been used interchangeably when researchers and the public have discussed citizen perceptions of the police (Cao and Hou 2001; Center for the Study of Democracy 2011; Devos et al. 2002; Jackson and Sunshine 2007; Kaariainen 2008). However, there are fundamental differences between these two factors that require clarification. Generally, the term 'trust' in the police or any government organization is closely affiliated with the maintenance of proper ethical standards, where as 'confidence' in public service agencies can be viewed as an indication that a specific entity is viewed as performing effectively. In essence, trust can be said to be associated with integrity, while confidence apparently is aligned with perceived performance.

In contrast, Uslaner (2005) differentiated between 'moralistic trust' and 'strategic trust,' delineating that 'moralistic trust' is based on expectations of behavior and 'strategic trust' relies on experiences and observations. It would appear, however, that 'moralistic trust' could be associated with trust (i.e. ethics), while 'strategic trust' could be construed to be related to actual organizational performance. Uslaner did not specifically differentiate between public trust and public confidence in the police, but appeared to present competing versions of trust, i.e. 'strategic' versus 'moralistic' trust, to portray the concepts of what are generally delineated as 'confidence' and 'trust' in government officials.

Tyler (2001) evaluated differences in public confidence in the police through the comparison of responses by majority and minority group members in the United

States. Tyler specifically conducted survey research in Chicago, Illinois and Oakland, California. This research was mainly oriented at measuring public perceptions of police performance and public confidence in the police organization. These surveys did include one item that specifically stated: "*The Police are generally honest.*" in an effort to potentially evaluate public trust in the police. But Tyler's resulting statistical analysis did involve a 10-item scale to gauge public confidence in the police, which actually incorporated the single item related to respondent trust in the police.

Tyler (2005) extended his research into disparities between white and minority residents as it related to public trust and confidence in the police in New York City. In this study, Tyler examined both '*institutional trust,*' which he described as "*beliefs about the degree to which the police are honest and care for the members of the communities they police* (Tyler 2005, p. 324), and '*motive based trust,*' defined as involving "*inferences about the motives and intentions of the police and reflects the concept of fiduciary trust, which is central to discussions among legal scholars* (Tyler 2005, p. 325). Tyler measured '*institutional trust*' through an 8-item scale that included statements that examined factors specifically related to perceptions of citizen confidence in the police, public trust in police leadership, police legitimacy, organizational dishonesty, among others; and gauged '*motive based trust*' upon respondent opinions related to three items: police empathy, concern for public needs, and the provision of "*honest explanations for their actions*" (Tyler 2005, p. 329). In his concluding discussion, Tyler combined institutional and motive based trust into his findings related to the concept of public '*trust and confidence*' in the police, but did not specifically delineate or define these terms within this research endeavor.

Jackson and Bradford (2010) examined the phenomena involving public trust and confidence in the police from a British perspective. Their primary thesis is that when attempting to measure public trust or confidence in the police, it would be best to incorporate four inter-related survey items into the scale to enhance the measurement of these concepts. Specifically, Jackson and Bradford recommended the creation of four separate indices to analyze: (1) trust in police effectiveness, (2) trust in police fairness, (3) trust in police engagement and shared values, and (4) overall confidence in policing in an effort to best measure general public trust and confidence in the police. In addition, Merry et al. (2012) also incorporated trust in police into a scale examining public confidence in the police in the United Kingdom.

In contrast, Van Craen (2013) examined public trust in the police in Belgium through the use of a one-item measure of trust that provided respondents with a 5-point Likert scale to directly report whether they trusted the police, which correlates to similar survey instruments utilized by Cao and Hou (2001); Cao and Zhao (2005); Kaariainen (2007); and MacDonald and Stokes (2006). It is therefore not uncommon for researchers analyzing public trust in the police to rely solely on a one-item measure or variable.

Mazerolle et al. (2013) conducted a meta-analysis of 30 studies related to police legitimacy and trust. This seminal examination utilized the terms related to citizen '*trust*' and '*confidence*' in the police interchangeably, and did not distinguish between the two concepts. It should be noted that this compilation of research studies had focused more on police legitimacy than on other issues. It is consequently difficult to draw conclusions about public "trust" in the police or the conceptualization of this concept (and public confidence in the police) from this meta-analysis when the term is routinely exchanged with the term '*confidence*' throughout the paper. It may have been beneficial to clearly define these terms, as will be done within this dissertation research, in order to make interpretation of the findings clearer and more relevant to practical applications. This generalization of terminology is often a contentious issue when assessing the value of meta-analysis based research.

In summary, it can be concluded that researchers have generally utilized the terms '*trust*' and '*confidence*' in the police interchangeably. In many cases, when the terms have been differentiated, some researchers have incorporated the concept of trust in the police into a multi-item scale or index in order to measure citizen confidence in the police. As such, it is likely that researchers will continue to not clearly differentiate between the two terms when conducting studies on police legitimacy.

Public Perceptions of Police: Global Perspectives

Generally speaking, developing nations in Eastern Europe, Central Asia, the Middle East, and Northern and Sub-Saharan Africa are plagued by limited trust in government authorities, including the police (Transparency International 2018). The most unstable countries, including those plagued by armed conflict with corresponding rule of law vacuum (e.g. Somalia, Sudan, Yemen, Afghanistan, and Syria), are often relegated to receiving the lowest scores in general corruption perception surveys. Nations with established democratic ideals and lower crime rates, such as those in North America (i.e. United States and Canada), western Europe (e.g. United Kingdom and the Scandinavian countries), and Australia and New Zealand tend to receive the highest grades and generally tend to be viewed as being the least corrupt.

When it comes specifically to the rule of law arena, trust in the administration of justice and law enforcement generally appears to score higher than other government and public service agencies. Globally 68% of individuals report that they have confidence in their local police. Results vary across the globe with rates of 82% in the USA and Canada, 80% in Western Europe and 80% Southeast Asia through 60% in Sub-Saharan Africa and 42% in Latin America and the Caribbean (Gallup 2018). Once again, confidence in the police appears to coincide with crime victimization rate and the extent of democratic practice.

In the United States, public confidence in the police stands at 57%, but the rate varies by race, as Whites have the highest confidence in the police with 61%, Hispanics at 45%, and Blacks at a disappointing 30%. More disturbing is that the rates for Hispanics (−14%) and Blacks (−5%) has actually declined dramatically over the last 5 years (Norman 2017).

In Europe, public trust in the police varies from high scores exceeding 85% in Switzerland and the four Scandinavian nations to scores below 40% as one moves farther east across Europe, including the Russian Federation and Belarus. It appears that lower crime rates and perceived lower levels of police and government corruption in Europe coincide strongly with higher trust in the police institution (Kaariainen 2007).

Conclusion

In conclusion, it would appear that a number of macro- and micro-level factors strongly influence public confidence and trust in the police. The macro-level variables generally associated with lower levels of public satisfaction in the police are regional armed conflict, political instability, higher crime rate, higher criminal victimization rate, perceptions of rampant police and government corruption, and lack of confidence in local democratic principles. The predominant micro-level factors correlated with lower levels of public trust in local rule of law practices include diminished or negligible involvement of citizens in the establishment of policing priorities and policies, preconceived beliefs that they will not be treated fairly when engaging elements of the criminal justice system, prior negative experiences with police and justice agencies, recent sensationalized events that tarnish the image of the police (whether accurate or not), race, ethnicity, lower socio-economic status, age, and membership in a politically underrepresented group.

It is therefore recommended that police administrators and government officials take the time to re-acclimate themselves with Peel's nine principles of policing (Lee 1901). The concept of *"the police are the public and the public are the police"* (Principle 7) has not lost its appeal or relevance after two centuries. Policing priorities, policies and actions should be guided by *'public approval'* (Principle 2). Front line police personnel should strive to *'secure and maintain the respect of the public'* (Principle 3) *'by constantly demonstrating absolute impartial service to the law'* (Principle 5). The use of force by police should be avoided, while *'persuasion, advice and warning'* (Principle 6) in an effort to *'secure the willing cooperation of the public'* (Principle 2) should be the guiding ideals.

It would accordingly be appropriate for law enforcement executives to consider the traditional form of community policing, which combines crime control through localized problem-solving with direct public input into organizational priorities and policies, as a legitimate option for enhancing legitimacy and increasing public trust and confidence in the police. Measuring the effectiveness of the police should not only include evaluation of index and other crime rates, and arrest and traffic enforcement data, but should incorporate public perception surveys that evaluate perceptions of trust, confidence, fairness and performance using a variety of variables. Technology may guide the future of policing and crime prevention, but it is the traditional doctrines of public policing (i.e. Peel's principles) and the later evolution to community policing (Albrecht 2012; Goldstein 1979; Trojanowicz 1982;

Trojanowicz and Bucqueroux 1994) that should continue to be comprehensively integrated into police agency ideologies and practices to enhance public input and improve agency transparency and legitimacy.

References

Albrecht, J. F. (2012). Analyzing the implementation and evolution of community policing in the United States and Scandinavia. In M. De Guzman, A. M. Das, & D. K. Das (Eds.), *Strategic responses to crime: Thinking globally, acting locally*. Boca Raton/Florida: Taylor and Francis/ CRC Press.

Bellman, A. (1935). A police service rating scale. *Journal of Criminal Law and Criminology, 26*, 74–114.

Bordua, D. J., & Tifft, L. L. (1971). Citizen interview, organizational feedback, and police-community relations decisions. *Law and Society Review, 5*, 155–182.

Brown, B., & Benedict, W. R. (2002). Perceptions of the police: Past findings, methodological issues, conceptual issues and policy implications. *Policing: An International Journal of Police Strategies & Management, 25*(3), 543–580.

Cao, L., & Hou, C. (2001). A comparison of confidence in the police in China and in the United States. *Journal of Criminal Justice, 29*, 87–99.

Cao, L., & Zhao, J. S. (2005). Confidence in the police in Latin America. *Journal of Criminal Justice, 33*(5), 403–412.

Center for the Study of Democracy. (2011). *Public trust in the criminal justice system – an instrument for penal policy assessment. Policy Brief No. 29*. Sofia: Center for the Study of Democracy.

Decker, S. H. (1981). Citizen attitudes toward the police: A review of past findings and suggestions for future policy. *Journal of Police Science and Administration, 9*, 80–87.

Devos, T., Spin, D., & Schwartz, S. H. (2002). Conflicts between human values and trust in institutions. *British Journal of Psychology, 41*, 481–484.

Donner, C., Makaly, J., Fridell, L., & Jennings, W. (2015). Policing and procedural justice: A state-of-the-art review. *Policing: An International Journal of Police Strategies and Management, 38*, 153–172.

Gallup. (2018). *Global law and order 2018*. Washington, D.C.: Gallup Analytics.

Goldstein, H. (1979). Improving policing: A problem-oriented approach. *NPPA Journal, 25*(2), 236–258.

Jackson, J., & Bradford, B. (2010). What is trust and confidence in the police? *Policing: A Journal of Policy and Practice, 4*(3), 241–248.

Jackson, J., & Sunshine, J. (2007). *Public confidence in policing: A neo-Durkhein perspective* (Vol. 47, pp. 214–233). Oxford: Oxford University Press.

Jackson, J., Bradford, B., Stanko, E., & Hohl, K. (2013). *Just authority? Trust in the Police in England and Wales*. London: Routledge.

Jesilow, P., & Meyer, J. A. (2001). The effect of police misconduct on public attitudes: A quasi-experiment. *Journal of Crime and Justice, 24*(1), 109–121.

Kaariainen, J. T. (2007). Trust in the Police in 16 European countries: A multilevel analysis. *European Journal of Criminology, 4*(4), 409–435.

Kaariainen, J. T. (2008). Why do the Finns trust the police? *Journal of Scandinavian Studies in Criminology and Crime Prevention, 9*, 141–159.

Kaminski, R. J., & Jefferis, E. S. (1998). The effect of a violent televised arrest on public perceptions of the police: A partial test of Easton's theoretical framework. *Policing: An International Journal of Police Strategies & Management, 21*, 683–706.

Klyman, F. I., & Kruckenberg, J. (1974). A methodology for assessing citizen perceptions of the police. *Journal of Criminal Justice, 2*, 219–233.

Lasley, J. R. (1994). The impact of the Rodney King incident on citizen attitudes toward police. *Policing and Society, 3*, 245–255.

Lee, W. L. M. (1901). *A history of police of England*. London: Methuan and Company.

MacDonald, J., & Stokes, R. J. (2006). Race, social capital and trust in the police. *Urban Affairs Review, 41*(3), 358–375.

Mazerolle, L., Bennett, S., Davis, J., Sargeant, E., & Manning, M. (2013). *Legitimacy in policing: A systematic review*. Oslo: Campbell Systematic Reviews.

Merry, S., Power, N., McManus, M., & Alison, L. (2012). Drivers of public trust and confidence in police in the UK. *International Journal of Police Science & Management, 14*(2), 118–135.

Norman, J. (2017). *Confidence in police back at historic average*. Washington, D.C.: Gallup Analytics.

Parratt, S. D. (1936). A critique of the Bellman police service rating scale. *Journal of the American Institute of Criminal Law and Criminology, 27*, 895–905.

Peak, K., Bradshaw, R. V., & Glensor, R. W. (1992). Improving citizen perceptions of the police: 'Back to the basics' with a community policing strategy. *Journal of Criminal Justice, 20*, 25–40.

Roche, S., & Oberwittler, D. (2018). Towards a broader view of police–citizen relations: How societal cleavages and political contexts shape trust and distrust, legitimacy and illegitimacy. In D. Oberwittler & S. Roche (Eds.), *Police–citizen relations across the world: Comparing sources and contexts of trust and legitimacy*. New York: Routledge.

Thurman, Q. C., & Reisig, M. D. (1996). Community-oriented research in an era of community policing. *American Behavioral Scientist, 39*, 570–586.

Transparency International. (2018). *Corruption perceptions index 2017*. Berlin: Transparency International.

Trojanowicz, R. C. (1982). An evaluation of a neighborhood foot patrol program in Flint, Michigan. In *East Lansing*. Michigan: Michigan State University.

Trojanowicz, R. C., & Bucqueroux, B. (1994). *Community policing: How to get started*. Cincinnati: Anderson Publishers.

Tuch, S. A., & Weitzer, R. (1997). The polls: Racial differences in attitudes toward the police. *Public Opinion Quarterly, 61*, 642–664.

Tyler, T. R. (2001). Public trust and confidence in legal authorities: What do majority and minority group members want from the law and legal institutions? *Behavioral Sciences & the Law, 19*(2), 215–235.

Tyler, T. R. (2005). Policing in black and white: Ethnic group differences in trust and confidence in the police. *Police Quarterly, 8*(3), 322–342.

Tyler, T. (2011). *Why people cooperate: The role of social motivations*. Princeton: Princeton University Press.

Tyler, T. R., & Sevier, J. (2014). How do the courts create popular legitimacy? *Albany Law Review, 77*, 101–143.

Tyler, T. R., Schulhofer, S. J., & Huq, A. Z. (2010). Legitimacy and deterrence effects in counter-terrorism policing. *Law & Society Review, 44*, 365–402.

Tyler, T., Goff, P., & MacCoun, R. (2015). The impact of psychological science on policing in the United States: Procedural justice, legitimacy, and effective law enforcement. *Psychological Science in the Public Interest, 16*, 75–109.

Uslaner, E. M. (2005). *Varieties of trust. FEEM Working Paper No. 69.05*. Milan: Fondazione Eni Enrico Mattei.

Van Craen, M. (2013). Explaining majority and minority trust in police. *Justice Quarterly, 30*(6), 1042–1067.

Weisel, D. (1999). *Conducting community surveys: A practical guide for law enforcement*. Washington, DC: US Department of Justice, Bureau of Justice Statistics, Monograph NCJ 178246.

Chapter 2
International Attitudes to Teaching Religion and Faith and the Policing of Minority Communities

Perry Stanislas and Kim Sadique

Introduction

Much research has been conducted to evaluate the nature and effectiveness of police training. However, there is the need for a more thorough evaluation of the role that the teaching of religion and faith issues play in the education and training of today's law enforcement officials across the globe, with specific attention paid to the context of histories of ethnic, racial, and other sectional conflicts and the attempts to reduce them. The chapter is exploratory in character and draws from initial data obtained from police trainers and researchers involved in police education and training and is a prelude to a more comprehensive survey on the treatment of religion and faith matters in different policing jurisdictions. The underlying assumption underpinning the research is the teaching of these issues as an indicator of the sensitivity to societal differences in efforts to effectively police diverse communities characterised by ethnic, racial, and other important cleavages.

Representative Bureaucracy and Minority Influence

One of the oldest and most common ways in which administrations have dealt with managing diverse communities, especially in the context of histories of political and economic tension and dominance, is the representative bureaucracy route, whereby a member or members of the marginalised group are employed or given positions within the institutions in society. Perhaps the most cynical, and not necessarily

P. Stanislas (✉)
Assistant Professor of Policing and Security, Rabdan Academy, Abu Dabi, UAE
e-mail: pstanislas@dmu.ac.uk

K. Sadique
De Montfort University, Leicester, UK

© Springer Nature Switzerland AG 2019
J. F. Albrecht et al. (eds.), *Policing and Minority Communities*,
https://doi.org/10.1007/978-3-030-19182-5_2

inaccurate, account of this practice is detailed by Machiavelli (1963) in his classic text 'The *Prince.*' According to Machiavelli's view, the appointment of members of dominated groups serves a largely symbolic legitimising function; in normalising the status quo in the eyes of the group from which they are drawn from, who are characterised by national, ethnic, or religious differences from those in power.

The weakness of this tactic is empirically elucidated by Subramaniam (1967) in his study of ethnic representation in India. Subramaniam argues that the values, beliefs, and worldview of minority members within public administrations are largely marginalised, due to in the first instance their small numbers and lack of organisational and cultural power which reduces their capacity to have significant influence on their environment (see Essed 1991). Moreover, minorities become assimilated and consciously strive for acceptance which can become an important element of their survival strategy. Allport (1987) noted this can take exaggerated or extreme forms which can be seen by the hostility of 'non Jewish Jews' to mainstream Jews in the US during the 1900s (Liebman 1979). In this instance, the former viewed themselves as being more advanced than their backward brethren, who were seen as holding onto ancient beliefs and practices which had no place in modern western society. Shedding traditional religious beliefs in a desire to become more accepted and assimilated into the dominant group is an essential element in minority strategies. According to Subramaniam, the representative bureaucracy approach simply changes the outward appearance of institutions in symbolic ways, with little import for their internal workings. An important example of this was the appointment of a Sikh Major General Kuldip Singh Brar to lead the controversial assault on the Sikh Golden Temple resulting in the massacre of large numbers of Sikhs as part of operation Blue Star (Tully 2014).

The dynamics elucidated by Subramaniam inter alia are particularly pertinent for ethnic minority police officers who are often expected to carry the historical weight of mitigating police racism, the exigencies and interests of their police superiors, and the often ill-informed and unreasonable expectations of the ethnic communities they come from and wider society (Cashmore 2002, Rowe 2016). Another route to making institutions more culturally and ethnically diverse and sensitive to the beliefs of other social groups, is through the education and training, and in this context of police officers specifically (Stanislas 2009). Religion and faith matters can feature within this process because of its importance for individuals and group social identity, communal attitudes, and behaviour (see Sadique and Stanislas 2016). The most obvious example of this is the growing importance of Islam to international law enforcement and other institutions (Hakeem et al. 2012, Mkutu 2017) or the need to understand crime motivated by witchcraft in particular parts of the world (Petrus 2016).

Definition of Religion and Faith

Religion according to Sadique (2014) refers to:

> 'a belief in [God(s), Humans, Nature, Self], that often requires faith in one or more of these having influence over our lives, that is demonstrated through certain practices, rituals, rites and 'ties fast' its followers to itself and other followers (in a non-geographical community) who share the same values.'

The term 'faith 'appears to be more simplistic referring to 'a specific system of religious beliefs.' Yet, in the context of understanding faith communities and multi-faith training and education there is no consensus as to what 'faith' actually means. In general it refers to communities that share a 'system of religious beliefs' and most commonly to those in the same (or near) geographical area. To confound the issue further, Weller (2005) notes the addition of 'inter-faith' to the lexicon and the use of these terms interchangeably renders unclear what is meant by each term. Weller (2001, 80) tries to delineate these terms, stating:

'When a society or an event or a project is described as 'multi-faith', it usually means that it includes a variety of religious groups. While the use of multi-faith highlights variety, the use of the term 'inter-faith' points more to the relationships between religions and the people who belong to them.'

For clarity, this chapter discusses faith communities and issues of multi-faith education and training in terms of awareness and understanding of the diverse range of religious/faith groups in each society (because this is the term used most often in relation to police training), rather than inter-faith relationships, although it is clear that these 'relationships' within and between faiths are central to social conflict/cohesion and policing thereof.

Religious beliefs can play a significant role in understanding opposition to new postmodern identities around the world, such as growing recognition of same-sex relationships in many societies, which in itself can become a source of conflict with those who hold traditional conservative values that the police have to negotiate in order to effectively carry out their duties (Stanislas 2013). In most societies the state police see themselves as representing the normative order and its religious influences. This can be seen by the Ugandan and Jamaican police where they were the principal tool of the state in tackling same-sex relationships, which was viewed as a form of sexual deviance (Stanislas 2016: 177–178). This inseparability between the dominant normative order, that include religious influences and state policing, can be seen in one of the less well-known roles of the early Metropolitan Police which involved clearing local neighbourhoods and the streets of drunks prior to Sunday church services.

Police, Conflict, and Effective Community Relations

Police concern with issues of religion and faith have their roots in conflicts which contributed to making the issue of community relations important in countries such as the US, England and parts of Britain, such as Northern Ireland; and also linked to the emergence of community policing (Grabosky 2009). However, elsewhere in developing countries such as, India the issue of religious and ethnic conflict has been intrinsic to that country since its birth as an independent nation (Weiner 1978, Varshney 2003). The increasing influence of human rights consideration in policing has led to greater sensitivity to matters around religion and faith. In particular, the Human Rights Standards and Practice for the Police (United Nations 2004) has numerous recommendations that indirectly and directly touch on religious matters. Among them are calls for:

- Law enforcement officials to demonstrate respect and preserve the human dignity and uphold the human rights of all individuals.
- Develop means to ascertain the specific needs of local communities and respond to them accordingly.
- The police must not discriminate on the basis of race, gender, religion, national origin inter alia.

Good practice in policing around matters involving religion and faith can be found and drawn from numerous sources. How each police jurisdiction responds to these issues is shaped by its own unique history and immediate political and cultural circumstances and challenges.

Methods

The methods used to inform this chapter were largely driven by convenience sampling (Bryman 2008). The authors contacted ten colleagues by mail who were trainers and researchers that specialised in police education and training matters in different countries. The purpose of the communication was to establish whether matters around religion and faith were included in the syllabi of the police training establishments they were associated or worked with, or addressed in other ways. In the majority of cases, the authors were able to contact these individuals directly, but in three cases third parties were approached to ascertain the information in question.

In terms of a sample, countries from the developing world primarily were chosen for this exploratory exercise given the existing working relations between the police institutions in question and the authors. Matters regarding policing diverse community and developing good community relations, and ideas and practices around these issues, are well-established in many advanced western liberal democratic policing jurisdictions. Examples of this are the US, Canada, Australia inter alia (see Stanislas 2014). Moreover, both authors have taught police officers and students interested in policing about many of the aforementioned issues at De Montfort University in England. The research sought to ascertain what activity in the areas of improving minority relations generally, and the role of religion and faith specifically, took place in the education and training of police officers in developing countries.

Of the 10 countries initially approached, responses were received from seven (70%) within the stipulated time frame. In one instance, two individuals were approached in one country i.e. India given the existence of numerous police training authorities at the state and regional level, unlike many countries that had single policing training authorities. According to Neyroud and Wain (2014: 120), there are

162 police training centres in India. The respondents chosen had knowledge of several police training authorities in India. The full study will survey both developing countries and advanced police jurisdictions. The majority of the countries included in the sample were chosen because of histories of ethnic and other tensions.

The countries included in this examination are:

- Trinidad and Tobago
- Guyana (South America)
- Kenya
- India
- South Africa
- St Lucia
- Britain

Summary of Country Findings

A common feature of the majority of the countries surveyed with a history of ethnic and other social group tension, such as India, Guyana, and Kenya is the great degree of sensitivity, if not nervousness, in speaking openly about these matters. In some cases the behaviour of the authorities can be described as duplicitous, which can clearly be seen in Kenya and highlighted in the recent presidential elections in August 2017 and repeat election of October 2017. The dominant ruling elite consists of the Kikuyu and Kalenjin ethnic groups who monopolise all state security and major economic institutions (Mwakikagile 2007; Mkutu 2017). Moreover, these elite have used their control of institutions to target and orchestrate state violence disproportionately against the Luo ethnic community which was evident during the presidential elections (Human Rights Watch 2017; The World 2017).

Any attempts to draw attention to these glaring facts of tribal dominance in Kenya is met with charges of trying to stir up ethnic tensions by the ruling elite, and its media, and has resulted in opposition politicians and critics being arrested on the grounds of 'hate speech' (Mwakikagile 2007). Kenya provides one of the clearest illustrations of how ethnic sensitivities are managed in many jurisdictions which is to use the full weight of the state machinery to silence discussions on the matter to mask a system of power and rewards based entirely on ethnicity (The World 2017). As a consequence, matters regarding ethnicity are unlikely to play any role in the formal activities or language of the Kenyan Police; especially in the context of training and education. In other countries, such as Guyana, and India matters regarding ethnicity and religion are equally extremely sensitive and not found on the police training syllabus. In Guyana, the ethnic makeup is similar to that of Trinidad and Tobago where members of the African and East Indian elite has played on ethnicity, similar to leaders in South Saharan African countries, in very cynical ways to buttress power and ensuring the survival of their regimes (Hintzen 2006).

While the South African policing education system can be viewed as being very progressive given its sensitivity to matters around human rights, anti-discrimination and minority relations, it stays clear from matters around religion. This is an outcome of the legacy of Apartheid and Afrikaner dominance which was closely related to the Protestant Church (Laloo 2008). The contemporary emphasis on constitutional secularity has made any teaching of religious matters as near taboo in South Africa which is reflected in police education and training matters, which according to sources has left the police service ill-equipped in understanding and effectively policing a very diverse society. Moreover, the reduction of the length of basic police training reduces the opportunity for these types of topics to be addressed.

Case Studies

St Lucia

The small Eastern Caribbean country of St Lucia historically has been a staunch Christian country with the Catholic Church dominating religious matters since the post slavery period (Jesse 1994). The Catholic Church has had a major influence on attitudes to morality, family life, and mainstream education, through its schools which were the first formally established educational institutions in the country (Harmsen et al. 2012). The Catholic Church was once an important influence on the Royal St Lucian Police Service and the behaviour of its officers, such as the highly-regarded Sgt Cyril from Castries, also known for his strong religious convictions which informed his attitude to policing (Stanislas 2017). According to the Joshua Project, 96% of St Lucians are Christians with the Catholic Church still maintaining its dominance in faith matters. This dominance has been eroded by the rise of more evangelic dominations of American origins who over the last couple of decades have made a presence on the island and the Caribbean region generally (Stanislas 2016: 175). Those who belong to Evangelical denominations constitute approximately 14% of the population.

The religious group who has caused the most anxiety for the St Lucian authorities are Rastafarians for a number of reasons. Rastafarianism has been described as a mixture of a Christian-based messianic cult and social movement that is based on preserving African identity, which was attacked and eroded as a consequences of slavery and colonial indoctrination (Gerloff 2006, Stanislas 2016: 174). One of the fundamental assertions of Rastafarianism is that the Jesus of the Christian bible was not white as depicted in western culture, nor was most of the earliest founders of the Christian faith (Beckford 1998, Spencer 2003). For example, the Ethiopian Orthodox Church is one of the oldest Churches in Christianity which preceded the establishment of churches in most parts of the world (Casper 2015). Doctrinally and ideologically Rastafarianism stands in stark opposition to the Christian and Roman Catholic Church in particular in St Lucia, which is depicted as the white slave master and colonialist in prayer, i.e. the religion of the oppressor.

As a consequence Rastafarians became the centre of a moral panic (Cohen 1980), as they were in neighbouring country of Dominica and other Caribbean islands. Very often this involved Rastafarians being subjected to fabricated criminal charges, as highlighted in the famous case in Dominica of Desmond Trotter accused of killing a white tourist (Williams 2010), and the passage of the infamous 1974 'Dread Act' where anyone wearing dreadlocks (i.e. a traditional African hairstyle worn by Rastafarians) in public could be arrested (Shillingford 2012). This environment resulted in Rastafarians being subject to constant media attention, misrepresentation, and discrimination and the focus for police harassment and violence; forcing them to retreat to mountainous and inaccessible rural terrain where they established their own camps and communities.

Farming and agricultural-related work was the primary economic means relied on by the Rastafarians to sustain themselves. During the run up to the St Lucian independence in 1979, the country experienced one of its worst bouts of social tension, and public disorder and violence with widespread militancy, from the trade unions in particular, a mass prison break, and acts of arson and sabotage which took place in the context of a revolution in the neighbouring island of Grenada that brought to power a left-wing government. Rastafarians were very active in these protests, given their historical enmity to colonial government and its oppressive police force (Harmsen et al. 2012).

The response of the embattled government was the establishment of the paramilitary Special Services Unit (SSU) (Wayne 2010: 357), due to concern that the mainstream police were unable to cope, which went about aggressively suppressing the public disorder. However, the SSU's most notorious actions occurred in 1981 in the ongoing moral panic, was reserved for the Rastafarian community that resided in the remote Mount Gimmie. A well prepared siege was put in place by the police and its newest division the SSU, resulting in the wholesale slaughter of unarmed and peaceful Rastafarians. To this day the numbers killed is unknown given very few members of that Rastafarian community survived to attest to the events (Unpublished interview). Rather than eliminating Rastafarianism the belief system spread throughout the island among marginalised youth.

While there are no official data on how large the Rastafarian faith and its proponents are in numerical terms, any visitor to St Lucia, and most Eastern Caribbean Islands will confirm its high visibility in terms of individuals, particularly the young who identify with it in terms of mode of dress, vernacular inter alia. Rastafarians are still harassed and victimised by the police and are easy visible targets for opportunistic officers looking for small amounts of marijuana, despite Rastafarians being among some of the most peaceful and law-abiding sections of St Lucian society. Members of this community are also subject to predatory police violence. During previous fieldwork on St Lucian policing one of the authors (Stanislas 2014, 2017), was given numerous accounts of violence against Rastafarians. In the course of one particular interview, the author was asked to feel the head of a young man, who during a stop and search process was hit in the head by a policeman with the butt of a gun, which had fractured his skull leaving a deep and permanent crevice that could be felt.

Education and Training of the Royal St Lucian Police Force

Great efforts have been made by the Royal St Lucian Police Force (RSLPF)[1] to transform important aspects of its training of police recruits in order to deemphasise the militaristic elements of colonial policing and its residues (Deosaran 2002, Stanislas 2014). This has seen the introduction of social sciences, and a greater emphasis in trying to understand society and the communities that the RSLPF have to work with. Human rights, community policing and customer relations have also been introduced, including very important components that address vulnerable groups, such as the mentally ill, in order to improve police interaction with citizens. An important feature of this changing ethos has been the opening up of police training to include academics, college tutors, and professionals such as mental health nurses, doctors inter alia. A stand out feature of contemporary training of RSLPF recruits is the recognition of sexuality and teaching new officers to interact respectfully with citizens with different sexuality (Stanislas 2014: 229–230). This development has to be applauded in a society where the influence of the Catholic Church, while not as powerful as in previous generations cannot be totally ignored. Missing from the groups included from special consideration and an important aspect of St Lucian life is the policing of Rastafarians. No particular educational or training input is given on this group, even though Rastafarians and their policing in theory can be subsumed in many of the other topics and issues addressed, such as improving community relations, there is no explicit mentioning of them. This failure weakens the ability of the RSLPF to understand key features and beliefs of Rastafarians and leaves their policing to be informed by ideas and sentiments derived from the social constructions of the institutions and interests who are hostile to them (Cohen 1980: 23–27).

Trinidad and Tobago

The Southern Caribbean twin countries of Trinidad and Tobago like its St Lucian counterpart have similar origins in terms of being heavily influenced by Christianity since its slave and colonial origins. However, this has been tempered by the presence of a significant East Indian population who were brought to the country as indentured labour. This has culturally impacted on the territory in important ways, such as the Hosay festival which is held annually for 10 days and is Muslim in origin. The dominance of Christianity on the police reflects African dominance and influence on this institution and can be seen by the Star of David which forms the

---

[1] Contrary to prevailing belief colonial police were often unable to entirely police colonised territories and relied on indigenous structures in the co-production of policing or as in the case of St Lucia in the Eastern Caribbean relied on autonomous community stakeholders.

https://www.youtube.com/watch?v=w96iaNgg9yA&t=1457s 28 February 2019 symbol of the Trinidad and Tobago Police Services (TTPS) and other practices; such as the saying of Christian prayers at important policing events.

According to the CIA World Fact Book (2017), the population of Trinidad and Tobago (T&T) is 1, 220, 479 making it one of the larger English-speaking Caribbean islands. In terms of its ethnic composition those of East Indian origins make up 35.5% of the population, with those of African descent constituting 34.2% and those of Mixed Other origins 15.3%, and individuals of Mixed East Indian and African descent making up 7.7% of the population. The history of ethnic competition is intense in the country with the Africans and Indian political elite resorting to tribal politics as their primary route in maintaining power; and similar to the South American country Guyana, which is populated by the same communities (Hintzen 2006). In terms of official religious affiliation T&T is relatively diverse. 32% of the population are Protestant (which broadly includes Pentecostal/Evangelist, Baptist and Anglican inter alia). Roman Catholics constitute 21.6% of the population, Hindus 18.2%, with Muslims constituting 5% of the population (CIA 2017).

However, these figures are misleading in so far as they do not indicate important changes which highlight dissatisfaction with the religious and normative status quo and movement away from traditional sources of authority with policing implications. The first is the increase of the Pentecostal and Evangelist movement which can be seen in St Lucia, Jamaica, and East Africa and indicates increasing material and economic strain on the population (Stanislas 2016). More troubling is the rise of militant Islam and radicalisation among predominantly young males of African descent in the country, many of whom are economically marginalised and were heavily involved in violent criminal and gang activity prior to conversion (Dearden 2016, Maharaj 2017: 178). Trinidad has become the hub for potential religiously-inspired violence in the Caribbean and Americas and a recruiting ground for the terrorist organisation ISIS (178–180).What is particularly interesting, while Rastafarianism has been one of the traditional vehicles which disaffected young males in St Lucia have used to channel their political and spiritual energies and is almost totally non violent, albeit very anti status quo. Trinidad and Tobago has a much longer history of violence and violent opposition to oppression and the status quo (see Brereton 2010). This can be seen by the general historically benign relationship between most St Lucians and their police, compared to the population of Trinidad and Tobago and their police. Violent social movements and belief systems appear to have greater appeal to the youth of the latter.

During the preparation for a training course in 2014 to test the operational responses of the TTPS to major critical incidents, led by the author and co-author of this book Professor James Albrecht, the Royal Canadian Mounted Police force raided the property of a T&T citizen and suspected terrorist and found details of plans to attack the Trinidad and Tobago Carnival, which is one of the largest events of its type in the world. What is particularly concerning is unlike other Caribbean countries, Trinidad has a long history of Islamic motivated violence, despite Muslims constituting a small minority in the country.

On July 26 1,990 a group of Muslim fanatics called Jamat al Muslimeem launched a carefully coordinated attack on the country's Parliament while in session, and its main television station, which they occupied and held individuals hostage for 6 days. The attack on Parliament was particularly violent and resulted in a police officer being shot dead and the Prime Minister being shot and beaten, along with six cabinet members receiving similar treatment, including the Minister of National Security; with MP Leo des Vignes dying from his injuries. In total, 24 people died as an outcome of these events (Report of the Commission of Enquiry 2004: 7, Gold 2014).

Education and Training of the Trinidad and Tobago Police Service

Similar to its St Lucian counterparts the TTPS is attempting to phase out its traditional mode of colonial- informed approach to recruit training, which emphasises order maintenance that is buttressed by the learning of public order and other legislation, tough physical training, use of weapons and strict military- type discipline (Stanislas 2014, Mathura 2018). The new approach to police education being adopted by the TTPS is in line with regional best practice and broader international trends in terms of the greater reliance on social science in understanding society, groups, and individual behaviour and involves more partners and stakeholders than hitherto. These changes have been accompanied by the improving educational calibre of those coming into the TTPS (Stanislas ibid., Mathura 2018) which has led to the usual discussions about the pros and cons of such developments.

What is particularly striking, is while there has been an increase in education of new recruits about the police's crime fighting role and crime matters generally, which is a response to Trinidad and Tobago having one of the highest crime and homicide rates in particular in the English Caribbean region that is driven by drugs and gang-related activity (United Nations Office of Drugs and Wallace 2012, Jaitman 2017). Little educational input is given to new TTPS recruits on radicalization and terrorism which underscores the largely reactive nature of this organization, despite the pioneering preventative work of individuals like Dr. Wendell Wallace (see Wallace 2013a, b). This hiatus is especially interesting and indicates the challenges of institutional learning given the history of Islamic radicalization in Trinidad and Tobago.

The Report of the Commission of Enquiry into the events in 1990 explicitly stated that one of its aims was to understand:

'The consequences of any historical, social, economic, political and other factors that may have contributed to the attempted coup.'

Despite these comments the reports emphasis in terms of its recommendation was on improving the effectiveness and efficiency of security agencies and their coordination and response. Very little emphasis was given on understanding the origins of the problems in question, in terms of why black males are more likely to become radicalized. As has argued elsewhere, in the context of East Africa (Mkutu et al. 2017), this silence by government on this and related issues is due to the awareness that important aspects of this problem is caused by their economic and social policies and intrinsic corruption, which have excluded key population groups, causing deep resentment. Hence the government and police's focus on hard policing responses in the form of: better coordination, improved intelligence-gathering and better security hardware is both convenient and self-serving.

Britain

The legislative framework and policing context of Britain has been heavily dominated by Christianity (and more directly the Church of England), with some of the earliest hate crime laws being articulated in the Criminal Libel Act 1819 (Blasphemy laws) which stated that the offence of Blasphemy was committed through the publication of: contemptuous, reviling, scurrilous or ludicrous matter relating to God as defined by the Christian religion, Jesus, the Bible or the Book of Common Prayer, intending to wound the feelings of Christians or to excite contempt and hatred against the Church of England or to promote immorality.

As noted above, Christianity has also underpinned the religious (and policing) landscapes in countries previously under colonial rule. Even today, Britain (or at least the British Government) would openly state that this is a Christian country. In a speech in Oxford in 2011 to mark the 400th Anniversary of the King James Bible, David Cameron averred "We are a Christian country and we should not be afraid to say so…Let me be clear: I am not in any way saying that to have another faith – or no faith – is somehow wrong" (BBC 2011). Mr. Cameron also said it was "easier for people to believe and practise other faiths when Britain has confidence in its Christian identity"(*ibid*). But this does not reflect the changing religious landscape seen in Britain over the last decade or so. In the UK, the 2011 Census figures show a decline from 37 million citizens (72%) identifying as Christian in 2001 to 33.2 million citizens (59%) in 2011, with those stating they were not religiously affiliated/no religion increasing from 7.7 million (10.3% to 14.1 million (25.7%) (Office of National Statistics 2011). Paganism is the 7th largest religion in the UK and the 2011 census recorded 76,459 people identifying as Pagan or adhering to a Pagan path such as Wicca, Druidism, Shamanism or Witchcraft. In 2008 the Home Office introduced the Pagan Oath for use in the courts, and in 2009 the Police Pagan Association was founded to 'tackle the issues surrounding Paganism in the police service and in the community' and to better represent and support police employees and their communities (policepaganassociation.org n.d).

Whilst Christianity as a whole is on the decline, like many of the countries included in this chapter, Britain has seen an increase in some Christian denominations, particularly the Pentecostal and Evangelical movements, as well as in those identifying as Muslim. It has also experienced similar problems with both the marginalisation and radicalisation of particular groups, often the former leading to the latter. The past and present of Britain is therefore marred by social problems (mis) attributed to religion in terms of terrorism, hate crime, child sexual exploitation and issues regarding 'faith' schools.

In terms of the policy context, the years of New Labour (1997–2010) saw a determined effort on the part of policy-makers to engage with faith communities. Dinham (2012) notes that this was driven firstly by the view of faith groups/communities as 'repositories of resources' which could be utilised for the public good, but also driven by an increasing anxiety about relationships 'between and beyond' faith communities and religious traditions following a number of incidents; in Burnley and Oldham in 2001 and later, as noted above the 7/7 terrorist attack on London in 2005. The scene was now set for the development of 'community cohesion' policies as a way of managing cultural and religious pluralism in Britain.

Community-cohesion policies were bifurcated with Active Citizenship, the engagement of people of all faiths and none in public activities, being used to foster 'good relations' and understanding across the spectrum of religious and ethnic differences and the Prevent strategy which sought to tackle religious radicalisation and violent extremism (particularly in terms of Islam). More recently under the Coalition government, the revised version of *Prevent* (Home Office 2015) has attempted to take account of Far- Right extremism and British nationalism and yet the focus is still clearly on Islam as the 'problem' and is grounded in a 'risk-based' approach (*ibid*).

Education and Training of the British Police

The launch of the Initial Police Learning and Development Programme (IPLDP) in 2005 was a response to the criticisms set out in Her Majesty's Inspectorate of Constabulary inspection report, Training Matters (HMIC 2002: 72), which concluded that current police training provision was 'not fit for purpose'. At the heart of the problem was 'insufficient community engagement' during initial training and a key recommendation from HMIC was that the training delivered to new recruits should be 'restructured to provide an in-depth understanding of the community to be policed' (HMIC 2002: 107).

The IPLDP was therefore specifically designed with community engagement at the heart of it, incorporating 80 h of community engagement activities as part of this initial training (Home Office 2005). It should be noted that although the current system of police officer training in Britain is 'fragmented' (Heslop 2010), with some police services working in partnership with academic institutions and others providing in-house training, the majority sent their officers on placements similar to those highlighted here.

Whilst placements are a conventional pedagogical approach in other areas of professional education such as youth work, nursing and social work, this was the first time that this method had been utilised in police officer training. The IPLDP consisted of a combination of classroom-based and experiential learning as well as reflective practice with the explicit aim of providing student officers with 'an understanding of other organisations, diverse communities and groups within their local policing areas' (Heslop 2011: 331, Stanislas 2009: 105). In the authors' academic institution up until 2014, police student officers undertook a module in Diversity and Community Engagement, within which the placements were situated. Additionally, there was specific input on religion and belief from a local Centre for Multi-Faith Engagement. Diversity and Community Engagement training was delivered (to varying degrees) to both student police officers and those training to become Police Community Support Officers (PCSOs) see Crisp (2014). As part of their studies, the student police officers and PCSOs were encouraged to reflect on their own 'values', 'beliefs' and their professional role policing 'in the community.'

Nationally, police education and training has recently been impacted by public sector funding cuts at the same time as a policy shift towards further 'professionalization' of policing (Stanislas 2014: 59–60, see College of Policing) and this has, in some cases, changed the content and length of degrees, local partnership training provision etc. Between 2014 and 2017, there was a noticeable absence of 'community engagement' within the police degree curriculum. Although some of the 43 Police Services continue to include education and training in the area of religion and belief the drivers for and focus of such training has in general shifted towards a more risk-based approach in light of the heightened 'terror threat levels'. Developing notion of 'suspect communities' and the role the introduction of the Prevention of Terrorism Act (Temporary Provisions) 1974 had on constructing the Irish Community as a 'suspect community', Pantazis and Pemberton (2009) suggest that recent legislative changes and political discourse have branded Muslims as the 'new' suspect community. Although police education and training regarding religion and faith has been seen (and was intended to) develop awareness and understanding of the diverse range of faith communities in Britain and foster 'good relations' and policing by collaboration not just by consent, the authors' argue that the focus on multi-faith awareness rather than inter-faith engagement exacerbates the notion of community-targeted policing of identified suspect communities.

In December 2017, new police degree curriculum guidance was sent to accredited policing degree HE providers by the College of Policing for mapping against current provision. Within this document was a section entitled Policing Communities. However, much of the language used in the initial mapping seen by the authors was focused around information gathering, intelligence and tension indicators regarding problems within and between, monitoring of and 'interventions' in communities. Only once was the term 'community engagement' referred to, and this was used in relation to 'identification of emerging issues, problems or concerns' and 'encouraging community ownership of community issues'. Nowhere does this document advise policing degree providers to re-establish placements or experiential learning opportunities to ensure student officers truly understand their communities. This indicates that the focus remains on intelligence and information gathering about, and in the policing of, 'suspect' or problematic communities.

Conclusion

The status of religion and faith matters in the developing countries of the English-speaking Caribbean was found to be very similar to that in South Africa, in so far as these issues play little role in the education and training of police officers. What is particularly interesting in the case of St Lucia and Trinidad and Tobago is that the marginalisation of poor young black males has contributed to their attraction to faith and religions, which tend to be particularly critical of the government and the status quo, and in the case of the latter, contributes to radicalisation and the possibility of violence which has already been experienced in that country. The lack of attention to matters around radicalisation and its attraction to particular sections of the population is especially worrying given the crucial role this territory plays in nurturing and exporting Islamic militants throughout the region and North America.

In the British context, while officially a religious country, committed affiliation and participation in organised religion seems limited to only newer formations, which are largely critical of the religious establishment and reflect postmodern changes in being more linked to the identity of local communities and their diverse needs. Unlike the two Caribbean countries in the case studies, British government has sought to address religious matters in the context of being responsive to changes to its demographic composition and some of the problems associated with it at the policy and institutional level. The police have been at the forefront of these developments given their pivotal role in the administration of justice and in providing services requiring sensitivity and understanding of people and their values. More recently, and in common with the police in Trinidad and Tobago, there has been a greater emphasis on the crime control model, which is largely driven by the desire for more and better quality intelligence, which in the British context has been achieved at the expense of more richer approaches to police education and learning on matters of religion and faith.

References

Allport, G. (1987). *The nature of prejudice*. Reading: Addison Wesley.

BBC. (2011). *David Cameron says the UK is a Christian country*, http://www.bbc.co.uk/news/uk-politics-16224394. 16 December 2011. Retrieved 23 Nov 2017.

Beckford, R. (1998). *Jesus is dread: Black theology and black culture*. Darton: Longman and Todd Ltd.

Brereton, B. (2010). The historical background to the culture of violence in Trinidad and Tobago, Caribbean Review of Gender Studies, Issues 4.

Bryman, A. (2008). *Social research methods* (3rd ed.). Oxford: Oxford University Press.

Cashmore, E. (2002). Behind the window dressing: Ethnic minority police perspectives on cultural diversity. *Journal Ethnic and Migration Studies, 28*(2), 327–341.

Casper, J. (2015) *Why Christians are fleeing one of Africa's oldest and largest Christian home*, www.christianitytoday.com June 18 2015. Retrieved 5 Nov 2017.

Cohen, S. (1980). *Folk devils and moral panics: The creation of mods and rockers.* Oxford: Martin Robertson.

Crisp, A. (2014). Getting back to peel: PCSO training in England and Wales. In P. Stanislas (Ed.), *International perspectives on police education and training.* London: Routledge.

Dearden, L. (2016). *Isis recruiting violent criminals and gang members across Europe in dangerous new 'crime terror nexus'.* www.independent.co.uk 10 October. Retrieved 6 Nov 2017.

Deosaran, R. (2002). *National Survey on fear of crime and community policing in St Lucia.* National Crime Commission.

Dinham, A. (2012). The multi-faith paradigm in policy and practice: Problems, challenges, directions. *Social Policy and Society, 11*(4), 577–587.

Essed, P. (1991). *Understanding everyday racism.* London: Sage.

Gerloff, R. (2006). The African diaspora in the Caribbean and Europe from pre-emancipation to the present day. In H. Mcleod (Ed.), *The Cambridge history of Christianity* (World Christianities c 1914–2000) (Vol. 9). Cambridge: Cambridge University Press.

Gold, D. (2014). *The Islamic leader who tried to overthrow trinidad has mellowed ... A little.* www.news.vice.com May 30 2014. Retrieved 5 Nov 2017.

Grabosky, P. (2009). *Community policing and peacekeeping.* Baton Raton: CRC Press.

Hakeem, F., Habermas, M., & Verma, A. (2012). *Policing muslim communities.* New York: Springer.

Harmsen, J., Ellis, G., & Devaux, R. (2012). *A history of St Lucia.* View Fort: Lighthouse Road.

Her Majesty's Inspectorate of Constabulary (HMIC). (2002). *Training matters.* London: Home Office.

Heslop, R. (2010). *Learning curve.* Police review, 20 Aug, pp. 18–21.

Heslop, R. (2011). Community engagement and learning as 'becoming': Findings from a study of British police recruit training. *Policing and Society, 21*(3), 327–342.

Hintzen, P. (2006). *The cost of regime survival.* Cambridge: Cambridge University Press.

Home Office. (2005). *Initial police learning and development programme central authority practitioner guidance: 'Community engagement and professional development units'.* London: Home Office.

Home Office. (2015). *Revised Prevent duty guidance: For England and Wales.* London: Home Office.

Human Rights Standards and Practice for the Police. (2004). *The office of the United Nations high commissioner for human rights.* Geneva: United Nations.

Human Rights Watch. (2017). *Kenyan elections 2017.* www.hrw.org. Retrieved 4 Nov 2017.

Jaitman, L. (2017). *The cost of crime and violence: New evidence and insights into Latin America and the Caribbean.* Inter American Development Bank.

Jesse, R. (1994). *Outlines of St Lucia's history.* Castries: The St Lucia Archaeological and Historical Society.

Laloo, K. (2008). The church and the state in apartheid South Africa, contemporary. *Politics, 4*(1), 39–55.

Liebman, A. (1979). *Jews and the left.* New York: Wiley.

Machiavelli, N. (1963). *The Prince.* Hertfordshire: Wordsworth Reference.

Maharaj, S. (2017). Globalization of the jihadist threat: Case study of Trinidad and Tobago. *Strategic Analysis, 41*(2), 173–189.

Mathura, M. (2018). *Public perception of police officers in Trinidad and Tobago.* Unpublished PhD Thesis, Demontfort University, Leicester.

Mkutu, K. (2017). *East African policing.* Wilmington Press.

Mkutu, K., Stanislas, P., & Mogire, E. (2017). Book conclusion: State and non state policing: The challenge of postcolonial political and social leadership: Building inclusive citizenship, safety and security in East Africa. In K. Mkutu (Ed.), *Security governance in East Africa.*

Mwakikagile, G. (2007). *Kenya: An identity of a nation.* New Africa Press.

Neyroud, P., & Wain, N. (2014). Police training and reform in India: Bringing knowledge-based learning to the Indian police service. In P. Stanislas (Ed.), *International perspectives on police education and training.* London: Routledge.

Pantazis, C., & Pemberton, S. (2009). From the 'old' to the 'new' suspect community: Examining the impacts of recent UK counter-terrorist legislation. *British Journal of Criminology, 49,* 646–666.

Petrus, T. (2016). Cultural beliefs, witchcraft and crimes in South Africa. In K. Sadique & P. Stanislas (Eds.), *Religion, faith and crime: Theories, identities and issues.* Basingstoke: Palgrave Macmillan.

Police Pagan Association. (n.d.). http://www.policepaganassociation.org/about/4587098215 Retrieved 6 Jan 2018.

Report of The Commission of Enquiry Appointed to Enquire into the Events into Surrounding the Attempted Coup De'Etat Which Occurred in the Republic of Trinidad and Tobago on 27th July 1990. Published March 2004.

Rowe, M. (2016). *Policing beyond McPherson.* Cullompton: Willan Publishing.

Sadique, K. (2014, May 15). The effect of religion on crime and deviancy: Hellfire in the 21st Century. Faith and criminal justice symposium, London South Bank University.

Sadique, K., & Stanislas, P. (Eds.). (2016). *Religion, faith and crime: Theories, identities and issues.* Basingstoke: Palgrave Macmillan.

Shillingford, H. (2012). *Let's discuss the period of the dread act.* http://dominicanewsonline.com/newsNovember19 2012. Retrieved 4 Nov 2017.

Spencer, W. (2003). *Looking for a dreadlocked Jesus,* www.christianitytoday.com August 1st 2003.

Stanislas, P. (2009). The policing experiences and perceptions of new communities in Britain. In M. Salah (Ed.), *Europe and its established and emerging communities: Assimilation, multiculturalism, or integration.* London: Palgrave.

Stanislas, P. (2013, May 5). Policing violent homophobia in the Caribbean and the British Caribbean disaspora. *Interventions: An International Journal of Postcolonial Studies.* https://doi.org/10.1080/1369801X.2013.798134.

Stanislas, P. (2014) Transforming St Lucian policing through recrcuit training in a   context   of high crime. In: Stanislas, P. (ed.) International perspectives on police education and training. Abingdon: Routledge, pp. 209-234.

Stanislas, P. (2016). Late modernity, religion, homophobia and crime: Police and criminal justice reform in Jamaica and Uganda. In K. Sadique & P. Stanislas (Eds.), *Religion, faith and crime: Theories, identities and issues.* Basingstoke: Palgrave Macmillan.

Stanislas, P. (2017). The changing perceptions of St Lucian policing: How St Lucian police officers view contemporary policing, police research and practice (Awaiting Decision).

Subramaniam, V. (1967). Representative bureaucracy: A reassessment. *American Political Science Review, 61*(4), 1010–1019.

The World. (2017). Ethnic tensions threaten to engulf post-war election Kenya. This Activist Sees a Way Out. www.pri.org. Nov 1 2017. Retrieved 4 Nov.

Tully, M. (2014). Operation blue star: How an Indian Army raid on the Golden Temple ended in disaster, www.telegraph.co.uk. 6 June 2014. Retrieved 4 Dec 2017.

Varshney, A. (2003). *Ethnic conflict and civil life: Hindus and Muslims in India.* New Haven: Yale University Press.

Wallace, W. (2012). Findings from a concurrent study on the level of community involvement in the police process in Trinidad and Tobago. *The Police Journal, 85*(1), 61–83.

Wallace Wendell, C. (2013a). Girls and gangs in Trinidad: An exploratory study. In R. Seepersad & A. M. Bissessar (Eds.), *Gangs in the Caribbean* (pp. 195–219). Cambridge Scholars Publishing.

Wallace Wendell, C. (2013b). Better to be alone than in bad company. In *A handbook about Gangs for Caribbean parents and children.* Kingston/Jamaica: Arawak Publications.

Wayne, R. (2010). *Lapses and infelicities: An Insider's perspective of politics in the Caribbean.* St Lucia: Star Publishing Co Ltd Lucia.

Weiner, M. (1978). *Sons of the soil: Migration and ethnic conflict in India.* Princeton: Princeton University Press.

Weller, P. (Ed.). (2001). *Religion in the UK 2001–03*. Derby: University of Derby.

Weller, P. (2005). Time for a change: Reconfiguring religion. In *State and society*. London: T. and T. Clark International.

Williams, A. (2010). Dread, Rastafari and Ethiopia, the definitive report on the history of the Rastafari in the Commonwealth of Dominica, Albert and Temple Ltd. https://joshuaproject.net/countries/ST. Retrieved 30 Oct 2017.

Chapter 3
Police Leadership During Challenging Times

Magne V. Aarset and Rune Glomseth

Part 1: The Work of the Police in New Demanding Contexts

The Context of Police Work is Undergoing Change, Leading to Demanding Challenges

The police services in a number of countries are undergoing changes. Traditional crime is declining in several European countries, while we can observe clear alterations in the types of crime occurring. For instance, organized crime, cross-border crime, various types of cybercrime, human trafficking and work-related crime have all been on the increase. Migration has also become a much more relevant issue in recent years. Over the same period, acts of terror have increased – many countries have been targeted by terrorist attacks. In addition to this general picture, natural disasters have grown more frequent. Crime is in the process of changing. The various communities that the police are set up to protect have become increasingly complex, leading to new and demanding challenges for the police and police leaders.[1]

In many countries, the police have been subjected to criticism, and their legitimacy has been challenged. Today, the media, politicians and people in general are directing a more critical light on the police than was the case a few decades ago. The police have faced criticism when operations fail, are drawn out, or are without results; when the police commit errors; when information emerges about police

---

[1] https://cult.is/rastafarians-in-the-hills-of-saint-lucia/ Retrieved 4 November 2012

M. V. Aarset (✉)
Norwegian University of Science and Technology (NTNU),
BI Norwegian Business School, Oslo, Norway
e-mail: magne.aarset@ntnu.no

R. Glomseth
Norwegian Police University College, Oslo, Norway

© Springer Nature Switzerland AG 2019
J. F. Albrecht et al. (eds.), *Policing and Minority Communities*,
https://doi.org/10.1007/978-3-030-19182-5_3

corruption or when the police use undue force against individuals or groups. In particular, governments want a well-organized, modern and competent police force that can fight crime and contribute to safety and security. At the same time, in several European countries, governments have implemented financial cutbacks. In recent years, openness, accountability, quality, efficiency and results have been significantly strengthened.[2]

In a number of countries, the police have undergone major changes and reforms. These changes and reforms have been characterized by the development of organizational culture, new working methods, an increased use of technology, stronger central management and result orientation. There has been a centralization of the police forces in Scotland, the Netherlands, Belgium and in the Scandinavian countries. Van Dijk et al. (2015) consider that this has involved restrictions on the police's mandate in the respective countries. The diversity within the police has increased. And finally, there is an increasing awareness in many countries that the fight against crime cannot be prevented and tackled by the police alone. This has meant that the police need to develop partnerships with other service providers in the public, private and third sectors. An interesting feature that has become increasingly evident in some countries is the development of productive cooperation between the police and various professional communities at universities.[3]

This has been done in order to utilize the professional expertise at the universities, but also to challenge the traditional perspectives, views and knowledge that have characterized the police in their perception of society, trends, crime, risks, and problem solving.[4]

The developmental trends outlined above show that the context in which the police operate has increased considerably in complexity (Mitchell and Casey 2007). This has led to new and greater challenges for police leaders. In a number of countries, the police are now at a turning point in terms of crime development, tasks, organization, working methods, technology, cooperation and, not least, context.[5]

In tandem with the main challenges described above, the police need to exercise and carry out good and effective prevention, investigations and emergency preparedness. The police must ensure safety and security, in a world where these values have come under pressure.

---

[2] One of the authors had an in-depth and chilling discussion with a member of the Dominican Police Forces who participated in a raid on a Rastafarian community similar to the assault on Mount Gimmie in St Lucia. One of the lasting memories from that discussion was his description of the killing of 'very attractive' Rastafarian woman from a middle class family and former university graduate who tried to save a child and duly shot dead. The police man's remarks 'what a waste' referred to the physical beauty of the young woman in question who was killed along with the child she was attempting to save. The police violence against generally law abiding Rastafarians is probably one of the ugliest periods in Caribbean policing history which has enjoyed little discussion outside Rastafarian communities.

[3] Rastafarians are well known for their use of marijuana.

[4] See Islamic State and the Mosques of Trinidad. www.dw.com. 25 March 2017. Retrieved 6 November 2017

[5] Michael Mathura PhD Thesis Police

The police have a monopoly on the legitimate use of physical force in society. This is an important and demanding responsibility, of which both employees and police leaders need to be fully aware. The responsibility, and the underlying tasks, will be put to the test when terror and insecurity threaten. The police are responsible for upholding various sets of important social values. Moreover, they are responsible for safeguarding democratic values, justice and human rights for individuals, groups and communities. Furthermore, the police are responsible for protecting economic assets through effective operations and services. And finally, professional values should characterize the operation and development of the police.

Police leaders are responsible for preserving democratic, economic and professional values in their capacity as leaders, in both the short and longer term. They should be able to master and deal with daily operations, emergency events and various types of crises, incremental developments and reforms, both separately and simultaneously. This comprises a large range of situations and management tasks. Against this background, we will argue that leadership both within and by the police has become more complex and challenging in recent years. At the same time, we believe that police leadership is a crucial resource in order to ensure the efficient operation and development of the police service, and essential if the police are to function efficiently with the level of quality and ethical standards that meet the demands and expectations of a liberal democracy.

Understanding Police Leadership

Leadership is an activity and a resource that is only partly linked to position and rank in the police. It is a resource that is needed at all levels in police organizations (Fleming 2015). Leadership is exercised at strategic, middle and senior levels, as well as on the front-line. Every police officer makes assessments and decisions, communicates, and thereby exercises leadership in their daily operations, when dealing with various problems and incidents. Effective leadership is important if the police organization is to be perceived as legitimate by both internal and external individuals. Effective leadership is also a prerequisite for police organizations to function effectively in an ever increasingly dynamic and complex landscape (Fleming 2015).

In his *Harvard Business Review* article "Skills of an Effective Administrator" (1955), Robert L. Katz found that managers needed three important skills: technical, human and conceptual. Northouse (2013) refers to this as the "Three-Skill Approach". Haberfeld (2013) refers to Swanson et al. (1998), claiming that police leadership may be understood by means of three sets of skills and/or competences. Swanson et al. describe similar managerial skills to those referred to by Katz in his 1955 article. We believe this approach to police leadership to be very useful.

In the Norwegian book on police leadership (Johannessen and Glomseth 2015), Glomseth writes the following: "The Police Leadership Qualifications Framework (PLQF), launched by the National Police Improvement Agency (NPIA) in England

and Wales, has formulated the following definition of police leadership: 'the ability to effectively influence and combine individuals and resources to achieve objectives that otherwise would be impossible' (Gibson and Villiers 2007: 7)". Gibson and Villiers claim that leadership may be perceived as "comprising five integrated levels: leading by example, leading others, leading teams, leading units and leading organizations" (Gibson and Villiers 2007: 7).

This approach is based on identifying the knowledge and skills necessary in order to maintain effective leadership roles and to exercise leadership. By following this model, police leaders can be educated and trained to perform competent leadership both individually and collectively in the police service.

Andreescu and Vito (2010) write that: "(police) leaders are expected to generate a sense of purpose that both motivates and directs followers so that they voluntarily make a meaningful contribution to the organization".

Haberfeld (2006) defines police leadership as follows: "The ability to make a split-second decision and take control of a potentially high-voltage situation that evolves on the street." Furthermore, she claims that "police leadership is the ability of each police officer, starting from the first day on the job, to take control of a situation on the street.

Any type of situation that requires assertion of control would fall under this definition. As police officers progress in their careers, the level and degree of control change. Due to the fact that police work is based on the mandate to use coercive force to achieve compliance, police leadership is about the ability to take control. (…) Police leadership will frequently be immersed in a clash between the concepts of doing things right and doing the right thing."

Golding and Savage (2008) distinguish between three types of police leadership:

- Command (commanding, instructing, ordering leadership)
- Leadership (leadership, leadership as interaction)
- Management (management/administration).

These three types may also be perceived as functions which police leaders must master in order to perform police leadership roles effectively and to solve various types of problems. Grint (2010, 21) accentuates these types of leadership, by claiming that leadership involves asking questions and inviting dialogue. Administration involves organizing processes and managing resources, while command-based leadership involves providing clear messages and instructions. Consequently, there are situations and problems that require different approaches in the exercise of leadership.

Grint relates the different types of management to three categories of problems: namely 'critical', 'tame' (ordinary) and 'wicked' (complex problems) (cited in Glomseth 2015: 149–150).

Moggré et al. (2017) claim that police leadership is considered as being more specific and context-sensitive than regular leadership, because of the continuous interaction with internal and external factors.

Police Leadership in Four Different Management Situations

Daily operational management concerns the daily running of a police unit, which is characterized by stable external conditions. Attention is focused on the organization's goals. Police officers undertake the regular tasks they have been allocated through the police operations center, and other police officers investigate the cases which they have been given. The police leaders need to ensure that the day-to-day operations run smoothly (Fig. 3.1).

Daily police operations constitute the main part of the police service's work, where tasks and problems need to be solved. The manner in which the organization addresses its tasks, develops working methods and practices, and how the police leaders gain experience, learn and develop, constitute the basis of the police service. The operational part of the police service probably uses the largest amount of resources.

Development management occurs in small steps and is a natural part of a police unit's activities. Tasks and problems are discussed and solutions reached, competence development is conducted, technology is developed and improved, and working methods are gradually altered. Employees cooperate with each other, and through this process they learn and develop. Development management means facilitating discussion, reflection and learning. Furthermore, it involves enabling situations where new and inexperienced staff can work together with those who are more experienced. It also means allowing employees to participate in and lead projects, coaching, mentoring, studying how other organizations function and learning from the practices of others. In addition, trimming work processes and the organization to exploit resources better will fall under this type of management, as well as the development and improvement of management processes.

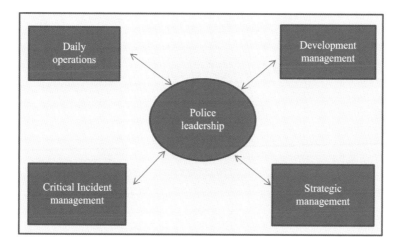

Fig. 3.1 The four main types of management in the police service. (Source: Glomseth 2015)

Strategic management in the police service may be understood in several ways. Strategic management can take place at all levels of the police organization when it is linked to an isolated task and solution. However, in this context, we understand strategic management as taking place at the organizational level; that is, where, for instance, the organization, an operating unit or a police district, need to carry out larger and more complex adjustments to adapt to the outside world. The 'outside world' may refer to a new and serious type of crime or threat. This may represent such a demanding challenge that the police service needs to reorganize, consolidate resources, or re-prioritize parts of its budget. Political decisions and new directions may result in a police district needing to change its strategy and priorities. This can also involve more comprehensive reforms, such as those facing the Norwegian police service today. Such situations, and other similar ones, require strategic leadership and management.

Finally, we will focus on *action-centered management* and *crisis management*, or what one might call *Critical Incident Management* (Alison and Crego 2008 and Turbitt and Benington 2015). The 22 July 2011 attacks required this type of management at all levels. The Torp Hostage Crisis on 28 September 1994, the Åsta Accident in 2000, the Nokas Robbery in April 2004, and the Lærdal Fire in January 2014, were all emergency situations characterized by great uncertainty and pressure of time, where decisions had to be made on the basis of limited and often uncertain information. In such crisis situations, the demands on and expectations of the police are very great from all quarters, and the consequences are also great. Outcomes and consequences will be seen as being related to police efforts (or lack thereof). These crisis situations place extremely great demands on police leaders, their competence, power to act, courage, wisdom and cooperation (Glomseth 2015: 162–164). In recent years, several countries have been hit by acts of terror; for instance, in Europe: London 2013; Brussels, 2014; Paris and Copenhagen, 2015; Berlin and Brussels, 2016; and London, Barcelona, Åbo and Manchester, 2017. This has led to great demands on personnel and leaders in the police.

Leadership, Management and Command

Grint, writing in Fleming (2015) refers to the complexity of police leadership. He has developed a model based on the concepts of leadership, management and command, in order to understand and explain various problems and decision-making processes. In the model, he also distinguishes between 'tame', 'wicked' and 'critical' problems. Grint uses the same concepts and categories as Golding and Savage (2008) – see (Fig. 3.2).

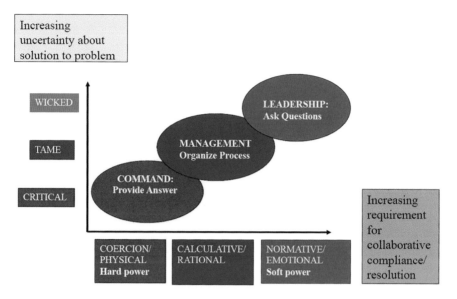

Fig. 3.2 Problems and decision styles. (Source: Grint 2005)

Part 2: Modeling Demanding Integrated Operations

Whatever situation a police leader is in, being wicked, tame and/or critical, today's work within the police force may thus be characterized as participation and/or leadership of operations involving personnel from different agencies or organizations, in addition to representatives of the general public. We will call such operations *demanding integrated operations*. What's typical with these integrated operations are that the different participants often have different "roles to play", and that they have rather insufficient knowledge and understanding of each other's roles. Furthermore, the different participants may have different background, both regarding knowledge of what's supposed to happen and experience from similar operations, different individual goals, and finally, sometimes surprisingly different perspectives of what's really going on.

This goes for almost any situation from a typical accident or fire to a terror attack where all the blue light organizations, the government, the media and representatives from the general public are involved. Participants in any such "operation" may have completely different primary goals and may see the situation from completely different angles. A random bystander may wonder how he can participate to help, while a police officer may be occupied with keeping the general public away from the crime scene. Someone from the fire department may be focusing on how to avoid that a fire is spreading to the next building, when the paramedics are trying to assist someone wounded.

These differences in goals, attention, focus, perception, and roles to play are of course just as it should be, but insufficient understanding of the roles of the other participants may cause actions that have adverse effect. Here, we claim that in such demanding integrated operations it's especially important, and difficult, to understand *what's really really going on*.

It is vital to see that this is not just important during crisis operations, but also during e.g. monitoring and control, and not at least regarding planning of possible critical operations. During planning (*Risk Management*), we try to foresee most of the possible scenarios that might occur, while during monitoring and control (*Issues Management*) we're searching for signals that might indicate that a dangerous scenario seems to be unfolding. In crisis situations (*Crisis Management*) the questions are what has happened and what is happening now (Aarset 2016). Something has occurred, but what – and what is the best response? Is it, and how is it, possible to reduce the possible undesirable events, and how is it possible to prevent further escalation? And what kind of consequences will the decisions that have to be taken in a split second, often based on limited and uncertain information, have on the goals of the other participants in the operation?

Consciousness

How safe and effective such operations are executed will among other things depend on the level of the participants' overall understanding of the situation, or the participants' consciousness. By consciousness we here mean our immediate awareness of ourselves and our environment (Passer et al. 2009). Consciousness is often understood as some kind of a summary, a mental "picture" of what's going on in our world. Therefore, consciousness is subjective, private, dynamic, self-reflective and vital for our understanding of ourselves and what we believe is going on. Thus, consciousness will control our attention and influence how we decide to act.

The concept usually addressed with respect to such demanding integrated operations is *situational awareness* (or situation awareness, meaning exactly the same). Smith and Hancock (1995) describe situational awareness as *externally directed consciousness*. According to Endsley (1995), participants in demanding integrated operations make bad judgments when their overall understanding of what's going on is insufficient, i.e. when acquisition and/or maintenance of situational awareness is insufficient.

Both leadership style, system design, artefacts (e.g. supportive tools) and procedures should therefore be formed to strengthen the participant's and the system's situational awareness. But to be able to do so, we need knowledge of how situational awareness may be acquired and maintained in different situations. To succeed in constructing systems and procedures that makes it possible to acquire and maintain situational awareness, and thereby reduce the probability of human failure, we will therefore study this concept here.

Situational Awareness

Situational awareness was originally introduced as a concept within military aviation when it was identified as crucial for military pilots during the first world war (Endsley 2000). The concept was however not given much attention within academic fields until the late 1980's (Stanton and Young 2000), and then mainly within civil aviation and air traffic control. Real attention from the academic field was not accomplished until a special edition of the journal *Human Factors* was published in 1995 focusing on situational awareness.

In the scientific literature, there are several definitions of situational awareness. There is thus still no general scientific agreement on how situational awareness best should be defined and modelled, and neither which of the suggested definitions that's most applicable. With the understanding that no models are correct, while some are useful, we'd like to list the following definitions anyway.

"(Situational awareness is) the combining of new information with existing knowledge in working memory and the development of a composite picture of the situation along with projections of future status and subsequent decisions as to appropriate courses of actions to take" (Fracker 1991).

"Situational awareness is the conscious dynamic reflection of the situation by an individual. It provides orientation to the situation, the opportunity to reflect not only the past, present and future, but the potential features of the situation. The dynamic reflection contains logical-conceptual, imaginative, conscious and unconscious components which enables individuals to develop mental models of external events" (Bedny and Meister 1999).

There is one definition of situational awareness that, especially in the applied field, has become more "popular" than the rest, though. We will focus shortly on this definition here because it also might be more intuitive and maybe easier to understand. As we shall comment on later, it has some drawbacks, though, but it's so often referred to that it is reasonable to introduce this model also here. Mica Endsley (1995) states that situational awareness is a cognitive product resulting from a separate process labeled *situation assessment* comprising the perception of the elements in the environment within a volume of time and space, the comprehension of their meaning, and a projection of their status in the near future (see Fig. 3.3).

Endsley's definition and model is describing situational awareness as the result of a separate cognitive process (situation assessment) which is creating an inner mental model of the actual environment. This understanding is forming the basis for decision making and action. Furthermore, the model in Fig. 3.3 illustrates several additional relationships influencing both the process of information gathering, comprehension and forecasting, as well as decision making and behavior. The model is also illustrating that individual factors as goals, expectations and abilities, and task and system factors as workload and complexity all are influencing acquisition and maintenance of situational awareness.

We are discussing this model here basically because it seems to be how we ideally think we should behave. The model does not indicate that prior knowledge and understanding will influence an actor's attention, though, which again will influence

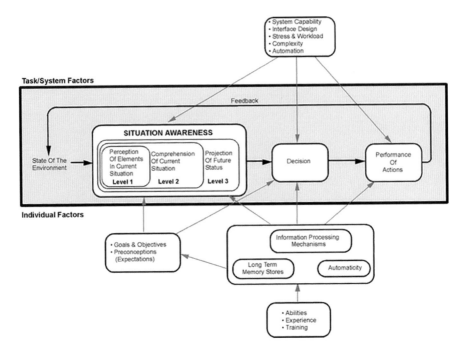

Fig. 3.3 Illustrasjon av Endsley's three level model

which information the actor will seek, and which impressions will be emphasized. This model may also promote a belief that the world is rich in information which objectively is presented to an observing actor – who is without preconceptions. Alas, maybe except a person like Sherlock Holmes, we believe no human being will act like this. Mostly, we don't perceive all signals that's available, and we even have a tendency "to see what we expect to see". We interpret the signals we observe based on our prior understanding (Plous 1993).

This model also has so many similarities to how our working memory is understood that it is an open question if situational awareness constitutes a separate term at all (see Fig. 3.4.) Before we proceed in our quest to define and explain what situational awareness actually is, and how the concept can be defined and applied, we therefore will point out some key memory-related relationships.

The Modal Model of Memory

Our memory contains everything we know and make us who we actually are. Memory constitutes three logical stages; encoding, storage and retrieval, as illustrated in the modal model of memory in Fig. 3.4 (Atkinson and Schiffrin 1971 as redrawn in Braisby and Gellatly 2005).

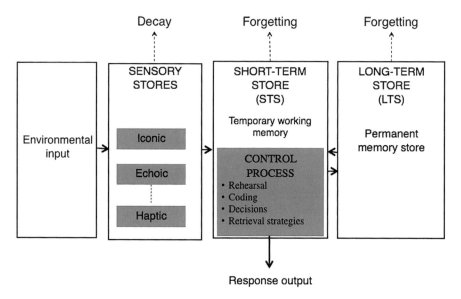

Fig. 3.4 The modal model of memory

The model illustrates that we receive information through our senses, which are then transferred to our working memory (which earlier on traditionally was named short-term memory). Working memory is coordinating our mental processes with transient stored information during cognitive activities such as planning, participating in or leading e.g. a demanding integrated operation.

After information is leaving one or more of our sensory stores, it must be represented by some code if it is to be kept in working memory and eventually transferred to the long-term memory store. Such memory codes are mental representations of some kind of information or stimulus, and have the form of visual codes, phonological codes, semantic codes or motor codes (Braisby and Gellatly 2005).

What we store in our long-term memory is thus processed information, as we perceive what we have sensed. Our memory works further so that we do not memorize isolated senses, we interpret new information in light of our previous experience and the context the senses are presented, and then construct and memorize larger scenarios (Braisby and Gellatly 2005). Retrieving such stored information from our long-term memory involves finding, activating and sometimes further processing pertinent memory representations.

Schema Theory

Schema theory was first introduced early in the 1900's (Head 1920 and Piaget 1926) and describes how individuals possess mental templates of past experience that are combined with information from the real world as the basis for actions. The schemata are the active knowledge structures that govern our attention, exploration and interpretation of the information available to us, which in turn are updated as a basis for further exploration.

Therefore, our expectation of what might happen is guiding what we decide to do, which information we're seeking and what information we actually become aware of. We seek to understand what we sense in light of our prior understanding, and we are continuously updating this understanding. Schema-based theories assume that this cognitive process is not only cyclic (rather than linear), but also parallel (as opposed to processing a stream of information at a time). The schemata are modified by new experiences, while they themselves affect information retrieval and interpretation. This seems to be in contrast to Endsley's model of situational awareness.

Bartlett (1932) introduced the concept of schema as active organization of earlier reactions and experience combined with information received by our senses. Furthermore, Bartlett argued that recall was a process of reconstruction and that memories showed evidence of consolidation, elaboration and invention, using material from other schemata.

Norman (1981) used schema-theory to explain human failures. Either, he suggested, we are:

- activating an erroneous schema (e.g. based on a similar experience)
- activating the wright schema too late or not at all (e.g. because we don't understand that a situation has changed)
- activating the wright schema too early (e.g. because we misunderstand a situation).

Neisser (1976) presented a model for this process as illustrated in Fig. 3.5. This model is based on schema, prior knowledge and selective perception.

Neisser's model illustrates that any actor in a given system has a cognitive map of the world, and especially a "smaller" cognitive map of the current environment (the triangle at the bottom left). This controls a top-down process, of several possible ways, where we seek to explore the environment (the triangle at the bottom right). With our senses we then manage to collect some, but not all, of the available information (the triangle at the top), which in turn leads to an update of our perception of what's happening (back to the triangle at the bottom left).

Adams et al. (1995) suggested that "Schema of the environment" in Neisser's perceptional cycle is illustrating "Working memory", and that "Individual cognitive map of the world" is illustrating "Long term memory" in the modal model of memory.

Smith and Hancock (1995) based their understanding of situational awareness on Neisser's perceptional cycle. They suggested the following definition; "Situational awareness is the invariant in the agent-environment system that generates the momentary knowledge and behavior required to attain the goals specified by an arbiter of performance in the environment, with deviations between an individual's knowledge and the state of the environment being the variable that directs situation

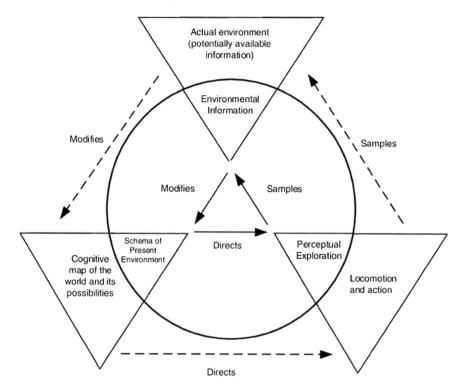

Fig. 3.5 Neisser's perceptional cycle

assessment behavior and the subsequent acquisition of data from the environment."

Studying this definition more in detail, we see that it points out conditions that concern a decision maker/agent (i.e. "an arbitrator of performance in the environment") in some situation (i.e. "in an agent-environment system"). Linked to this decision maker in the current situation there are two concepts; the variable (that change during "a circle" in Neisser's perceptional circle) and the invariant (that doesn't change).

The variable is related to the deviations that exist between the decision maker's understanding of what is happening and what really happens (i.e. "deviation between the individual's knowledge and the state of the environment"). This deviation will typically vary as the process evolves. As illustrated in Fig. 3.5, this deviation will affect what tools the decision maker seeks to utilize, what information he manages to understand and how he interprets this information (i.e. "conducts a situation-based assessment and subsequent acquisition of data from the environment").

Smith and Handcock define situational awareness as what is constant in the agent-environment system that generates the momentary knowledge and behavior required to attain the goals specified. That is to say that if the decision maker has a correct understanding of what's going on, then he won't change neither how he decides to collect information, his perception nor his interpretation of what's going on (i.e. "being invariant").

What we can see based on the models and the definitions we have mentioned so far is that situational awareness can be perceived both as a product of a process, as a process in itself or as a mixture of both.

- As a process, i.e. it is the state of the perceptual cycle at any given moment, the process of gaining awareness (e.g. Fracker).
- As a product, i.e. it is the state of the active schema, the product of awareness and the conceptual frame or context that governs the selection and interpretation of events (e.g. Endsley).
- As both a process and a product, i.e. it is the cyclical resetting of each of the other, the combination of the two (e.g. Smith and Hancock).

Situational Awareness in Collaborative Systems

When performing demanding integrated operations, there is typically a group of people who jointly perform activities to achieve a goal. We shall define a team as a distinguishable set of people who interact dynamically, interdependently and adaptively toward a common goal, who have each been assigned specific roles or functions to perform and who have a limited life span of membership (Salas et al. 1995).

We will classify the activities to be carried out by such a team as either teamwork or taskwork. Teamwork is activities where the behavior of the actors is affecting each other, or they coordinate their behavior in relation to each other to reach the system's partial or overall objective. Taskwork means activities where the actors are performing individual activities separately and (in part) independently of input from the other actors.

When performing demanding integrated operations, the actors (agents) and the tools that are available (artefacts) will form a so-called *joint cognitive system* (Hollnagel and Woods 2005). Furthermore, cognitive processes will occur and be distributed in this joint cognitive system. It is not trivial to define situational awareness in such situations, and it is clear that situational awareness associated with such a system is somewhat more than just "a sum of the individual's understanding."

When researchers have attempted to define situational awareness for a team, focus has typically been on what is called *shared situational awareness*. The idea behind this wording is that there is a "part" of the current situation that all (or some) of the team understand in the same way. This is usually illustrated as shown in Fig. 3.6.

Endsley (1995) defines shared situational awareness as "the degree to which each team member has the same situational awareness on shared situational awareness requirements". However, as discussed above, we point out that situational awareness depends both on the individual's starting point and prior knowledge, and that the individual actors typically have different backgrounds and experience. This indicates

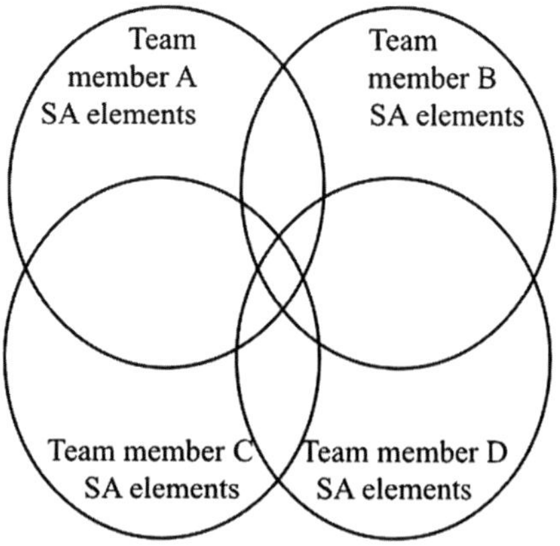

Fig. 3.6 Illustration of shared situational awareness

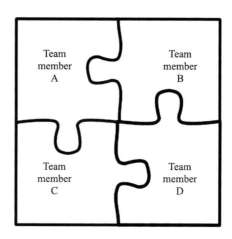

Fig. 3.7 Illustration of compatible situational awareness (Stanton et al. 2006)

that shared situational awareness not at all is easy to acquire and maintain, if possible at all. Such a common understanding can therefore be too strict to ask.

A less strict, and perhaps more realistic, relationship we may wish for a team to achieve may be what Stanton et al. (2006) calls *compatible situational awareness* (see Fig. 3.7). Here we see that in order for a team to achieve compatible situational awareness, it is sufficient that the different actors have an understanding of what is happening that is consistent with the understanding the others have.

It is this interpretation Salmon et al. have build on when they defined *distributed situational awareness* (Salmon et al. 2009). Their model (Fig. 3.8) uses schema theory as its basis and treats distributed situational awareness during demanding integrated operations as "a systemic property that emerges from the interaction (referred to as situational assessment transactions) between system elements (human and non-human)" (Salmon et al. 2009). They view distributed situational awareness as "the system's collective knowledge regarding a situation that comprises each element's compatible awareness of that situation."

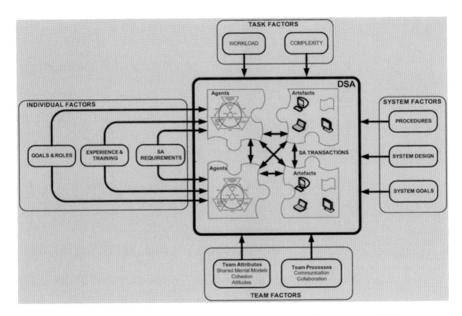

Fig. 3.8 Model of distributed situational awareness according to Salmon et al. (2009)

According to the model depicted on Fig. 3.8 four groups of factors, in addition to the individual situational awareness as illustrated by Neisser's conceptual circle, are influencing a system's distributed situational awareness. When a demanding integrated operation is to be planned or executed, these are the factors we suggest should be optimized.

System Factors

The system factors first of all include the overall objective of the operation, the sub-goals of the system, and the constraints which the operation is to be executed within. The design of the system is including "the interface design of the artefacts that are used to present situational awareness information to the agents within the system", the structure of the network of agents, and the communication channels that are available (Salmon et al. 2009). Furthermore, the system factors include the procedures established for the operation, and the redundancy implemented in the system.

Individual Factors

Each agent within such a system as described here will have individual goals, constraints and roles to play during a demanding integrated operation. These will all influence the agent's individual situational awareness. According to Neisser's perceptual model, all agents will furthermore have their own subjective prior knowledge and understanding of what's going on, and at any time their own subjective situational awareness requirements. Both the prior knowledge and the situational awareness requirements will be influenced by the agent's competence and commitment, established through e.g. experience and training.

Team Factors

The team competence and commitment will also influence the distributed situational awareness. These are depending on e.g. leadership, mutual performance monitoring, and redundancy behavior. Furthermore, the team factors may be split into team attributes and team processes. Team attributes include e.g. shared mental models, cohesion, and attitudes, while team processes include communication and collaboration.

Task Factors

There are several task factors that influences the distributed situational awareness, as e.g. task design, complexity, workload and different kind of constraints (time, place, environment, etc.) for the execution of the tasks.

Acquisition and Maintenance of Distributed Situational Awareness

The model in Fig. 3.8 provides us with a tool to organize our thoughts when we are trying to improve the probability of success of a demanding integrated operation. The model may be utilized for directing actions to improve acquisition and maintenance of distributed situational awareness, and thereby improving both efficiency and reliability.

Part 3: Techniques for Improving Distributed Situational Awareness

Leaders should facilitate for acquisition and maintenance of distributed situational awareness both during planning, monitoring and control, and execution of demanding integrated operations. For leaders to be able to accomplish this, we suggest utilizing the following illustrative techniques, in addition to individually and collective training; objective hierarchies, Structured Analysis and Design Technique (SADT), agent-based flow charts (ABFC), and Neisser's perceptual cycle model.

Objective Hierarchy

As illustrated also on Fig. 3.8, it's of vital importance to identify and share the vision (overall or main objective) of an operation (Aarset 2016). To clarify, a main objective should be subdivided into several more detailed sub-objectives or sub-goals and constraints. Such sub-goals can be organized in a meaningful way by using a hierarchical structure, although such a hierarchical structure will rarely be entirely unambiguous. Furthermore, this can easily result in sub-goals that vary strongly in terms of clarity and level of detail, and the sub-goals can even be mutually conflicting.

Also, such a specification can often lead to important parts of the vision or main objective disappearing. Therefore, be careful not to forget important factors when attempting to specify the vision. On the other hand, an overly extensive or detailed subdivision can lead to the main idea behind a vision being pulverized. Sometimes, this structuring of objectives can be very complex, while at other times it can be quite simple. Anyhow, it will improve the agent's consciousness, which basically is the general idea.

The desired level of detail will usually depend on what this specification is to be used for. If it is only intended for use in a planning phase, a less detailed specification will probably suffice. It is recommended to specify the objectives to one level lower than the level at which you wish to define targets and attributes. The level below the "attribute level" can then be used to justify the values assigned to the attributes or be seen as means of achieving the targets (Aarset 2016).

Whether we wish to define the individual sub-items as constraints (barriers) or sub-goals is often a matter of preference, but a preference that should be addressed. A constraint (barrier) is a factor that must not be exceeded under any circumstances, but that we don't necessarily wish to improve beyond meeting that constraint. A (sub-)goal is typically something we would like as much (or as little) of as possible (Aarset 2016).

If, for example, quality and time are of importance, then time as a sub-goal and quality as a constraint will suggest executing the operation as quick as possible, as long as the quality is acceptable. Quality as a sub-goal and time as a constraint are suggesting executing the operation of as high quality as possible, as long as the time frame is not exceeded (Fig. 3.9).

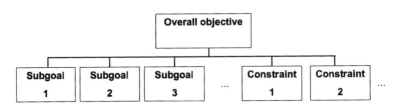

Fig. 3.9 The hierarchical breakdown of a main objective with pertaining targets and attributes

For attributes, measuring if the (sub-)goals are met or the constraints are exceeded, to be useful in an analysis, they should satisfy the following requirements. The attributes should be (Aarset 2016):

- *operational*, so that they can tell us with a certain amount of precision the extent to which the objective has been achieved
- *complete*, so that they cover all aspects of the objective
- *disjoint*, so that the same factors are not measured in several attributes at the same time
- *minimal*, so that the dimension of the issue is kept as small as possible
- *quantifiable*, so that we can both assign a probability to the different values the attribute can have and specify preferences between these values.

Unfortunately, it is not always easy to find good attributes that, together, satisfy all the above-mentioned requirements. It is also easy to argue that no attribute will be able to fully measure the extent to which an objective has been achieved. It is common, therefore, to instead define "proxy" (or contingent) attributes. A proxy attribute is an attribute that only reflects the objective, but that does not directly measure the extent to which the objective itself has been achieved (Aarset 2016).

SADT-Charts

To illustrate (part of) the system design and the overall flow of phases during a demanding integrated operation, we suggest drawing a flow chart – and more specifically, a *SADT chart* (Marca and McGowan 1988). (This technique is also known as a part of the IDEF family of programs.)

SADT is an abbreviation of Structured Analysis and Design Technique. SADT charts have a lot in common with traditional (functional) flow charts. They also use activity boxes and arrows that, among other things, indicate the order in which activities are to be carried out. There are several software packages for computers that help in drawing and organizing SADT sheets. (The software package usually comes with a good introduction.)

Each activity to be performed is represented by an activity box, and each activity box is given a name and an alphanumerical designation called a node number. The name of the activity box is a verb that describes the activity the box represents. The node number identifies the box and describes the box's position in the SADT chart.

In SADT sheets, the side from which the arrows point at the activity box has a specific meaning. An ICOM system is normally used, where ICOM is an abbreviation for Input, Control, Output and Mechanism. Here, "Input" or input data stands for something that is changed by or is starting the activity in the box. "Output" or output data is a result of or something produced by the activity. "Control" decides when and how the activity is to be performed and is not changed by the activity. "Mechanism" indicates the agents or artefacts (i.e. actors, subsystems, departments

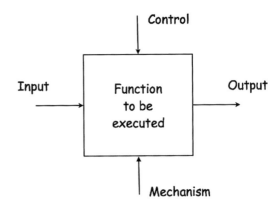

Fig. 3.10 Example of an activity box with ICOM arrows

or units) that perform the activity. A comment, which could be a noun, a designation containing a noun or a verb, is linked to each arrow. An activity box can have several ICOM arrows on each side (Fig. 3.10).

The construction of SADT charts is most often done using a "top-down" procedure. You start with an activity box, often called "A – 0". This box indicates the highest level of the activity to be described.

The activity in this box, named the parent box, is then specified in more detail in several underlying activity boxes. Input data in the parent box are input data in one or more of the activity boxes at the level below. However, the input arrow can also be, for example, the Control for one of the activity boxes at the level below. The same applies to the other arrows from the parent box.

Further analysis of the ICOM arrows at the level above or below is sometimes not desirable. In such situations, you create a "tunnel" instead. If you do not want to include an ICOM arrow at the level below, you put brackets around the arrow nearest to the activity box. If you do not want to include an ICOM arrow at the level above, you put brackets around the arrow furthest from the activity box.

Agent-Based Flow-Charts

SADT charts are practical for illustrating the "flow" of an operation. The internal communication between the different agents and/or the artefacts may on the other side be difficult to see from such an illustration. As this communication often may be vital to avoid human failure, we will introduce an alternative way of illustrating which functions are part of an activity and in what order they are to be performed. We therefore introduce and recommend utilizing so-called *agent-based flow charts* (ABFC) (Aarset 2016).

As the name indicates, the emphasis here is on visualizing the connection between the different agents (i.e. actors, subsystems, departments or units), and how they relate to each other. Using such agent-based flow charts, it is often more difficult to see how a function is performed from beginning to end, but it is significantly easier to see what information and what resources each agent needs to be able to perform his sub-functions, and what information and what result each agent should pass on. It is also often easier to see where and to which other agents this result is to be sent.

The agents that make up the system are identified from the mechanism inputs in the SADT sheets. An agent-based flow chart is then constructed for each agent. Each such agent-based flow chart is constructed by listing all the functions that shall be performed by this agent in a box placed in the middle of the chart. Then identify for each of these functions separately whether or not the function needs input data (information, commands or similar) from another agent. These input data are marked by drawing smaller boxes from each of the other agents to the left of the main box and marking which input data these agents will transfer to the agent in focus here.

Correspondingly, boxes are created on the right of the main box for those of the other agents that are to receive something from this agent. A schematic illustration is shown in Fig. 3.11.

It can be seen as a good test of any group of procedures to check if there is a corresponding "out-put arrow" to each "in-put arrow". Because if some agent is expecting input from some other agent (or artefact), there has to be some agent (or artefact) that needs to have this as an output communication in their procedure.

To improve acquisition and maintenance of distributed situational awareness during execution of demanding integrated operations, we therefore is suggesting to construct an objective hierarchy (including both main objective, sub-goals and constraints), identify and discuss such flow-charts as SADT charts and agent-based flow charts, and seek to improve understanding of human behavior by utilizing the concept of distributed situational awareness (including Neisser's perceptual circle) as illustrated in Fig. 3.8 in Salmon et al. (2009).

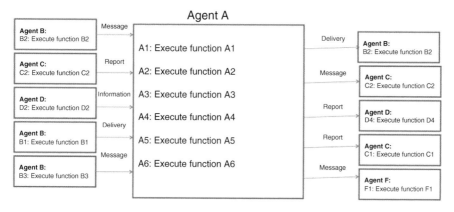

Fig. 3.11 Schematic example of an agent-based flow chart

Part 4: A Short Illustration of the Techniques

From the Police Emergency Preparedness System, Part 1, Norway – Emergency Management Manual (PEPS I) (2007), we see that during a major incident, the police levels of command should be structured as strategic level, operational level and tactical level as illustrated on Fig. 3.12.

At the very high level the objective hierarchy of a police operation may be as illustrated on Fig. 3.13.

A preplanned operation, again at a high level, may be divided into three phases as illustrated in Fig. 3.14. (Here, realistic Command and Mechanism arrows have only been included for the Preparation phase.)

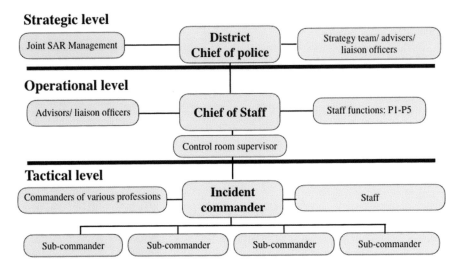

Fig. 3.12 Level of commands

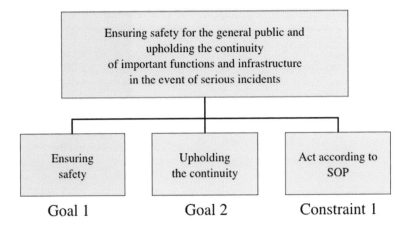

Fig. 3.13 A simple objective hierarchy

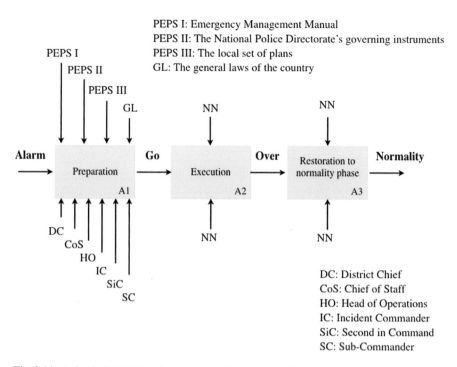

Fig. 3.14 A simple SADT chart for a preplanned police operation

If we focus on the incident commander (IC), we may illustrate the functions he or she is expected to execute during the preparation phase, and the respective interface between the IC and the other agents active in this phase, by introducing the ABFC in Fig. 3.15.

Performing a more thorough analysis we would have been more specific in the objective hierarchy and extending the description of the operation by producing more and more detailed SADT and ABFC flow-charts. Now, comparing with the distributed situational awareness model in Fig. 3.8, we may observe that these kinds of illustrations may improve vital parts of what that model identifies as required to acquire and maintain situational awareness.

- *System factors*: Procedures, system design and system goals may all be visualized with an objective hierarchy, some SADT charts and some ABFCs.
- *Individual factors*: Individual goals may be visualized with an objective hierarchy to be compared with the system goals and roles may be visualized with an ABFC. Neisser's perceptual circle may improve understanding of individual SA requirements, while Experience and Training are handled as of today.
- *Team factors*: Both team processes (communications, collaboration) and team attributes (shared mental models, cohesion, attitudes) may benefit from the visualization of the ABFCs.

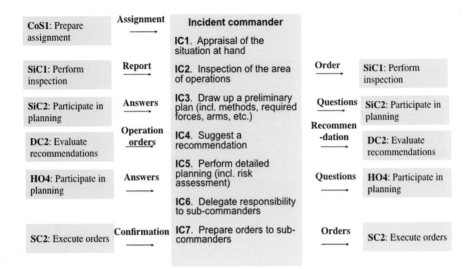

Fig. 3.15 An agent-based flow-chart

- *Task factors*: The process of identifying both workload and complexity in an operation may also benefit from the visualization of the operation by SADT charts and ABFCs.

Thus, utilizing these relatively simple techniques of visualization may considerable improve the distributed situational awareness of an operation – which again is improving both the efficiency and the reliability, and reduce the risk of human failure.

References

Aarset, M.V. (2016). *Risk, issues and crisis management*, Electronic book, http://terp.no.

Adams, M. J., Tenney, Y. J., & Pew, R. W. (1995). Situation awareness and the cognitive management of complex systems. *Human Factors, 37*, 1.

Alison, L., & Crego, J. (Eds.). (2008). *Policing critical incidents. Leadership and critical incident management*. Oxon: Routhledge.

Andreescu, V., & Vito, G. F. (2010). An exploratory study on ideal leadership behavior; the opinions of American police managers. *International Journal of Police Science and Management, 12*(4), 567–583.

Atkinson, R. C., & Shiffrin, R. M. (1971). The control of short-term memory. *Scientific American, 225*(2), 82–90.

Bartlett, F. C. (1932). *Remembering: A study in experimental and social psychology*. Cambridge: Cambridge University Press.

Bedny, G., & Meister, D. (1999). Theory of activity and situation awareness. *International Journal of Cognitive Ergonomics., 3*, 63–72.

Braisby, N., & Gellatly, A. (2005). *Cognitive psychology*. London: Oxford University Press.

van Dijk, A., Hoogewoning, F., & Punch, M. (2015). *What matters in policing? Changes, values and leadership in turbulent times*. Bristol: Policy Press, University of Bristol.

Endsley, M. R. (1995). Towards a theory of situation awareness in dynamic systems. *Human Factors, 37*, 1.

Endsley, M. R. (2000). Theoretical underpinnings of situation awareness: A critical review. In M. R. Endsley & D. J. Garland (Eds.), *Situation awareness analysis and measurement*. New York: CRC Press.

Fleming, J. (Ed.). (2015). *Police leadership. Rising to the top*. Oxford: Oxford University Press.

Fracker, M. (1991). *Measures of situation awareness: Review and future directions* (Report No. AL-TR-1991-0128). Wright Patterson Air Base: Armstrong Laboratories, Crew System Directorate.

Gibson, A & Villiers, P. (2007). Leading for those we serve, NPIA/Home Office.

Glomseth, R. (2015). Towards a profession of police leadership. In S. O. Johannessen & R. Glomseth (Eds.), *Politiledelse*. Oslo: Gyldendal Akademisk.

Golding, B., & Savage, S. (2008). Leadership and performance management. In S. O. Johannessen & R. Glomseth (Eds.), *Politiledelse*. Oslo: Gyldendal Akademisk.

Grint, K. (2005). *Leadership: Limits and possibilities*. Houndmills/Basingstoke: Palgrave Macmillan.

Grint, K. (2010). *Leadership. A very short introduction*. Oxford: Oxford University Press.

Haberfeld, M. R. (2006). *Police leadership*. New Jersey: Pearson Prentice Hall.

Haberfeld, M. R. (2013). *Police leadership. Organizational and managerial decision making process* (2nd ed.). Boston: Pearson.

Head, H. (1920). *Studies in neurology* (Vol. I). London: Oxford University Press.

Hollnagel, E., & Woods, D. D. (2005). *Joint cognitive systematics: Foundations of cognitive systems engineering* (Electronic book). Boca Raton: CRC Press.

Johannessen, S. O., & Glomseth, R. (2015). *Politiledelse*. Oslo: Gyldendal Akademisk.

Katz, R. L. (1955). Skills of an Effctive administrator. *Harward Business Review, 33*(1), 33–42.

Marca, D., & McGowan, C. L. (1988). *SADT: Structured analysis and design technique*. London: McGraw-Hill.

Mitchell, M., & Casey, J. (2007). *Police leadership & management*. Sydney: The Federation Press.

Moggré, M., den Boer, M., & Fyfe, N. R. (2017). Police leadership in times of transition. *Policing*, 1–10.

Neisser, U. (1976). *Cognition and reality: Principles and implications of cognitive psychology*. San Francisco: Freeman.

Norman, D. A. (1981). Categorization of action slips. *Psychological Review, 88*, 1–15.

Northouse, P. G. (2013). *Leadership. Theory and practice* (6th ed.). Thousand Oaks: Sage.

Passer, M., Smith, R., Holt, N., Bremner, A., Sutherland, E., & Vliek, M. (2009). *Psychology. The science of mind and behaviour*. Berkshire: McGraw-Hill.

Piaget, J. (1926). *The language and thought of the child*. New York: Meridian Books.

Plous, S. (1993). *The psychology of judgment and decision making*. New York: McGraw-Hill.

Salas, E., Prince, C., Baker, D., & Shresta, L. (1995). Situation awareness in team performance: Implications for measurement and training. *Human Factors, 37*, 1.

Salmon, P. M., Stanton, N. A., Walker, G. H., & Jenkins, D. P. (2009). *Distributed situation awareness. Theory, measurement and application to teamwork*. Surrey: Ashgate.

Smith, K., & Hancock, P. A. (1995). Situation awareness is adaptive, externally directed consciousness. *Human Factors, 37*(1), 137–148.

Stanton, N. A., & Young, M. S. (2000). A proposed psychological model of driving automation. *Theoretical Issues in Ergonomics Science, 1*(4), 315–331.

Stanton, N. A., Stewart, R., Harris, D., Houghton, R. J., Baber, C., McMaster, R., Salmon, P. M., Hoyle, G., Walker, G. H., Young, M. S., Linsell, M., Dymott, R., & Green, D. (2006). Distributed situation awareness in dynamic systems: Theoretical development and application of an ergonomics methodology. *Ergonomics, 49*, 1288–1311.

Swanson et al. (1998) in Haberfeld, M.R. (2013). Police leadership. Organizational and managerial decision making process, 2nd, Boston: Pearson.

Turbitt, I. & Benington, J. (2015) Testing adaptive leadership theory in practice: The policing of the dumcree demonstrations in Northern Ireland in Brooks, S & Grint, K (eds.) (2010): The new public leadership challenge, Houndmills\Basingstoke: Palgrave Macmillan.

Chapter 4
Promoting Enhanced Public Participation and Community Engagement in Policing

James F. Albrecht

Introduction

Law enforcement agencies across the Americas and in many democratic nations have implemented a number of law enforcement strategies over the last five decades in an effort to reduce crime, violence, and the fear of crime. In North America, from the 1960s through the mid-1990s, these efforts had proven to be relatively ineffective as crime rates increased dramatically. However, the use of technology and a proactive enforcement-oriented approach during the late 1990s has resulted in notable decreases in crime and reported improvements in community quality of life across most of the United States (US), Canada, the United Kingdom (UK), and many other nations. By combining timely crime analysis with a 'zero tolerance' approach, and through effective leadership and management strategies that hold local police commanders accountable for crime control, many police departments have observed dramatic declines in serious and violent crime. As a result, the 'get tough on crime' mindset has rapidly replaced the neighborhood and public oriented approaches fostered by the traditional models of community policing. As such, many law enforcement agencies have shifted their deployment focus from one supporting the 'left realism' community focused theory of justice to one that has firmly grasped the 'right realism' crime and disorder control based ideology.

What has been most disturbing to government and police officials has been the significant decline in trust and confidence in law enforcement organizations, as sensationalized allegations of ethnic profiling and police brutality have become routine. This public scrutiny, often from members of the minority communities, has damaged the reputations of not only those directly involved, but of the law enforcement profession at large. A criminal justice philosophical paradigm shift, from a 'right realism' enforcement-oriented strategy to one advocating 'left realism' and the

J. F. Albrecht (✉)
Department of Criminal Justice and Homeland Security, Pace University,
New York, NY, USA

© Springer Nature Switzerland AG 2019
J. F. Albrecht et al. (eds.), *Policing and Minority Communities*,
https://doi.org/10.1007/978-3-030-19182-5_4

direct involvement and input of the community and the crime victim, may be in order. It is therefore recommended that any future criminal justice and police reform endeavors incorporate direct public engagement and the 'left realism' perspective into any prospective policy proposals. This transition aligns with the recent recommendations made within the report by the President's Task Force on 21st Century Policing (2015) in the United States, the emphasis on prioritizing community policing and enhanced citizen and engagement across the United Kingdom (City of London Police 2014; United Kingdom Home Office 2015), and the continuing shift toward public and victim involvement in policing, rule of law and crime prevention practices across Canada (Canada Department of Justice 2015)

Criminological Explanations for Increasing Crime Rates

Once regional crime statistics began to be collected and recorded on a national level in the USA in the 1960s, it became easier for the public to take note of crime trends, and in particular, the generally increasing violence rates. At the same time, the movement for social justice had not only taken form, but was moving at full speed across America. In addition, through the 1970s, criminological explanations for crime had continued to emphasize the examination of the individual offender, e.g. rational choice theory (Becker 1968), routine activities theory (Cohen and Felson 1979), etc., in attempting to explain contributing and motivating factors behind deviant conduct and criminal actions. In the 1980s, new theoretical perspectives arose that again questioned the role of society itself as a principal influence in clarifying criminality. This new form of radical criminology resulted in a number of novel theories. Two interrelated paradigms include critical criminology and the 'left realism' theory of justice, both of which follow the leftist, socialist and neo-Marxist traditions (Tierney 1996).

Critical Criminology

The critical criminological theory maintains a number of recurrent concepts, which include:

a) Crime must be viewed in the context of capitalist society,
b) Capitalism supports an atmosphere of class conflict,
c) Social control and law are related to materialism,
d) Effective societal change must involve a move away from capitalism to socialism, and
e) Individualized explanations for criminal theory should be eliminated (Tierney 1996).

As such, individuals who are commonly called 'criminals' are actually considered 'victims' of capitalist society's tendency to maintain power, wealth and comfort within the elitist class. And it is postulated that this upper class has created a mechanism called the criminal justice system, with its repressive laws, to preserve their monopoly on social control. Ultimately, the solution would be to create an egalitarian society where justice is applicable equally to all (Quinney 1974).

For a contemporary example of related criticism of the criminal justice process in the United States, Pontell et al. (2014) posit that the influence of major players in the American banking industry on government officials restrained the proper prosecution of apparent financial crimes that led to the greatest recession of the American stock exchanges and a dramatic decline in the national (and even global) economy, often without punitive repercussions. It could therefore be stated that the general public were the true victims, as many lost large amounts from their savings and pensions, while the elitist class involved in the financial industry were ultimately found again to be "above the law."

The 'Left Realism' Theory of Justice

In contrast to the assertion by critical criminologists that America be transformed from a capitalist society into a Marxist 'utopia' (Quinney 1974), the 'left realism' theory of justice retained the socialist perspective, yet promoted that crime and crime prevention must be taken seriously, and that a practical approach had to be considered in an effort to correct the injustices imposed by society, and prevent the injuries and damages incurred through criminal victimization. In line with the perceptions of critical criminologists, while the elitist class is blamed for the definition of criminal acts, much of the crime is being committed by working class and impoverished males. But with each of these criminal infractions, there are the unfortunate victims, and the majority of the victims of property and predatory crime are mainly from the middle and more often from the lower classes. At the same time, the criminal justice system has shifted its emphasis to the offender and upon the general effect of crime on society at large. As such, the role and input of the victim has overwhelmingly been eliminated, and the attention granted to the individual victimization in the past has been reduced. On the other hand, criminologists who support the 'left realism' perspective believe that both the offender and the victim are significant concerns within the crime problem, and that any sociological analysis must incorporate both of those parties, and other factors, into the search for an effective resolution (Tierney 1996).

Those who promote the left realism theory of justice advocate that critical criminologists must also take crime and crime prevention seriously, at the same time as challenging the 'right realism' emphasis on stringent crime and disorder control. In summary, Tierney (1996) noted that the 'left realism' theory of justice makes an attempt to:

1. Build an accurate picture of crime and its impact on victims;
2. Develop causal explanations of criminality;
3. Trace the relationship between offenders, victims, and formal and informal controls; and

4. Develop 'progressive' yet realistic policies aimed at the reduction of victimization rates, especially among vulnerable, lower socio-economic groups.

Without a concerted effort from the 'left' (i.e. activists and politicians who are politically liberal) to stress the victimization of the working and impoverished classes, it has been proposed that the 'right' (i.e. those who are politically conservative) will control the issue in the public and political arenas, and the 'get tough on crime' approach, which reportedly has devastatingly targeted racial minorities and individual from the lower social classes, will continue to receive the enhanced attention of government and law enforcement administrators (Schwartz and DeKeseredy 2010).

The theory of left realism highlights the social interactions involved in crime control endeavors by portraying the complex relationships between the significant actors within the 'square of crime.' These four critical variables include the offender, the victim, the police (and the entire criminal justice mechanism), and the community (Young 1992). Within this theory of justice, there are four primary elements necessary for the development of criminality. On one side are the agents for social control and on the other side is the criminal act. Social control agents include the police, other criminal justice actors and the public/community. The criminal act, particularly as it relates to predatory crime, involves the offender(s) and the victim(s). Altogether, the offender must engage in deviant behavior that harms/hurts a victim and these actions would elicit a formal response by the criminal justice mechanism to enforce the law. And finally, the act itself must be acknowledged as a legal transgression by the informal contributor to the square of crime, the community. As such, all of the elements must be present and all must collectively interact to produce crime (Young 1992).

The critical actor within Young's 'square of crime' is the public. Since the victims belong to the community, the responses to crime should be undertaken at the local level (Matthews 1992). As such, advocates of left realism recommend some form of cooperative community network be implemented to counter crime, but at the least, there should be public input into the management and philosophical practices of the police. This mandate is apparently in line with the community policing practices that promote public involvement, engagement, and feedback. Other options proposed to enhance community input have included restorative justice practices, victim-offender mediation processes, target hardening, and youth, family and victim support mechanisms (Matthews 1992). Ultimately, primary crime prevention and rehabilitation should take priority over the contemporary emphasis placed on punishment and incarceration.

The 'Right Realism' Theory of Justice

In contrast, the 'right realism' theory of justice, advocated most commonly by the politically conservative, is oriented toward crime prevention and punishment, with little energy and support granted toward seeking the root causes of crime and deviance (Wilson 1975). The right realism perspective relies on a number of criminological theories, i.e. rational choice theory (Becker 1968), routine activities theory (Cohen and Felson 1979), among others, to stake the claim that offenders voluntarily engage in illegal conduct and as such, should face the appropriate penalty for their illicit actions. Retribution and incapacitation are viewed as the primary correctional options.

As a result, stringent crime control, proactive law enforcement, and incarceration are the preferred options to ensure a safe society. Strong efforts at preventing contact between an offender and a potential victim is viewed as a clear path to crime deterrence. For the supporters of the right realism theory, the arrest and high volume police-suspect engagement approaches commonly observed in proactive police agencies across the United States, Canada and the United Kingdom are the proposed and preferred tactics for effective crime prevention.

Examining Successful Endeavors to Strengthen Police-Public Engagement

The left and right realism theories of justice can be better appreciated through a case study approach by examining and highlighting related practices observed in the United States, the United Kingdom, and Canada. In addition, specific legislation and policies enacted to improve public engagement and victim participation into criminal justice procedures within these western democracies will be outlined, and relevant empirical findings will be highlighted. Finally, practical recommendations will be proposed that could potentially incorporate the left realism ideology into contemporary policing and criminal justice strategies.

The New York City Police Department

First, an analysis of the policies and organizational strategies utilized by the New York City Police Department, as an example and consistent trend setter of American municipal law enforcement, may provide insight into the fluctuation in theoretical justice philosophies that have been incorporated into mainstream policing tactics and practices in the United States and other western nations over the last five decades.

The New York City Police Department (NYPD) is a municipal law enforcement agency tasked with serving the metropolitan area of New York City, which encompasses more than 350 square miles (i.e. 907 square kilometers) of terrain. With a residential population approaching nine million, and a cadre of NYPD enforcement personnel close to 36,000,[1] the primary functions of the NYPD emphasize public

---

[1] In 2019, the NYPD consisted of approximately 36, 000 police officers and an additional 9000 unarmed traffic enforcement and school safety officers.

safety and security. Over the last 50 years, the NYPD has continued to revise its crime control and public service models, with the ultimate goal of reducing serious and violent crime and deterring terrorism. Many of these measures have been incorporated into other large American municipalities.

Applying the 'Left Realism' and 'Right Realism' Philosophies to the NYPD

The New York City Police Department has implemented a number of enforcement philosophies since 1960 in an effort to counter rising crime, street violence, and public fear (Albrecht 2012). The reactionary deployment of police resources in the 1960s and 1970s had proved to be ineffective. The randomized nature of vehicle patrol failed to deter crime or lead to increased arrest rates. The NYPD had no distinct (or effective) crime reduction policy in place until the early 1980s. One could conclude that the NYPD had implemented a 'soft' version of the right realism perspective in the 1960s and 1970s, which generally had incorporated the law and order mandate.

With drug related violence escalating in the 1980s, the NYPD initiated community policing as a proactive crime reduction, problem solving strategy. Initially limited to 10 police officers in each police station, this evolved into the agency wide deployment protocol in 1990. Noteworthy crime control results were limited before showing signs of nominal effectiveness in the mid-1990s. Of greater importance, the community policing concept permitted community residents (i.e. police station community council) to designate the priority problems to be addressed by the local police commander, and therefore had a direct impact on the deployment of local police station resources. These initiatives had commenced a transition toward a stronger left realism organizational ideology. As such, although NYPD investigative efforts into serious crime cases were not overwhelmingly affected, street level enforcement and deployment were in the control (albeit limited) of neighborhood representatives. In addition, it was the police station community council that gauged the effectiveness of the local NYPD performance each month. In addition, each community policing beat officer, deployed on neighborhood foot patrol, was directed to contact each person who filed a NYPD criminal complaint or incident report to determine if more information about the event could be discerned and to see if the victim wanted any further specific action taken. Both victim and community feedback and input (and the bases of the left realism concept) had become essential aspects of NYPD endeavors from the 1980s through the mid-1990s (Albrecht 2012).

However, a new development involved the 'get tough on crime' mandate, which commenced in 1994 as the result of the strong demand by New York City's residents for the police to aggressively address community complaints involving 'quality of life' infractions.[2] The resulting 'zero tolerance' directive authorized the arrest of all offenders regardless of the seriousness of the crime or offence. This initially was the

---

[2] Quality of life issues included begging, public intoxication, loud noise, street level drug dealing and usage, graffiti, etc.

responsibility of community policing personnel, but with a significant and clear reduction in serious and violent crime by the end of 1994, all patrol and investigative personnel were directed to engage in increased enforcement activity (i.e. arrests and court and traffic summonses). The responsibility for coordinating long term problem solution to crime and disorder complaints moved from the front line police officer (under the traditional community policing approach) to the local police station commander.[3] Timely crime analysis permitted police resources to be mobilized to crime and disorder 'hot spots' (as highlighted on crime maps). At the same time, however, precinct level priorities were designated by the police station commander, and community participation became superficial at best. With steeply declining crime rates, this enforcement oriented ideology had become the organizational philosophical norm, which continues to the present date (Albrecht 2012). One could easily conclude that the NYPD has since 1994 undertaken an enforcement strategy that strongly grasps the right realism philosophy.

Following the tragic World Trade Center events of September 11, 2001, the NYPD developed similar proactive tactics to counter the threat of future terrorist attack. Intelligence gathering efforts that targeted members of the Muslim community throughout the New York City tri-state area[4] were quickly commenced and had since been enhanced. Once again, the counter-terrorism deployment protocol did not seek input from Muslim, Middle Eastern or other community representatives. As a direct result, the right realism approach continues to be the predominant ideology in the terrorism fighting initiatives and crime control efforts of the NYPD and most American state and local law enforcement organizations.

Transitioning to Direct Public and Victim Engagement

Most American metropolitan police departments over the last 50 years have transitioned from a soft version of right realism with the (clearly ineffective) law and order reactive deployment strategy observed in the 1960s and 1970s; then slowly but dramatically had transformed into an impressive public participation model, involving community policing, that incorporated aspects of the left realism perspective, in the 1980s and first half of the 1990s; and finally have resorted to and have generally maintained a proactive, enforcement-oriented approach involving their crime control and counter-terrorism endeavors since 1994 and continuing to contemporary times. With minimal community input or feedback and little interaction with victims (other than

---

[3] It was noted that front line patrol and community police officers had difficulty in developing lasting solutions to reported problems and crime trends due to their general levels of police inexperience. In addition, it was clearly much easier for the tenured police station commander to re-deploy resources and develop long term strategies than it was for a new police officer to develop effective problem-solving strategies for local crime and disorder complaints.

[4] The tri-state area includes New York City and the New York, New Jersey and Connecticut commuter regions.

recording police incident reports), most contemporary American police departments remain deeply entrenched in the right realism perspective of justice. And, given the reported successes of the 'get tough on crime' approach as it relates to crime control in the USA, the United Kingdom, and other nations, it is unlikely that the philosophical 'realism' pendulum will dramatically swing in the 'left' direction unless there is dramatic public demand to move in that direction. However, given the frequent criticism placed on policing practices in many urban American, British and Canadian municipalities, specifically from underrepresented minority groups, the time for a philosophical paradigm shift that will incorporate the input of all factions of society into policing and criminal justice policy and practices, in line with the left realism theory of justice, may be at hand. These options also align with the final recommendations noted within the Final Report of the President's Task Force on 21st Century Policing (2015), which closely examined contemporary affairs in law enforcement practices across the United States. In an effort to increase public trust in the police, this critical report specifically highlighted the need for enhanced citizen-police engagement:

> "Law enforcement agencies should, therefore, work with community residents to identify problems and collaborate on implementing solutions that produce meaningful results for the community. Specifically, law enforcement agencies should develop and adopt policies and strategies that reinforce the importance of community engagement in managing public safety. Law enforcement agencies should also engage in multidisciplinary, community team approaches for planning, implementing, and responding to crisis situations with complex causal factors" (President's Task Force on 21st Century Policing 2015, p. 3).

The report additionally highlights the relevance of social media and the internet to keep the public informed in real time of relevant incidents, crime trends and community events. Clearly this transition is in line with the basic tenets of the left realism perspective.

Examining Community Policing and Citizen-Police Engagement in Practice

After this introduction, a number of examples of community policing and citizen and crime victim engagement options and legislation from the United States, the United Kingdom and Canada should enhance understanding and provide direction for potential policy recommendations aimed at incorporating the left realism theory of justice into current criminal justice practices.

Examining Community Policing in the US, the UK, and Canada

The American federal government viewed the potential for the community policing concept so highly that in 1994 it created the Office of Community Oriented Policing Services to provide guidance and funding to US police departments with the goal of incorporating community policing practices into all law enforcement agencies across the country. Specific expenditures were initially approved to support the hiring of an additional 100,000 community policing foot patrol officers nationally to counter the expanding street crime and violence rates that had been plaguing America's largest cities. Over the last two decades, the US Department of Justice COPS Office has funded the hiring of more than 125,000 community policing officers in more than 13,000 local, state and tribal police departments across the US (US Department of Justice COPS Office 2015).

Around the same time, government leaders in the United Kingdom, faced not only with increasing crime rates, but with repeated allegations of racially discriminating policing practices, ushered in the Community Safety Act of 1998. The highlight of this new law enforcement philosophy involved the 'neighborhood policing model,' which involved using career and volunteer police resources to address crime and disorder priorities identified by the local community and to reduce fear of crime. The neighborhood policing teams routinely relied on a 'zero tolerance' enforcement strategy with a 'problem-oriented policing' approach (McLaughlin 2007).

The Solicitor General of Canada, as early as 1990, had advocated community policing as the "most appropriate police response to crime and disorder problems in modern Canadian society" (Normandeau and Leighton 1990, p. iv). Police personnel were instructed to engage in proactive, problem solving to address community crime and disorder concerns, while deployed on neighborhood foot patrol and in local police mini-stations (Normandeau and Leighton 1990). However, in contrast to the United States and the United Kingdom, Canada maintained a rather decentralized approach, and permitted the Royal Canadian Mounted Police and local law enforcement agencies to individually and independently coordinate specific community policing practices.

It is not hard to conclude that in the 1990s, community policing practices were in place in most western democracies.

Common Community Policing Practices

Engaging the public in providing input into law enforcement policies and practices can take many forms. Examining tactics that have been proven to enhance the police-community dynamic in the past may be the best method for developing contemporary strategies. One does not have to go further than the variety of community policing tactics in the United States, the United Kingdom and Canada that have been viewed as being successful in improving public involvement in safety and security measures, and in providing options for community input into local policing priorities. Some of the most common community policing practices, as observed in western democracies, have included:

1. Strengthening police-community partnerships;
2. Police collaboration with neighborhood residents and other public and private agencies;

3. Media outreach and cooperation;
4. Proactive problem solving;
5. Geographic assignment of police personnel to fixed beats or areas;
6. Crime prevention approach;
7. Addressing disorder and improving neighborhood quality of life;
8. Distribution of traffic safety and crime prevention material;
9. Improving school safety;
10. Distribution of real time crime data to police personnel and community members;
11. Development of a protocol to permit two way communication between the police and community via community meetings, the internet, and social media;
12. Use of community volunteers;
13. Establishment of a neighborhood watch and / or community patrol program;
14. Citizen police academies; and
15. Use of citizen surveys to measure fear of crime and trust in police as alternate measures of police organizational effectiveness.

Ultimately the consideration of any of these options into contemporary law enforcement protocols and endeavors must also acknowledge the roles that technology and social media play in modern society.

Public Perceptions of Community Policing Practices

Two criminologists, Goldstein (1990) and Trojanowicz (1988), independently conducted the initial research on community policing pilot programs in the United States. Their findings about these law enforcement strategic deployment options, which eventually were generally referred to as community policing, appeared to improve citizen satisfaction in police and the job satisfaction of patrol officers, and promoted a problem-solving approach which advocated the development of long-term solutions to crime trends. Forced to make ideological changes due to the increasing crime rates across the United States in the 1980s and 1990s, police executives in large cities across America, e.g. San Diego, New York City, and Chicago among others, implemented small community policing pilot programs (Albrecht 2012), which later expanded to more complex agency-wide strategies within most police departments across the United States. During the 1990s, a number of research studies that evaluated the implementation of community policing in American police agencies noted significant results, the most notable being increased confidence and trust in the police (Scott and Goldstein 2005 and Lord et al. 2009). Since the 1990s, the community policing concept quickly became a global phenomenon and was expanded to the United Kingdom (Quinton and Morris 2008), Canada (Friedman 1992), and elsewhere (Albrecht 2012).

Victim Involvement in the Criminal Justice Process

While the primary goal of this paper is to highlight options for increased public involvement and participation in policing practice, the second consideration would involve efforts to re-integrate the victim back into the criminal justice process. This is another tier advocated by the left realism philosophy. Generally speaking, other than the initial police report and interview, and an occasional related court appearance, crime victims are rarely involved directly in the various steps of the criminal justice mechanism. Victim input and restitution continue to be rare in both policy and practice, although laws have repeatedly been created to enhance protections for the crime victim.

The direct involvement of a crime victim in criminal justice processes is critical to reducing the resultant frustrations routinely encountered by victims of crime. A victim's sense of justice directly impacts their perception of procedural legitimacy (Reisig and Lloyd 2008; Sunshine and Tyler 2003). It is therefore imperative that victims be granted the opportunity to regain their sense of security and that their status as victim be acknowledged by criminal justice actors (Orth 2003). As a result of these sentiments, efforts have been made to initiate the enhanced involvement and input of crime victims throughout the criminal justice processes through the implementation of related legislation and government regulation.

One of the more significant pieces of federal legislation created by the United States Congress was the 'Justice for All' Act of 2004 (H.R. 5107 – Public Law 108-405 2004). Part of this law modified the federal criminal code to grant crime victims specific rights which include:

1. The right to be reasonably protected from the accused;
2. The right to reasonable, accurate, and timely notice of any public court proceeding or any parole proceeding involving the crime, or of any release or escape of the accused;
3. The right not to be excluded from any such public court proceeding, unless the court, after receiving clear and convincing evidence, determines that testimony by the victim would be materially altered if the victim heard other testimony at that proceeding;
4. The right to be reasonably heard at any public proceeding in the district court involving release, plea, sentencing, or any parole proceeding;
5. The reasonable right to confer with the attorney for the Government in the case;
6. The right to full and timely restitution as provided in law;
7. The right to proceedings free from unreasonable delay; and
8. The right to be treated with fairness and with respect for the victim's dignity and privacy.

As with community policing, the US government provided funding to ensure that the relevant sections of this legislation were properly enacted and effectively operational. Federal grants to state, tribal, and local prosecutors' offices, law enforcement agencies, courts, jails, and correctional institutions, and to qualified public and private entities were made available to develop, establish, and maintain programs for the enforcement of crime victims' rights. In addition, budgeting was set aside for the improvement of the Victim Notification System, which enables federal law enforcement to make sure that crime victims receive timely notification of all court proceedings, parole and probation hearings, and any release hearings. The primary shortcoming of this Congressional Act was that it applied these rights only to those crime victims whose cases were being processed through the American federal courts (US Department of Justice Office for Victims of Crime 2006).

Many American states have developed their own protocols for assisting and supporting victims of crime. New York State, for example, has implemented the Office for Victims Services to ensure that certain key rights are provided to crime victims (New York State Crime Victims Board 2007). This legislation specifically stipulated that crime victims have the "right to be involved in certain stages of the criminal justice process" and the "right to make a statement at the time of the defendant's sentencing, if you are the victim of a felony," among other mandates. Generally similar guidelines are in place in all American states and territories.

In line with these American guidelines, the Ministry of Justice in the United Kingdom has enacted the 'Code of Practice for Victims of Crime' (UK Ministry of Justice 2015), which provides extensive rights to victims of crime, which include such options as "(r)eferral to organizations supporting victims of crime; (u)pdates about the police investigation," and "the right to make a Victim Personal Statement (VPS) to explain how the crime affected the victim," in addition to other provisions. It is obvious that government officials in the United Kingdom, through the enactment of this important law, have strongly considered the concerns of the crime victim. The relative novelty of this legislation, however, makes it difficult to assess the impact and direct effects since the law's implementation.

The Canadian government has also recently enacted the Canadian 'Victims Bill of Rights' (2015) that granted the following rights and protections to crime victims, including the "right to information about the status of the investigation and the criminal proceedings," the "right to convey their views about decisions to be made by authorities in the criminal justice system that affect the victim's rights," and the "right to present a victim impact statement and to have it considered," along with other stipulations that enhance victim understanding and participation in the criminal justice and restorative processes. Once again, given the law's temporal immaturity, it is presently challenging to identify the benefits and costs of these provisions at this time.

It is evident that many western democracies, as noted above, have strongly considered and addressed the relevance of the victim within the criminal justice system. However, each of these impressive legislations has overlooked a very critical element as it relates to one of the more commonly applied practices observed in the criminal justice process, particularly in the United States. The vast majority of criminal cases are rather quickly adjudicated through the application of a plea bargain (i.e. a defendant is granted the opportunity to plead guilty to a lesser offense in return for a shorter incarceration or other less punitive sentence). It is not very clear in any of the victim's rights statutes noted above, whether a crime victim has input into this commonly occurring and crucial decision making stage. In practice, this appears unlikely, and any notice of the defendant's punishment would likely provide little consolation to the victim of a criminal incident. As such, the benefits of these comprehensive legal acts may often be viewed as being moot, rather than helpful, to those who have unfortunately been impacted by a criminal offense.

Practical Recommendations for Enhanced Public and Victim Engagement

As the result of this thorough evaluation of policies and legislation related to community policing and the enhanced participation of the public and crime victims into the criminal justice practices, a number of policy recommendations can be proposed.

Given the frequent calls from certain factions of the media and the community-at-large for criminal justice reform, the challenge for both policy maker and administrator involves the development of proposals that would maintain the crime control perspective, while considering options for enhanced public and victim engagement throughout the criminal justice processes. It is likely that the left realism theoretical philosophy may provide insight and guidance into potentially effective strategies for accomplishing these objectives. As such, a number of practical recommendations can be proposed.

In order to avoid the main criticism of the advocates of the conflict theory, i.e. that elitists develop criminal statutes in an effort to maintain control over the lower social classes, it may be appropriate for all newly proposed criminal legislation to undergo community debate and public approval. Many states, including California, provide the option for public referendums to be voted upon by the voting eligible population, normally at the time of annually scheduled political elections, to decide on the implementation of new legislation. This option could be considered for all newly proposed criminal law in an effort to allow for public input into this critical stage of the criminal justice process.

The police in many jurisdictions, as the result of crime analysis and the streamlined collection of criminal intelligence, have become quite effective in their crime prevention and crime control endeavors. The challenge, then, will be to propose steps to enhance public involvement in crime control and to provide greater support to crime victims. The lessons learned from the community policing experiences in western democracies, as noted above, should provide guidance into which strategic aspects would prove to be the most effective in ensuring public input and insight into local policing efforts. A neighborhood police-community council, jurisdictionally aligned within police station boundaries, and elected, not appointed, by public vote, could be tasked with identifying the priorities to be addressed by regional law enforcement personnel. Monthly police-community council meetings should be announced and posted, through social and traditional media, and open to all local residents and business persons. The attendance of local police command staff, fully prepared to discuss contemporary crime and disorder concerns, should be made mandatory.

Citizen exposure to police practices, through citizen police academies, public ride-alongs, and the use of trained community volunteers to supplement full-time personnel, should be strongly considered as a means to promote cooperation and transparency. In addition to the official police agency website, popular social media options should be utilized to provide public access to crime statistics; distribute crime prevention material and crime trend information; outline the concerns raised during police-community council meetings; and afford the means for supplying feedback and input to local and regional police command staff.

In addition to sharing information about local and regional crime rates, the public should be regularly surveyed by an independent professional entity to assess local perceptions of: public trust in the police, fear of crime, police effectiveness, neighborhood quality of life, and other relevant factors. The results of this survey should be reported to local, regional, and national police authorities; local and regional government officials; interested media; and prominently posted on the police department's official website.

In an effort to address the concerns of the crime victim at the earliest phase of the criminal justice process, the local police agency should be obligated to provide each victim with a copy of the official police incident report (with necessary redactions) in a timely fashion. Mandatory notice of developments at all later stages of the investigation, prosecution and court processes should be provided to every crime victim; and ample steps should be made to ensure the safety of crime victims and witnesses at all times, including at the completion of any judicial or correctional measures. In addition, any requests for restitution should be coordinated by the local criminal and civil courts on behalf of the crime victims concerned.

The above proposals would permit law enforcement executives to continue with effective crime control and prevention endeavors, while allowing for local community insight and input into policing practices and priorities. Police commanders should be measured not only on their ability to reduce crime rates, but also on the public perceptions of organizational transparency and legitimacy and fear of crime.

Transforming Contemporary Policing

There have been many calls for criminal justice reform in Canada, the United Kingdom and globally over the last decade, and even more so across the United States of America within the last few years, predominantly from advocates for ethnic and racial minority groups in populated metropolitan centers. Many of the calls for the transformation of policing practices have demanded enhanced community engagement and even direct involvement of the public into the development of revised policing strategies and policies. The time for change may be at hand, and the 'left realism' philosophy may provide critical substance to these reform initiatives.

As a reminder, government officials and police department administrators should never forget that, at the conception of the police profession in 1829, Sir Robert Peel (Lee 1901) made it clear within the first two of his critical principles of law enforcement that all police agencies are obligated to *"recognize always that the power of the police to fulfill their functions and duties is **dependent on public approval of their existence, actions and behavior, and on their ability to secure and maintain public respect**,"* and to *"recognize always that to secure and maintain the respect and approval of the public means also the **securing of the willing co-operation of the public** in the task of securing observance of laws."* It is obvious, particularly in the contemporary era when so much public scrutiny has been placed on policing practices, that police administrators must strongly consider incorporating the direct involvement and engagement of the public into the development of local law enforcement and public safety priorities and practices.

Conclusion

It is imperative that the public-at-large maintain considerable input and insight into criminal justice and law enforcement practices in any democracy. Certain aspects of the 'left realism' ideology of justice administration may provide the inspiration for the requested reforms apparent in contemporary policing, many of which should enhance the levels of transparency and legitimacy that the public demands from the law enforcement and criminal justice officials serving their respective communities. Mandating that the public provide direct input into identifying police priorities and in judging the overall effectiveness of the police agency serving their jurisdiction, and directing that the role of the crime victim be enhanced within each segment of the criminal justice process would take big steps in that direction.

In order to assess the value of these proposed recommendations and the efficacy of the outlined policies and legislation already created for the distinct reason of empowering the public and crime victims in criminal justice practice (in the United States, Canada and the United Kingdom), there is the obvious need for specific research to measure and evaluate these endeavors. There unfortunately has been limited contemporary assessment of these measures and therefore there is the need for substantial research to analyze the potential for left realism in modern rule of law practices.

In conclusion, the 'left realism' perspective clearly can play a major role in contemporary policy reform measures being considered by government and criminal justice leaders interested in matching public demands with rule of law reorganization. There is a variety of policy and legislative options already in place in established democracies that could provide substance and consideration for countries and jurisdictions that are considering the left realism philosophy as the foundation for enhancing practical and perceived enhancements to police and criminal justice performance and transparency, and to increase public trust and confidence in those processes. After all, public service should imply that government workers serve the public (and not the respective agency's and employees self interests).

References

Albrecht, J. F. (2012). Analyzing the implementation and evolution of community policing in the United States and Scandinavia. In M. De Guzman, A. M. Das, & D. K. Das (Eds.), *Strategic responses to crime: Thinking globally, acting locally*. Boca Raton: CRC Press.

Becker, G. (1968). Crime and punishment. *Journal of Political Economy, 76*(2), 196–217.

Canada Department of Justice. (2015). *Police discretion with young offenders*. Ottawa: Canada Department of Justice.

Canadian Victims Bill of Rights, S.C. (2015). c. 13, s. 2. Ottawa: Parliament of Canada.

City of London Police. (2014). *Community policing*. London: City of London Police.

Cohen, L., & Felson, M. (1979). Social change and crime rate trends: A routine activity approach. *American Sociological Review, 44*(4), 588–608.

Friedman, R. R. (1992). *Community policing*. New York: Springer Publishers.

Goldstein, H. (1990). *Problem-oriented policing*. New York: McGraw Hill Publishers.

H.R. 5107 – Public Law 108-405. (2004). *The justice for all act of 2004*. Washington, D.C.: US Congress.

Lee, W. L. M. (1901). *A history of police in England*. London: Methuan and Company.

Lord, V. B., Kuhns, J. B., & Friday, P. C. (2009). Small city community policing and citizen satisfaction. *Policing, 32*(4), 574–594.

Matthews, R. (1992). Replacing 'broken windows:' Crime, incivilities and urban change. In R. Matthews & J. Young (Eds.), *Issues in realist criminology*. London: Sage Publications.

McLaughlin, E. (2007). *The new policing*. London: Sage Publications.

New York State Crime Victims Board. (2007). *A guide to crime victims compensation in New York state*. Albany/New York: New York State Crime Victims Board.

Normandeau, A., & Leighton, B. (1990). *A vision of the future of policing in Canada: Police challenge 2000*. Ottawa: Solicitor General of Canada.

Orth, U. (2003). Punishment goals of crime victims. *Law and Human Behavior, 27*(2), 173–186.

Pontell, H. N., Black, W. K., & Geis, G. (2014). Too big to fail, too powerful to jail? On the absence of criminal prosecutions after the 2008 financial meltdown. *Crime, Law and Social Change, 61*(1), 1–13.

President's Task Force on 21st Century Policing. (2015). *Final report of the President's task force on 21st century policing*. Washington, DC: Office of Community Oriented Policing Services.

Quinney, R. (1974). *Crime and justice in America: A critical understanding*. London: Little, Brown and Company.

Quinton, P., & Morris, J. (2008). *Neighborhood policing: The impact of piloting and early national implementation*. London: Home Office.

Reisig, M. D., & Lloyd, C. (2008). Procedural justice, police legitimacy, and helping the police fight crime: Results from a survey of Jamaican adolescents. *Police Quarterly, 12*(1), 42–62.

Schwartz, M. D., & DeKeseredy, W. S. (2010). The current health of left realist theory. *Crime, Law and Sociological Change, 54*, 107–110.

Scott, M., & Goldstein, H. (2005). *Shifting and sharing responsibility for Public safety problems*. Washington, DC: Office of Community Oriented Policing Services, US Department of Justice.

Sunshine, J., & Tyler, T. R. (2003). The role of procedural justice and legitimacy in shaping Public support for policing. *Law and Society Review, 37*(3), 513–547.

Tierney, J. (1996). *Criminology: Theory and context*. Hertfordshire: Prentice Hall Publishers.

Trojanowicz, R. C. (1988). *The meaning of community in community policing*. East Lansing: National Neighborhood Foot Patrol Center, School of Criminal Justice, Michigan State University.

UK Home Office. (2015). *2010–2015 Government policy: Policing*. London: United Kingdom Home Office.

UK Ministry of Justice. (2015). *Code of practice for victims of crime*. London: UK Ministry of Justice.

US Department of Justice COPS Office. (2015). *COPS fact sheet: 2015 COPS hiring program.* Washington, D.C.: US Department of Justice.

US Department of Justice Office for Victims of Crime. (2006). *OVC fact sheet: The justice for all act.* Washington, D.C.: US Department of Justice.

Wilson, J. Q. (1975). *Thinking about crime.* New York: Vintage Books.

Young, J. (1992). Realist research as a basis for local criminal justice policy. In J. Lowman & B. MacLean (Eds.), *Realist criminology: Crime control and policing in the 1990s.* Toronto: University of Toronto Press.

Part II
Sensitive and Controversial Issues

Chapter 5
Policing and Special Populations: Strategies to Overcome Policing Challenges Encountered with Mentally Ill Individuals

Theresa C. Tobin

Introduction

The intersection of the criminal justice system and the public health system has increased in recent years, mostly as a result of the deinstitutionalization process of those with mental illness in the 1950s. In the United States, deinstitutionalization occurred by reducing the population of individuals residing in mental institutions by releasing patients, shortening the length of stay and reducing both admissions and readmission rates to the facility. As of 2012, the number of patients in state-run psychiatric facilities was 35,000 (Mencimer 2014). This number represents less than a tenth of the number of patients that were in state-run psychiatric facilities in 1955. The aim of deinstitutionalization was to move the care of patients in the state-run psychiatric institutions to less isolated community mental health services. Many of these individuals were increasingly cared for at home or in halfway houses, group homes, clinics and regular hospitals.

One of the unintended consequences of closing these state-run mental hospitals, without ensuring that all patients were connected to services was homelessness, which became a national issue upon deinstitutionalization. Not all of the formerly hospitalized individuals had the resources to live independently and moved to the streets, making up a growing portion of the homeless population. A 2015 survey based on a one-night count of people sleeping on the streets estimated that 564,708

T. C. Tobin (✉)
Molloy College, Rockville Center, NY, USA

New York City Police Department, New York, NY, USA

© Springer Nature Switzerland AG 2019
J. F. Albrecht et al. (eds.), *Policing and Minority Communities*,
https://doi.org/10.1007/978-3-030-19182-5_5

people in the United States were homeless (436,921 of them adults). Of these, 104,083 (24%) were identified as severely mentally ill.

According to the National Alliance on Mental Illness (2015), when a person is in a mental health crisis, they are more likely to encounter police than get medical help. Given this statement and the mental health crisis that has arisen in the United States, part of the solution resides in the collaboration of both the mental health system and the criminal justice system collaborating to address the growing issue of people with mental illness and the response by police departments nationwide. This intersection requires new strategies by both systems, but in particular for those situations in which the police are the first responders to people requiring mental health services. In many places in the United States there has been a growing desire to train police officers on mental health as law enforcement, often the first responders to people with mental illness, has become the de facto provider or connector to mental health services. Many people believe that this has led to the criminalization of mental illness. Although there are issues to be addressed jointly by the public health system and the criminal justice system, the focus of this chapter is on what law enforcement around the country is doing in response to the growing number of calls for people in mental health crises, ranging from children with developmental disabilities to those adults diagnosed with bipolar disorder.

Context

The prevalence of mental illness in the United States is widespread, crossing ethnic, gender and age groups. In a 2015 report, the National Alliance on Mental Illness (NAMI) reported that one in five adults experience a mental health condition every year, and one in twenty live with a serious mental illness such as schizophrenia or bipolar disorder. The 2016 National Survey on Drug Use and Health (NSDUH) reported that one in one hundred (2.4 million) American adults live with schizophrenia, 2.6% (6.1 million) of American adults live with bipolar disorder, 6.9% (16 million) of American adults live with major depression, and 18.1% (42 million) of American adults live with anxiety disorders. These statistics give perspective to the enormous need for community mental health programs, as deinstitutionalization in the 1950s in the United States removed people with severe mental illness from state managed care to community outpatient mental health clinics (Jimenez 2010).

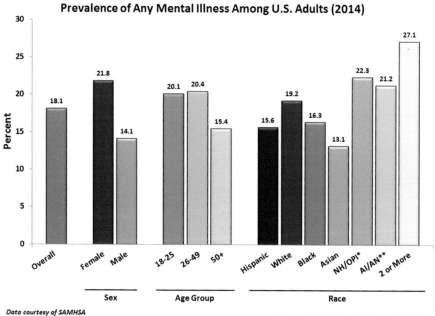

Prevalence of Any Mental Illness Among U.S. Adults (2014)

Data courtesy of SAMHSA

*NH/OPI = Native Hawaiian/Other Pacific Islander
**AI/AN = American Indian/Alaska Native

Background

On September 24, 1987, Memphis police officers responded to a call and encountered a man, later identified as Joseph DeWayne Robinson, a person with mental illness, who was high on cocaine. He was cutting and stabbing himself with a foot-long butcher knife, inflicting as many as 120 wounds on his body. The call for assistance came from Mr. Robinson's mother. As four police officers surrounded him outside his apartment in the LeMoyne Gardens public housing project, the 27 year-old man lunged toward them. The officers discharged their firearms ten times and Mr. Robinson died. This incident – between responding police officers and a person with mental illness – spurred an outcry from mental health officials and advocates who said the police did not know how to handle people with mental illness, especially those in the crisis situations. The National Alliance for Mental Illness lead the charge and were among a group of advocacy groups willing to work with the Memphis Police Department to improve the department's response to mental health crisis calls.

Major Sam Cochran became the Memphis Police Department's choice to coordinate the department's new response. He is known nationally for developing the Crisis Intervention Team (CIT) model which was introduced in 1988 and now is considered "best practice" for law enforcement agencies worldwide. The purpose of the CIT training is to improve the responding officers' ability to safely intervene to people with mental illness, provide linkage to mental health services, and when appropriate, divert the individual from the criminal justice system (Compton et al. 2015).

New York City

In 2017, the New York City Police Department received close to 169,000,911 calls for "emotionally disturbed person."[1] Of prime importance was the final disposition of calls, which included:

- the EDP being brought to/or refusing the hospital;
- these incidents were classified as unnecessary, which includes the dispositions of gone on arrival, unable to gain entry, and unfounded;
- non-crime situations which were handled or referred to a different agency;
- a crime report prepared;
- a non-crime condition being corrected; and
- an arrest.

The dispositions for the calls in 2017 are illustrated in the pie chart below. The disposition of those incidents which were classified as "unnecessary" would include a situation in which a person was walking down the block speaking in an exaggerated manner to no one, causing a person to call 911 only to find out upon the arrival of the police, that the person was speaking on their cell phone via Bluetooth. Generally, the call disposition of "handled or referred to a different agency" refers to those cases in which an Emergency Medical Services responded and handled the call prior to the NYPD's response. An example of "a non-crime condition being corrected," would be a person who is directing traffic at an intersection and is told by police to stop doing so because it unnecessarily places the person in danger and the person complies.

---

[1] The New York City Police Department defines an emotionally disturbed person as, "A person who appears to be mentally ill or temporarily deranged and is conducting himself in a manner which a police officer reasonably believes is likely to result in serious injury to himself or others." New York City Police Department Patrol Guide Procedure 221–13 p. 1.

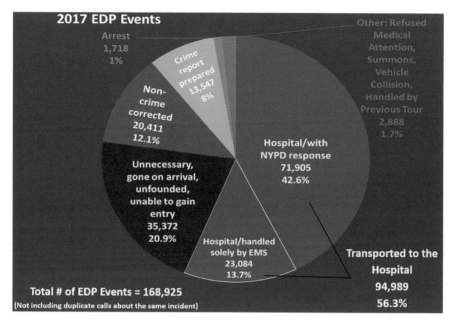

911 Calls to the New York City Police Communications Division for Emotionally Disturbed Persons

As is noted in the above table, the majority of EDP calls result in the individual being transported to the hospital, followed by those calls deemed to be unnecessary, gone on arrival, unfounded or unable to gain entry. One percent of the calls (1718) resulted in an arrest.

Changing Response

In 2014, the New York City Police Department made a commitment to seek out the best practices nationwide of how police departments were responding to people with mental illness and various other people with special needs. In partnership with the Department of Health and Mental Hygiene (DOHMH), personnel from the NYPD visited several cities that had noteworthy training, programs and innovative approaches to addressing these issues. Among the cities visited were Los Angeles, Tempe, Phoenix, Houston and Tucson. The purpose was to examine what other jurisdictions were doing, determine if it could be adjusted to work in New York City and speak to the first responders, both police offices and in some cities, mental health clinicians, about what they believed was working and what could be improved upon.

The exposure was both informative and invigorating. Based on observations, sitting through some of the crisis intervention team trainings and responding with trained officers, the NYPD created its own Crisis Intervention Team training which began in the summer of 2015. There are some staples that were part of each cities training. Among them were: keeping the class size small so that each participant would be involved; ensure that there is interaction with consumers of mental health services and class participants; and, have each trainee participate in scenario based training.

Some of these ideas are wonderful in concept, but posed issues in operationalization. For instance, having a class size of thirty participants is great, but with a department comprised of over 35,000 uniform members, with the goal of training all, the task required creative thinking. Other ideas were a sure fit for the NYPD. Having trainees participate in scenario based training was ideal in the NYPD's new Police Academy located in College Point, Queens. The designers of the academy had the foresight to build in scenario-based space which includes a bank, an apartment, a bodega, a café, and a portion of a subway car, among other mock scenario rooms.

NYPD's CIT Program

In partnership with DOHMH's training academy, the Center for Urban Community Services (CUCS), and NYPD instructors, the CIT training curriculum was developed. The course is 4 days and co-taught by a certified clinician and a tenured NYPD Police Academy instructor. Each day after the first, a review of each topic presented on the previous day is conducted and clarification of any issues that require further discussion is provided. Instructors encourage and sustain an open discussion format with the trainees. The following is an overview of the program, including the various modules incorporated.

Introduction

The program begins with an introduction to the Crisis Intervention Team (CIT) Training Program, informing the participants that the training is based on the Memphis Model, and designed to efficiently and effectively assist individuals in the community who are in crisis due to mental health, behavioral health, or developmental disorders. CIT is a collaborative program with a broad reach that relies strongly on community partnerships and a vibrant crisis intervention system that understands and responds to the needs of the community and law enforcement officers alike. CIT training encourages officers to utilize the mental health crisis facilities located throughout the city in order to redirect individuals away from the criminal justice system, when appropriate. Upon completion of CIT training, officers are provided with a printed directory of local, state and national social service providers that can be offered to individuals in crisis or their family members as an additional resource. Moreover, officers are oriented to the services offered by the NYPD, other city agencies and other field-based care coordination models. CIT training focuses intently on the safety of the person in crisis, the officers involved, and the general public by teaching officers a best practices approach to de-escalating persons in crisis within the Department's response framework with voluntary compliance as the end goal. CIT training aims to reduce the stigma related to mental illness and decreases the need for further involvement within the criminal justice system by ending the revolving door many individuals in crisis routinely find themselves in.

NYPD Protocols

The NYPD's policy, procedures and tactics are reviewed. This module provides officers with an overview of the Department's emotionally disturbed person incident response framework and includes policies, procedures, and tactical recommendations as outlined in the NYPD's Patrol Guide's Tactical Operations. The trainees are reminded that the ultimate goal in these critical incidents is to gain the voluntary compliance of the subject while ensuring the safety of the public and responding officers. This is accomplished through the effective use of de-escalation techniques; a term of art that includes a wide array of skills including crisis communication techniques, emotional response regulation (both for the officer and the subject), and proper tactical management of the incident scene. Furthermore, the trainees are reminded of the Department's general use of force policy, availability of protective equipment, and less lethal device options. Emphasis is added on the need to collaboratively create and employ a coordinated tactical response plan with de-escalation and the deceleration of pace as the primary considerations. The training also promotes and reinforces that the proper handling of these critical incidents increases the Department's standing in the community as a legitimate and procedurally just agency that places a high priority on the safety of its citizens whom the NYPD is called upon to help in a time of crisis. Towards that end, the training reinforces these skills during the subsequent scenario-based exercises where the instructors specifically critique the trainee's performance as it pertains to de-escalation and their employment of a coordinated tactical plan that includes but is not limited to: deceleration, protective equipment, less lethal force options, firearms control, zones of safety,[2] isolation and containment, and leveraging the knowledge and skills of specialty units and supervision when needed. Trainees are also instructed on the

___
[2]Zone of Safety is the distance to be maintained between the EDP and the responding member(s) of the service. This distance should be greater than the effective range of the weapon (other than a firearm), and it may vary with each situation (e.g. type of weapon possessed, condition of EDP, surrounding area, etc.). A minimum distance of twenty feet is recommended. An attempt will be made to maintain the "zone of safety" if the EDP does not remain stationary. New York City Police Department Patrol Guide Procedure 221–13 p. 1.

benefits of conducting a post-incident supervisor-led debriefing of the incident with the purpose of improving our collective response to these critical incidents by analyzing the team's performance and identifying training issues or other deficiencies.

Each day of the course has scenario-based training which are held in mock environments. The state-of-the art NYPD Police Academy has mock-environment training rooms including a precinct station house, multi-family residence, grocery store, restaurant, park, court room, bank, and a subway car and platform. The focus of the scenarios is to provide the opportunity for the trainees to put into practice the best tactics, de-escalation skills and engagement skills they have acquired in the lecture component of the training. Reviews of the scenario and safety instruction are included prior to the exercise commencing. Professional actors are employed to role-play the disorders the trainees have just learned and then by acting them out, the trainees are taught how to identify the disorder, use the appropriate tools to deescalate and gain voluntary compliance. Instructors conduct a supervisor-led discussion detailing the scenario-based training regimen and the safety protocols involving the professional actors and Police Academy facility. Attentive observation, team-centered feedback, and the acceptance of constructive criticism are emphasized. The role of the safety officer is clearly described to the trainees along with the paramount importance of firearms-related security. Following is an example of a scenario utilized during the post-traumatic stress disorder module.

Scenario-Based Training

When teaching students about post-traumatic stress disorder, an overview of the illness is given. The following information is given regarding the pathology. Traumatic events can have long-lasting negative effects. Sometimes our biological responses and instincts, which can be life-saving during a crisis, leave people with ongoing psychological symptoms because they are not integrated into consciousness. Because the body is busy increasing the heart rate, pumping blood to muscles for movement and preparing the body to fight off infection and bleeding in case of a wound, all bodily resources and energy get focused on physically getting out of harm's way. This resulting damage to the brain's response system is called Posttraumatic Stress Response or Disorder, also known as PTSD. PTSD affects 3.5% of the U.S. adult population—about 7.7 million Americans—but women are more likely to develop the condition than men. About 37% of those cases are classified as severe. While PTSD can occur at any age, the average age of onset is in a person's early 20s.

Additionally, the symptoms of PTSD are also taught, indicating that people experiencing PTSD may have intrusive memories, which can include flashbacks of reliving the moment of trauma, disturbing dreams and scary thoughts. They may also utilize avoidance, which can include staying away from certain places or objects that are reminders of the traumatic event. A person may also feel numb, guilty, worried or depressed or having trouble remembering the traumatic event. Additionally the person may experience dissociation which can include out-of-body experiences or feeling that the world is "not real" (derealization) or be hypervigilant, which can include being startled very easily, feeling tense, and the person may have trouble sleeping or outbursts of anger. The medications prescribed for PTSD, namely antidepressants (Prozac, Wellbutrin), Alpha- and Beta Blockers (propranolol, atenolol), and mood stabilizers, are also taught to the participants so that they may become familiar with the names of the medications prescribed for various mental illnesses.

One of the scenarios used for PTSD involves two actors inside an apartment. One actor has PTSD from a previous trauma which can include military service, serious assault, rape, child abuse, robbery, or terrorist attack. The actor has not been taking their prescribed medication due to side effects and is utilizing alcohol to mitigate symptoms. The other actor will be a family member who is currently living with actor suffering from PTSD. The two actors will engage in a disagreement and the actor with PTSD will display a flashback. The 911 call will come over as a noise complaint from a neighbor.

At this point, two of the class's participants respond to the scene. The instructor will be looking for active listening skills (emotional labeling, open ended questions, paraphrasing, minimal encourages, etc.) utilized during the scenario. Additionally, the instructor will be looking for the officers to reorient the subject and speak in a calm tone. The officers should be as concrete as possible when orienting the actor with PTSD. For example, the officers should introduce themselves by rank and name and state that they are police officers with the NYPD. The officer should also ask the family member about any information regarding medical or psychiatric history of the subject, as well as asking if any medication is prescribed and whether or not it is taken. Tactically, the officers should ask the family member if there are any weapons in the house, acknowledging that the family member may not know for sure. When the officers approach the subject they should proceed with caution and look for the subject's hands for any weapon or instrument that could cause injury. When the actor with PTSD comes out of the flashback and appears to be embarrassed, the officers should reassure the actor that they are okay.

Based on the participant's ability to deescalate the situation, there are different potential outcomes. One may be that the actor suffering from PTSD may go into a bedroom and the scenario is transformed into a barricaded/armed person situation and different NYPD protocols are put in motion. Another may be that an ambulance is called and the actor voluntarily goes to the hospital. The key topics that are reviewed are: the effective utilization of crisis communication skills; the proper identification of all potential resources at the scene for gathering possible intelligence about the actor with PTSD prior to engaging or moving forward with the scenario; a coordinated tactical plan; the appropriate de-escalation techniques; utilization of the necessary equipment; and, the implementation of the proper NYPD procedure given the situation.

Peer Panel

One of the most important modules is the peer panel discussion. A group of peer panelists with lived experience relating to mental illness visit the training environment. They share details with the trainees about their personal experiences with mental illness and how their disorder has affected them and their family. Panelists also debrief their experiences in dealing with law enforcement officers while they were in crisis and how those officers performed; both positive and negative aspects of these experiences are discussed. An instructor facilitated discussion is then conducted where each panelist is encouraged to engage the trainees in an authentic and thought provoking manner. As part of the panel discussion the concepts of police legitimacy, procedural justice, stigma, and implicit bias are introduced. The panelists also assist the instructors in highlighting the significance of the NYPD performing in a procedurally just way when responding to critical incidents involving persons in crisis, one that is viewed as fair, impartial, and transparent and that acknowledges the community's voice in the method of getting an individual the assistance they require.

Crisis Communication

Using a behavioral influence model developed by Dr. Gregory M. Vecchi, formerly a Special Agent in the Federal Bureau of Investigation who served as the Chief of the Behavioral Sciences Unit and as a negotiator in the Crisis Negotiation Unit, the Behavior Change Stairway Model (BCSM)[3] establishes the foundation of the crisis communication skills that are utilized throughout the CIT training program. The skills are adapted from crisis and hostage negotiation training and are grounded in extensive research on how to effect a behavioral change. The training emphasizes the use of communication techniques in a calm and courteous manner with the ultimate goal of changing the subject's behavior and gaining their voluntary compliance. Voluntary compliance is achieved through the utilization of a variety of de-escalation and communication techniques that are outlined below. This module entails both a lecture presentation and numerous interactive elements where the trainees practice the skills being reviewed.

The core topics discussed include the following:

Active Listening – An important set of crisis communication skills that greatly contributes to each of the below elements. Active listening is the most critical set of skills a person needs to effectively communicate during a crisis situation.

---

[3] Vecchi, G. M., Van Hasselt, V. B., & Romano, S. J. (2005). Crisis (hostage) negotiation: Current strategies and issues in high-risk conflict resolution. Aggression and Violent Behavior, 10(5), 533–551.

Deceleration and utilization of time – Officers are instructed on how to slow the pace of an incident and not rush towards a quick resolution, whenever possible. Rapidly made decisions, when not required due to an immediate safety concern, lessen an officer's reaction time, prompts an uninformed decision making process, and may provoke an individual who is already in a crisis state. Decelerating the process contributes to achieving a successful outcome by allowing time for more informed decisions to be made that include the person in crisis as the primary stakeholder in the overall process.

De-escalation – Slowing the process down through active listening and crisis communication naturally de-escalates a critical incident and reduces the effect of the emotions the subject is experiencing. These emotions directly influence the subject's actions and must be addressed.

Additionally, the emotional contagion experienced by responding officers is also addressed as they are active participants in the incident and are subject to making poor decisions due to their own emotional fluctuations and perceived challenges to their ego. The final component of de-escalation discussed in this module includes the importance of proper tactical management of the incident scene and the effective utilization and deployment of necessary resources (NYPD and others) which help minimize any potential uses of force, if required.

Participants are also taught about empathy and rapport. Basic psychology and negotiation research demonstrates that in order to change a person's current behavior you need to understand their perspective. This is what true empathy entails. Engaging the subject in a respectful and positive manner builds rapport and increases our legitimacy with the subject and any other persons involved or observing the incident. In order to change a person's behavior and gain voluntary compliance, the officer must be able to positively influence, not manipulate, the individual to change their current behavior and actions. The purpose of demonstrating empathy and building rapport is to eventually influence the person to the point of behavioral change, getting them to voluntarily do what the officer needs him or her to do at that time. Through this process, the officer's actions clearly demonstrate a willingness to help the individual through the process by listening and offering assistance. For responding officers, a critical incident frequently entails a feeling of lack of control over the situation and its participants. The officer, by effectively utilizing the above skillset and techniques, can often regulate the incident and reestablish a sense of order without diminishing their own tactical control over the scene or using force on the subject. Throughout this module, repeated connections are made to the policy, procedure and tactics module in order to underscore the importance of employing a coordinated tactical plan containing de-escalation and deceleration techniques while simultaneously maintaining full situational awareness.

An introduction to both the mental health and criminal justice system is given on the second day of training. This provides trainees with a brief examination and overview of the mental and behavioral health industry, the laws governing the taking of persons into protective custody, and how these issues intersect with the criminal justice system. Instructors address the issues of limited access to and the use of mental health services, mental illness stigma and attitudes towards individuals with mental health issues, recidivism rates, and the frequency of calls for service.

Modules

The following are the mental and behavioral modules covered over the rest of the course. Each module has various scenarios that will be employed in the mock scenarios.

Psychotic Disorders – In this module the clinicians define psychosis and provide statistics on its prevalence in society. They also explain how psychosis affects an individual cognitively and behaviorally. The central mental illness discussed during this module is schizophrenia. The trainees are provided with a list of indicators of the illness and guidance is provided on how to effectively communicate with someone who is symptomatic. The trainees participate in an auditory hallucination exercise which aids in building empathy and rapport between law enforcement and this population. The exercise entails the participants using MP3 players which simulate typical schizophrenia symptoms (e.g. voices) playing constantly in their ear; they are then asked to perform simple tasks. It has proven to be a very effective exercise, as the trainees are not capable of performing the tasks.

Mood Disorders –This module provides the trainees with the knowledge, skills, and abilities to recognize the signs and symptoms of commonly occurring mood disorders and how to safely and effectively render assistance to those persons in crisis. The major disorders that are presented in this module are depression and bipolar disorder. The impact of these and similar disorders among the homeless population is discussed. The trainees are advised that persons with bipolar disorder can have intermittent periods of psychosis and are reminded to employ proper crisis communication strategies and tactics, when applicable.

Suicide Indicators and Prevention – The purpose of this module is to provide the trainees with an overview of suicide that includes the features of ideation, common risk factors, assessment tools, intervention techniques, and prevention strategies. Each year more than 34,000 individuals take their own life, leaving behind thousands of friends and family members to navigate the tragedy of their loss. Suicide is the 10th leading cause of death among adults in the U.S. and the 3rd leading cause of death among adolescents. Suicidal thoughts or behaviors are both damaging and dangerous and are therefore considered a psychiatric emergency (NAMI 2015).

The trainees are instructed to communicate clearly and to deliberately ask the individual in crisis if they want to kill themselves, if they have a plan, and if so, why they want to carry it out on this particular day. The class reviews several positive communication strategies and how to decipher what a protective factor (a reason to live such as family, education, work, etc.) is versus a hot button issue (a topic that will drive the person further into crisis). The impact of suicidal tendencies among the homeless population is also discussed during this presentation. Suicide risks among law enforcement officers are examined and the numerous resources available to assist with handling such a crisis are presented.

Personality Disorders – This module provides officers with the knowledge, skills, and abilities to recognize the signs and symptoms of commonly occurring personality disorders. The major disorders discussed are borderline personality and narcissistic personality disorders. The training program stresses that personality disorders are deeply ingrained maladaptive patterns of thinking and behaving that are inflexible and which generally lead to impaired relationships with others. Communication strategies are discussed and the trainees are advised on the most effective methods to interact with an individual they suspect of having a personality disorder.

Anxiety Disorders – This module presents the signs and symptoms of generalized anxiety as well as several sub-types of common anxiety disorders. The trainees are provided with direction on effective methods for rendering assistance to individuals experiencing intense anxiety. Panic attacks are discussed in depth and the trainees are taught several communication strategies that are effective with this population.

Post-Traumatic Stress Disorder – This module provides the trainees with the knowledge, skills, and abilities to recognize the signs and symptoms of post-traumatic stress disorder and acute stress disorder in an individual experiencing a crisis. Statistics outlining the prevalence of post-traumatic stress disorder among US military veterans and law enforcement officers are discussed. The trainees are provided with direction on effective methods for rendering assistance to individuals with post-traumatic stress disorder.

Mindfulness – This module discusses the basic concepts of mindfulness and examines valuable connections to the work of law enforcement officers. Specifically, a model called Mindfulness Based Stress Reduction is reviewed along with information about the demonstrated efficacy of mindfulness in promoting officer wellness. A brief guided mindfulness exercise created specifically for law enforcement is conducted and information about additional exercises is provided.

Developmental Issues and Childhood / Adolescent Behavior Disorders – The purpose of this module is to provide officers with the knowledge, skills, and abilities to recognize the signs and symptoms of young members of the community who are in crisis. Generally, these mental health issues originate in childhood and may involve a significant impairment of function in different areas that may continue through adult life. The specific disorders covered are conduct disorder, oppositional defiant disorder and antisocial personality disorder. The NYPD's policies and procedures regarding juvenile detention and arrest are also reviewed as many of these critical incidents occur in public schools. The trainees are provided with direction on effective methods for rendering assistance to adolescents in crisis.

Autism Spectrum Disorder – This module provides information about the signs and symptoms of someone living with Autism Spectrum Disorder. Generally, the most significant impairments are in the areas of communication and adaptability to change or unforeseen circumstances. The trainees are provided with general guidelines for effective communication and incident scene management. Additionally, a discussion about the impact Autism Spectrum Disorder has on caregivers and family is facilitated. This module has a particular emphasis since the disappearance of Avonte Oquendo, an autistic 14 year-old boy who went missing from his Long Island City school in Queens on October 4, 2013. The NYPD, working with other governmental agencies, took extraordinary steps. Over 100 NYPD officers were assigned to search for him, the Metropolitan Transportation Agency (MTA) took the unprecedented step of halting overnight track maintenance and ordered at least 200 workers to instead scour the tunnels for him and the NYPD Harbor Unit combed the shoreline. It wasn't until January 17, 2014 that searchers began finding clothing and body parts on a set of rocks along the shoreline in College Point. The following week the Medical Examiner confirmed that the remains where those of Avonte Oquendo. The population of people with autism grows, as the Centers for Disease Control and Prevention (CDC) estimates autism's prevalence as 1 in 59 children in the United States, which includes 1 in 37 boys and 1 in 151 girls,[4] and police interactions increase, the more skills police are taught, the better these interactions will be.

Alzheimer's Disease and Other Dementias –This module reviews several different types of dementia that may be encountered by the trainees while carrying out their duties. The emotional impact of losing one's memory is discussed as it can manifest quite seriously during crisis situations. As with Autism Spectrum Disorder, an examination of the impact on caregivers and family is provided for the officers. The class reviews several positive communication strategies for dealing with someone suffering from dementia. Additionally, the NYPD is examining the ways in which technology can aid in tracking individuals with Alzheimer's when they go missing.

Substance Use Disorder and Co-Occurring Disorders –The purpose of this module is to provide the trainees with the knowledge, skills, and abilities to recognize the signs and symptoms of individuals experiencing a crisis due to impairment by a legal or illegal substance. The prevalence rate of substance abuse and co-occurring disorders is discussed. The trainees are given communication strategies that will assist in determining if the individual has a mental health disorder and / or a substance abuse disorder. A discussion is facilitated about how there is a greater risk of violence and suicide when a subject abuses a substance. Synthetic cannabinoids and opioid pain medications are discussed in detail as this is a current phenomenon impacting many of our local communities. The link between substance abuse and the homeless population is also discussed. Finally, the impact of substance use on law enforcement professionals is discussed along with information about what treatment and recovery options are available. The trainees are provided with direction on effective methods for rendering assistance to individuals with substance use disorder.

---

[4]Centers for Disease Control April 27, 2018 / 67(6); 1–23 (2017).

Participant Feedback

Upon completion of the course, participants are requested to anonymously complete a 14 question survey via survey monkey. The survey requests their feedback on the course instructors, the NYPD instructors and clinicians, actors and peer panelists, and in regards to their ability to communicate the content of the course effectively, as well as the opportunities for the participants to ask questions and express their thoughts and ideas. Other survey questions request their opinion as to the relevancy of the course to their work on patrol and whether it will improve most NYPD officers' ability to interact with a person in crisis. Additionally, comments of the course are sought and often provide helpful insights.

The course is consistently well received, with the overwhelming stating that they would recommend the course to other members of the NYPD, as well as the participants belief that the course will have a positive impact on the Department and its relationship to the community. Here are some of the comments posted after attending the course:

- Learning key points about different psychiatric disorders, how we can identify those disorders, and things we can do or say to deescalate encounters with people in crisis is valuable. The most valuable however, was the focus on our own physical and mental wellness, being that we encounter crisis both in our personal lives and every day at work. Excellent course!
- Scenarios were great, lots of useful information.
- Provides really good foundation on mental health issues removing the stigma associated with mental health. The instructors are top notch and it was a very informative course.
- This is the second time I've done this training and I still find it very intriguing. The scenarios are done very well and have helped me in the field already when I encountered someone with autism.
- I thought hearing from the peer panelists was a great idea because it allows us to hear about their own personal experiences. It also helps us see them in other than crisis moments where we see them as people and not just EDPs.
- The panelists showed the human side of mental illness and brought a personal level that I have not seen before.

Since the course began in the NYPD in June, 2015 all lieutenants and sergeants – the NYPD's front line supervisors have all been trained in CIT. The dispatcher at the NYPD Communications Division automatically directs that the patrol supervisor and the Emergency Service Unit to respond to any call of an emotionally disturbed person. While the Emergency Service Unit is equipped with a host of equipment that can be utilized, the patrol supervisor's vehicle is also equipped with less lethal devices to assist in the containment and control of an EDP. The only time a patrol unit can take the EDP into custody without the specific direction of a supervisor is when the EDP is unarmed, not violent and is willing to leave voluntarily. In all other cases, where the EDP's actions do not constitute an immediate threat of serious physical injury or death to him/herself or others, the officers will attempt to isolate and contain the EDP after establishing a zone of safety until the arrival of the patrol supervisor and Emergency Service Unit. An ambulance will also be requested. As the aim is to help officers effectively handle EDP situations, it is the NYPD's goal to train all members of the department in CIT.

Success Stories

On a frigid January night, officers responded to an incident in the Bronx involving an emotionally distressed woman armed with several knives. The radio dispatcher advised the responding patrol officers that a woman with a history of psychological issues was threatening to kill her father. At the scene the 40 year-old woman in crisis was actively threatening her father's life and daring the officers to shoot her. While maintaining their zone of safety, officers attempted to calm the distraught woman by using numerous communication techniques including reassuring her that they did not intend to harm her. The officers, some who were Crisis Intervention Team trained, worked together combining de-escalation strategies with physical tactics. While one officer continued to seek voluntary compliance by communicating with the woman, while two other officers provided tactical cover. Additional units, including Emergency Service Unit, arrived on the scene and after repeated attempts to get the woman to drop the knives were not successful, an officer utilized their Department issued taser. The woman dropped the knives and was safely subdued. The woman was brought to the ambulance and transported to the hospital. A later conversation with the distressed woman's family revealed that she had intended for the police to kill her when she called 911.

In another instance, police officers responded to a hospital to assist a distressed person in the waiting rom. They observed a 37 year-old woman holding two large knives pressed to her throat. One of the responding officers reflected on how his training in the CIT training helped him and the other officers calm the situation. By maintain their emotional and situational control, the officers immediately attempted to establish a dialogue with her. The officers slowed the situation down by utilizing crisis communication skills including active listening in order to de-escalate the tense situation. Their patience and training paid off when the lady calmed down and dropped the knives to the floor. The woman was then removed to a psychiatric unit for evaluation.

In a story which made media headlines, a newly trained CIT police officer responded to the scene of a suicidal woman on the Upper West Side of Manhattan. The woman, zipped inside of a sleeping bag, with a hood over her head, was standing on a three inch wide ledge below, dangling from the window. She was wrapped in the sleeping bag because she "didn't want to make a mess" (Musumeci and Balsamini 2016). The officer engaged the woman in conversation using flowers as the topic of conversation after the suicidal woman told the officer wanted flowers from Central Park. The officer, Nina Friberg, was able to engage the heavily sedated woman in conversation for approximately 10 min until Emergency Services Unit officers arrived.

Officer Nina Friberg, 35, was among the first rescuers at the scene. She engaged the desperate woman in conversation about flowers in Central Park for 10 min until Emergency Services Unit officers arrived. Because the woman had climbed out of the window through a stairwell in the building, there were no adjoining windows which forced the responding Emergency Service Officer, Detective Randy Miller, to lie on his stomach on the landing of the stairwell in order to see her. As the woman became to doze off, she let go of one hand holding onto the windowsill. At this point, Detective Miller saw her knuckles start to turn white, and he grabbed her hand. Other Emergency Services Officers pulled her to safety through a window one story below. Detective Miller stated it was a coordinated effort and credits Officer Friberg's ability to keep the suicidal woman talking that allowed for them to grab and save her.

Looking to the Future

So, where do we go from here? As the calls for a police response to people with mental illness continues to increase, there are several innovative programs which, although only in their pilot phase, give hope to increasing peaceful and voluntary resolution. In partnership with DOHMH, the NYPD has begun several new initiatives.

In March 2016, the NYPD and DOHMH created co-response teams, comprised of two NYPD uniform officers and one DOHMH clinician. The units respond to referrals from police commanders, service providers, and NYC-Well, another new initiative described below. The co-response teams are utilized as a preventive measure, reaching out to people known to have a mental illness and are exhibiting escalating violence. Since its inception, the co-response teams have had over 1000 contacts, with the vast majority resulting in a positive outcome.

The co-response team is directed by the Triage Desk, which receives real-time information and is staffed by a DOHMH clinician and an NYPD officer. Once a referral is received, the person's health history is obtained by the clinician and, due to the Health Insurance Portability and Accountability Act (HIPPA), shared only with the responding clinician in the field. Additionally, the person's interaction with the police is also obtained by the Triage Desk officer. This report contains information on how often the person received help from the NYPD for an injury or other health related issues in New York City, had a vehicle accident, as well as a criminal justice history, indicating arrests, warrants and summonses. This information is also relayed to the responding co-response team, to best prepare an appropriate response by the team.

NYC-Well is New York City's 24 h connection to free, confidential mental health support. It enables people to speak to a counselor via phone, text or chat and get access to mental health. At any hour of any day, in almost any language, from phone, tablet or computer, NYC Well is the community's connection to get the help needed. It provides:

- Suicide prevention and crisis counseling
- Peer support and short-term counseling via telephone, text and web
- Assistance scheduling appointments or accessing other mental health services
- Follow-up to check that a person has connected to care and it is working for the person.

Lastly, the NYPD is working with DOHMH in developing diversion centers. These centers are being designed to provide alternatives for officers responding to people with mental health and substance abuse issues. Currently, the only options for officers are to either arrest people when there is a low level offense, but the underlying cause is some mental health issue or bring the person to the hospital. The diversion centers will be fully staffed with medical personnel and case managers and operate 24 h a day/7 days a week, 365 days a year. The potential of the diversion centers has many people in the NYPD optimistic in changing how both the public safety and public health systems respond to people in behavioral crisis.

References

Compton, M. T., Broussard, B., Reed, T. A., Crisafio, A., & Watson, A. C. (2015). Surveys of police chiefs and sheriffs and of police officers about CIT programs. *Psychiatric Services, 66*(7), 760–763. https://doi.org/10.1176/appi.ps.201300451.

Jimenez, J. (2010). *Social policy and social change: Toward the creation of social and economic justice*. Los Angeles: Sage.

Mencimer, S. (2014, April 8). There are 10 times more mentally ill people behind bars than in state hospitals. Mother Jones.

Musumeci, N. & Balsamini, D. (2016, April 9). Hero cop saves would-be suicide jumper from 10th floor leap. New York post. Retrieved from https://nypost.com.

National Alliance on Mental Illness. (2015/2017). *Home page.* Retrieved from https://www.nami.org.

Chapter 6
Ethnicity and Other Demographics Associated with Perceived Police Fairness

S. Hakan Can

Introduction: Ethnicity and Other Demographics Associated with Perceived Police Fairness

In theory, police action symbolizes the collective will of society to suppress disorder and crime, but history also suggests that conflict may occur between police officers and the community members they serve. Blacks frequently assume that the police engage in racial profiling as a means to stop, search, and question them more frequently than other racial/ethnic groups (Engel 2008; Weitzer and Tuch 2002), and past research has documented that such discriminatory practices by police are experienced more by racial minority individuals (Howell et al. 2004; Kent and Jacobs 2005; Smith and Holmes 2003; Weitzer et al. 2008). Historically, the civil protests that occurred in the 1960s by minority groups and their advocates were partly the result of unequal treatment of Black citizens by the police (Bayley and Mendelsohn 1969), with the growing belief that police organizations more racial representative of their communities would be less likely to engage in such discriminatory practices (President's Commission on Law Enforcement and Administration of Justice 1967). A similar historical pattern has affected the Hispanic population. As border security and control of illegal immigration become key policy objectives in Congress, the potential for unfair treatment of Hispanics by police may have increased. In fact, it may be that Hispanics now distrust police even more than do Blacks, especially in the Southwest where border concerns are more prominent. Unfortunately, no available study of perceptions of police fairness includes consideration of such regional differences.

S. H. Can (✉)
Penn State University, Schuylkill, PA, USA

Past Research on Variables Associated with Perceived Police Fairness

Past research consistently finds racial differences in perceptions of police fairness. In general, Whites report more trust in police than do minority ethnic groups (Buckler et al. 2008; Cao and Garcia 2005; Schuck and Rosenbaum 2005; Weitzer et al. 2008), although most available studies have focused on comparisons of Black and White individuals with less inclusion of Hispanics (Franklin 2010; Murty et al. 1990). The Comparative Conflict Theory (Hagan et al. 2005) suggests that the reason that ethnic minority individuals hold more negative views of police is because they have experienced more discriminatory police practices (such as "racial profiling"). Alternatively, the Group Position Theory (Blumer 1958) suggests that socioeconomic status is the more important variable that influences perceptions of police fairness, with more economically well-off groups (often Whites) holding the most favorable views toward the police, while the less economically well-off groups (often Hispanics, Blacks) holding less favorable views toward police. Additionally, recent media coverage of conflicts and shooting deaths between White police officers and Black community members in cities across the United States (Nicholson-Crotty et al. 2017; Klahm et al. 2016; Nix et al. 2017) may also increase the percentage of Black individuals reporting low levels of perceived police fairness, and recent media coverage of border conflicts between police and illegal immigrants from Mexico (Durán 2009; Sadler et al. 2012) may increase the percentage of Hispanic individuals reporting low levels of perceived police fairness.

Besides ethnicity and socioeconomic status, past research has identified other variables that are associated with perceptions of police fairness by members of the community. For example, age has been found to be associated with attitudes toward police, with older individuals usually holding more positive views of police (Hurst et al. 2000). Also, gender has been found to be associated with attitudes toward police, with females more likely to hold positive views toward police and courts (Brunson and Miller 2006; Mast 2004; Weitzer and Tuch 2002). Additionally, prior experiences with police or the court system have been documented to be associated with decreased perceptions of police fairness (Buckler et al. 2008; Tyler and Huo 2002), with these prior legal experiences being quite varied and including being the defendant in a criminal case, the defendant in a civil case, or the plaintiff in a civil case.

One variable that has not yet been examined for its association with perceptions of police fairness is region of the country. Regional differences potentially may affect an individual's perception of what is expected and reasonable behavior on the part of police. For example, past research has documented that media coverage of police injustice and other forms of "vicarious experience" may influence an individual's later perception of police fairness. Perhaps individuals from different regions of the United States experience differences in the types of crimes that are most prevalent, in the types of police action taken, and in the extent of media coverage of these police-community relationships, all of which could influence their perceptions of police fairness more than does their ethnicity alone.

Purpose of the Present Study

The purpose of the present study was to examine ethnic differences (Black, White, Hispanic) in perceptions of the fairness of police action, while controlling for other variables suggested by past research to also be associated with perceptions of police fairness (age, gender, income, prior legal experience), with a separate look at these variable relationships for two regions of the United States (Southwest, Pennsylvania). More specifically, perceptions of police fairness were measured for how "reasonable and therefore legal" police searches were perceived to be for actual Supreme Court cases (determined by the Court to be legal and appropriate), with a focus on both searches of the defendant's home, and searches of the defendant's vehicle. On the one hand, one of the most recently contentious areas of policing is the issue of racial profiling and police discretion in conducting vehicle stops (Engel 2008), with research suggesting that police are more likely to stop and search Blacks and Hispanics rather than Whites (Alpert et al. 2005; Borooah 2011; Engel and Calnon 2004; Engel and Johnson 2006; Rojek et al. 2012). These findings for vehicle searches may suggest that more significant racial differences (and perhaps other demographic differences) in perceived police fairness would be found for vehicle searches than for home searches. On the other hand, individuals may have a higher expectation of privacy in their homes as opposed to their vehicles in public venues, so perhaps racial differences (and other demographic differences) in perceived police fairness would be more prominent for home searches than for vehicle searches.

One new feature of the present study is that it adds to the limited set of studies that compare three racial groups (Black, Hispanic, White) in their perceptions of the fairness of police action. Another new feature of the present study is that, in its examination of racial differences in perceptions of police fairness, it controls for a number of other demographics suggested by past research to be associated with attitudes towards police (age, gender, income, prior police experience), with separate examinations of these variable relationships for two regions of the United States (Southwest, Northwest). It was hypothesized that ethnic differences in perceived police fairness would be found to be similar to those found in previous research, with White individuals reporting more police fairness than Black and/or Hispanic individuals. Additionally, it was hypothesized that other demographic variables (such as age, gender, income, and/or prior legal experience) would be also found to be significantly associated with perceived police fairness. Finally, it was hypothesized that regional differences in associations between ethnicity and perceived police fairness would be found, suggesting that ethnicity may not be the sole or primary demographic variable predictive of attitudes towards police.

Methods

Participants and Procedures

During the 2015 academic year, an anonymous survey was returned by undergraduate students from two regions of the United States. One region was the Southwest,
with 359 students from Texas A&M University at San Antonio returning the surveys, and the other region was the Northwest, with 702 students from two campuses
of the Pennsylvania State University (Schuylkill, Harrisburg) returning the survey.
The Texas location included 334 students who provided all variables used in the
present study (10.8% Black, 24.0% White, 65.3% Hispanic; 181 women, 153 men;
mean age = 29.5 years, SD = 8.1). The Pennsylvania location included 643 students
who provided all variables used in the present study (30.8% Black, 56.8% White,
12.4% Hispanic; 243 women, 400 men; mean age = 21.0 years, SD = 3.0). (See
Table 6.1 in the Appendix for descriptive statistics of study variables.) Surveys were
administered at all locations during normal class hours across a variety of academic
programs and included students majoring in criminal justice, business, education,
and the natural sciences. Students were offered extra credit points toward their final
semester grade, but they were not required to complete the survey, and they could
earn similar extra credit points by doing other small projects.

Measurement

Demographic variables – Students were asked to report their race/ethnicity as
Hispanic, African-American (Black), Asian, American-Indian, White (non-
Hispanic), or other. Only those reporting either Hispanic, Black, or White were
included in the present study. Students also reported their gender (female, male),
their age in years, and their income using six possibilities, which we later coded to
a six-point Likert scale (0 = $15 K and below, 1 = above $15 K to $25 K, 2 = above
$25 K to $35 K, 3 = above $35 K to $45 K, 4 = above $45 K to $55 K, 5 = above
$55 K). Finally, students were asked to report (0 = no, 1 = yes) whether they had
experienced any of four roles in the legal system during the past 5 years (plaintiff,
defendant, juror, witness), with their score for "prior legal experience" calculated as
the number of these four roles they reported.

    Perceived police fairness – Student perception of the fairness of police action
was measured by asking them to use a five-point rating for how "reasonable and
therefore legal" they believed police action was (0 = strongly disagree, 1 = disagree,
2 = neutral, 3 = agree, 4 = strongly agree) in eight actual Supreme Court cases of
home searches, and in seven actual Supreme Court cases of vehicle searches. Students
were not told that the case descriptions came from Supreme Court cases, and they
were not told Court decisions for any of the cases. The use actual court cases (Kessler
2009) rather than fictional vignettes (Rossi and Anderson 1982; Piquero 2012) is

relatively uncommon in criminological research. From the United States Supreme Court Media OYEZ database, we selected a random sample of 17 cases involving police searches of homes or vehicles between the years 1999–2009. The facts of each case were summarized succinctly to reflect its central issues. Each participant's score for perceived police fairness in home searches was calculated as the mean rating given to the eight home cases. Each participant's score for perceived police fairness in vehicle searches was calculated as the mean rating given to the seven vehicle cases. Examples of the home and vehicle cases are described below:

(HOME) "Police officers, with a warrant, knocked on the door of suspected drug dealer X. They waited between 15 and 20 s, and when X did not come to the door, they smashed it open with a battering ram."

(HOME) "Responding to a complain about a loud party, police arrived at a house where they saw minors drinking alcohol outside and heard shouting inside. As they approached the house, they saw a fight through the window involving a juvenile and four adults. The officers announced their presence, but the people fighting did not hear them, so they entered the home."

(VEHICLE) "Person X was apprehended by Arizona state police on an outstanding warrant for driving with a suspended license. After the officers handcuffed X and placed him/her in the squad car, they went on to search his/her vehicle, discovering a handgun and a plastic bag of cocaine."

(VEHICLE) "When X approached the United States and Mexico border, Customs inspectors noticed his hand shaking. An inspector tapped on X's gas tank with a screwdriver and noticed the tank sounded solid. A drug-sniffing dog alerted to the vehicle. After a mechanic disassembled the car's fuel tank, inspectors found 37 kilograms of marijuana bricks."

Data Analysis

One goal for data analysis of the present study was to compare student samples from the two regions of the United States (Texas, Pennsylvania) for perceived police fairness. T-tests were therefore used to compare students from Texas and Pennsylvania in their mean rating for how "reasonable and therefore legal" they perceived police searches to be for the eight home cases, and for the seven vehicle cases.

Another goal for data analysis was to examine ethnic differences in perceptions of police fairness, controlling for other demographic variables suggested by past research to be associated with attitudes toward police. Separately for participants from each region (Texas, Pennsylvania), a 3 × 2 ANCOVA was used to compare perceived police fairness (in home searches, in vehicle searches) across three ethnicities (Black, White, Hispanic), across two genders (female, male), with covariates including age, income (using the six-point Likert rating) and prior legal experience (the number of four legal roles in the past 5 years). Dependent variables for these ANCOVAs were the mean rating for how "reasonable and therefore legal" were the eight home searches, and the mean rating for the seven vehicle searches.

Results

Regional Differences in Perceived Police Fairness

T-tests found no significant differences between Texas and Pennsylvania student participants in their perceptions of police fairness in home searches ($t = 1.62$, $df = 975$, $p = .105$; Texas mean = 2.49, $SD = .58$; Pennsylvania mean = 2.43, $SD = .57$). However, t-tests revealed that Texas participants reported significantly greater perceptions of police fairness in vehicle searches ($t = 6.34$, $df = 975$, $p = .000$; Texas mean = 2.72, $SD = .61$; Pennsylvania mean = 2.45, $SD = .67$).

Demographics Associated with Perceived Police Fairness in Home Searches

For perceived police fairness in home searches, the ANCOVA for Texas participants revealed that income was the only significant demographic variable, with higher income associated with more perceived police fairness in home searches ($r = .13$, $n = 334$, $p = .014$). For Texas participants, ethnicity, gender, age, and prior legal experience were unrelated to perceptions of police fairness in home searches. However, for Pennsylvania participants, the ANCOVA found ethnicity to be significantly associated with perceived police fairness in home searches, with paired comparisons revealing that White individuals perceived more police fairness than did either Black or Hispanic individuals ($t = 4.42$, $df = 561$, $p = .000$; $t = 3.83$, $df = 443$, $p = .000$; respectively), with no differences between Black and Hispanic participants ($t = .78$, $df = 276$, $p = .436$). In addition, Pennsylvania participants with older age reported more perceived police fairness in home searches ($r = .20$, $n = 643$, $p = .000$). (See Table 6.2. in the Appendix.)

Demographics Associated with Perceived Police Fairness of Vehicle Searches

For perceived police fairness in vehicle searches, the ANCOVA for Texas participants found no significant effects for any of the demographics considered (ethnicity, gender, age, income, prior legal experience). However, for Pennsylvania participants, the ANCOVA found ethnicity to be significantly associated with perceived police fairness in vehicle searches, with paired comparisons revealing that White individuals perceived more police fairness than did Black individuals ($t = 3.67$, $df = 561$, $p = .000$), marginally more than Hispanic individuals ($t = 1.75$, $df = 443$, $p = .081$), with no differences between Black and Hispanic participants ($t = .77$, $df = 276$, $p = .443$). In addition, Pennsylvania participants with older age and more prior legal experience reported more perceived police fairness in vehicle searches ($r = .13$, $n = 643$, $p = .000$; $r = .10$, $n = 643$, $p = .014$). (See Table 6.3. in the Appendix.)

Discussion

The purpose of present study was to provide a more detailed analysis of how ethnicity affects perceptions of police fairness using actual Supreme Court cases of police vehicle and home searches. New features of the present study were that comparisons of ethnicity were made across three ethnic groups (Black, White, Hispanic) instead of the two typically compared in previous research (Black and White), that these ethnic comparisons also controlled for individual demographic variables suggested by past research to be associated with perceptions of police fairness (gender, age, income, prior exposure to the legal system), and that these examinations of how ethnicity is associated with perceived police fairness were conducted separately for two very different regions of the United States (Texas, Pennsylvania). Overall, results from the present study suggest that ethnicity may not be the primary demographic associated with perceptions of police fairness, with *learned* personal and regional experiences just as important as predictors.

According to both the Comparative Conflict Theory (Hagan et al. 2005) and the Group Position Theory (Blumer 1958), we anticipated that Black or Hispanic individuals would hold more negative views of police fairness than would White individuals. However, only for Pennsylvania participants but not Texas participants of the present study did Whites report more perceived police fairness in home and vehicle searches than did Blacks or Hispanics. Additionally, other demographic variables besides ethnicity were found to be significantly associated with perceived police fairness in the present study. For example, regional differences were found in the present study, with Texas participants perceiving more police fairness in vehicle searches than did Pennsylvania participants. One interpretation for this finding could be that the Texas border location and its need for vehicle checks by police, as well as recent media coverage to increase fear concerning illegal immigrants (Huddleston 2016) may have prompted citizens of this region to be more supportive of police action to protect them. As in past research (Hurst et al. 2000), older age was also associated for Pennsylvania participants with more perceived police fairness in both home and vehicle searches. Also as in past research (Buckler et al. 2008; Tyler and Huo 2002), prior experience with the legal system was associated for Pennsylvania participants with more perceived police fairness in vehicle searches. Finally, as suggested by Group Position Theory (Blumer 1958), higher income was associated for Texas participants with more perceived police fairness in vehicle searches.

Results from the present study suggest that ethnicity may not be the sole nor primary demographic variable associated with positive attitudes toward police. Present results also suggest that citizens may *learn* to have better perceptions of police fairness. Perhaps when individuals are exposed to regionally-relevant crime (as Texas students might be concerning vehicle searches needed at the Texas-Mexican border), they may increase their reliance on police for protection, and increase their perceived trust in the fairness of these police actions. Perhaps when individuals are exposed to the actual procedures of the legal system (by serving as plaintiffs, defendants, jurors, or witnesses in criminal or civil court cases), they reduce some of their stereotypes about police officers that have developed from sensationalized news coverage of police misconduct or from exaggerated social media conversations about it ("groupthink").

Study Limitations and Directions for Future Research

One limitation of the present study was that it only included participants from two regions of the United States (Southwest, Northeast). Especially because these regions were shown to have significant differences in perceived police fairness, future research should examine these comparisons for a wide variety of regions including the Northwest, the Southeast, and the Midwest, and including exclusively rural areas, suburban areas, and urban areas. Future research should also examine more precisely how participants have been involved with the legal system to determine which particular experiences tend to be associated with increased or decreased trust in police fairness. These experiences could include the number of days they have been in court in various roles (plaintiff, defendant, juror, witness), the percentage of court cases decided in their favor, the dollars they spent on attorneys, the number of days they have been incarcerated, the number of traffic tickets they have received, the number of times they have called 911 for emergencies, and the number of violent crimes they have witnessed in their neighborhood. Future research could also examine how programs to increase positive police-community relationships (Police Athletic League or other athletic projects, Operation Conversation, All Star Project etc.) can improve citizen attitudes toward police fairness.

Appendix

Table 6.1 Descriptive statistics of study variables for participants from Texas (N = 334) and Pennsylvania (N = 643)

Texas	Pennsylvania			
Variable	N	(%)	N	(%)
Ethnicity***				
Black	36	(10.8%)	198	(30.8%)
White	80	(24.0%)	365	(56.8%)
Hispanic	218	(65.3%)	80	(12.4%)
Gender***				
Female	181	(54.2%)	243	(37.8%)
Male	153	(45.8%)	400	(62.2%)

Variable	Mean	(SD)	(range)	Mean	(SD)	(Range)
Age***	29.54	(8.07)	(18–55)	21.02	(3.04)	(18–48)
Income (0–5 rating)***	1.62	(1.58)	(0–5)	37	(.99)	(0–5)
Prior legal experience***	34	(.65)	(0–3)	1.23	(.57)	(0–4)
(# of 4 types)						
HOME search fairness	2.49	(.58)	(.63–4.00)	2.43	(.57)	(0–4)
(mean 0–4 rating)						
VEHICLE search fairness***	2.72	(.61)	(.43–4.00)	2.45	(.67)	(0–4)
(mean 0–4 rating)						

*$p < .05$, **$p < .01$, ***$p < .001$

Table 6.2 Results of 3 × 2 ANCOVAs to examine demographic variables associated with perceived police fairness in home searches, shown separately for Texas students (N = 334) and Pennsylvania students (N = 643)

Texas				
Effect	*F*	*(df)*	*p*	Effect size
Ethnicity	.15	(2, 325)	.865	
Gender	.61	(1, 325)	.437	
Ethnicity × gender	.19	(2, 325)	.838	
Age	.02	(1, 325)	.897	
Income	4.03	(1, 325)	.046	.012
Prior legal experience	.13	(1, 325)	.714	
Pennsylvania				
Effect	*F*	*(df)*	*p*	Effect size
Ethnicity	7.28	(2, 643)	.001	.022
Gender	1.58	(1, 643)	.210	
Ethnicity × gender	1.00	(2, 643)	.342	
Age	9.32	(1, 634)	.002	.014
Income	.82	(1, 634)	.367	
Prior legal experience	2.62	(1, 643)	.106	

Table 6.3 Results of 3 × 2 ANCOVAs to examine demographic variables associated with perceived police fairness in vehicle searches, shown separately for Texas students (N = 334) and Pennsylvania students (N = 643)

Texas				
Effect	F	(df)	p	Effect size
Ethnicity	1.05	(2, 325)	.353	
Gender	.06	(1, 325)	.809	
Ethnicity × gender	.79	(2, 325)	.455	
Age	1.23	(1, 325)	.268	
Income	1.24	(1, 325)	.266	
Prior legal experience	1.04	(1, 325)	.308	
Pennsylvania				
Effect	F	(df)	p	Effect size
Ethnicity	3.59	(2, 634)	.028	.011
Gender	2.47	(1, 634)	.116	
Ethnicity × gender	.38	(2, 634)	.682	
Age	4.48	(1, 634)	.035	.007
Income	.05	(1, 634)	.826	
Prior legal experience	4.35	(1, 634)	.037	.007

References

Alpert, G. P., MacDonald, J., & Dunham, R. G. (2005). Police suspicion and discretionary decision making during citizen stops. *Criminology, 43*(2), 407–434.

Bayley, D., & Mendelsohn, H. (1969). *Minorities and the police: Confrontation in America.* New York: Free Press.

Blumer, H. (1958). Ethnicity prejudice as a sense of group position. *Pacific Sociological Review, 1*(1), 3–7.

Borooah, V. K. (2011). Racial disparity in police stop and searches in England and Whales. *Journal of Quantitative Criminology, 27*, 453–473.

Brunson, R. K., & Miller, J. (2006). Young black men and urban policing in the United States. *British Journal of Criminology, 46*, 613–640.

Buckler, K., Unnever, J. D., & Cohen, F. T. (2008). Perceptions of injustice revisited: A test of Hagan et al.'s comparative conflict theory. *Journal of Crime and Justice, 31*(1), 35–57.

Cao, L., & Garcia, V. (2005). Ethnicity and satisfaction with the police in a small city. *Journal of Criminal Justice, 33*(2), 191–199.

Durán, R. J. (2009). Legitimated oppression: Inner-city Mexican American experiences with police gang enforcement. *Journal of Contemporary Ethnography, 38*(2), 143–168. https://doi.org/10.1177/0891241607313057.

Engel, R. S. (2008). A critique of the outcome test in racial profiling research. *Justice Quarterly, 25*(136), 22.

Engel, R. S., & Calnon, J. M. (2004). Comparing benchmark technologies for policecitizen contacts: Traffic stop data collection for the Pennsylvania state police. *Police Quarterly, 7*, 97–125.

Engel, R. S., & Johnson, R. (2006). Toward a better understanding of racial and ethnic disparities in search and seizure rates. *Journal of Criminal Justice, 34*, 605–617.

Franklin, T. W. (2010). The intersection of defendants' ethnicity, gender, and age in prosecutorial decision making. *Journal of Criminal Justice, 38*(2), 185–192.

Hagan, J., Payne, M. R., & Shedd, C. (2005). Ethnicity, ethnicity, and youth perceptions of injustice. *American Sociological Review, 70*, 381–407.

Howell, S., Perry, H., & Vile, M. (2004). Black cities, white cities: Evaluating the police. *Political Behavior, 26*, 4568.

Huddleston, K. (2016). Border checkpoints and substantive due process: Abortion rights in the border zone. *Yale Law Journal, 125*(6), 1744–1756.

Hurst, Y., Frank, J., & Browning, S. (2000). The attitudes of juveniles toward the police. *Policing, 23*, 3753.

Kent, S. L., & Jacobs, D. (2005). Minority threat and police strength from 1980 to 2000: A fixed-effects analysis of nonlinear and interactive effects in large cities. *Criminology, 43*(3), 731–760.

Kessler, D. K. (2009). Free to leave? An empirical look at the fourth Amendment's seizure standard. *Journal of Criminal Law and Criminology, 99*(1), 51–87.

Klahm, C. F., Papp, J., & Rubino, L. (2016). Police shootings in black and white: Exploring newspaper coverage of officer-involved shootings. *Sociology of Crime, Law and Deviance, 21*, 197–217.

Mast, M. S. (2004). Men are hierarchal, women are egalitarian: An implicit gender stereotype. *Swiss Journal of Psychology, 63*, 107–111.

Murty, K., Roebuck, J., & Smith, J. (1990). The image of the police in black Atlanta communities. *Journal of Police Science and Administration, 17*, 250–257.

Nicholson-Crotty, S., Nicholson-Crotty, J., & Fernandez, S. (2017). Will more black cops matter? Officer race and police-involved homicides of black citizens. *Public Administration Review, 77*(2), 206–216. https://doi.org/10.1111/puar.12734.

Nix, J., Campbell, B. A., Byers, E. H., & Alpert, G. P. (2017). A bird's eye view of civilians killed by police in 2015. *Criminology & Public Policy, 16*(1), 309–340. https://doi.org/10.1111/1745-9133.12269.

Piquero, N. L. (2012). The only thing we have to fear is fear itself: Investigating the relationship between fear of falling and white collar crime. *Crime and Delinquency, 58*(3), 362–379.

President's Commission on Law Enforcement and Administration of Justice. (1967). *Task force report: The police*. Washington, DC: GPO.

Rojek, J., Rosenfeld, R., & Decker, S. (2012). Policing ethnicity: The racial stratification of searches in police traffic stops. *Criminology, 50*(4), 993–1024.

Rossi, P. H., & Anderson, A. B. (1982). The factorial survey approach: An introduction. In P. H. Rossi & S. L. Nock (Eds.), *Measuring social judgments* (p. 1567). Beverly Hills: SAGE.

Sadler, M. S., Correll, J., Park, B., & Judd, C. M. (2012). The world is not black and white: Racial bias in the decision to shoot in a multiethnic context. *Journal of Social Issues, 68*(2), 286–313. https://doi.org/10.1111/j.1540-4560.2012.01749.x.

Schuck, A. M., & Rosenbaum, D. P. (2005). Global and neighborhood attitudes toward the police: Differentiation by ethnicity and type of contact. *Journal of Quantitative Criminology, 21*(4), 391–418.

Smith, B. W., & Holmes, M. (2003). Community accountability, minority threat, and police brutality: An examination of civil rights criminal complaints. *Criminology, 41*(4), 1035–1063.

Tyler, T., & Huo, Y. (2002). *Trust in the law*. New York: Russell Sage Foundation.

Weitzer, R., & Tuch, S. (2002). Perceptions of racial profiling: Ethnicity, class, and personal experience. *Criminology, 40*(2), 435–455.

Weitzer, R., Tuch, S. A., & Skogan, W. A. (2008). Police-community relations in a majority black city. *Journal of Research in Crime and Delinquency, 45*(4), 398–428.

Chapter 7
The Impact of Police Shootings in the United States on Police-Community Relations

Hasan Arslan

Introduction

Policing is not an easy job to do. It is "a costly, complex enterprise whose practitioners intervene with citizens 24 h a day on matters ranging from homicide to blaring radios" (Travis and Brann 1997). The most important job for any officer is to preserve human life, while maintaining order. It is a noble and respected task with grand accountability and responsibility. Thus, police officers work under constant stress; face dangerous circumstances and attempt to resolve difficult life matters for their communities. "These include responding to unpredictable situations, periods of work that range from inactiveness to extremely stressful activity back to periods of less stressing activity, instantaneous decision making, the court system, and the use of force" (Dantzker 2005; 277). Thus, constant confrontation with such social problems put some officers under psychological strain. "An officer's day is generally a constant flow of stressful events, either on the street or inside the walls of the precinct" (Tejada and Gorling November 2017). In fact, due to existing overwhelming pressure, some officers might develop some level of medical or mental issues like anxiety, and post-traumatic stress disorder throughout their careers. Suicide is a leading killer of law enforcement officers (Violanti et al. 2013). Under constant and changing job environment, police officers exercise enormous discretions while dealing with pressure, stress, and hard split-second decisions. The reality of officer-involved shooting is one of those discretions in the life of police. Although the use of force by law enforcement officers happens on rare occasions, it puts an enormous strain on the police-community relations.

"The actual number of civilians killed by police is unknown as only 3% of our nation's 18,000 police departments voluntarily submit this information to federal agencies" (Davis and Lowery 2015). However, the media scrutiny and public

H. Arslan (✉)
Western Connecticut State University, Danbury, CT, USA
e-mail: arslanh@wcsu.edu

© Springer Nature Switzerland AG 2019
J. F. Albrecht et al. (eds.), *Policing and Minority Communities*,
https://doi.org/10.1007/978-3-030-19182-5_7

awareness have increased tremendously, and have resulted in a nationwide debate about race and policing, particularly following the police-involved shootings in Ferguson, New York City, Baltimore, Sacramento, and numerous other places in recent years. Indeed, some believed the recent increase of violent crimes in major cities might be due to the phenomena called the "Ferguson Effect," following the 2014 shooting by a police officer of an unarmed black suspect in Ferguson, Missouri. However, then FBI director James Comey rejected that particular term but accepted the fact that the "Viral Video Effect" blunts police work (Lichtblau 2016, May 11). "This instant access to recordings of real-world interactions between law enforcement and the community members they serve has enabled a larger segment of the population to engage in the discussions surroundings use of force" (Dziejma and De Sousa, April 2017; 22). Indeed, several officer-involved shootings were captured in digital video, either by police cameras or citizen's smartphones. It is noteworthy to add the media's selective approach to shooting incidents, which also impact police-community relations. "It's not that the news media has not acknowledged that heart-break or that it's done a bad job of covering these stories as they happen. But we need to get more of the story behind the story. We need more serious and informed coverage of the issues that drive these weekly — and, seemingly, daily — tragedies" (Ryan 2016, July 18). As a result, many large police departments started "the use of police officer body-worn cameras (BWCs) which are designed to record the interactions between police and citizens with the intention of moderating police and ostensibly, also citizen behaviors" (Headley et al. 2017).

Police training has grown exponentially since the late 1960s (National Research Council 2004), while at the same time, recent changes in policing have resulted in an increase in the duties and responsibilities of police officers on the street. James J. Fyfe, an author and nationally recognized expert policing, and the former top training official in the New York Police Department, apparently changed the direction of police practice and legal doctrine on the use of deadly force policies. In 1988, Fyfe stated that police use of deadly force accounted for the death of nearly 100 suspects per year in the United States. However, this number increased significantly; "available data indicate that about 600 criminals are killed each year by police officers in the United States. Some of these killings are in self-defense, some are accidental, and others are to prevent harm to others" (Miller 2006: 239). One of the main questions posed by all, that is, by the police and the community, is how many police shootings are too many, or too little. Obviously if it is your child, then it is way too many. Does the current trend on reporting of police shootings by the media portray an accurate picture or is the sensitization of the media reporting on certain events causing a public frenzy? It is hard to answer. However, let's remind ourselves that "the basic tenant of U.S. law enforcement is that the police cannot be successful if they do not enjoy the support and confidence of the people they serve" (Engel and Serpas April 2017; 30).

There is currently no national public database that tracks every officer-involved shooting in the United States. Indeed, during a summit on reducing violent crime convened by the United States Justice Department, the former head of Federal Bureau of Investigation (FBI), James Comey stated, "*it is unacceptable that the*

Washington Post and the Guardian newspaper from the UK are becoming the lead source of information about violent encounters between [US] police and civilians" (Tran 2015, October 8). "The repeated and failed calls made by scholars and policy-makers for nearly 40 years begs the question of why a national police deadly force database still has not been developed" (White 2015; 224). Whether it is due to concerns that such data might be misinterpreted and misused, but still for police training and education purposes, a national database seems to be the most effective solution. Nevertheless, despite the fact that editorials and periodicals scrutinize police policy, past police practices, police brutality and misconduct in general, they fail to focus on what actions the offender was engaging before the officer decided to use deadly force. Most editorials and periodicals scrutinize police policy, past police practices, police brutality and misconduct in general and yet they fail to focus on what actions the offender was engaging before the officer opted to use deadly force. The research is clearly insufficient when it comes to shedding any light on the details of the fatal encounter between the officer and the subject. In fact, little scholarly research has studied the predefined indicators of a police shooting like mental health status, weapon possession, type of aggression, type of police call, car pursuit, foot chase, the specific location, number of rounds fired by officer, etc. Researchers must approach it with a high curiosity that reflects 'the devil is in the detail' metaphor. The following questions and many more should thus be examined:

• Does training on de-escalation or other alternative police tactics result in diminished use of force outcomes in police-citizen encounters?
• Do use-of-force training programs reduce injuries to officers, subjects, and bystanders?
• To what degree is training technology incorporated into the use of force training programs and what is its impact on the efficacy of the training program?
• What is the effect of the use of force training on officer perceptions?
• What is the impact of the use of force training on officer decision-making?

The value of these questions is undeniable and acknowledges that national data does not currently exist that would permit the revision of police training curriculums to address strategies that could lead to a reduction in the police use of deadly force. "There must be sound research and science provided in response to this and other pressing questions regarding law enforcement's use of force, and sooner rather than later" (Engel and Serpas April 2017; 30). Finally, on October 12, 2016, the U.S. Department of Justice announced enabling public collection of use of force data. The press release stated:

"Accurate and comprehensive data on the use of force by law enforcement is essential to an informed and productive discussion about community-police relations," said Attorney General Lynch. "The initiatives we are announcing today are vital efforts toward increasing transparency and building trust between law enforcement and the communities we serve. In the days ahead, the Department of Justice will continue to work alongside our local, state, tribal and federal partners to ensure that we put in place a system to collect data that is comprehensive, useful and responsive to the needs of the communities we serve."

The FBI's initiative, the National Use-of-Force Data Collection reporting portal, is a significant step to address some of the many questions both for the academics and practitioners concerning police training and the standardization of the use of force policies. Most police departments train their recruits on when and when not to shoot; actual and accurate data never guide the police training. Mostly and simply, officers were told to use their discretion in every incident. However, if "data-guided training" would become a frequent reality of the officer training, potential strategies to alter fatal outcomes in many cases would be taken into consideration for many officers. The data-guided use of force training would enable us to provide the necessary steps that are needed to improve instruction and tactics for the police officer.

In every police shooting case, there are always two perspectives: those of the officer and the subject. However, in between these two figures, a combination of many things happens in less than a minute in many times. Statistically, the use of force by law enforcement officers occurs on rare occasions. There were 17,895 law enforcement agencies employing a total of full- and part-time employees with general arrest powers of about 810,000 in 2008 (Reaves 2012). In February 2017 issue, *The Police Chief* journal published by the International Association of Chiefs of Police (IACP), asked its member law enforcement agencies their last updated use-of-force policies. The results were printed in the April 2017 issue, which displayed the following: 42% updated within the last 6 months followed by 29% 1–2 years ago, 13% with 5+ years ago. Almost 7% of the reported law enforcement agencies indicated that they had not changed their policies at all.

Nevertheless, it is an acknowledged fact that officer-involved shooting incidents strain relationships between the police and the community. Whether it is an on- or off-duty shooting, police discretion on the use of deadly force is a tough and a rare decision, and involves a split-second action under a tense situation. All experts note that in any violent and shootout moment, things escalate fast and that there is little time to adequately assess the situation on how a police officer can act, and most importantly, work in accordance to departmental policy on deadly force (Springer n.d.). According to a report published by the San Diego County District Attorney's office, based on the data analysis of 358 incidents that have occurred between 1993 and 2012 in San Diego County, "nearly half (45%) of the shootings took place immediately upon arrival on-scene; 65% of the incidents occurred within three minutes or less of arrival on- scene; the majority of the incidents (280) occurred within 2 h of on-scene arrival" (2014). Multiple factors lead to a fatal encounter, therefore; the vantage point from many angles may not be available in many of those cases; nevertheless, officer-involved shootings are the most visible outcome of police training and carry significant implications for the need to assess the use of force policies. The realities and results of these policy issues involve fatal consequences and community perceptions, which suggest that it happens too many times (Eligon 2015, November 18). For this matter, every excessive use of force incident reflects negatively on the shining armor of the police shield and badges for many police officers. Sometimes, the scale of the event and the burden itself leaves a dent on the image of the police in general. The loss of human life whether carrying a badge, law-abiding citizen or a person engaging in a criminal act is too vital not to be analyzed in depth. Regardless, such shootings put an enormous strain on police-community relations. And with tensions running high, citizens often raise concerns and questions on all incidents of use force by the police whether excessive or not. Such concerns and criticism pose the question of whether better of training of police officers would reduce such incidents. Society subjects the police officers to higher expectations; citizens prefer to see police more guardians of their community, rather than warriors (Rahr and Rice 2015). Therefore, the public is quick to allege to law enforcement administrators that such high-profile events are the result of either poorly trained and, or the result of not adequately disciplined police officers who had used excessive or unnecessary force in those incidents.

Researchers who study the use of deadly force nationally have difficulty determining how many police shootings occur across the country and over time. That means that trends on who police shoot are hard to identify, and clues to make needed changes in police training and practices may go undetected. One of the practical solutions that will give officers additional skills and tools is the better use of analytics; that is, data developed to understand better the circumstances involved in all police shootings. Data should drive understanding, decisions, policing strategies, and training for officers and emphasize how to avoid the unnecessary use of force; that is, assuming that such choices could be altered.

Investigative journalists wrote most reports on police shootings for local or regional newspapers. "The lack of reliable statistics about police shootings is a nationwide problem" (Bay State Examiner, 2014, February 16; Lennard 2012, December 10). Currently, data collected by the Federal Bureau of Investigation (FBI) is narrow and inadequate in that it only reports mostly on annual officer fatality rates (fbi.gov/crimestats, n.d.). Moreover, the FBI does not collect data that can distinguish or reveal whether any of the armed suspects wanted to commit suicide (suicide by cop) or were mentally unstable or intoxicated during that fatal confrontation. Furthermore, by collecting data on the mechanics and factual elements of a police shooting, researchers and police administrators will be able, to assess the level of data on such as gun possession, gun use and mental status of the shooter from a different angle, etc.

There clearly needs to be a standardized deadly force reporting mechanism. One of the practical solutions to the dilemma of the police shooting is to improve data collection systems with a new open-source format that would count shooting incidents by police around the country. Creating a "state-of-the-art" information database that enables meaningful organization and categorization of information can seriously underline the scale of this media magnet problem. Hopefully, with the completion of the national use-of-force data collection, this would be addressed with valid and reliable research.

This chapter aims to assist the essence of what should be in a law enforcement-training curriculum as a whole, and which should ultimately demonstrate how effective training programs address the use of deadly force policy issues. A data-guided training program should guide police officials in better understanding the nature of moments/factors/elements that precede a shooting, such as lethal and non-lethal forms of weapon possession or display of a weapon which might likely heighten the tension between any subject and the police officer. Other factors include a shooter's affiliation with a gang or lack of mental ability at the time of the shootout, which would tend to worsen the escalation of the sequence of events. Therefore, the creation of a multi-level relational database system would undoubtedly benefit many interest groups, including law enforcement agencies, policymakers, the press and the public itself.

Literature Review

There are very few prior studies that have analyzed the officer-involved shootings in multi-variable perspective. As stated earlier, little scholarly research on police shootings focusing on precursor variables is available because most research has been done by the newspapers mainly on city or local level scope. Others examine the consequences of the deadly use of force for involved police officers; more specifically, they focus on the aftermath of a shooting and officers who pull the trigger during the fatal confrontation (Fooksman 2006; Xiong 2013). The issue is mostly presented as a mental and public health issue. According to the Oregonian newspaper, which produced an analysis of the studies of 29 police shootings that had occurred between 1988 and 1991 in the state of Oregon, the publisher noted that in two-thirds of the cases, the suspect who had been shot was under the influence of drugs or alcohol while one-third of the suspects had suicidal tendencies (1992). In a separate analysis, the San Diego County District Attorney's Office also revealed the following (2014):

> "Drugs and/or mental health issues were very common in the subjects. Either some evidence of drug use and/or mental health concerns was present in 81% of the cases (290 of 358 total). Sixty-six percent (242) of the subjects had drugs in their systems, including many with multiple substances in their system (18 subjects being under the influence of three or more drugs)."

According to American Association of Suicidology, the term 'suicide by cop' has been defined as "the suicidal subject engages in a consciously, life-threatening behavior to the degree that it compels a police officer to respond with deadly force" (Suicidology.org). It can be well understood that when facing an armed individual, officers often do not know if the individual's firearm is loaded or not, more specifically, there is also often no way of knowing the intention of an armed suspect. Indeed, it was asserted in this article that many people who were involved in an officer-involved shooting had some mental health conditions. A 1990 survey found more than half of respondents reporting violent behavior during the prior year met Diagnostic and Statistical Manual of Mental Disorders – Third Edition (DSM-III), criteria for at least one psychiatric disorder (Swanson et al. 1990). A 2009 systematic review confirmed these associations (Fazel et al. 2009). Two scholars, Fisher and Lieberman revealed that violence for severe mental illnesses, such as schizophrenia, bipolar disorder and depression, increased by 2 to four-fold. They emphasize the importance of proper mental health treatment in reducing the risk for violence involving mentally ill people (2013).

David Klinger's outstanding research on the development of a concrete understanding of officers' involvement in shootings is one of the few to mention here. Klinger mainly addressed the issue of an officer's experience during and after shootings. The researcher interviewed eighty municipal and county police officers, who reported on 113 different cases where they shot citizens during their careers. One of the primary findings of the study was that "nearly half of the shootings occurred while the officers involved were working general patrol assignments, and a minority of the shootings occurred during tactical operations" (2001).

Similar to Klinger's study, McElvain and Kposowa (2008) examined the characteristics of officers involved in shootings and found that male officers are more likely than female officers to fire their weapons, and college-educated officers are less likely to shoot than officers with no college education. Furthermore, the risk of an officer being involved in a shooting decreases with age.

One of the earliest studies is a book titled "Police Defensive Handgun Use and Encounter Tactics" by Brian Felter (1988). According to Felter, "the use of deadly force by police often occurs (80% of the time) with seven yards or less separating the officer and suspect; the incident is over within 3 s; and the average number of shots fired, by all those involved in the incident, is less than three" (1988).

As indicated above, most studies examine the gun violence issue in more local contexts. In addition to study at Oregonian newspaper above, in Boston, researchers attempted to uncover distinctive developmental trends in gun assault incidents over a 29 year period and found that "gun violence is intensely concentrated at a small number of street segments and intersections rather than spread evenly across the urban landscape between 1980 and 2008" (Braga et al. 2010). Michael White analyzed the role and potential influence of external environmental factors on police shooting behavior in Philadelphia (2003). Jeffrey S. Adler approached the issue a bit differently by discussing the history of police brutality in Chicago from 1875 to 1920 (2007).

The San Diego County District Attorney's office published a study that they conducted themselves over a span of 20 years. It is one of the most comprehensive studies that was done locally, which investigated officer-involved shootings from 1993 to 2012. The majority of the information comes from reports compiled by law enforcement investigators, forensic analysts, and medical examiners. The study did not merely focus on the analysis of actors involved in the shooting by providing demographic data but also presented statistics on other characteristics of the shootings as well. For example, use of less lethal force, nature of the call, type of the initial contact, pursuits and response times, etc. Indeed, the San Diego study also revealed data on the factors of drug/alcohol use by subjects.

Perkins and Bourgeois (2006) investigated perceptions of police misuse of deadly force by looking at two studies:

"Study 1 showed that as the number of officers decreased and the number of shots increased, perceptions of misuse of force were augmented. The number of shots per officer significantly predicted perceptions of misuse of force. Study 2 investigated the effects of social dominance orientation, blind patriotism, and right-wing authoritarianism. Results showed a significant interaction between the number of officers, the number of shots fired, and social dominance orientation."

The Washington Post has been compiling a database of every fatal shooting in the United States by a police officer in the line of duty since Jan. 1, 2015. In addition to demographics of the officer and the subject along with geographic details, unlike previous media reports and newspaper collections, the Post also includes the following variables: the use of body camera by the officer, weapon possession, mental illness and fleeing the scene. The newspaper has been compiling the information from local news reports, law enforcement websites and social media and independent databases such as Killed by Police and Fatal Encounters (2018).

Finally, the state of Texas has continued to lead this initiative by collecting official data on police shootings. According to House Bill 1036, law enforcement agencies are required to report all shooting events:

> "Each report details the demographics of both the officer and the other party involved in the shooting, the incident that led to the shooting, and whether the victim was exhibiting a deadly weapon. However, the reports either the officers' or suspects' names to be identified, keeping the data to be strictly used for trend analysis and policy decisions" (Mulder 2015, October 4).

Even with the current and recent data collection efforts by few national media outlets and crowd-sourced websites, the specific additional questions are not collected thoroughly. Information on below factors is often still lacking:

- number of hits on intended targets by officers
- the caliber of weapons used by officers
- the distance at which shots were fired
- number of "bunch shootings" in such events

In sum, none of the aforementioned studies directly address the issue by examining data within a national police shootings data. It is evident that a relational database on nationwide officer-involved shootings in many layers could be hugely beneficial in better understanding the phenomenon and in training of police officers as part of their curriculum. However, there is a precedent to performing content analysis on open sources and storing shootings data in a relational database. Hale (2006) did a similar project for worldwide terror incidents. While the attributes were different, they were collected using content analysis open sources and propose using a relational database to study trends and patterns. Hale points out that "most of the research lacks a comprehensive database approach" and that this approach offers to link a large number of variables and provide the organization and structure required to investigate valuable patterns and trends" (2006).

Relational Database Design on Studying the Use of Force

The relational database is a type of database management that stores data items in the form of organized formally described tables, merely a new kind of data design (as noted above), which can do multiple functions. This new design reduces everything into numbers and provides a perfect angle to give a full picture; essentially enabling one to link related incidents with groups, individuals, places, properties, etc. It can also store extensive collections of data in a single location, support multiple users, indicate valuable relationships, and can be organized and updated with ease (Hale 2005, p. 31). Both the scholar and the practitioner have great flexibility and thus are able to flush every piece of detail out of the open source document while working with the relational database. The current state of the database is at a point where it is feasible to populate it with the data that is currently collected as shown in Fig. 7.1.

Providing reliable data to researchers is crucial because many police departments do not keep separate records of officer-involved shootings. When one looks at the available data on police shootings, one can only find limited information or datasets with only partial capacity. Most notably, the available information touches surface level data like age, gender, and race of the shooter, but almost no information is revealed on any trends and patterns of the shooter's profile. The Relational DB model enables criminal justice scholars to do data mining on large datasets and also

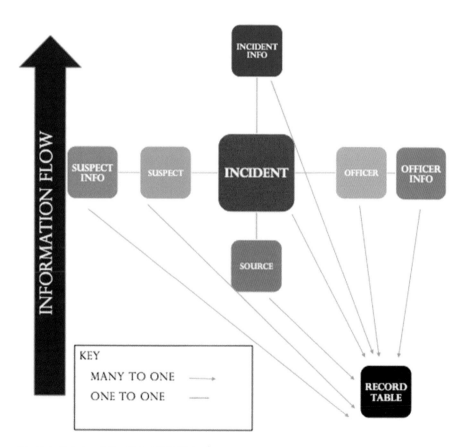

Fig. 7.1 Relational diagram of SHOT database

empowers practitioners to discover trends on the situational factors in an officer-involved shooting in the United States. For this matter, a 'relational database' on police shootings with predictive capability, as well as being an efficient investigative, tool has never been wholly achieved so far in the United States. Both the scholar and the practitioner would have excellent flexibility and thus be able to flush every piece of detail out of the open source document while working with the relational database. In addition to using data-driven teaching models, "training should incorporate scenarios, role-playing, and simulations-with instructors who consistently emphasize the lessons both inside and outside the classroom" (Lawrence and Rosenbaum November 2017; 14)

Statistics Help Officer Training (SHOT) Database

There has been an interdisciplinary effort to develop a prototype of a comprehensive database to define and consolidate information of police shooting incidences throughout the United States. One such attempt took place at Pace University in New York called the SHOT (Statistics Help Officer Training) project, which is a joint effort of the Departments of Criminal Justice and Security and Information Technology within the Dyson College and Seidenberg School, respectively. There are two primary objectives in this project: (1) to improve data systems for studying officer-involved shootings by building a data repository of police shootings from open sources and making the findings from the data through a publicly accessible internet interface; and (2) using open source data to increase transparency, build community trust, and support innovation. With the creation of a relational database system, this project additionally aims to achieve early warning systems and improve internal accountability in police departments. The design and the variety of subsidiary variables within the SHOT capture the minutia of officer decision-making during a deadly encounter. The database attempts to complete the missing variables that are not available within many of the public databases mentioned above. The database clearly has the potential of being a valuable resource for law enforcement officials in order to better understand the dynamics of a police-involved shooting encounter and to have a historical reference of police behaviors in such cases. This information will undoubtedly help police officers serve their community better as well as to provide a categorized dataset to scholars and academia to examine precursor variables during a shooting incident. The SHOT database demonstrates how a national database on police shootings can be used by researchers and police executives to develop a data-driven policy decision on the use of force practice. It could potentially provide answers to different questions concerning descriptive, inferential, incident-cause analysis, target, and geospatial analysis. Some significant analytical questions below show the value of the SHOT system for potential future scholarly products, as well as have the potential to provide enough information for professionals, practitioners, and policymakers within the criminal justice system.

Descriptive

1. In how many of those shooting cases does a suspect use or brandish a gun?
2. How have many officer-involved shootings (local-state-federal) occurred since 2000?
3. How many rounds does an officer fire and what is the average number of the bullet hitting at the suspect during a deadly encounter?
4. Where in the U.S. have these shootings been taking place since 2000?

Inferential

5. What is the relationship of suspects with guns and shooter or police officer fatality?
6. Is experience of a police officer a factor in gun violence?
7. Is location a factor in gun violence (urban, rural, region, etc.)?
8. Are age, gender, and race of the shooter a factor in fatality ratio?
9. Are there predictive factors that lead to incidents in which police use deadly force?
10. How much mental illness of the subject and the officer played a role in police shootings?
11. What is the correlation between the types of aggression (altercation, physical attack, brandishing a weapon and firing a gun) shown by the subject and the officer's decision making?
12. How many of the police shootings resulted in lawsuits? How much American taxpayers are impacted by such litigations?

More specifically, the second objective of the SHOT database emphasizes increasing transparency within a police department and aims to build community trust and support innovation. The relational database system or data-guided instruction focuses on the recognition of the need for training to shift more toward education where empirical knowledge provides guided insight. The implications of a relational database system are a significant innovation in the preparation of the police officer in local, state and regional level. State/local level legal statutes guide the essence of police use of force. For example, in New York State, Penal Law Article 35 explicitly outlines when the use of force can be used. It should be noted that such legislation leads to the essence of dealing with unintended consequences; that is, what does it mean to the average officer on patrol, (e.g., *"Sergeant, can you provide us with an example(s), etc.).* Questions of this nature lead to a discussion on the difference between training *("do this")* versus education *("why we do this?")*. There are apparent issues with police education in the United States. One of the assertions of data-driven police training is to point out the lack of standards as it often relates to police education, policy and practice. It should be acknowledged that the highly regarded International Association of Chiefs of Police does develop suggested model policies, but since these are recommended, that is where these procedures often stay.

The SHOT database has the potential to provide considerable insight into the issue of the most tragic police-suspect confrontations. Four main elements are the core of the open source data collection for SHOT DB[1]:

1. *Incident variables* answer the fundamental questions of what, when, where, and how. They provide factual information about shooting patterns of police officers as well. It is this minutia that enables police supervisors to envision specific strategies for better officer tactic and training.
2. *Subject variables* refer information related to the shooter or armed assailant. It provides vital information regarding moments before use of deadly force policy by a police officer. Variables like shooter's weapon's type, mental status, nature of aggression, gang affiliation or prior criminal record and attempting to flee from the scene most likely serve as precursor indicators of police discretion on the use of force.
3. *Officer variables* mostly include demographic information about police officers, who are involved in a shooting. The criterion for data entry asserts that a shooting incident must end either with a fatality or injury of the shooter. This section mainly describes officer's experience, affiliation, assignment and the nature of police response along with other demographic variables.
4. *Source variables* play a crucial role in SHOT database collection strategy. It collects the shooting variables from twelve different open sources.[2]

An Examination of the Preliminary Results of the SHOT Database

It is crucial to analyze the OIS cases with a more thorough examination of any trends and patterns. The data may be useful in ways to enhance officer safety and community relations. Below are the preliminary findings from the SHOT database.

---

[1] **Incident Variables:** Date (day, month, season, year), Approximate time (early morning, morning, noon, afternoon, evening, night and midnight), number of officers on the scene, number of officers, who fired their guns, number of rounds hit the target, part of target being hit (head/neck, torso, limbs), Lawsuit?, Geographical info (region, state, city, address, location type, Lat/Lon coordinates), source.

    Subject Variables: age, race, gender, fatality, mental status, weapon possession, type of aggression, use of vehicle, occurrence of any foot or car chase, gang affiliation, nationality, fatality/injury.

    Officer Variables: race, gender, experience, affiliation, department type, assignment, status (on/off duty) and type of police call, fatality/injury..

[2] **Source Variables:** Book, Broadcast Transcripts, Governmental reports, Court Document, Dataset, Journal, Magazine, Mailing List, Newspaper, NGO Report, Website, Wire Report, World News Connection

The SHOT database gathered a dataset of 4283 officer-involved shootings (OIS) that have occurred in 50 states between January 2000 and December 2017 in the United States. Figure 7.2 displays the almost steady incline in the distribution of shootings∗ since 2000. Of the total events, 73.3% were fatal, where 3139 people lost their lives; 95.5% of the subjects being shot by police during these deadly encounters were male, and only 1.2% of the subjects were immigrants from various countries. 104 of the subjects also had gang affiliations at the time of the OIS. Frankly, the escalation to use deadly force is very rapid in the majority of the incidents, mostly less than 3 min. Almost one fifth (758) of the incidents involved car pursuits, whereas another one-sixth (682) forced police officers to take part in foot pursuits before the shooting. Sadly, almost 50% of both chases ended up with fatalities. A small number of OIS (157) involved both a vehicle and a foot pursuit as well.

The distribution of OIS is almost equally distributed within all four seasons; however, Autumn with 27% has the highest percentage than the rest of them with a few more points. The deadliest month is November with 301 fatalities, whereas the lowest is April with 73 deaths within 18 years of police shootings (Table 7.1). The percentage of shootings in a given year that was fatal ranged from a low of 1.4% (2000) to a high of 18.7% (2015). Similar to seasons, there is not a single day of the week that strikes out significantly (Table 7.2). The range of shootings for 7 days seems to embedded in 14% with various minor point difference from each other; however, the number of shootings is a little higher on Thursday (14.9%) and Fridays (14.8%).

Age was missing for 178 subjects; the average age of all subjects involved in OIS was almost 34 years old, ranging from 4 to 107. Male subjects ranged in age from 12 to 107, whereas female subjects ranged from 4 to 92. The mode for age is 25, and over half (60%) of all subjects were between the ages of 20–39.

More than 70% of the subjects had documented no mental health issues, and sixty-two exhibited unstable behavior at the time of the incident (Fig. 7.3). 11% (468) of the incidents fit into the category "suicide-by- cop," situation where the subject acts erratically and wants police to shoot him or her. Mental health concerns

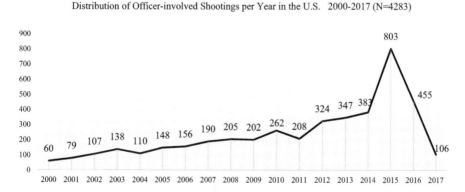

Distribution of Officer-involved Shootings per Year in the U.S. 2000-2017 (N=4283)

Fig. 7.2 Distribution of police shootings in the United States per year

Table 7.1 Distribution of OIS per month

Months	Injured	Killed	#	%
Jan	87	259	346	8%
Feb	83	223	306	7%
Mar	109	269	378	9%
Apr	93	214	307	7%
May	108	223	331	8%
Jun	96	219	315	7%
Jul	89	271	360	9%
Aug	106	270	376	9%
Sep	104	251	355	8%
Oct	77	321	398	9%
Nov	84	318	402	9%
Dec	108	301	409	10%
Total	1141	3139	4283	100%

Table 7.2 Distribution of OIS per days of the week

Days	Injured	Killed	Total
Fri	170	462	632
Tue	157	457	614
Sat	159	452	611
Mon	150	451	601
Sun	160	450	610
Thu	188	449	637
Wed	160	418	578
Total	1144	3139	4283

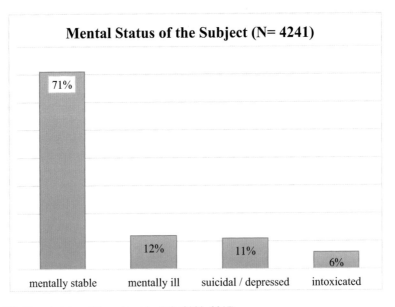

Fig. 7.3 Mental status of the subject in OIS (2000–2017)

Table 7.3 Cross tabulation of fatality and race by regions

U.S. Region	Race	Injured	Killed	Total
Midwest	*Missing*	*85*	*72*	*157*
	Asian	0	15	15
	Black	24	147	171
	Hispanic	4	36	40
	White	38	178	216
	Total	151	448	599
Northeast	*Missing*	*51*	*31*	*82*
	Asian	1	5	6
	Black	23	117	140
	Hispanic	12	35	47
	White	43	118	161
	Total	130	306	436
South	*Missing*	*90*	*80*	*170*
	Asian	4	25	29
	Black	173	342	515
	Hispanic	71	151	222
	White	96	412	508
	Total	434	1010	1444
West	*Missing*	*104*	*166*	*270*
	Asian	11	63	74
	Black	42	226	268
	Hispanic	133	441	574
	White	136	463	599
	Total	426	1359	1785

were present in 12% of the cases (534). Only 6% (239) of the subjects had been reported to be under the influence of drugs, including many with multiple substances in their system.

Race stands at the center of the controversy. The media frequently reports when members of two different race categories are involved in the shooting. More specifically, an unarmed black man killed by a white officer stirs a considerable controversy for the sake of trust between communities. 1/7th (674 incidents) of the Race variable is missing. Table 7.3 demonstrates the distribution of subject fatalities by race in four regions of the United States. Overall, the White race has a 60% ratio of death alone; there is, however, some variation per region. While White (599) and Hispanic (577) subjects have higher fatality counts than others in the West; the Black subjects (515) is higher than White subjects (508) in the South. In regards to age, young Black male (20–29) has significantly higher fatality rate than any others. Both the White male and female subjects (626) have higher deaths at the age 40 and above.

There are close to 2000 law enforcement agencies involved in the OIS according to SHOT database. Regarding the officers' assignments, the vast majority (82.9%)

Table 7.4 Part of subject
body where the bullets struck

Body Shots	#	%
Torso	3368	78.6
Lower body	276	6.4
Limbs	265	6.2
Head/neck	205	4.8
Upper body	99	2.3
Full body	42	1
Head/limbs	28	0.7
Total	4283	100

were on-duty patrol/uniformed officers. The remainder were split between tactical operations (e.g., *Emergency Response Team & SWAT*) which had 5%, State Troopers with 3.2%, plainclothes accounting for 3% and followed by Vice & Gang Squads with 1%. The rest consists of the combination of various units and agencies. Six percent (253) of the OIS cases involved more than one law enforcement agency such as local police departments assisting county/sheriff's office or state troopers being present on the scene with local police. In 65% of the incidents, only one officer fired his or her weapon. In 42.4% of the cases, the shooting officer was the only officer present; two officers were present in 31.8% of the cases. As part of their training, officers target the body center mass when they fire their guns. In more than 2/3 of the cases (78.6%), police hit the torso of the subject (Table 7.4).

There are twenty different call types during where shootings happened. *Domestic disturbance* cases with 17% are the most frequent police calls that officers responded to prior to an officer-involved shooting followed by the *traffic-related* calls with 12.8%, which starts merely with a simple traffic stop and escalates quickly to the deadly use of force. Other dangerous calls for officers finding themselves in the OIS situation are *Welfare check* with 7.1%, and *Person-with-a-gun* with 7%. However, it is evident that Patrol (uniformed) officers from local police departments are most at-risk for becoming involved in a shooting while responding to a family dispute or traffic-related calls.

In half of the cases, the subject possessed a firearm and 23% cases he/she fired the gun, whereas nearly half of the times, the subject brandished some form of weapon in the arrival of the officer to the scene. However, in certain situations, the subject neither carried a form of weapon (15%), nor posed a threat (11%) to the officer or a third person (Table 7.5; Fig. 7.4).

Most shootings occurred in the Western region of the U.S. with 42%. California and Nevada have the highest ratio of shootings in the West. The South has 34% of the OIS with Texas and Florida being the top two states in the region. The Midwest comes third with 14% and then the Northeast region with 10%. The nature of the location, meaning the physical setting where the OIS occurred, varied widely. Most were outdoors, predominantly taking place on the roads, streets and parking lots (74.5%). Most indoor shootings took place in residential locations, like apartment buildings and houses (40%).

Table 7.5 Weapon possession by subject

Weapon Possession/Type	#	%
Firearm	2114	50%
Sharp edged / bladed weapon	764	18%
Unarmed (no weapon)	663	15%
Other	392	9%
Replica / fake gun	169	4%
Bludgeoning weapon	154	4%
Total	4256	100%

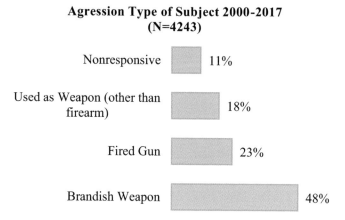

Agression Type of Subject 2000-2017 (N=4243)

Nonresponsive — 11%

Used as Weapon (other than firearm) — 18%

Fired Gun — 23%

Brandish Weapon — 48%

Fig. 7.4 Types of aggressive behavior demonstrated by subject

Conclusion

"Patrol officers are expected to fulfill a wide range of functions, including preventing crime, helping victims and others in danger, resolving conflicts between parties, managing the movement of people and vehicles, creating a feeling of safety in the community, and a host of other services" (Lawrence and Rosenbaum, November 2017; 14). The most critical and also sensitive factor shaping the police role is the ability to use force, which separates the police from other public service actors. The discretion of use of force, however, comes with limitations; it is either limited by the law, or it can only be implemented within the official capacity. Multiple factors influence the police officer's discretion: the seriousness of the crime, the demeanor of the subject, the immediate environment of the incident, and finally the official departmental policies along with the local political culture. Once the escalation begins in a situation, the direction of the use of force continuum always rises. It is like walking on thin ice, once it cracks, every rapid and rushed move would fasten the breaking of the ice. The impact of police shooting resembles the sound of that

Fig. 7.5 Distribution of officer involved shootings per regions of the U.S. (N = 4283)

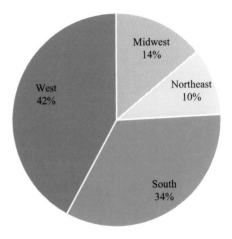

crack on ice; it will tear apart the community-police relationship if it is not managed well (Fig. 7.5).

Policing in a democratic society requires that law enforcement personnel be accountable for their actions based on the principles of legality, subsidiary, and proportionality. Effective control with rulemaking has been evidenced in policies regarding the use of deadly force. When police go beyond reasonable force to use excessive force during an arrest or in precipitous response, citizens become victims of police, and the publics confidence in the police agency can plummet (McEwen 1996). Since abolishing the ability to use discretion in each case is not the rational and proper way to examine the police behavior; thus, enhancing the professional judgment of police under scrutiny would be the appropriate action to do. Whether the public is aware or not about the fact that "officers see, hear, and face things that most people will not witness in their lifetimes, and the resulting cumulative impact of stress and traumatic events witnessed by officers can wreak havoc on their physical, emotional, and psychological health" (Johnson and Brown, November 2017; 12) does not always draw attention of the average citizen. That is why officers must be adequately trained and carefully vetted at all times. To heal the wounds caused by police shootings in recent years will require the change of direction in police training, which is supported by data-driven analyses. Educating police on analytics and the resultant findings might be the initial concrete sign of steps to build a stronger trust between the people and law enforcement.

References

Adler, J. S. (2007). Shoot to kill: The use of deadly force by the Chicago police, 1875–1920. *Journal of Interdisciplinary History, 38*(2), 233–254.

Braga, A., Papachristos, A., & Hureau, D. (2010, March). The concentration and stability of gun violence at micro places in Boston, 1980–2008. *Journal of Quantitative Criminology, 26*(1), 33–53.

Dantzker, M. L. (2005). *Understanding today's police* (4th ed.). Monsey: Criminal Justice Press.

Davis, A. C., & Lowery, W. (2015, October 07). *FBI director calls lack of data on police shootings 'ridiculous,' 'embarrassing'*. The Washington Post. Retrieved from https://www.washingtonpost.com/national/fbi-director-calls-lack-of-data-on-police-shootings-ridiculous-embarrassing/2015/10/07/c0ebaf7a-6d16-11e5-b31c-d80d62b53e28_story.html?utm_term=.3383f836ab86.

Dziejma, S. & De Sousa, D. (2017, April). National Consensus Policy on use of force: How 11 leading enforcement leadership and labor organizations arrived at one policy. The Police Chief. 84(4), 22–26.

Eligon, J. (2015, November 18). One slogan too many methods: Black lives matter enters politics. *The New York Times*. Retrieved from http://www.nytimes.com/2015/11/19/us/one-slogan-many-methods-black-lives-matter-enters-politics.html?_r=0.

Engel, R. S., & Serpas, R. (2017, April). How research could improve development and training. *The Police Chief, 84*(4), 28–36.

Fazel, S., Gulati, C., Unsell, L., Geddes, J. R., & Grann, M. (2009). Schizophrenia and violence: Systematic review and meta-analysis. *PLoS Medicine, 6*, el000120. [PMID: 19668362].

Felter, B. (1988). *Police defensive handgun use and encounter tactics*. Engle- wood Cliffs: Prentice-Hall.

Fisher, C. E., & Lieberman, J. A. (2013). Getting the facts straight about gun violence and mental illness: Putting compassion before fear. *Annals of Internal Medicine, 159*(6), 423–424.

Fooksman, L. (2006, December 4). Repeat shootings haunt officers – Effects can be traumatic, lasting for police who open fire. *South Florida Sun-Sentinel (Fort Lauderdale, FL)*. 1A. Retrieved on January 8, 2013 from http://articles.sun-sentinel.com/2006-12-04/news/0612040158_1_police-officer-shootings-two-officers.

Hale, W. C., (2005). Twenty-first century terrorism, twenty-first century answers: The why and how of collection, analysis, and dissemination of open source intelligence (Doctoral dissertation, Sam Houston State University). *Dissertation Abstracts International*.

Hale, W. C. (2006). Information versus intelligence: Construction and analysis of an open source relational database of worldwide extremist activity. *International Journal of Emeregency Management, 3*(4), 280–297.

Headley, A. M., Guerette, R. T., & Shariati, A. (2017). A field experiment of the impact of body-worn cameras (BWCs) on police officer behavior and perceptions. *Journal of Criminal Justice, 53*, 102–109.

Johnson, O., & Brown, J. (2017, November). Suicide awareness and prevention for law enforcement professionals. *The Police Chief, 84*(11), 12–13.

Lawrence, D. S., & Rosenbaum, D. P. (2017, November). Teaching procedural justice and communication skills during community-police encounters. *The Police Chief, 84*(11), 14–15.

Lennard, N. (2012, December 10). Half of people shot by police are mentally Ill, investigation finds. Retrieved on May 26, 2014 from http://www.salon.com/2012/12/10/half_of_people_shot_by_police_are_mentally_ill_investigation_finds/.

Lichtblau, E. (2016, May 11). F.B.I. Director says 'Viral Video Effect' blunts police work. *The New York Times*. Retrieved http://www.nytimes.com/2016/05/12/us/comey-ferguson-effect-police-videos-fbi.html?_r=0.

McElvain, J. P., & Kposowa, A. J. (2008). Police officer characteristics and the likelihood of using deadly force. *Criminal Justice and Behavior, 35*(4), 505–521.

McEwen, T. (1996, April). National data collection on police use of force. *U.S. Department of Justice, Office of Justice Programs*. Retrieved from https://www.bjs.gov/content/pub/ascii/NDCOPUOF.TXT.

Miller, L. (2006). Officer-involved shooting: Reaction patterns, response protocols, and psychological intervention strategies. *International Journal of Emergency Mental Health, 8*(4), 239–254.

Mulder, B. (2015, October 4). "Online database sheds light on statewide officer involved shootings." *Midland Reporter-Telegram*. Retrieved on May 1, 2016 from http://www.mrt.com/news/state_and_national/article_f05dcae6-695f-11e5-aec9-2bf15c467b36.html.

National Research Council. (2004). Fairness and effectiveness in policing: The evidence. Committee to review research on police policy and practices. In W. Skogan & K. Frydl (Eds.), *Committee on law and justice, division of behavioral and social sciences and education.* Washington, D.C.: The National Academy Press.

Perkins, J. E., & Bourgeois, M. J. (2006). Perceptions of police use of deadly force. *Journal of Applied Social Psychology, 36*(1), 161–177.

Rahr, S. & Rice, S. K. (2015, April). From warriors to guardians: Recommitting American police culture to democratic ideals. *New Perspectives in Policing* [National Institute of Justice]. Retrieved from https://www.ncjrs.gov/pdffiles1/nij/248654.pdf.

Reaves, B. (2012). Hiring and retention of state and local law enforcement officers, 2008 – Statistical tables. Bureau of Justice Statistics (BOJ).

Ryan, M. (2016, July 8). How the media can help make sense of a senseless week. *The Variety.* Retrieved on March 21, 2018 from http://variety.com/2016/tv/opinion/police-shootings-frontline-documentary-nra-philando-castile-alton-sterling-1201810789/.

Springer, B. (n.d.) Police Shooting. *Virginia COPS – The state organization for law enforcement officers in Virginia!* Retrieved on May 18, 2014, from http://www.virginiacops.org/Articles/Shooting/shoot.htm.

Swanson, J. W., Hölzer, C. E., Ganju, V. K., Jono, R. T., (1990). Violence and psychiatric disorder in the community: Evidence from the epidemiologic catchment area surveys. Hospital & Community Psychiatry, 4l: 76l–770.

Tejada, J., & Goerling, R. (2017). Mindful policing – A new approach to officer wellness and safety training and education. *The Police Chief, 84*(11), 48–51.

The Oregonian. (1992, April 25). *Police shootings: Who, what and how many.* Retrieved from http://www.theppsc.org/Archives/DF_Articles/Files/Oregon/92-Oregonian_Study.htm.

Tran, M. (2015, October 8). "FBI chief: 'unacceptable' that Guardian has better data on police violence." The Guardian newspaper. Retrieved May 7, 2016 from http://www.theguardian.com/us-news/2015/oct/08/fbi-chief-says-ridiculous-guardian-washington-post-better-information-police-shootings.

Travis, J. & Brann, E. (1997, November). Measuring what matters – Part two: Developing measures of what the police do. *National Institute of Justice Research in Action.* Office of Justice Programs. Retrieved from https://www.ncjrs.gov/pdffiles/167255.pdf.

Violanti, J. M., Robinson, C. F., & Shen, R. (2013). Law enforcement suicide: A National Analysis. *International Journal of Emergency Mental Health and Human Resilience., 15*(4), 289–298.

White, M. D. (2003). Examining the impact of external influences on police use of deadly force over time. *Evaluation Review, 27*(1), 50–78.

White, M. D. (2015). Transactional encounters, crises driven reform, and the potential for aNational police deadly force database. *Criminology & Public Policy, 15*(1), 223–235.

Xiong, C. (2013, January 8). Shootings often haunt the police officers involved. *Star Tribune (St. Paul, MN).* Retrieved on May 29, 2014 from http://www.startribune.com/local/stpaul/186108491.html.

Chapter 8
Search and Seizure Jurisprudence: Community Perceptions of Police Legitimacy in the United States

S. Hakan Can and Durant Frantzen

Introduction

Over the last few decades major shifts in demographics have occurred in various parts of the United States, most notably in the Southwest. In large part these changes are a result of mass immigration of Hispanic immigrants, particularly from Central America and Mexico (Grieco and Rytina 2011; Guzmán 2001). Much debate has occurred in the area of immigration policy and the need to implement more resources to border security in border regions (Stacey et al. 2011). At the state level, Arizona's Support Our Law Enforcement and Safe Neighborhoods Act of 2010 is a recent example of legislation that affords police more authority to stop, search, and arrest suspected illegal immigrants. Concerns about illegal immigration and the debate about effective policy have been the focus of media attention and are premised on the notion that Hispanic immigrants are prone to violence and crime (Rumbaut and Ewing 2007; Steen et al. 2005). However, the extent to which majority-Hispanic communities in the Southwest border region differ in their perceptions of police legitimacy compared to other regions of the U.S. has not been well-documented in the literature.

Police action symbolizes the collective will of society to suppress disorder and crime, but our history also well documents discrimination and oppression on the part of police against minorities (Smith and Holmes 2003; Stucky 2005; Kent and Jacobs 2005). In terms of police-community relations, prior research has shown that the racial and ethnic composition of a community largely influences the quality of relations police have with their citizens (Weitzer et al. 2008; Weitzer and Tuch 2005; Howell et al. 2004), however, much of this research does not include majority-Hispanic

S. H. Can (✉)
Penn State University, Schuylkill, PA, USA

D. Frantzen
Texas A & M University, College Station, TX, USA

© Springer Nature Switzerland AG 2019
J. F. Albrecht et al. (eds.), *Policing and Minority Communities*,
https://doi.org/10.1007/978-3-030-19182-5_8

125

communities (Murty et al. 1990). Various perspectives exist on the relationship between the racial and ethnic composition of the community and perceptions about the police. For example, Hagan et al. (2005) comparative conflict theory argues that African Americans and Hispanics are more likely to hold negative views toward the criminal justice system compared to whites. This view is premised on the history of discriminatory practices (e.g., racial profiling on the part of the police) toward minority groups. Accordingly, Hagan et al. (2005) maintain that perceptions of justice are gradient—African Americans will hold the most negative views toward the system and whites the most favorable, with Hispanics occupying a middle ground. This view assumes that African Americans would hold the most negative views of the police despite changes in the racial and ethnic composition of the community (Weitzer and Tuch 2006; Howell et al. 2004).

Over the last decade or so, however, the Hispanic population has risen dramatically. In the Southwest, for example, Hispanics have become the fastest growing ethnic group in the country, and represent a considerable portion of the overall Hispanic population in the United States (Massey and Capoferro 2009). Other populations in regions of the U.S., such as the northeast, have shown more stable immigration patterns and thus may hold different perceptions toward the police. What remains an open question is whether Hispanics in border communities view police searches differently than do African Americans given the recent enactment of controversial immigration and border security-related policies that threaten their existence (Provine and Sanchez 2011; McDowell and Wonders 2010).

This study examines public perceptions of police search policies in two communities that differ considerably according to race and ethnicity. Using a case scenario approach, the study examines regional differences in perceptions of police legitimacy as defined by U.S. Supreme Court cases involving police searches and seizures. A related issue unexplored in previous research is whether perceptions of the legality of vehicle stops and searches vary according to race and ethnicity and the demographic make up the community. Do African Americans and Hispanics perceive searches and seizures of vehicles as less legitimate than do Whites and do these perceptions vary according to place? Given that most research on police search practices has focused on vehicle stops, we created a separate measure to explore differences in racial perceptions of police search policies in the two data collection sites.

Theoretical Framework

The common finding in most of the research on police-community relations is that African Americans and Hispanics are less likely to trust the police compared to whites (Cao and Garcia 2005; Schuck and Rosenbaum 2005; Weitzer et al. 2008). Two bodies of literature provide the background for understanding the interrelationship between racial perceptions and the criminal justice system. From an institutional actors' perspective, Blalock's (1967) racial threat theory maintains that minorities are more likely to be feared by whites, and therefore, viewed as threatening to their social and economic status. Historically, this view has been intensified through racial stereotypes by the media that depict Blacks as the "typical street criminal" (Franklin 2010, p.694) most prone to violence, particularly in large urban areas. In addition, research has indicated that Hispanics share many of the same economic disadvantages as Blacks, such as unemployment, poverty, and lack of education, and therefore represent a similar threat to society (Healey 1995; Mata 1998).

Closely related to this view is Blumer's (1958) group position thesis, which provides a model for understanding dominant group attitudes toward minority groups. According this view, the population distribution of a community structures the way in which groups perceive other groups as well as those in positions of power and control. Britt (2000) contended that those in positions of power and control were more likely to perceive lower levels of racial threat in more homogenous cities and higher levels of racial threat in more heterogeneous cities. Extending the logic of the group position thesis to police-community relations, dominant groups would maintain the most favorable view of the police, while the minority group would hold a less favorable perspective. A common finding in this line of research is that whites tend to justify police misconduct toward minorities, particularly blacks, resulting in what has been described as a form of "rational discrimination" (Weitzer and Tuch 2002, p. 437). As a result, Whites view African Americans as having a stronger inclination toward violence and crime (Hurwitz and Peffley 1997) and rationalize police mistreatment of African Americans based on these perceptions (Weitzer 2000).

Alternatively, Hagan et al. (2005) comparative conflict theory argues that perceptions of injustice are gradient, meaning that African Americans hold the most negative views, followed by Hispanics, and then whites. According to their perspective, racial minorities develop negative views of the criminal justice system through "cognitive landscapes" that manifest from negative experiences with the police at the community level (Buckler et al. 2008, p. 37). In contrast to the group position thesis, their theory holds that racial attitudes toward the legal system do not vary according to the demographic composition of the communities. The authors argue that because African Americans have long experienced negative treatment and discrimination by the police, they have become desensitized through a process of persistent exposure to the police and are thus more likely to regard negative treatment as normal. In sum, they contend that Hispanics are less likely to be discriminated against given their lighter skin tone, but suffer from some of the same abusive practices that African Americans have endured.

Racial and Ethnic Differences in Attitudes Toward Police Searches

Whether real or perceived, African Americans frequently assume that the police engage in racial profiling as a means to stop, search, and question citizens (Engel 2008; Weitzer and Tuch 2002, 2005). These perceptions are largely reflective of the historical treatment of minority citizens, specifically African Americans, by the criminal justice system (Bayley and Mendelson 1969). In part, the civil protests that occurred during the 1960s by minority groups and their advocates were a result of unequal treatment of African American citizens by the police. Legislators called for more diversification of police staffs, contending that a police organization that is representative of its community is less likely to engage in discriminatory practices against minority groups (President's Commission on Law Enforcement and Administration of Justice 1967). A similar pattern has affected the Hispanic population. As border security and illegal immigration continue to be key policy objectives in Congress, the potential for unfair treatment of Hispanics by the police remains elevated. Further, Hispanics may in fact be more likely to distrust the police than African Americans, particularly in the Southwest. Prior to the passage of SB 1070, state legislation and policing strategies threatened the civil liberties of legal as well as non-legal Hispanic residents living in states such as Arizona and Texas. Previous research has documented the potential net-widening effects of anti-immigrant legislation leading to "ethno-racial profiling" (Provine and Sanchez 2011, p. 471). The authors describe some of its consequences as follows:

Job hunting, particularly in a time of recession and high unemployment has become hazardous and problematic for Latinos, whose right to work is questioned and challenged by employers weary of being accused of hiring undocumented workers. Day labourers, many of whom are of Latino origin, are under suspicion and some municipalities have prohibited them from congregating in public areas to offer labour services. Law-enforcement agencies in Arizona have occasionally enforced these ordinances, arresting Latino men who, despite being American citizens, are subjected to stops on the basis of their use of language, their attire or choice of location (p. 471–472).

It is unclear to what extent changes in immigration policy have affected minority groups' perceptions of the police, particulary given differences in their demographical representation in various communities.

Vehicle Stops

Arguably the most contentious area of policing is the issue of racial profiling and police discretion in conducting vehicle stops. In *Whren v. U.S.* (1994), the U.S. Supreme Court held that police may conduct a pretextual traffic stop on the basis of a traffic violation to investigate criminal activity. In effect, the Court ruled that the ultimate motivation of the stop is not the important issue, only whether there is legal justification for police intervention. Despite the the Court's inattention toward extralegal factors, there is a well-documented line of research on police traffic stops indicating that police are more likely to stop and search Hispanics and Blacks than Whites (Alpert et al. 2005; Rojek et al. 2012; Borooah 2011; Engel and Johnson 2006; Engel and Calnon 2004).

Weitzer and Tuch (2005) noted that "blacks may be more vulnerable than Hispanics to traffic stops by police because their skin color heightens their visibility" (p. 1025). To date, research has not addressed the relationship among race and perceptions on the type of search conducted. Do African Americans and Hispanics perceive the same level of legitimacy in search policies relating to vehicle searches compared to other forms of searches, e.g., residential and person? Given that most research on search rates has focused on vehicle stops, we created a separate measure to compare differences in racial perceptions on the legality of vehicle searches in the two data collection sites.

The Present Study

Public opinion of the police is largely based on whether citizens view police action as legitimate. Further, the manner in which police searches and seizures are conducted have a profound impact on how citizens view the police (Brunson 2007; Brunson and Miller 2006). According to the Supreme Court, police searches and seizures must be based on the concept of reasonableness, and are contingent upon "the place to be searched and the item to be seized" (*Groh v. Ramirez*, 2004, p.551). To date, the reasonableness standard has received very little empirical attention despite its significance to police work. The limits of police action are governed by what police officers perceive to be reasonable given the totality of the circumstances (*U.S. v. Arvizu* 2002). In theory, if the Supreme Court has accurately interpreted the "reasonable person standard," then citizens' opinions about search issues should represent the degree to which the legal process has impacted police behavior and satisfaction with their services.

This study uses U.S. Supreme Court decisions of police searches and seizures to determine the extent to which citizens' views of the police vary by race and ethnicity and by region of the U.S., net of control variables. We examine these perceptions in two regions of the country—Pennsylvania and Texas. The comparison of two communities with markedly different demographics provides an opportunity to assess the major tenets of both the group-position perspective as well as comparative conflict theory. Given the controversy surrounding immigration policies and associated crime control strategies, we explore the views of Hispanics toward case law governing police searches and seizures. In this community, Hispanics are the dominant ethnic group. Therefore, if the group position theory holds true, Hispanics should maintain the most favorable view toward the police compared to Whites and African Americans. Conversely, we would expect that in communities with more stable immigration trends and less exposure to border violence, such as the Northeast, perceptions of police search policies will be more closely associated with comparative conflict theory and its tenets. Therefore, in the Northeast, we expect that African Americans will hold the least favorable view of the police, followed by Hispanics and Whites most likely to view police search policies as legitimate.

Method

Sample and Procedure

During the 2014–2015 academic year, a survey[1] was distributed to undergraduate students attending Pennsylvania State University (PSU)-Schuylkill and Harrisburg and Texas A&M University-San Antonio (TAMU-SA), each representing markedly different demographic populations. According to the 2010 U.S. Census Bureau, the San Antonio population is described as 58.3% Hispanic, 7.8% African American, 31.3% White (non-Hispanic), and other (2.6%). Schuylkill County, Pennsylvania, which is located approximately 100 miles from Philadelphia, consists of 93.8% White (non-Hispanic), 3.0% African American, 2.3% Hispanic, and 1% other. In contrast to most 4-year universities, TAMU-SA only offers upper-division courses and is thus considered non-traditional. The student population ($n = 3468$) is majority Hispanic (62%), followed by white (27%), and African American (11%), and the average student age is 31.Alternatively, the combined student population of Penn State-Schuylkill and Harrisburg is predominantly white (63%), followed by African American (18%), and then Hispanic (6%), with an average age of 22. Students declaring themselves as multi-racial or multi-ethnic accounted for 13% of the population across the Penn State campuses.

Surveys were administered during normal class hours across a variety of academic programs to include students majoring in criminal justice, business, education, and the natural sciences at both universities. Students were not required to complete the survey—in most cases points were offered to volunteers as extra credit toward their final semester grade. A total of 1235 completed surveys were returned; however, 96 students refused to participate ($N = 1331$).

Measures

Dependent Variable

The use of facts from court cases (Kessler 2009), as opposed to vignettes (Rossi and Anderson 1982; Piquero 2012) is relatively uncommon in criminological research. Whether case facts accurately depict the context of a police search is a topic that can

---

[1] We field-tested the instrument with a group of ten police officers and made some changes prior to deploying it to the study population. All of the participants acknowledged that the scenarios represented the "most essential facts" of the search once alterations had been made. Kessler (2009) used a similar approach to gauge perceptions of citizens on whether they felt "free to leave" after having been confronted by a police officer while riding a bus or walking on the sidewalk. Building on this instrument, we were careful to include as many of the key legal issues of each search as possible: (1) whether consent, plain view, or any other exceptions to the normal probable cause requirement applied to the search, and (2) whether the facts arising to probable cause or reasonable suspicion were sufficiently identified.

be debated. Despite limitations to this approach, there is a body of research that documents a relationship between perceptions of events and actual behavior (Pogarsky 2004). Further, the complexity of police searches may be best represented by this form of measurement, and Supreme Court cases are well-suited for this study given the universal applicability of the law to all U.S. law enforcement officers.

We selected a random sample of 20 U.S. Supreme Court cases involving police searches and seizures occurring between the years 1999–2009. The population of cases ($N = 48$) consisted of the U.S. Supreme Court Media OYEZ database of cases aggregated by legal issue and year. The facts of each case were summarized to reflect the main legal issue and its key facts. An example of one case scenario is depicted as follows:

Person X was apprehended by Arizona state police on an outstanding warrant for driving with a suspended license. After the officers handcuffed X and placed him/her in the squad car, they went on to search the vehicle and discovered a handgun and a plastic bag of cocaine.

Students were asked to respond to each case summary on a scale of 0–4 (0 = strongly disagree, 1 = disagree, 2 = neutral, 3 = agree, and 4 = strongly agree) as to whether they believed "the search or seizure was reasonable and therefore legal." The search scale score was the combined score for all cases included in the scale for each sample. Of the 20 cases represented on the survey, five were reverse coded to reflect the Court's decision that the search was unreasonable. Factor analysis of the scale showed substantial evidence of a single factor and alpha reliability was good ($\alpha = .69$). We then computed a separate scale composed of cases involving vehicle searches. These 7 items represented the vehicle search scale, which showed modest reliability ($\alpha = .51$).

Independent Variables

We constructed a series of dummy variables to assess racial and ethnic group differences in perceptions toward police search policies. To measure the effect of prior contact with the legal system, we included four questions that asked participants about their involvement in the court system during the past 5 years. These questions were measured dichotomously: "I have been a plaintiff in a criminal or civil case" (1 = yes, 0 = no), "I have been a defendant in a criminal or civil case" (1 = yes, 0 = no), "I have served as a juror in a criminal or civil case" (1 = yes, 0 = no), and "I have been a witness in a criminal or civil case" (1 = yes, 0 = no). We also included an item to gauge perceptions of police search policies based on perceived fairness during prior police encounters, measured on a scale of 0–4.

Several control variables were included in the models to measure the independent effect of race and court system involvement on our dependent measures. Gender (male = 1, 0 = female). Previous research indicates that as people grow older they tend to hold more positive views toward the police (Hurst et al. 2000). Studies also show a similar trend in citizens' attitudes toward the court system—people gain more positive views of the court system with age (Wortley et al. 1997). Most prior research indicates males and females typically do not significantly differ in their views toward the police, but when the interaction between race, age, and gender is considered, gender becomes a significant variable. Specifically, young, Black males are the most likely to hold negative views of the police (Weitzer and Tuch 2006) and that females are less biased in their views toward the court system compared to males (Mast 2004).

Research is mixed on the effects of social class and attitudes toward the police and the court system. While findings are typically insignificant for whites, studies have shown that middle class Blacks and Hispanics are more likely to view the police negatively compared to lower class Blacks and Hispanics (Wortley et al. 1997; Weitzer and Tuch 2002). To assess the independent effects of income across both samples, income level was included as an ordinal variable (15 K and below = 1, above 15 K to 25 K = 2, above 25 K to 35 K = 3, above 35 K to 45 K = 4, above 45 K to 55 K = 5, and above 55 K = 6). Years of employment (over 50% of one calendar year = 1 yr) was also included and measured as a continuous variable.

Two final control variables were included in the models to account for differences in student populations. Since many of the participants were criminal justice majors or actively employed in a criminal justice agency we anticipated more positive attitudes toward the police and the court system among these groups. Prior research has shown that police officers, in particular, tend to be more authoritarian compared to non-officers (Culhane et al. 2008). Therefore, student major (criminal justice/criminology = 1, other = 0) and occupation (1 = currently employed in CJ field = 1, 0 = other) were included in the models.

Analytical Strategy

This study included two separate analyses. First, a series of OLS regression equations were estimated to explore the independent effects of region as well as race and ethnicity on our general measure of police legitimacy. We introduced the independent variables in four stages (models) to show the incremental effects of region, race/ethnicity, legal contact, and other demographic variables. Next, we repeated the same analysis for our measure of the measure of police legitimacy as reflected through vehicle search cases as decided by the Court. When using a combination of variables measured at both the continuous and dichotomous levels, the assumption of homoscedasticity may be violated due to significantly different levels of variance that affect linearity among the variables. However, the Durbin-Watson test for violations of homoscedasticity showed no problems across the models. Another potential problem that affects OLS regression models is multi-colinearity among the variables. A preliminary analysis of the variable inflation factors and tolerance levels was conducted; however, the analysis showed no problems with multi-collinearity among the variables.

Aside from racial differences between the two samples, students at TAMU-SA were older; were predominantly female; reported a higher mean income; and were slightly more likely to be currently employed in the criminal justice field. In terms of overall perceptions of police legitimacy, Northeastern respondents were significantly more likely to agree with the case law governing police searches and seizures compared to those in the Southwest. Interestingly, as it relates to vehicle searches and seizures, respondents from our Southwestern community were significantly more likely to agree with the Court's case law.

Results

Weitzer (2000) suggested that more research is necessary to examine individual perceptions toward the police and how these views vary across communities. This study is one of the few to examine regional differences in perceptions of police legitimacy; and employs a contextual measure that is reflected through search and seizure cases decided by the U.S. Supreme Court. First, we examine regional as well as racial and ethnic differences with respect to our overall measure that is based on searches of persons, places, and vehicles. Next, we investigate these effects as they relate specifically to vehicle searches and seizures. Our last point of inquiry concerns the partitioned effects of these variables according to region. The standardized beta coefficient for the variable region is statistically significant, even when legal background and control variables are introduced in the sequence of models. More specifically, respondents in our Northeastern community were more likely to agree with the legality of Supreme Court decisions governing police searches and seizures. Additionally, the models show that relative to Whites, African Americans are substantially more likely to hold opinions that are at odds with our measure of police search legitimacy. Similarly, Hispanics appear to be somewhat in disagreement with our measure of police legitimacy, and appear to occupy a middle-ground between Whites and African Americans. Several of the legal background and contact variables are significant in the models. Consistent with previous research, those respondents who had been treated fairly by the police in the past were more likely to hold views that were in accordance with our dependent measure (Terrill and Resig 2003; Fagan and Davies 2000). Additionally, those who had been a defendant or a juror in a criminal or civil case were more likely to maintain positive views of case holdings. Of the remaining variables, individuals with greater years of experience working in the criminal justice system were more likely to agree with the Court's opinions.

The results of the regression models included the same predictor variables on perceptions of vehicle search and seizure legality. Initially, the variable for region appears statistically significant in model one and remains so through model three. However, when all variables are included in model four these effects diminish. This finding is at odds with the outcome observed from our general measure of police search legality. Second, only the coefficient for race (African Americans) is statistically significant and remains fairly stable in models two through four. In other words, Hispanics appear to maintain beliefs that are more closely aligned with Whites as it relates to laws governing vehicle searches and seizures. African Americans, on the other hand, also are more likely to disagree with the Court's legal opinion compared to these groups. And like the results using the overall measure search legality, the individual's prior experience as a juror and treatment by the police continue to be salient predictors in the models.

Interaction Effects

Because differences were discovered in the overall models, the data for each region was analyzed separately to explore interaction effects. When the results for each region are examined independently, a somewhat different perspective emerges. Indeed, the influence of race and ethnicity on attitudinal measures of police searches and seizures is most evident in the Northeast. These effects are largely consistent with the additive models—African Americans in the Northeast, relative to Whites, tend to hold the most negative views of case law governing police searches and seizures, followed by Hispanics. Moreover, our respondents in the Southwest showed no significant differences our either outcome of interest. This finding highlights the importance of taking into context the regional effects on attitudes toward police practices.

Beyond racial and ethnic differences, Northeasterners' responses were also mediated by legal contact and background variables such as having served as a juror or defendant in the last 5 years. Further, our measure of prior treatment by the police is the only factor that remains consistently and positively related to our dependent measure in both regions.

The results also show regional differences in perceptions according to employment, major, gender, and age. While respondents with prior criminal justice system experience were more likely to agree with the Court's opinions in the Northeast, no significant differences were found among respondents in the Southwest. Paradoxically, the student's gender and reported major had a negative effect on overall perceptions in the Northeast and a positive effect on each dependent measure in the Southwest. Age was only a salient predictor in Northeasterners' attitudes to the general search measure.

Discussion

A common assumption in police-community relations research is that racial and ethnic differences in attitudes toward the police are relatively stable across communities. Comparative conflict theory holds that African-Americans will maintain the most negative views toward the police, followed by Hispanics, and then Whites.

Moreover, the theory asserts that Hispanics should hold more favorable views toward the police than African-Americans but less than Whites. However, recent political and social developments have impacted the Hispanic population in significant ways. Politicians have criticized anti-immigration legislation such as Operation Secure Communities and Arizona's Support Our Law Enforcement and Safe Neighborhoods Act of 2010 as unfairly targeting Hispanics. Moreover, although federal immigration law applies with equal force across the U.S., the majority of the population affected by these policies resides in the Southwest. This study fills a gap in the police-community relations literature by comparing racial and ethnic differences in perceptions of the legality of police searches and seizures in a Hispanic-majority and White-majority community.

Perhaps the most salient finding from this study is that respondents' views differed as they related to vehicle and overall measures of police search legality. In the Northeast, African Americans and Hispanics were significantly less supportive of general police search policies compared to Whites. Indeed, as Comparative Conflict Theory predicted, African-Americans held the least favorable views of police search legality followed by Hispanics. These findings suggest that where immigration patterns are relatively stable, perceptions of racial injustice are gradient according to race and ethnicity.

In keeping with the group position thesis, we predicted that Hispanics would retain the most favorable views of police search policies in the Southwest, despite the escalation in border violence in this region and recent federal and state immigration policies targeting Hispanics. However, our findings showed that racial and ethnic perceptions of police search legality did not differ significantly in the Southwest. It is somewhat surprising that African-Americans in the Southwest did not significantly differ from Whites in our analysis. This finding may be attributed to the use of scenarios to measure perceptions of search legality as opposed to general social surveys. Whereas the former presents a more objective measure of one's opinion regarding search legitimacy, the latter is inextricably tied to preconceived notions of bias that are heavily influenced by one's social surroundings (Tyler and Huo 2002; Kaminski and Jefferis 1998).

Weitzer and Tuch (2002) noted that African-Americans "may be more vulnerable than Hispanics to traffic stops by police because their skin color heightens their visibility" (p. 1025). Our study provided support for this notion with one caveat—the extent to which racial attitudes are related police search policies is mediated by region. In the Northeast, African-Americans were less supportive vehicle search and seizure policies compared to Whites, but Hispanics did not significantly differ from Whites in their support for these policies. In the Southwest, however, our findings indicated that neither Hispanics nor African-Americans significantly differed from Whites on their perceptions of vehicle search legality. These results are incongruous with past research indicating that African-Americans as well as Hispanics tend to be stopped by the police more frequently than Whites and treated more harshly during these incidents (Harris 2002).

However, our findings in relation to perceptions about the legality of vehicle stops are in some ways similar to results from prior research. The literature in this area reveals that African Americans are generally more critical of the legal justification for traffic stops compared to Whites. When viewed from the lens of Comparative Conflict Theory, Hispanics are ostensibly more sensitive to police contact than are African-Americans, partly due to the latter group's tendency to regard police encounters as "business as usual." When data was partitioned by region, results showed that individuals who had experienced positive encounters with the police in the past were also more likely to hold favorable perceptions of police search policies. These results imply that one's experiences with the police have enduring effects on conceptions of police legitimacy; and that race or ethnicity may not always influence police-community relationships.

Previous research has typically relied on general social surveys (see Weitzer et al. 2008), observational data (Rojek et al. 2010) or records from police traffic stops (Rojek et al. 2012) to gauge attitudes toward the police. This study employs a new methodological design using fact-based scenarios of seminal police search and seizure cases. Reflecting on the results of this study, the scenario-approach may tend to reveal opinions that are less susceptible to bias and one's social environment compared to previous approaches. Although differences according to race were found in the Northeast, no such differences were revealed in the Southwest. Another possible explanation for the null results in the Southwest is that southern states in general tend to be more conservative in their views on political issues, and that such views may be more pervasive within Hispanic-majority communities despite surges in border violence and controversial immigration reform. Future research employing legal cases to examine public opinion is warranted to explore more deeply the relationship between ones' political views and perceptions regarding the legitimacy of police searches; and specifically, how these views differ according to race and ethnicity.

The results of this study suggest that police have much to gain with respect to equal treatment of citizens during vehicle stops and other encounters. For example, citizen's beliefs and experiences with the police can influence their motivation to report crimes and cooperate as witnesses. In addition, positive perceptions of the police are more likely to facilitate more effective community-based programs that prevent and deter criminal activity. This study highlights the importance of place in understanding the connection between race and ethnicity and perceptions of police legitimacy. Further, it reveals that the validity of theoretical frameworks such as Comparative Conflict Theory and the group position thesis are nested in the local and regional aspects of crime and social control agents' response to crime.

Appendix

Table 8.1 Descriptive statistics for variables in study by region of country

	Southwest (n = 533)	Northeast (n = 703)	
	Frequency/Mean	Frequency/Mean	Difference in means
Independent variables			
Plaintiff	.09	.10	.007
Defendant	.12	.13	.02
Juror	.06	.11	.05**
Witness	.10	.09	−.01
Police contact	2.68	2.47	−.21**
Employment (years)	9.85	2.94	−6.90**
Employed (CJS)			−.05**
Income level	1.68	.36	−1.33**
Major (CRIM/CJ)			−.05
Gender (male)			.22**
Age (years)	30.42	20.93	−9.49
Race			
Hispanic			
African American			
White			
Dependent variables			
Case score	44.64		3.79**
Vehicle case score	18.64	17.64	1.00**

Note: A t-test was used to measure mean differences between regions for the independent variables. A Mann-Whitney U test was used for the dependent variable (Case Score). Descriptive and bivariate statistics for the variable Race/Ethnicity are reported in the Results section
*$p < .05$
**$p < .01$, using a two-tailed t-test

Table 8.2 OLS regression predicting perceived legitimacy of searches and seizures

Independent and control variables	Model 1	Model 2	Model 3	Model 4
Region (1 = PSU)	.21**	.21**	.23**	.26**
	(.51)	(.62)	(.61)	(.79)
Hispanic		−.09**	−.09**	−.10**
		(.68)	(.66)	(.79)
African American		−.16**	−.17**	−.17**
		(.68)		(.66)
Plaintiff			.02	.01
			(.89)	(.94)
Defendant			.07*	.07*
			(.83)	(.85)
Juror			.06*	.07**
			(.89)	(.92)
Witness			.02	.02
Police contact			.22**	.22**
			(.22)	(.23)
Employment length				.04
				(.06)
Employed in CJS (1 = yes)				.08**
				(1.02)
Major (1 = CJ/CRIM)				−.03
				(.53)
Income				.03
				(.23)
Gender (1 = male)				.04
				(.54)
Age				---
				(.06)
Intercept	44.64	46.17	41.01	39.73
Adjusted R^2	.04	.07	.12	.14

Note: For the variable Race, White is the reference group. The standardized coefficients are reported for the independent variables with the standard errors in parentheses
*$p < .05$
**$p < .01$

Table 8.3 OLS regression predicting perceived legitimacy of vehicle searches and seizures

Independent and control variables	Model 1	Model 2	Model 3	Model 4
Region	−.12**	−.10**	−.08*	−.06
	(.23)	(.29)	(.29)	(.37)
Hispanic		−.02	−.02	−.04
Black		−.12**	−.13**	−.13**
		(.32)	(.31)	(.33)
Plaintiff			.02	.01
			(.42)	(.44)
Defendant			.07*	.08*
			(.39)	(.40)
Juror			.05	.06*
			(.42)	(.44)
Witness			−.02	−.02
			(.42)	(.44)
Police contact			.19**	.19**
			(.11)	(.11)
Employment				.08
				(.03)
Employed in CJS				.05
				(.48)
Income				.02
				(.11)
Major				—
				(.25)
Gender				.02
				(.26)
Age				−.04
				(.03)
Intercept	18.64	18.94	16.93	16.79
Adjusted R^2	.01	.02	.06	.06

Note: For the variable Race, White is the reference group. The standardized coefficients for the independent variables are reported with the standard errors in parentheses
$^*p < .05$
$^{**}p < .01$

Table 8.4 OLS regression for partitioned data by region and type of search

Variable	Northeast				Southwest			
	General		Vehicle		General		Vehicle	
	β	SE	β	SE	β	SE	β	SE
Hispanic	−.09*	1.26	−.09*	.54	–	–	–	–
AA	−17**	.92	−.15**	.41	–	–	–	–
Juror	.10**	1.28	.09*	.56	–	–	–	–
Defendant	–	–	.10*	.57	–	–	–	–
Police contact	.24**	.37	.22**	.16	.20**	.24	.15**	.15
Employed in CJS	.12**	1.82	.08*	.80	–	–	–	–
Major	−.07*	.79	–	–	.10*	.56	.10*	.35
Gender	.09*	.83	.08*	.36	–	–	−.11*	.34
Age	.09*	.16	–	–	–	–	–	–
Adjusted R^2	.15		.11		.06		.04	

References

Alpert, G. P., MacDonald, J., & Dunham, R. G. (2005). Police suspicion and discretionary decision making during citizen stops. *Criminology, 43*, 407–434.

Bayley, D., & Mendelsohn, H. (1969). *Minorities and the police: Confrontation in America.* New York: Free Press.

Blalock, H. M. (1967). *Toward a theory of minority-group relations.* New York: Wiley.

Blumer, H. (1958). Race prejudice as a sense of group position. *Pacific Sociological Review, 1,* 3–7.

Borooah, V. K. (2011). Racial disparity in police stop and searches in England and Whales. *Journal of Quantitative Criminology, 27,* 453–473.

Britt, C. L. (2000). Social context and racial disparities in punishment decisions. *Justice Quarterly, 17*(4), 707–732.

Brunson, R. K. (2007). Police don't like black people: African American young men's accumulated police experiences. *Criminology and Public Policy, 6,* 71–102.

Brunson, R. K., & Miller, J. (2006). Young black men and urban policing in the United States. *British Journal of Criminology, 46,* 613–640.

Buckler, K., Unnever, J. D., & Cohen, F. T. (2008). Perceptions of injustice revisited: A test of Hagan et al.'s comparative conflict theory. *Journal of Crime and Justice, 31*(1), 35–57.

Cao, L., & Garcia, V. (2005). Race and satisfaction with the police in a small city. *Journal of Criminal Justice, 33*(2), 191–199.

Culhane, S. E., Hosch, H. M., & Heck, C. (2008). Interrogation technique endorsement by current law enforcement, future law enforcement, and laypersons. *Police Quarterly, 11*(3), 366–386.

Engel, R. S. (2008). A critique of the outcome test in racial profiling research. *Justice Quarterly, 25,* 1–36.

Engel, R. S., & Calnon, J. M. (2004). Comparing benchmark technologies for police-citizen contacts: Traffic stop data collection for the Pennsylvania state police. *Police Quarterly, 7,* 97–125.

Engel, R. S., & Johnson, R. (2006). Toward a better understanding of racial and ethnic disparities in search and seizure rates. *Journal of Criminal Justice, 34,* 605–617.

Fagan, J., & Davies, G. (2000). Street stops and broken windows: *Terry,* race, and disorder in New York City. *Fordham Urban Law Journal, 28,* 457–490.

Franklin, T. W. (2010). The intersection of defendants' race, gender, and age in prosecutorial decision making. *Journal of Criminal Justice, 38*(2), 185–192.

Grieco, E. M., & Rytina, N. F. (2011). U.S. data sources on the foreign born and immigration. *International Migration Review, 45*(4), 1001–1016.

Groh v. Ramirez. (2004). 540 U.S. 551.

Guzmán, B. (2001). *The Hispanic population (census brief 2000: C2KBR/01–3).* Washington, DC: U.S. Census Bureau.

Hagan, J., Payne, M. R., & Shedd, C. (2005). Race, ethnicity, and youth perceptions of injustice. *American Sociological Review, 70*, 381–407.

Harris, D. (2002). *Profiles in injustice.* New York: New Press.

Healey, J. (1995). *Race, ethnicity, gender, and class.* Thousand Oaks: Pine Forge Press.

Howell, S., Perry, H., & Vile, M. (2004). Black cities, white cities: Evaluating the police. *Political Behavior, 26*, 45–68.

Hurst, Y., Frank, J., & Browning, S. (2000). The attitudes of juveniles toward the police. *Policing, 23*, 37–53.

Hurwitz, J., & Peffley, M. (1997). Public perceptions of race and crime: The role of racial stereotypes. *American Journal of Political Science, 41*, 375–401.

Kaminski, R., & Jefferis, E. (1998). The effect of a violent televised arrest on public perceptions of the police. *Policing, 21*, 683–706.

Kent, S. L., & Jacobs, D. (2005). Minority threat and police strength from 1980 to 2000: A fixed-effects analysis of nonlinear and interactive effects in large cities. *Criminology, 43*(3), 731–760.

Kessler, D. K. (2009). Free to leave? An empirical look at the fourth Amendment's seizure standard. *Journal of Criminal Law and Criminology, 99*(1), 51–87.

Mast, M. S. (2004). Men are hierarchal, women are egalitarian: An implicit gender stereotype. *Swiss Journal of Psychology, 63*, 107–111.

Massey, D. S., & Capoferro, C. (2009). The geographic diversification of American immigration. In D. S. Massey (Ed.), *New faces in new places: The changing geography of American immigration* (pp. 25–50). New York: Russell Sage.

Mata, A. G. (1998). Stereotyping by politicians: Immigrant bashing and nativist political movements. In C. R. Mann & M. S. Zatz (Eds.), *Images of color, images of crime* (pp. 151–167). Los Angeles: Roxbury.

McDowell, M., & Wonders, N. (2010). Keeping migrants in their place: Technologies of control and racialized public space in Arizona. *Social Justice, 7*(2), 54–72.

Murty, K., Roebuck, J., & Smith, J. (1990). The image of the police in black Atlanta communities. *Journal of Police Science and Administration, 17*, 250–257.

President's Commission on Law Enforcement and Administration of Justice. (1967). *Task force report: The police.* Washington, DC: GPO.

Provine, D. M., & Sanchez, G. (2011). Suspecting immigrants: Exploring links between racialised anxieties and expanded police powers in Arizona. *Policing and Society, 21*, 468–479.

Piquero, N. L. (2012). The only thing we have to fear is fear itself: Investigating the relationship between fear of falling and white collar crime. *Crime and Delinquency, 58*(3), 362–379.

Pogarsky, G. (2004). Projected offending and contemporaneous rule-violation: Implications for heterotypic continuity. *Criminology, 42*, 111–136.

Rojek, J., Alpert, G. P., & Smith, H. P. (2010). Examining officer and citizen accounts of police use-of-force incidents. *Crime and Delinquency, 58*(2), 301–327.

Rojek, J., Rosenfeld, R., & Decker, S. (2012). Policing race: The racial stratification of searches in police traffic stops. *Criminology, 50*(4), 993–1024.

Rossi, P. H., & Anderson, A. B. (1982). The factorial survey approach: An introduction. In P. H. Rossi & S. L. Nock (Eds.), *Measuring social judgments* (pp. 15–67). Beverly Hills: SAGE.

Rumbaut, R. G., & Ewing, W. A. (2007). *The myth of immigrant criminality and the paradox of assimilation: Incarceration rates among native and foreign-born men.* Washington, DC: Immigration Policy Center, American Immigration Law Foundation.

Schuck, A. M., & Rosenbaum, D. P. (2005). Global and neighborhood attitudes toward the police: Differentiation by race, ethnicity and type of contact. *Journal of Quantitative Criminology, 21*(4), 391–418.

Smith, B. W., & Holmes, M. (2003). Community accountability, minority threat, and police brutality: An examination of civil rights criminal complaints. *Criminology, 41*(4), 1035–1063.

Stacey, M., Carbone-Lopez, K., & Rosenfeld, R. (2011). Demographic change and ethnically motivated crime: The impact of immigration on anti-hispanic hate crime in the United States. *Journal of Contemporary Criminal Justice, 27*(3), 278–298.

Steen, S., Engen, R. L., & Gainey, R. R. (2005). Images of danger and culpability: Racial stereotyping, case processing, and criminal sentencing. *Criminology, 43*(2), 435–468.

Stucky, T. D. (2005). Local politics and police strength. *Justice Quarterly, 22*(2), 139–169.

Terrill, W., & Reisig, M. (2003). Neighborhood context and police use of force. *Journal of Research in Crime and Delinquency, 40*, 291–321.

Tyler, T., & Huo, Y. (2002). *Trust in the law*. Russell: Sage Foundation.

United States v. Arvizu, 534 U.S. 266 (2002)

Weitzer, R. (2000). Racialized policing: Residents' perceptions in three neighborhoods. *Law and Society Review, 34*(1), 129–155.

Weitzer, R., & Tuch, S. (2002). Perceptions of racial profiling: Race, class, and personal experience. *Criminology, 40*(2), 435–455.

Weitzer, R., & Tuch, S. A. (2005). Racially-biased policing: Determinants of citizen perceptions. *Social Forces, 83*(3), 1009–1030.

Weitzer, R., & Tuch, S. A. (2006). *Race and policing in America: Conflict and reform*. New York: Cambridge University Press.

Weitzer, R., Tuch, S. A., & Skogan, W. A. (2008). Police-community relations in a majority-black city. *Journal of Research in Crime and Delinquency, 45*(4), 398–428.

Wortley, S., Hagan, J., & Macmillan, R. (1997). Just desserts? The racial polarization of perceptions of criminal ill Injustice. *Law and Society Review, 31*, 637–676.

Part III
North American Perspectives

Chapter 9
Diversity and Policing in Canada

Richard Parent and Catherine Parent

Introduction: The Policing Landscape in Canada – Recruitment and Training

In Canada, policing is the largest component of the criminal justice system with a budget of over $14 billion. As the second largest country in the world, there are approximately 69,000 police officers serving a population of roughly 35 million people. 60% of all police officers are employed within five Canadian police services—the Royal Canadian Mounted Police (RCMP), the Toronto Police Service, the Ontario Provincial Police (OPP), the Sûreté du Québec (SQ), and the City of Montreal Police Service (Service de police de la Ville de Montréal, or SPVM). Stand-alone municipal police services in Canada represent the remaining 40% of the police personnel (Statistics Canada 2017a). In 2015, there were a total of 176 municipal police services of which 117 police services had fewer than 25 staff. In the far north, Nunavut, the Northwest Territories and the Yukon utilize the services of the RCMP for policing (Statistics Canada 2016).

Recruiting Strategies

Career positions within Canadian policing are seen as attractive due to the level of pay, benefits, and the job satisfaction that comes from assisting members of the public. Police recruits and police services recognize that Canada is a multicultural

R. Parent (✉)
Simon Fraser University, Vancouver, Canada
e-mail: rparent@sfu.ca

C. Parent
Diversity and Policing in Canada, Vancouver, British Columbia, Canada
e-mail: cparent@telus.net

© Springer Nature Switzerland AG 2019
J. F. Albrecht et al. (eds.), *Policing and Minority Communities*,
https://doi.org/10.1007/978-3-030-19182-5_9

country with a vast range of diverse communities. Historically, police officers have been overwhelmingly Caucasian males. It is only in the past 25 years that police services have actively recruited women, Indigenous people as well as visible and cultural minorities, and, more recently, members of the lesbian, gay, bisexual, and transgender (LGBT) community. As the Canadian landscape began to change police services recognized the need to hire individuals from diverse communities and in particular, those that are under-represented within the police service.

In keeping with Sir Robert Peel's principles of 1829, Canadian police services have focused upon the principle that the public are the police and the police are the public and should therefore reflect the diversity of the community. It has also been suggested that police services with diverse representation of officers, similar to that of the community they serve, may have better communication skills to listen; explain and interact more frequently in ways that will enhance the relationship between the community and the police (Ben-Porath 2007, p. 7, 10, 15; Szeto 2014, p.9).

In an effort to promote diversity, a smaller number of Canadian police services have adopted employment equity practices that give preference to an individual of a target group. In essence, when two equally qualified candidates suitable for hiring, the individual from the target group will be hired first. This practice allows a police service to achieve its desired target numbers effectively within a shorter period of time (Employment Equity Act 1995).

Most police services have avoided employment equity practices and have developed or are developing other strategies to encourage applications from qualified individuals of all cultures, backgrounds and walks of life. These agencies tend to be localized municipalities with a focus upon customer service and community engagement. Ethics, professionalism and community policing are emphasized within this model of service delivery, all of which further influence recruiting strategies (Parent and Parent 2018).

Gender and Policing

It was not until 1974 that women became involved in regular front-line police duties. Toronto's police service was one of the first Canadian police services to actively incorporate and promote women in policing; however, female officers did not initially have all of the rights of male officers. Women were not permitted to ride in patrol vehicles until 1959, and it was not until 1974 that they were allowed to carry revolvers (which were carried in handbags specifically designed for this purpose) (Toronto Police Service 2017). Since the 1990's, the number of women have been steadily increasing within most Canadian police services. Great strides have been made in the hiring, retaining, and advancing of female police officers. Today, women are found serving in all facets of Canadian policing, positively impacting the policing of the community. Women have also taken on the challenge of running police services, serving in a variety of ranks including as senior administrators and police chiefs.

One of the more significant events regarding women in policing occurred in March 2018 when it was announced that a women would be appointed as the Commissioner for Canada's largest police service, the Royal Canadian Mounted Police (RCMP). Commissioner Designate Brenda Lucki became the first ever female officer to command the historic federal police service, rising through the ranks with 32 years of policing experience (Prime Minister of Canada 2018).

Equal representation of women in policing still has a long way to go. Although women comprise approximately 48% of the labour force and roughly 51% of the Canadian population, female police officers accounted for just 20.8% (14,332) of the national police population in 2015 (Mazowita and Greenland 2015). Nonetheless, women continue to be increasingly represented in the higher ranks of police services. Women represented 13% of senior officers in 2016, the highest proportion ever recorded when compared with 6% in 2006 and less than 1% in 1986 (Statistics Canada 2016). In the past 15 years the proportion of female officers within the non-commissioned and senior officers' ranks has almost tripled. The growth of women in policing in recent years is a long term trend. This is in contrast to the number of male officers which interestingly decreased in 2016.

The Canadian province of Quebec had the highest percentage of female police officers at 24% in 2011. The lowest proportions of women police officers were found in the Yukon, Northwest Territories, and Nunavut, with women accounting for roughly 14% of total police officers in each area (Statistics Canada 2011). In Toronto, Canada's largest city, female officers made up 18% of police personnel in 2011. Of the 5776 police officers in Toronto, 1063 are female.

Women also comprise more than half of civilian staff. As of 2015, more than half (57.3%) of women employed by police services were in civilian positions, accounting for 67.8% of civilian personnel. In comparison, 85.6% of men employed by police services were sworn police officers, while the remaining 14.4% of men were civilian personnel (Mazowita and Greenland 2015).

In sum, while women continue to make inroads into Canadian law enforcement, the journey has been long, challenging and difficult. Recruitment strategies designed to attract women into law enforcement have in reality met with moderate success. Sexual harassment, workplace bias, and bullying continue to challenge the careers of women within law enforcement. Further changes within policing are necessary if women are to fully assume an equal role with their male counterparts in Canada.

The LGBT Community

Since 2000, gay and lesbian officers have been acknowledged and welcomed within Canadian police services. More recently, members of the bisexual and transgender community have been included in the police ranks. This has served to enhance the diversity of policing by expanding the representation of diverse individuals from the communities. Several police services actively recruit officers from the Lesbian, Gay, Bisexual, Transgender (LGBT) community. Most police leaders publically acknowledge and support the employment of LGBT police personnel. This acceptance has been facilitated by human rights legislation and positive workplace laws and policies, including the creation of hate and bias crime units in many police services. Even with this support, many LGBT officers continue to be cautious of coming out and publicly stating their sexual orientation (Whitelaw and Parent 2018; pp. 257–259).

There also appears to be differences among law enforcement services regarding the degree to which some officers feel comfortable having their co-workers know about their sexual orientation. Many police officers may feel that their sexual orientation is a private matter. There is also concern that some police officers will not work with an openly gay, lesbian, bisexual, or transgender officer on the street. Fear and lack of trust between partners might occur and, in extreme cases, individual officers may not provide the necessary backup that could literally save an officer's life. Even with major inroads into the police subculture, stereotypes and fears still exist and need to be dismantled. Although the Canadian police subculture has progressed significantly during recent years, further evolution is needed to reflect the changing times within contemporary society (Whitelaw and Parent 2018, pp. 257–259).

Indigenous Peoples

Although Indigenous peoples are considered to be the "first nations" within Canada there has historically been little attempt to recruit Indigenous individuals within police services. Indigenous people have also been reluctant to pursue a police career largely due to negative past experiences that include a general mistrust of government and government representatives such as the police. This situation has shifted in the past 20 years with Canadian police services actively seeking Indigenous recruits and making attempts to build relationships and trust within Indigenous communities.

The RCMP has been the most successful Canadian police service in recruiting Indigenous people within their organization. The Aboriginal Policing Program (APP) is an RCMP initiative that spans across the nation, fostering positive relationships with Indigenous peoples while promoting recruitment. The Aboriginal Pre-Cadet Training (APTP) program is one example within the APP, involving the selection of twenty-eight participants from across Canada attending the RCMP training academy in Regina, Saskatchewan. The successful candidates are young people, aged 19–29 and are of Indigenous ancestry that are provided police training in the area of problem solving, law, public speaking, physical fitness, police defensive tactics, drill, & cultural awareness.

The 3 week training program serves as an outreach into Indigenous communities, providing youth with the opportunity to interact with officers in a positive setting that may ultimately lead to individuals pursuing careers with the RCMP. The youth are paid a wage during the training program and upon completion, are sent to an RCMP Detachment in their home province. The youth will then spend the summer months assisting regular police officers with various aspects of community policing duties. The basic requirements for eligibility into the APTP program include:

- Be a Canadian citizen
- Be of First Nation, Metis or Aboriginal Descent
- Be of good character
- Be between 19–29 years of age
- Have completed Grade 12 or equivalent
- Be in good physical condition
- Have a valid BC's Drivers Licence
- Be able to pass an enhanced reliability security check

Source: Royal Canadian Mounted Police (2017a).

In the province of Ontario, the Ontario Provincial Police (OPP) has created the Aboriginal Policing Bureau (APB) in response to the various needs of Indigenous people and Indigenous communities. Within the province, legislation allows for Indigenous communities to create their own police services. Known as First Nation Constables, the officers are supported and jointly administered by the OPP. There are currently 19 First Nation communities in the province of Ontario that have adopted this model, utilizing a collaborate approach to recruitment and policing. The creation of autonomous Indigenous police forces within Ontario has enhanced the opportunities available to Indigenous persons seeking a career within policing (Whitelaw and Parent 2018: pp. 259–260).

Visible Minorities

In 2016, roughly 7.6 million individuals identified as a visible minority, representing 22% or roughly one-fifth of Canada's population. This figure is a five-fold increase from 1981, when visible minorities were less than 5% of the population. While minority groups have always existed in Canada, police recruiting practices tended to promote a profession that was comprised of white males. Since the 1990s police services have made great strides in attempting to hire recruits that reflect the demographics of the community being served. Diversity hiring continues to increase across Canada most notably in large urban areas. However, this process has been challenging. For example, only 12% of the police officers in Toronto were identified as visible minorities (Statistics Canada 2017a).

Although police services are attempting to diversify personnel within their ranks, they are unable to keep up with the rapid changes occurring within the country. In 2016, Canadian census data on ethnicity and immigration, noted that large numbers of immigrants are moving to Canada's major cities that include Toronto, Vancouver and Montreal. As a result, Greater Toronto now has fewer "whites" (Caucasians) and Indigenous peoples (48.6%) than "visible minorities" (51.4%). The term "visible minority" is utilized by Statistics Canada, in contrast to the term "people of colour" that is often used in the United States.

Similar to Toronto, the western city of Vancouver has an equal numbers of Caucasians compared to visible minorities. Statistics Canada data noted that although these cities continue to grow, there is an exodus of locals from these major centers. The locals tend to be Caucasians. As a result, the cities of Toronto, Montreal and Vancouver are projected to have fewer people of European origin with an ever increasing population of immigrants that tend to come from Asia, the Middle East, South America and Africa (Statistics Canada 2017b). The gravitation of foreign born migrants to Canada's three biggest cities has created local infrastructure challenges in areas that include English-as-a-second-language programs, housing and public health care.

Police services in Canada's major urban areas are struggling to keep up with this rapid and significant shift in demographics that will require a shift in the police services provided to the community. Across the nation, Canadian police services are being challenged to reflect community diversity among their ranks. Significant numbers of visible minorities and Indigenous populations do not have full representation within their police services. Indeed, a recent review of various police services in Canada noted the following:

- In the western city of Vancouver, some 54% of Vancouverites are from minority groups (predominately Chinese and South Asian), but only 22% of its police service matches that profile.
- In Edmonton, Alberta, 35% of citizens are visible minorities or Indigenous, yet those groups are represented in less than 10% of its police service.
- In the province of Ontario, while 57% of the Peel Region near Toronto is diverse, the Peel Police Service has only 19% non-white officers. Similarly in York Region, also neighbouring Toronto, 44% of the population is diverse, but only 17% of the police service.
- In Quebec City and Gatineau, Quebec, just over 1% of officers are diverse, whereas the diversity within their communities is multiple times more diverse at 5 and 12.7%, respectively.
- The Sûreté du Québec (SQ), Quebec's provincial police, stands out as a public institution in need of diversity. This provincial police agency serves more than 2.5 million people in the province of Quebec, yet less than 1% of its officers are not Caucasian. It was noted that between 2007 and March 2015, the SQ hired 735 new police officers; however, only 5 of the recruits were from cultural communities different from English or French native speakers (Leavitt 2016).
- In Canada's largest and most northern territory, Nunavut, roughly 12% of the police service is Indigenous; however the territory is made up of almost 90% Indigenous people. *Source*: Marcoux et al. 2016

It is within this setting that Canadian police services are attempting to increase minority-hiring without the lowering of entrance standards by utilizing employment equity practices in the recruitment of officers. As mentioned, employment equity provides preference to a visible minority or member of a target group where two equally qualified candidates exist. Typically, one individual is from a visible minority and the other is a male Caucasian. If two highly qualified individuals are considered equal during the hiring process, the tie tends to be broken in favour of the visible minority applicant. This process varies and is dependent upon the specific needs of the police service and the extent to which the police service currently reflects the diverse makeup of the community it serves.

The hiring of an inferior applicant from a target group, for the main purpose of achieving a quota, is seen as a disservice to the public and to the target group represented by that individual. Interestingly, the current demand for new police recruits and their relatively limited supply suggests that suitable candidates will be hired regardless of employment equity practices. Most police services are focused upon recruiting initiatives that increase the number of applications received (Whitelaw and Parent 2018, p. 260).

Canada's federal police service, the RCMP, is actively attempting to increase minority hiring in order to reflect the diverse population of Canada and to strengthen relationships with local communities. In order to achieve this goal the RCMP is attempting to provide applicants with equal and fair opportunities that are in alignment with employment equity policies and federal legislation. As a federal agency, the RCMP views employment equity measures as contributing directly to effective community policing, quality of service and police/minority relations. On their web page the RCMP state that they are an organization moving towards:

- An organizational culture in which diversity is the recognized norm;
- A learning strategy which embraces diversity;
- All policies and practices are adapted to the reality of diversity at all levels;
- Continual communications to address diversity
- Ongoing monitoring of recruitment, selection, management and career development of the designated groups;
- Career development programs for designated groups and the needs of the RCMP;
- Organizational investment for diversity issues;
- Measure management performance on diversity;
- Training programs to improve competencies in Diversity Management at all levels of decision making;
- Training and development on Diversity Management to become an integral part of all promotion processes;
- Regularly report on diversity issues through the balanced scorecard

Source: Royal Canadian Mounted Police (2016).

Even though police services are focused upon hiring minorities, challenges to recruiting remain. For example, visible minorities may hold negative perceptions of police personnel based upon on their experiences in their country of origin. Immigrants may also hold the view that law enforcement is not an honorable profession and discourage their children from applying to policing suggesting that they seek more reputable occupations (Jain et al. 1999, p.55).

In an attempt to address this concern, police services in Canada have implemented various community initiatives aimed at increasing support for law enforcement, enhancing communication and, building public trust. For example, initiatives such as the "Coffee with a Cop" program strengthen community relationships and encourage visible minority interest in police services by allowing front-line officers to speak directly with the public. Other initiatives include door-to-door visits, police consultative committees and "get acquainted" sessions that serve to enhance relationships with visible minorities while encouraging potential recruits for the police service (Parent and Parent 2018). A common theme to these programs is that they serve to break down barriers, reduce fear of the police and increase police legitimacy.

Nonetheless, while police services continue to make inroads into minority communities, recruiting initiatives continue to fall far short of reflecting the diversity of Canadian society. As society shifts and continues to change, police recruiting requires a continued focus upon communities that are underrepresented among the police.

Fostering Diversity Within the Workforce – Community Policing

As stated, police services across Canada are actively seeking female applicants and applicants from visible ethnic minorities with the view that these individuals will not only influence and shape the delivery of police services but more importantly, police culture. In addition to recruiting initiatives, most police services across Canada have adopted a community policing model that reflects diversity within all aspects of police operations. Community policing serves to create partnerships between the police and the local community, working in a collaborative fashion to share and direct the delivery of police services.

An important part of this process is policing by consent. When law enforcement occurs with the consent of the general public, it implies that officers have demonstrated a sincere concern and thus are permitted to exercise authority to manage conflicts, maintain social order, and solve problems in the community. In other words, police have earned the legitimacy to conduct policing. The public perceives that the actions of the officers should be consistently ethical, fair, unbiased, and beyond reproach (Tyler and Jackson 2013, p. 7–9, 12). When this occurs, officers are perceived by the public as acting with integrity, fairness, and respect. Often referred to as *procedural justice*, police actions must be considered legitimate and in accordance with the rule of law.

Police officers also need to have a sense of community and intimate knowledge of the area that they police. Officers need to know about the cultural and demographic changes that are occurring around them and how those changes will impact upon the decisions they make. By being aware of societal trends and local community factors, officers are better equipped to interact and partner with the community in developing solutions and in delivering services. For example, cultural and religious appreciation enables effective working relationships with community members shifting the police service's role to one of providing support, guidance and assistance in matters of safety and security.

A fundamental component of fostering community policing principles within the police service is training. Officers require training that will allow them to carry out the various tasks within a community-based policing framework. For example, training curriculum for recruits and in-service personnel must reinforce the core values of the police service. Officers must also have an awareness and understanding of the social, economic, and political make-up of the community. Training should foster a genuine appreciation and respect for the cultural diversity of the community being policed.

Some police services in Canada have provided implicit bias awareness training to personnel in an attempt to address inconsistencies within the delivery of police services. The training is provided to civilian and police personnel, fostering an awareness of the inherent bias that individuals may have in regards to race, religion, gender, age, and sexual orientation. Implicit bias may distort an individual's perception and subsequent treatment, either in favour of, or against, an individual or group of individuals. Reducing the influence of implicit bias is important to building relationships between police services and the diversity that exists within Canadian communities (Whitelaw and Parent 2018: pp. 265–267)

Indigenous Peoples and Policing Initiatives in Canada

Indigenous people occupy a special place within Canadian society and have unique policing needs. The initial contact by Europeans some 500 years ago ultimately led to the displacement of many Indigenous peoples from their lands with forced relocation to smaller territories or land reserves. As Canadian society evolved, most Indigenous peoples became further marginalized. Historically, relations between Indigenous peoples and the police have frequently been characterized by a high degree of mutual suspicion and hostility. Often discriminated against, Indigenous people have just reason to be cautious about governments (and their law enforcement agencies) that have attempted to force them to assimilate, and to adopt European cultural perspectives (Parent and Parent 2018).

Indigenous communities confront a variety of social and policing problems that are distinctive and typically more serious than those in non-Indigenous communities. For example, in 2016, Indigenous people made up roughly 4% of the Canadian population but comprised 25% of the federal prison population. In the Prairie Provinces, 48% of federal inmates are Indigenous people and over 36% of women in Canadian prisons are of Indigenous descent (Correctional Investigator Canada 2016). Issues such as colonialism and the disproportionate presence of poverty are frequently cited to explain why so many Indigenous people become involved with the criminal justice system and police.

Previous steps to resolve the crime and policing challenges with Indigenous peoples either provided marginal results or failed. Most Indigenous communities have expressed the desire for a different approach to policing, one that would be more reflective of Indigenous community issues and concerns.

Along with a new approach to law enforcement, alternative models of community justice may better serve Indigenous peoples by incorporating traditional practices and providing a reduction in incarceration rates. In recent years, community justice or restorative justice principles have attempted to address these concerns and have played a significant role in Indigenous communities. In 1999, the Supreme Court of Canada (SCC) recognized the importance of these principles within the landmark decision of *R. v. Gladue* (1999). In this decision the Supreme Court directed Canadian courts to take meaningful steps to reduce the frequency of incarceration when sentencing Indigenous offenders. Sentencing judges are directed to consider all non-jail options that are appropriate and available, during the assessment of the Indigenous offender.

In 2012, the Supreme Court of Canada in the ruling of *R. v. Ipeelee* (2012 S.C.C. 13), emphasized that:

> To be clear, courts must take judicial notice of such matters as the history of colonialism, displacement and residential schools and how that history continues to translate into lower educational attainment, lower incomes, higher unemployment, higher rates of substance abuse and suicide and, of course, higher levels of incarceration for Aboriginal Peoples[.] Failing to take these circumstances into account would violate the fundamental principle of sentencing.

Several government task forces and commissions of inquiry have also suggested that in the past, police acted in a discriminatory fashion against Indigenous people. The Ipperwash Inquiry into the 1995 Ontario Provincial Police shooting of Dudley George is but one example of the reoccurring conflict between Indigenous peoples and police.

Dudley George grew up on the Stony Point Indigenous Reserve. On September 4, 1995, Dudley George and other Indigenous people occupied Ipperwash Provincial Park to protest the refusal of the Canadian government to return ownership of the Stony Point Reserve. Two days after the occupation of the park an altercation occurred between protestors and the Ontario Provincial Police resulting in the fatal shooting of Dudley George who was unarmed at the time of his death.

The incident prompted a comprehensive government inquiry into why the police had shot and killed an unarmed Indigenous person during a land claim dispute. The purpose of the inquiry was to report on events surrounding the death of Dudley George and to make recommendations that would prevent similar tragic events in the future. On May 31, 2007, the Commission of Inquiry's final report was released noting:

- The disputed land should be returned immediately to the Stony Point First Nation, which should also receive compensation.
- Ontario should establish a permanent, independent, and impartial agency to facilitate and oversee the settling of land and treaty claims.
- Ontario should improve public education about its land claim policies, as well as Aboriginal burial and heritage sites.
- Access to the Ontario land claims process should depend on whether the documentation filed by the First Nations provides clear evidence that there has been a breach of the legal obligations of the Crown.

- The Ontario Provincial Police should establish a formal consultation committee with major Aboriginal organizations in Ontario.
- Provincial police should establish an internal process to ensure racist and culturally insensitive behaviour by police is dealt with publicly.
- The province should establish and fund an Ontario Aboriginal Reconciliation Fund.

Source: Ipperwash Inquiry Report 2007).

The Ontario Provincial Police (OPP) responded to the Ipperwash inquiry by developing a "Framework approach" in defining and guiding the police response to various incidents that may occur on Indigenous lands. The Framework approach provides flexibility in how to manage individual conflict situations while establishing consistency, meeting policing core duties as well as statutory and common law responsibilities. Of importance is that this approach emphasizes accommodation and mutual respect for differences, positions and, interests of involved Indigenous and non-Indigenous communities and the police service. The strategies that are developed support the minimal use of force by police, to the fullest extent possible.

The OPP Framework identifies three stages of potential conflict that can occur: pre-incident, incident and post-incident. Actual incidents occurring on Indigenous lands are further defined as:

- A *major incident* is an occurrence that, by circumstance, requires employees, equipment and resources beyond those required for normal police service delivery; for example civil disturbances or disasters such as an airplane crash.
- A *critical incident* is a high-risk incident requiring mobilization of an integrated emergency response; for example an active shooter, a hostage taking or a barricaded person. Typically, in these instances, a tactical team will be deployed in conjunction with an incident commander and crisis negotiators.
- An *Indigenous critical incident* is any critical or major incident where the source of conflict may stem from assertions of inherent, Indigenous or treaty rights; or that is occurring on a First Nation territory; or involving an Indigenous person(s), where the potential for significant impact or violence may require activation of an integrated emergency response unit (OPP 2013: 4–6).

The Framework approach emphasizes peacekeeping as a means to minimize violence, keep and restore public order, maintain neutrality, facilitate rights and work toward trusting relationships. Equally important, the Framework establishes that the OPP will investigate and take appropriate action in response to civil disobedience and unlawful acts, using discretion, a carefully measured approach and only the level of force necessary to ensure the safety of all citizens and to maintain/restore peace, order and security. The use of force is always a last resort. In keeping with the objectives of peacekeeping, police may exercise considerable discretion with respect to how and when enforcement initiatives are undertaken. (OPP 2013: 5).

Indigenous protests and occupations should be considered a separate and unique form of protest within Canada. As demonstrated by the Ontario Provincial Police Framework approach, there is a need for specific strategies and responses to

Indigenous related events including a dedicated and specially trained police response. The objectives of the police service and the police leaders during the event must be to minimize the potential for violence, facilitate constitutional rights and, to restore public order. Also key to the resolution of the event is the need to maintain and facilitate positive and trusting relationships with individuals in both the Indigenous community and the non-Indigenous community.

In sum, day-to-day policing activities in Indigenous communities should be based upon a "cultural foundation" thereby establishing legitimacy. Police officers that understand and appreciate Indigenous issues and, work closely with Indigenous communities, will be better to identify and defuse potentially violent confrontations. The police service will be more effective and the Indigenous community is more likely to view the policing activities as having legitimacy (Ipperwash Inquiry Report 2007: 179–180).

The findings of the Ipperwash inquiry also suggest that there is a need to place greater emphasis upon training police personnel to utilize communication and tactical skills that are associated with crisis intervention. The components of this training need to emphasize the importance of Indigenous history, customs, traditions, legal issues and community dynamics. Police officers require training that will allow them to interact in a calm and controlled manner when confronting individuals that may be angry or emotional due to the complexities associated with Indigenous issues. An informed and comprehensive front-line intervention strategy has greater chance of successfully resolving face-to-face confrontation in a peaceful manner. Indeed, the suggested approach to resolving issues with Indigenous peoples transcends to all diverse communities providing valuable lessons learned and suggested best practices.

Independent Indigenous Police Services

Independent Indigenous police services are a unique aspect of North American policing and have existed for several decades. In the United States, these services are typically known as "Tribal Police". In Canada, the term "First Nations Police" is used to describe autonomous law enforcement entities that are emerging within the context of Indigenous self-government. Also of note is that the term "Indigenous" was recently substituted for the term "Aboriginal".

In Canada, the First Nations Policing Policy (FNPP) is a tripartite agreement that has been negotiated with the federal, provincial or territorial governments, and Indigenous First Nations. These agreements allow First Nations to develop and administer their own police service. The First Nation also has the option of entering into a Community Tripartite Agreement (CTA) in which the First Nation utilizes its own dedicated contingent of officers within an existing police service such as the Royal Canadian Mounted Police or the Ontario Provincial Police (Whitelaw and Parent 2018: 24).

Indigenous police officers typically have the same powers and expectations as other police in Canada. They are expected to enforce the *Criminal Code of Canada,* federal and provincial statutes, as well as band bylaws on reserve lands. Activities of Indigenous police services are overseen by reserve-based police commissions or by the local band council. In some provinces oversight agencies will provide a level of review for Indigenous police services is areas such as the use of force or a police shooting.

Across Canada, there were 186 First Nations policing program agreements in place in 2015, providing policing services to roughly 65% of First Nation and Inuit communities. Serving a population of approximately 422,000 in 453 communities, a total of 1299 police officer positions exist and receive funding under the FNPP. Within this setting, there are multi-community agreements, such as Nishnawbe-Aski, providing First Nations policing to 35 communities. There are also single-community services, such as at Six Nations, providing policing services to a population of roughly 10,000 in the province of Ontario (Whitelaw and Parent 2018: 24).

In addition to sworn police officers, Indigenous communities may employ Band constables to enforce traffic and municipal bylaws. These individuals are not fully sworn police officers and their powers are limited. Nonetheless, Band constable positions serve to provide the flexibility to address the unique needs and concerns of an Indigenous community. For example, in the northern Canadian territory of Nunavut, the city of Iqaluit has established a Municipal Enforcement Division. One of the preferred qualifications for individuals seeking the position of enforcement officer is the ability to read and write Inuktitut (Parent and Parent 2018: 24).

Indigenous Communities and Canadian Police Services

As mentioned, various police services across Canada have implemented training and cultural sensitivity that is specific to Indigenous peoples. In addition, several Indigenous communities have developed community-based criminal justice services and programs to meet the unique need of Indigenous peoples. Working with various levels of government and police services, Indigenous peoples are establishing partnerships and positive relationships with non-Indigenous police services. Police services such as the RCMP have also created internal programs such as the National Aboriginal Policing Services (NAPS) as a means of establishing stronger relationships with Indigenous peoples in Canada. On the RCMP webpage, Canada's federal police service states:

The RCMP: Serving Canada's Indigenous People

Since the earliest days of the North-West Mounted Police in the 1870s, the RCMP has been a law enforcement partner of Indigenous communities. The RCMP continues to develop a unique and important relationship with Indigenous people in Canada.Contributing to safer and healthier Indigenous communities is one of the five strategic priorities of the RCMP. Delivering culturally competent police services provides the foundation necessary to build relationships and partnerships with the more than 600 Indigenous communities the RCMP serves.

- The RCMP's shared and unique history with Canada's Indigenous peoples allows an environment in which it can work collaboratively to improve community health and wellness. The RCMP is committed to continue building upon these relationships as it encourages, sustains, and fosters honest and open dialogue among its Indigenous partners. Working together, the RCMP is in a position to assist and advocate for Indigenous communities at a local and national level. The RCMP contributes to safer and healthier Indigenous communities by:
- promoting and encouraging the recruitment of Indigenous people as potential employees and police officers.
- working collaboratively with the communities to ensure enhanced and optimized service delivery by developing relevant and culturally competent police services.
- contributing to the development of community capacity to prevent crime through ongoing social development.
- maintaining and strengthening partnerships with Indigenous communities, our policing and government partners, stakeholders, and Indigenous organizations.
- promoting and using alternative/community justice initiatives for Indigenous people.
- demonstrating value for service through the development, management, and evaluation of the detachment performance plan created in collaboration with the local Indigenous communities.
- contributing to public policy development and implementation to assist in building safer and healthier Indigenous communities.

National Indigenous Policing Services (NAPS)

The RCMP's National Indigenous Policing Services (NAPS) is responsible for planning, developing, and managing the organization's strategies and initiatives. NAPS works closely with Indigenous groups to develop innovative policing approaches that meet their distinctive needs. NAPS oversees a number of Indigenous programs and initiatives, including the following:

- Commissioner's National Indigenous Advisory Committee;
- Indigenous Perceptions Training;
- Inuit Perceptions Training; and
- Annual Performance Plans, which address an offence or negative social issue that concerns the community.

NAPS also provides support on the First Nations Policing Policy to its partners at Public Safety Canada.

Serving First Nations, Inuit and Métis groups

The RCMP maintains ongoing dialogue with the:

- Assembly of First Nations;
- Inuit Tapiriit Kanatami (Canada's national Inuit organization);
- Métis National Council;
- National Association of Friendship Centres;
- Native Women's Association of Canada; and the
- Congress of Indigenous Peoples.

Source: RCMP (2017b): http://www.rcmp-grc.gc.ca/aboriginal-autochtone/index-eng.htm

In sum, most police service within Canada have a genuine desire to build positive relationships with Indigenous people and their communities however this is a unique process requiring time, commitment, and care. Along with understanding and appreciating the unique aspects of Indigenous people, Canadian law enforcement services are adjusting street-level policing to incorporate the cultural and religious practices of all individuals.

For example, in 2016, the Vancouver Police Department (VPD) drafted policy on how officers are to correctly handle cultural or religious items. The respectful and inclusive policy applies to all individuals and typically will occur when an officer is searching an arrested individual.

The policy notes: "In the course of their duties officers may be required to search arrested persons in possession of cultural, religious or spiritual items. These items may pose unique considerations for officers when balancing the need to ensure safety, enforce the law and conduct criminal investigations with preserving the person's dignity and respecting the sanctity of their culture or religion."

VPD policy and training includes photographs and explanations regarding the significance of various cultural or religious items and applies to:

- Cultural Considerations in Searches of a Person
- Indigenous Medicine Bags
- Searches of a Person Wearing a Burqa, Hijab, Niqab, or other covering veil
- Searches of a Jewish Person in Possession of Religious Items

Source: Vancouver Police Department (2016).

Summary and Conclusion

In Canada, a focus upon community policing has resulted in changes regarding the recruitment of new officers. Police services are increasingly expected to reflect the diversity of the communities they police. This has resulted in an emphasis on hiring women, Indigenous peoples and visible and cultural minorities, as well as gays, lesbians, bisexual, and transgender individuals. Suggestions have also been made for increasing the numbers of women and visible minorities in policing by modifying traditional hiring criteria. However, for the most part, police services in Canada tend to hire the best applicant giving preference to a target group only when faced with two equal applicants for a single position.

Along with recruiting initiatives to increase diversity, there has been an emphasis placed on promoting women within the ranks and into senior officer positions. Women are increasingly involved in leadership roles and within the executive level of police services adding another dimension to Canadian policing. Although great attempts have been made to increase the proportion of women within policing since the 1970's, progress has occurred at a glacial pace.

Police training has provided the best catalyst for progressive change. The core values associated with community policing permeates recruit and in-service training within most Canadian police services. Police officers are trained and expected to be fair, impartial and unbiased in the services that they provide. The community is presented as one that is composed of diverse individuals that are to be respected. Police personnel need to understand and work with the emerging diversity in Canada's ever changing communities by establishing partnerships and fostering relationships.

While Canadian police services continue to make in-roads into the challenges associated with diversity there is room for further improvement. Satisfaction levels with police performance are often reflected in public opinion surveys, and by the number and degree of complaints lodged against officers. A 2013 survey revealed that Canadians felt police were doing a fairly good job at being approachable and easy to talk to (73%), ensuring the safety of citizens (70%), promptly responding to calls (68%), treating people fairly (68%), enforcing the laws (65%), and providing information on crime prevention (62%) (Cotter 2015). The findings of the 2013 survey suggest that police in Canada could do far better. The lessons learned from policing Indigenous peoples in Canada may serve as a valuable template for policing diverse communities, today and in the future.

References

Ben-Porath, Y. (2007, October 25–27). Policing Multicultural States: Lessons from the Canadian Model Presented at Immigration, Minorities and Multiculturalism in Democracies Conference in Montreal.

Cotter, A. (2015). Spotlight on Canadians: Results from the general social survey public confidence in Canadian institutions. *Statistics Canada, Cat. no. 89-652-X.* http://www.statcan.gc.ca/pub/89-652-x/89-652-x2015007-eng.htm.

Correctional Investigator Canada. (2016). Annual report of the office of the correctional investigator, 2015–2016. Retrieved from: *http://www.oci-bec.gc.ca/cnt/rpt/pdf/annrpt/annrpt20152016-eng.pdf.*

Employment Equity Act. (1995). Retrieved from: http://laws-lois.justice.gc.ca/eng/acts/e-5.401/FullText.html.

Ipperwash Inquiry Report. (2007). Commissioner Sidney B. Linden. Government of Ontario. Volume 2.

Ontario Provincial Police. (2013). *Annual report on the framework approach 2007–2012*. A framework for the police preparedness for aboriginal critical incidents. Retrieved from http://www.scribd.com/doc/199455930/OPP-Aboriginal-Critical-Incidents.

Jain, H. C., Agócs, C., & Singh, P. (1999). Recruitment, selection and promotion of visible minorities and aboriginals in selected Canadian police services.

Leavitt, S. (2016, March 24). Quebec's police forces still overwhelmingly white. *CBC News*. Retrieved from: www.cbc.ca/news/canada/montreal/quebec-police-hiring-visible-minorities-1.3502667.

Marcoux, J., Nicholson, K., Kubinec, V., & Moore, H. (2016, July 14). Police diversity fails to keep pace with Canadian populations. *CBC News*. Retrieved from: www.cbc.ca/news/canada/police-diversity-canada-1.3677952.

Mazowita, B., & Greenland, J. (2015). Police resources in Canada, 2015. *Juristat*. Cat. no. 85- 002-X. Ottawa: Canadian Centre for Justice Statistics. Retrieved from: www.statcan.gc.ca/pub/85-002-x/2016001/article/14323-eng.htm.

Parent, R., & Parent, C. (2018). *Ethics and Canadian law enforcement*. Toronto: Canadian Scholars' Press.

Prime Minister of Canada. (2018). Prime minister announces new commissioner designate of the royal Canadian mounted police. Retrieved from: https://pm.gc.ca/eng/news/2018/03/09/prime-minister-announces-new-commissioner-designate-royal-canadian-mounted-police?fe.

Regina v. Gladue (1999) *S.C.R. 688*.

Royal Canadian Mounted Police. (2016). Employment equity. Towards a diverse workforce of excellence. Retrieved from: http://www.rcmp-grc.gc.ca/ee-eme/index-eng.htm.

Royal Canadian Mounted Police. (2017a). Aboriginal Policing Services. Retrieved from: http://bc.rcmpg-grc.gc.ca/ViewPage.action?siteNodeId=2087&languageId=1&contentId=51216.

Royal Canadian Mounted Police. (2017b). Serving Canada's Indigenous People. Retrieved from: http://www.rcmp-grc.gc.ca/aboriginal-autochtone/index-eng.htm

Statistics Canada. (2011). *Police resources in Canada, 2011. Cat. no. 85–225-X. Ottawa*.

Statistics Canada. (2016). *Police resources in Canada, 2015*. Cat. No. 85–002-X. Ottawa.

Statistics Canada. (2017a). *Police resources in Canada, 2016*. Cat. No. 85-002-X. Ottawa: Minister Responsible for Statistics Canada. Retrieved from: http://www.statcan.gc.ca/pub/85-002-x/2017001/article/14777-eng.htm.

Statistics Canada. (2017b). *2016 Census topic: Population and dwelling counts, November 15, 2017*. Ottawa: Minister responsible for statistics Canada. Retrieved from: *http://www12.statcan.gc.ca/census-recensement/2016/rt-td/population-eng.cfm*.

Szeto, J. K. (2014). Policing diversity with diversity: Exploring organizational rhetoric, myth, and minority police officers' perceptions and experiences. *Theses and Dissertations (Comprehensive)*. 1674. Retrieved from: http://scholars.wlu.ca/etd/1674.

Toronto Police Service. (2017). *Equal partners*. Retrieved from: http://www.torontopolice.on.ca/publications/files/misc/history/4t.html.

Tyler, T. R., & Jackson, J. (2013). Future challenges in the study of legitimacy and criminal justice. In J. Tankebe & A. Liebling (Eds.), *Legitimacy and criminal justice: An international exploration* (pp. 83–104). Oxford: Oxford University Press.

Vancouver Police Department. (2016). *Service and policy complaint (2016–115) on handling of cultural or religious items*. Vancouver Police Department Report to the Vancouver Police Board. Retrieved from: http://vancouver.ca/police/policeboard/agenda/2016/0616/1606C01-2016-115-SP-Handling-of-cultural-Items.pdf.

Whitelaw, B., & Parent, R. (2018). *Community-based strategic policing in Canada*. Toronto: Nelson.

Chapter 10
The Impressive Impact of *Project Illumination* on Police-Community Relations in Charleston, South Carolina

Robert Jacobs, Margaret Seidler, Kylon Middleton, Gregory Mullen, and Gregory Whitaker

CHARLESTON
ILLUMINATION
PROJECT

Introduction to the Charleston Illumination Project

In 2015, events, both locally and nationally, highlighted the eroded relationships between police departments and the communities they serve. Charleston was given a unique opportunity to build upon the goodwill and unity displayed in the wake of the shootings during a Bible Study at Mother Emanuel African Methodist Episcopal (AME) Church.

R. Jacobs · K. Middleton
Charleston Illumination Project, Charleston, SC, USA

M. Seidler (✉)
Charleston Illumination Project, Seidler & Associates, Charleston, SC, USA
e-mail: Margaret@margaretseidler.com

G. Mullen
Clemson University, Clemson, SC, USA

G. Whitaker
Trident Technical College, Charleston, SC, USA

In that spirit, the Illumination Project was born just weeks later, designed to engage the community upstream of inevitable challenges. This approach lessened the likelihood of damaging reactions between police and the community they serve during stressful situations. The Project was made possible by the Charleston Police Fund, a local non-profit, which solicited and managed funds from local leaders in health care, tourism and private citizens.

The mission of the Illumination Project remains to further strengthen citizen/police relationships grounded in trust and legitimacy. Its groundbreaking process is founded on the principles and practices of "Polarity Thinking™." A strategic and systemic approach, it is anchored throughout the process using "both/AND" principles. It was uniquely designed to positively leverage the natural tensions that exist in complex societal systems, instead of them devolving into unproductive debates and potentially dangerous situations. Here people can transcend the all-too-typical *either/or, win/lose arguments* as they address situations in which both parties have valid perspectives and "two rights" actually exist and need each other over time. For example, tensions much like a human's basic need to both Inhale and Exhale.

During Year One of the Project, we engaged 857 citizens in small group facilitated conversations, from which 86 strategies were created, most of which are now fully implemented. In Years Two and Three, we expanded the Project focus using Charleston's history to delve into complicated issues of race. Here police also participate, just without being the focus of the discussion so that learning and discovery take place with citizens. We have also partnered with the National Law Enforcement Museum in Washington, DC to bring this process to the nation!

History of Charleston, South Carolina

Settled by English colonists in 1670, Charleston grew from a colonial seaport to a wealthy city by the mid-eighteenth century. Through the mid-nineteenth century, Charleston's economy prospered due to its busy seaport and the cultivation of rice, cotton, and indigo. Prosperity was in large part due to the enslaved population of West Africans brought through the port for centuries.

In April of 1861, Confederate soldiers fired on Union-occupied Fort Sumter in Charleston Harbor, thus signaling the beginning of the Civil War with its resultant end to the practice of enslaved labor. Charleston was slow to recover from the devastation of the war. However, its pace of recovery became the foundation of the City's greatest asset – its vast inventory of historically significant architecture. Short on capital after the war, Charleston was forced to repair its existing damaged buildings instead of replacing them.

After the Civil War, the City gradually lessened its dependence on agriculture and rebuilt its economy through trade and industry. Construction of the Navy Yard in 1904, just north of the City's boundaries, pushed Charleston vigorously into the twentieth century. During the first few decades of the 1900's, industrial and port activities increased dramatically. Later, major sources of capital came from the Charleston Naval Base, the area's medical industry and the tourism industry.[1]

Charleston is one of the fastest-growing cities in the United States. The greater Charleston area has one of the highest growth rates in America as more people move from surrounding counties to enjoy the city's rapidly improving economy.[2]

Today, approximately seven million people visit Charleston annually, generating an estimated economic impact of $7.37 billion. About 5% of the population is Hispanic, and just 1.5% of Charleston races identify as two or more races. These racial demographics for Charleston actually mirror the racial make-up of the state of South Carolina, which is 68.3% white and about 28% black, according to the 2018 census estimates more than 148,000 city residents.[3]

History of the Charleston Police Department

In the early colonial period, police protection for the citizens of Charleston was performed by the Town Watch, a paramilitary unit. After incorporation in 1783, Charleston formally established the City Guard, another paramilitary force. From 1846–1855, the City Guard was reorganized several times and finally emerged in 1856 as a uniformed police force under the administration of Mayor Porcher Miles.

Prior to the close of the Civil War, martial law was enacted in Charleston, and the city police force disbanded. Civil police forces were revived and reorganized, however, in 1865 following the election of P. C. Gaillard, these forces served as a counterpoint to the federal authorities until the end of martial law in 1877. The election of Mayor W. W. Sale that same year marked the introduction of a solid city police organizational system of officers and men, divided between the main station and the upper station, a system that was continued by succeeding administrations.[4]

Today, the department employs 458 sworn police officers and 117 civilians. Providing a high level of public service is the police department's mission. The Charleston Police Department was the first municipal law enforcement agency in the State of South Carolina to be accredited by the Commission on Accreditation for Law Enforcement Agencies (CALEA) and now holds the CALEA Gold Level.[5]

---

[1] http://www.charleston-sc.gov/index.aspx?NID=110

[2] http://worldpopulationreview.com/us-cities/charleston-population/

[3] http://www.charleston-sc.gov/index.aspx?NID=110

[4] https://www.ccpl.org/records-charleston-police-department-1855-1991

[5] https://www.charleston-sc.gov/police

Need for Enhancing Police-Community Relations

The story of enhancing police-community relations in Charleston accelerated in April 2010, with the city of Charleston Police Department. Polarity Thinking was applied to support a relatively new Chief, Gregory Mullen, in gaining support for the department's first ever strategic plan. Successful work with the police leadership led to a deepening appreciation of the polarity and on-going need for having officers both Enforce the Law AND Maintain Community Support.

In light of police shootings in 2014 and 2015, even one in an adjacent municipality, Charleston watched as riots often erupted across the country. In the wake of the Charleston massacre during the Bible Study at Mother Emanuel AME Church in June 2015, Charleston did not have riots, in large part due to the bonds that were formed before there was a crisis. Given the community's response of unity, Chief Mullen felt an obligation to honor those who lives were taken and those who had professed forgiveness at the bond hearing for the perpetrator.

Within minutes of the massacre, officers reached out to community influencers deep and wide. These were citizens with whom they had already built relationships, confidence, and trust. They shared what they knew and began the process of calling people together. In the days following the massacre, outsiders descended on Charleston with intentions to protest as a way of proving support. The community's response was to request they leave. What the community and its police officers had created together in the previous 8 years made an undeniable difference in the face of this unimaginable tragedy.

With the confidence of several years of experience by city leaders and police command staff using the principles of Polarity Thinking, Chief Mullen created a plan for what he named the Illumination Project. So we embarked on a ground-breaking effort to ask citizens how to Strengthen Relationships with Police in order to both preserve Public Safety AND safeguard Individual Rights.

The mission of the Illumination Project is to further strengthen citizen/police relationships grounded in *trust and legitimacy*. Trust is a vital ingredient in all healthy relationships, especially one with the inherent tension in U.S. communities of Public Safety (taking care of the "whole") AND Individual Rights (taking care of the "part"). Legitimacy speaks to a core element of the citizen and police relationship – police exercising their authority appropriately and citizens believing they are being treated fairly.

Outcomes We Set Out to Achieve

- Enhance community-police relationships throughout the community and across the entire Charleston Police organization.
- Give voice to all segments of our community in a way that promotes calm and measured exploration of issues and ideas.

- Agree upon changes that preserve both societal values of Public Safety and Individual Rights.
- Increase the capacity of community and police to have civil, meaningful dialogue when addressing difficult issues.
- Celebrate and nurture those aspects of the police-community relations that are working well.
- Develop specific, concrete, implementable plans that are measured for success.

A five-phase process guided decisions and actions throughout the initial year:

Phase 1 | Plan the Project
Phase 2 | Develop the Steering and Resource Groups to provide Leadership
Phase 3 | Engage the Community
Phase 4 | Set up Measures to Evaluate the Project
Phase 5 | Make the Model Available for the Rest of the Nation

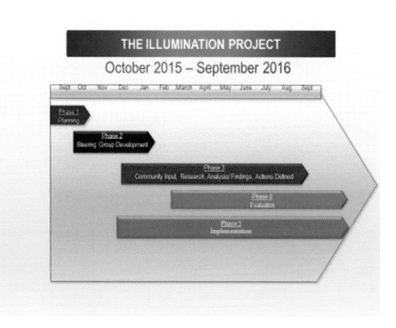

The Illumination Project[6] provided an avenue for Charlestonians to do something positive and to move forward together. Before going public, training was provided to the most diverse group of ninety-nine community influencers ever assembled in Charleston. Their charge was to encourage and guide community

---

[6] http://www.charleston-sc.gov/DocumentCenter/View/12061

engagement so a Strategic Plan could be developed by asking citizens how to Strengthen Relationships with Police in order to both <u>Preserve Public Safety</u> AND <u>Safeguard Individual Rights</u>.

Below is what we called a Polarity Map™, developed by the Steering Group to guide community input to achieve the Benefits/Results of focusing on both. The green rectangle at the top is the "Greater Purpose Statement," or a common goal that both people who have a strong Public Safety point of view and those who emphasize Individual Rights can agree is worth achieving. The red rectangle at the bottom of the boxes is known as the "Deeper Fear," or the worst case of what could happen if this polarity or tension becomes an on-going power struggle between Public Safety and Individual Rights. The orange boxes represent the benefits of focusing on Public Safety (upper left) and the cost of over-focusing on Individual Rights to the relative exclusion of Public Safety (lower right). The opposite diagonals illustrate the benefits of focusing on Individual Rights and over-focusing on Public Safety. The goal of leveraging the polarity well, or channeling its tension in positive and productive ways is to gain and maintain the "upsides" or benefits of each pole and minimize the "downsides" or costs of over-focusing.

Polarity Map, created by the 22-member Steering Group, which guided the Illumination Project process.

The Police are Listening and Citizen Voices Matter

The heartbeat through the Illumination Project are the small group facilitated "Listening Sessions." The purpose of a Listening Session is to seek ideas and opportunities to improve relationships *pro-actively* between police and the citizens they serve through mutual support. Sessions are facilitated to make sure each voice is heard to generate thoughts and ideas.

Within the city limits of Charleston, we hosted 34 *signature* public listening sessions. These sessions engaged more than 850 citizens in conversations about their hopes and fears in our community when it came to strengthening citizen/police relationships. Next, we asked for ideas about what improvements could be made by both police and themselves as citizens.

To gain community support of the Listening Sessions, we tapped into the special expertise of Chandra Irvin, a Master of Divinity and peace agent. With Chandra's support, we took an innovative path by engaging faith communities in their places of worship monthly, an additional way to engage large numbers of citizens, explore commonalties, learn, and pray for our community's continued success.

From January through July, we held Listening Sessions wherever citizens met. The Charleston Branch of the NAACP President, Dot Scott, became a public advocate of the process, which was a tremendous boost for recruiting parts of the community that would normally not participate in the Project.

Along with a cadre' of volunteer facilitators, conversations were civil with each person having an equal voice at the table. Watching relationships being built in the moment was particularly rewarding. People sitting and having conversations were unlikely to have ever met and certainly not to talk about such controversial topics.

Below are the questions that were asked:

Questions # 1 and # 2 *Building Respectful Partnerships*

We recognize the issues facing our society, at the forefront across our country, involving citizen and police encounters that led to tragedy. In light of the current environment, *what are your concerns about building respectful partnerships in the Charleston community between citizens and police? What are your hopes?*

Question # 3 *Action Ideas for the Future*

What suggestions do you have for <u>police</u> to further strengthen relationships with citizens that both preserve Public Safety AND safeguard Individual Rights? For example, ideas about what police could start doing, stop doing, continue doing and do more (any of these).

Question # 4 *Action Ideas for the Future*

What suggestions do you have for <u>citizens</u> to further strengthen relationships with police that both safeguard Individual Rights AND preserve Public Safety? For example, ideas about what citizens could start doing, stop doing, continue doing and do more (any of these).

These efforts brought forth more than 2200 ideas and comments for police and citizens and to our surprise, these ideas were very nearly evenly split between police and citizen actions. In each session, all participants were asked to designate suggested priorities.

Listening Session Ideas/High Priorities

The highest prioritized summaries of ideas for actions for both citizens and police from Listening Sessions are below. The number in parentheses is equal to the number of people in the Sessions that put a high priority on the item as a good one to implement.

Police ideas – priority actions	Citizen ideas – priority actions
• Police procedures 265	• Know and follow law 356
• Community engagement 252	• Community policing (includes citizen review board) 267
• Community policing (includes citizen review board) 243	• Respect authority and stop stereotyping officers 255
• Communication 173	• Community engagement 232
• Treat citizens equally/Stop profiling 163	• Youth programs 192
• Better training for officers 125	• Be informed and hold media accountable to share positive stories 129
• Youth programs 79	• Communication with officers 80
• Training for citizens to understand police roles an laws 72	• Officer appreciation 62
• Transparency 59	• Humanize officers 34
• Media 48	• Continue listening session conversations 23
• Technology 40	• Law enforcement career 6
• Continue listening session conversations 13	
• Collaborate with local PD 4	
• Officer appreciation 4	

The Illumination Project Strategic Plan

The Plan has five goals that are related to recent National Studies in effective policing. Each goal has objectives, strategies and important measures of success.

Of the 86 strategies in the Plan:

- *66 came directly from Listening Session ideas/comments*
- *12 came from three National Policing Studies assessment*
- *8 came from city of Charleston Police staff*

Of the 86, **TOP TEN** strategies are listed by Goal Category. These were selected by the Steering Group and Community Resource Group for immediate implementation in 2016.

Goal: Develop better understanding between police and the community

Objective: Police Contribute to Creation of Diverse partnerships to Enhance Community Safety

Strategy: Collaborate with citizens who are disproportionately impacted by crime to develop crime reduction strategies to improve relationships and gain cooperation

Measurement: Identify the top 5 crime prone neighborhoods within the city based on crime analysis data; conduct listening sessions within these neighborhoods to build a mutual understanding and strategy to address crime; measure change in crime rates; measure change in relationships by involving neighbors to conduct a door-to-door survey

Goal: Build mutually respectful, trusting relationships between citizens and police

Objective: Citizens Take a Leadership Role in Creating a Safe Community

Strategy: Continue Listening Sessions in all parts of the community:
- (a) **Identify a citizen team made up of local community influencers to continue the work ahead**
- (b) **Train citizen team in presentation skills and how to facilitate Listening Sessions**
- (c) **Define team responsibilities so they can be direct links to the community to help develop crime reduction strategies to improve relationships and gain cooperation among citizens who are disproportionately impacted by crime**
- (d) **Host annual listening sessions in each patrol team, schools, Camp Hope and difficult-to-reach groups such as low income areas, ex-felons, individuals who are incarcerated regarding citizen/police understanding and relationships**
- (e) **Conduct annual public community listening sessions to assess progress and hear new issues or concerns**
- (f) **Create internal risk-free listening sessions for officers to express issues and concerns involving community support and relationships**

Measurement: Identify and train community influencers to comprise the team by April 2017; develop roles and responsibilities for the Team by August 2017; number of Listening Sessions held annually; facilitators' self-report competence and confidence in leading sessions

Goal: Train police and citizens to understand each other's roles and responsibilities

Objective: Police Apply Current Research and Citizen Feedback to Police Training, New Equipment and Policy and Procedures to Minimize Negative Citizen/Police Encounters

Strategy: Expand CPD training curriculum for officers and supervisors with consideration of the following topics:

(a) **Concepts in unconscious bias, problem solving, and partnership building, cultural sensitivity**
(b) **Procedural Justice Principles (Internal and External)**
(c) **Officer Wellness**
(d) **Language skills**
(e) **Cultural differences and norms within diverse groups**
(f) **Communication/people skills/conflict resolution skills for/with citizens**
(g) **Guardian Mindset concept**
(h) **Generational differences**
(i) **Enhanced Constitutional Law with a specific focus on the legal parameters of officer-initiated contacts using classroom and scenarios based formats**
(j) **Scenario based training on decision-making and real-life situations**
(k) **Crisis Intervention Team concepts for all officers (during Block-Training program)**
(l) **Supervisory skills and practices to investigate Use of Force incidents**
(m) **Basic and advanced Community Policing curriculum**
(n) **Interacting with mentally ill and emotionally-challenged citizens**

**Fair and Impartial Policing Training – implementation already in progress

Measurement: Increase the training hours per officer by 8 h in 2017, 2018, and 2019 to address priority topics listed above based on officer self-report and supervisor input; number of advanced training hours provided in the listed topic areas each year; internal processes implemented dealing specifically with officer safety, wellness, and morale

Strategy: Promote de-escalation as a core principle in all CPD training

Measurement: Add de-escalation principles and concepts to all applicable training courses as identified by CPD's senior staff and Training Director; identify subject matter experts to deliver education and training for de-escalation; number of officers trained in advanced de-escalation techniques and principles

Objective: Citizens Provide Input/Feedback for Police Training, New Equipment and Procedures, when Needed, to Minimize Negative Citizen/Police Encounters

Strategy: Provide input for a process to make it easy and secure for citizens to make a complaint and or/provide a compliment about a police officer; use a variety of methods which includes a notification letter of the complaint and disposition

Measurement: Liaison group's assessment of the current Administrative Investigation Policy; modifications made to the current policy based on the Group's input; number of complaints received and the method of complaint making; number of compliments received

Goal: Develop Police Department policies and procedures to improve relationships

Objective: Police Provide Opportunities for Citizen Access and Understanding of Police Policies and Procedures

Strategy: Create, train, and equip a Police Citizen Advisory Council (PCAC), ensuring transparency and broad participation in member selection including community activists, neighborhood leaders, educators, retired professionals from criminal justice, legal, and victim services, researchers, and youth, using input from elected leaders, community members and police employees

Measurement: Research conducted on similar groups in the US; Citizens represent a broad cross-section of criteria defined by elected leaders, community members and police employees, media coverage that increases transparency; knowledge and understanding of ethics and principles of policing

Strategy: Implement an impartial Police Citizen Advisory Council that works with the police to develop and evaluate policies and procedures involving priority issues such as:

(a) **Use of Force**
(b) **Administrative investigations**
(c) **Hiring, evaluation and promotional processes with increased importance of community policing principles**
(d) **Release of information during critical incidents**
(e) **Develop criteria and timelines for release of information that both informs the public and considers investigative needs**
(f) **Receipt of citizen complaints**
(g) **External review of citizen and police concerns**

Measurement: PCAC By-Laws and Organizational Structure designed with stake-holder input; Structure approved by City Council by December 2016; Educate PCAC members in police policy, procedures, practice and the complexities involved in the profession; Council holds findings in confidence to protect the rights of offi-cers and to ensure transparency in the process

Objective: Citizens De12monstrate Respect for Police

Strategy: Identify, where needed create, then disseminate instructional mate-rial, both using traditional methods and social media, to youth and adults about proper protocols to follow during citizen/police encounters to reduce the likelihood of conflict and confrontation

Measurement: Brochures, videos, PSAs, and presentations created for dissemina-tion; number of each of the above disseminated

Goal: Expand the concept of community-oriented policing in all segments of our community

Objective: Police Expand Opportunities for Joint Problem Solving/pro-Active Engagement

Strategy: Expand citizen/police interaction in challenged neighborhoods dur-ing non-crisis or enforcement situations by increasing communication about current programs and community outreach opportunities

Measurement: Conduct surveys in Community Action Team (CAT) areas to identify and prioritize citizen concerns; conduct quarterly community conversations to share progress toward problem resolution; Number of current and new outreach initiatives in each area; participants engaged in community events

Objective: Citizens Take Advantage of Expanded Opportunities for Joint Problem Solving/Pro-Active Engagement

Strategy: Develop and implement a Chief's Young Adults Advisory Council (17–25 age range) to provide input into community issues, problem-solving and create programs that support ongoing, positive interaction between youth and police officers

Measurement: Advisory members identified, selected, and trained by June 2017; Quarterly meetings held; number of problems identified and solutions devel-oped; number of programs developed, attendance at programs, evaluation of participant learning and attitude improvements from attending programs

Research

In order to determine the current attitudes and perceptions of citizens and police during Year One of the Illumination Project, the Joseph P. Riley Center at the College of Charleston conducted two surveys. In this report we describe a summary of the findings. The subject of this survey research is the Charleston Police Department. Their main survey asked citizens in the Charleston area about their views on the police, police department practices, and their interactions with police officers. A second survey asked police officers about their views on a similar set of issues. Although most Americans expressed confidence in police in national surveys, that confidence has declined to a 22 year low. When compared to police in general however, we found that the Charleston Police Department receives significantly higher marks. When asked about specific policing issues, most citizens agreed that the CPD does a satisfactory job (including questions about accountability, making the right decisions, honestly, fairness, and transparency). In all, we believe there is clear evidence that Charleston area residents have confidence in the CPD. As one would expect, however, the surveys reveal significant differences of opinion by race. On many issues related to whether the police do a satisfactory job, Blacks are closer to the "neutral" position (on a sliding agree/disagree scale) while Whites are closer to the "agree" position. (Because of a limited response rate, we were unable to examine the views of Latinos as a separate category). Although popular opinion views these gaps as immutable, one of our more encouraging findings is that the gap between Whites and Blacks can be almost entirely undone by positive interactions with the police. Finally, we found that how citizens view the police has real world consequences. Controlling for a range of factors, the biggest determinant of whether a citizen is willing to report crimes to the police or work on a community policing project is their opinion of the police. All in all, the results reveal significant levels of support for the CPD but also suggest some areas for improvement.

Lessons for the Future

Highlights

- Diverse leadership is needed to engage diverse citizenry
- "Both/and" Thinking opens conversations, Right Vs. Wrong Thinking polarizes them
- Small group facilitated conversations foster civility
- Giving equal voice leads to credibility that voices matter
- People are eager to participate when given a welcoming invitation
- The "win" is in the dialogue; good dialogue always leads to good results
- Untraditional and lasting relationships are fostered as a product of the process
- Access to a much larger base for advocacy begins with small efforts

Lesson Details

1. The people who really lead the city need to lead the project. Easy and obvious formal leaders come to mind. We found the informal leaders in the neighborhoods, on street corners and in community centers to be at least, if not more, important to our success.

2. Persevere. We found this to be above and beyond other community work we have done in the past. The number of stakeholders and complexity of the work continued to grow throughout the project, sometimes at what felt like exponential rates. When we were tested the most is when others pulled more than their fair share to make things work, regardless of job title or role in the project.

3. Not enough can be said about the importance of vision and leadership. Chief Mullen saw the power and possibilities in asking police and citizens to improve their own relationships. The polarity of Direction and Participation was well leveraged throughout the process. Clear boundaries, processes and roles were defined early in the project. Paradoxically people had more freedom to participate in the work in many ways because of this structure. As a mentor of ours once said, "Structure is really helpful; it gives you something to deviate from." Vision and leadership were not the sole purview of Chief Mullen either. Members of the leadership teams, facilitators, consultants, researchers and people joining each Listening Session shared their own visions for the project and future relationships. All were welcomed to lead in this effort and all were welcomed to participate.

4. Prepare to be changed by the process. Emotionally. Logistics, meeting designs and rooms, flyers to increase attendance and more are required to succeed. These are all tasks. You'll become familiar with your checklist for every Listening Session you hold. And then there are the conversations that you hear from people sitting in their circle. The fear they have walking outside their home. The challenges they have felt in their past relationship with police. The difficulty they have living paycheck to paycheck. The pride they feel in how they are raising their children. The good deeds they do for others for no other reason than that they need to be done. These stories, repeated so many times, make their way into your heart. Hearing them over and over can leave you feeling both motivated and powerless at the same time. We thought we understood and had empathy for those less fortunate than ourselves. The process transformed us. We now see so much more of the reality in the world – both the good and the bad.

5. You're going to make some new friends. Whether they are members of one of the leadership teams, facilitators, or participants, they all have the same greater purpose. You'll find people who know people you know, and others who are brand new friends. New best friends may be waiting for you in the process. We found that by staying open to the possibilities, the kind of people we met were as diverse as the communities in which we lived.

6. Find a great team. These may be people with whom you've worked before or new colleagues where you are partnering together for the first time. Our definition of a great team included having each other's back, ensuring excellence in all we did, and supporting each other in doing the work we each did well. Train your facilitators who conduct the Listening Sessions and debrief for shared learning and improvement. This is the foundation of trust-building.

7. This is very serious business…and don't forget to find time to enjoy each other and the work along the way. The gravity of the work is substantial. Some people feel that their basic human dignity is being challenged. Others have a fear of facing life and death situations in their own neighborhoods and homes. This project was intense because the issues were intense. Yet we found that a healthy helping of positive energy went a long ways toward making the tough times better. Whether it was a mad rush to get Listening Session data ready for a Steering Group meeting or bonding with some of the most interesting characters that make Charleston, Charleston, when we acknowledged the difficulties and focused on what was working we got the best results.

8. Learn, apply, repeat. Many times we found ourselves saying "Boy, we sure wish we had another chance to…" And of course in most cases we did. Our final version of materials used in the Listening Sessions had the word "accessible" in the title. Had we started with that in the title would it have been easier for the early groups to grasp the work we were asking them to do or did we need to improve the materials to such a point as they earned the title of accessible? Either way, continuous improvement was the watchword of the day. If something was good at one stage of the effort, the question became how could it become great for the next one? Learn, apply, repeat.

9. Leave a trail for others to follow. From the beginning it was a goal of the Illumination Project to become a national model. When we had things clear enough to do our work, we often paused to make them clearer yet for others who might be creating Illumination Projects in their own cities. We have a vision that while we can continue to learn from others around the country doing this important work, they too will be able to learn from us.

10. Expect a great deal of yourself and others….and be surprised at how much more everyone is willing and able to give to a common cause. A project of this scope and scale is a significant undertaking. Our common greater purpose of further strengthening citizen and police relationships with trust and legitimacy became the glue that held us together. Especially through the most challenging times. We have been surprised by the progress we have made in the past year in pursuing the noble goal of leveraging the polarity of individual rights and public safety.

11. Realize that beginning community work through police relationships is an effective entry point for addressing other issues. The police have a reach into a community unlike any other since their main mission, safety, is a common greater purpose that all members of the community support.

12. Information = commitment. The more people know about the process in which they are engaged, the more informed their decisions are within that process.

The Illumination Project was designed and managed to share information whenever and however possible. The overall process was described at the beginning of each Listening Session. Every idea for police and citizens to improve their relationship were captured, themes identified and this information posted on a public website. Email addresses were collected at Listening Sessions and at events where the Illumination Project was publicized. Project newsletters were regularly sent to these addresses with the latest project updates and links to the newest documents that had been compiled. The old adage that "Information is power," has some truth to it. With the Illumination Project, that power was shared far and wide building commitment to the project and most importantly between citizens and police of Charleston to further improve their relationship.

The Illumination Project, if it is to realize its full potential, needs to become a regular way of working and living in the city of Charleston. When it becomes this type of ongoing process we will both have completed our work and at the same time ensured the work to further improve the relationship between citizens and police, with trust and legitimacy will never end.[7]

2017 Broadening the Base Locally

Lasting positive relationships were another result of this approach which carried us into Years Two and Three of the Project. Here the police were part of the overall discussion rather than being the focus of the discussions, using Charleston's history to delve into complicated issues of race.

We learned a lot in Year One. We learned that a police department can serve as a portal into many parts of a community and we learned that relationships, never previously imagined, can be formed. Using this momentum, we hosted 17 Listening Sessions in 2017, mostly focused on racial history in Charleston. More than 1100 citizens participated. Police were always present and part of the experience including our signature facilitated small group discussions. Police effectiveness issues have moved from the foreground since the Strategic Plan is in place and being ardently implemented. Now, broader topics create shared experiences for our police, and continue building deeper understanding for stronger relationships with the community. All the while, police continue to enforce the law to provide a safe place for all.

We also made our way into the local Latino community through local activists and faith communities. Listening Sessions follow a different format because we found that local congregational leaders are key for communicating with a culture of folks from outside our country.

---

[7] http://www.charleston-sc.gov/DocumentCenter/View/12061

Conclusion

Charleston, South Carolina is a city grounded and in some ways, bound by history and tradition. We seceded from the Union in 1861; decades later we experienced poverty and neglect and now Charleston is becoming a modern and progressive community where both young and old wish to call home.

We want to continue to honor the lives lost in the Mother Emanuel tragedy, now and in the future. We aspire to show the nation that listening to each other for understanding and appreciating our different experiences, as well as our similarities, as human beings is a way we truly create *One Nation, Under God.*

In 2017, we were humbled to be invited to be part of the video exhibits in the National Law Enforcement Museum in Washington, DC. Now in 2018, we have partnered to create the Affinity Project, an amazing blending of the Museum's artifacts with our community-oriented process. With the partnership, we are excited beyond belief about the potential for our country's future when it comes to Strengthening Citizens and Police relationships.

Note: See http://www.theilluminationproject.org for additional background information.

Suggested Reading

Jacobs, R. (1994). *Real time strategic change: How to involve an entire organization in fast and far-reaching change*. Oakland: Berrett-Koehler.

Johnson, B. (1994). *Polarity management: Identify and solving unsolvable problems*. Amhurst: HRD Press.

Johnson, B. (Unpublished). *And: Leveraging polarity/paradox/dilemma*. Sacramento: Polarity Partnerships.

Seidler, M. (2014). *Power surge: A conduit for enlightened leadership*. Amhurst: HRD Press.

Chapter 11
Policing Native American Lands in the United States

Robert Morin and Colleen Morin

Introduction

Police functions in the United States are carried out at the federal, state and local levels of government. Police functions are also carried out in Indian country. Policing in Indian country is a very complex subject matter area as well as being controversial. Indians and Indian country occupy a very special position in terms of history, legislation, and judicial decisions. This chapter will examine the development of federal Indian policy, Indian country criminal jurisdiction, policing in Indian country, as well as the future of policing in Indian country.

Federal Indian Policy

Policy issues involving Indian tribes are complicated by the unique position assumed by Indians under the federal system of government in the United States. Traditionally, Indian tribes have been considered sovereign entities, and federal regulation of Indian affairs was governed under treaties entered into between the federal government and Indian tribes (Kronowitz et al. 1987). An Indian tribe, as an individual sovereign, was considered to be capable of making and enforcing its own laws outside the federalist structure. This traditional policy position concerning Indians has been radically transformed over the course of the past 200 years. No unitary doctrine draws together the field of Indian law and policy (Turner 1988). Federal Indian

R. Morin (✉)
Western Nevada University, Carson City, Nevada, USA
e-mail: robert.morin@wnc.edu

C. Morin
University of Nevada, Reno, Nevada, USA

policy has been cyclical. The federal government has vacillated between the two conflicting policies of self-determination and assimilation (Turner 1988).

Assimilation seeks to limit or extinguish the federal-tribal trust relationship and self-determination seeks to preserve the relationship as well as promote tribal autonomy (Wilkinson and Biggs 1977). Indians and their tribes have been forced to contend with these two opposing position of the federal government for a period of approximately 100 years. Federal Indian policy has cycled twice between assimilation and self-determination. Each instance of changed policy has resulted from a Congressional decision to repudiate the policy approach concerning Indians taken by a previous Congress. Congress has assumed almost unfettered authority to govern Indian affairs in accordance with the Indian Commerce Clause of the U.S. Constitution, the sole specific Constitutional grant of Congressional power concerning Indians (Laurence 1981).

The theories of Francisco de Victoria dominated the foreign policy of the European nations when they first colonized America and established the basic framework of the relationship between Indians and colonists in America (Kronowitz et al. 1987; Kalish 1996). Victoria's theories provide that Indians were free and rational peoples who possessed inherent natural legal rights. Victoria's theory further provided that the rights held by Indians under international law included the right to own property and the right to be free of European authority as long as the Indians did not provoke a war (Kalish 1996). Europeans powers divided America according to which country had the recognized right to acquire land from the Indians and not according to which country actually possessed what piece of land. European nations adhered to Victoria's theory that Europeans could legally acquire Indian lands and exert political domination over Indians only upon the consent of Indian tribes. Victoria's theories of international law provided the foundation for Europeans to establish and conduct relations with Indian tribes on the basis of negotiated treaties (O'Brien 1991).

British law explicitly recognized tribal sovereignty and provided that Indian tribes be treated as distinct political sovereigns (Smith 1993). Indian affairs were controlled by local, individual colonies without any real interference from the central government during most of the colonial period. Each colony had the freedom to formulate and pursue its own policy with Indian tribes in this area. Tribal-colony conflict developed over a period of time based upon conflicting interests. Colonists were interested in pursuing trade and acquiring land. Indian tribes were interested in minimizing the adverse impact of the arrival of the colonists on tribal autonomy (Worthen and Farnsworth 1996). The British government realized that local, colonial control of Indian affairs might not be in the best interests of the national government.

The French and Indian War ended in 1763 when Britain and France executed The Peace of Paris and Britain initiated an effort to centralize control of Indian affairs in the national government. The Proclamation of 1763 granted the national government, as opposed to local colonial governments, the power to control and slow the westward movement of white settlers (Worthen and Farnsworth 1996).

Actions taken by Britain such as the Stamp Act of 1765, the Sugar Act of 1764, and the Townshend Acts, produced conflict and political tensions between the national and local governments which overshadowed Indian policies in colonial America (Worthen and Farnsworth 1996). The Revolutionary War broke out and Indian tribes viewed the American Revolution with uncertainty. The newly independent United States assumed management of Indian affairs upon the departure of the British. The United States, based upon principles inherited from the British, considered Indian tribes to be sovereign, foreign nations. During the drafting of the Articles of Confederation, the only real debate concerning Indians addressed the apportionment of governmental power between the state and national governments in the handling of Indian affairs (Kronowitz et al. 1987). The governmental handling of Indian affairs was addressed in Article IX of the Articles of Confederation. This provision provided Congress with the exclusive authority to control Indian affairs; however, this provision also provided the states with full legislative authority to control their geographic areas. Under the Articles of Confederation, the Confederation Congress did not possess the governmental power to restrain states from dealing with Indian tribes and possessed no effective enforcement power in order to restrict Indian tribes to trading exclusively with the national government (Worthen and Farnsworth 1996).

From its inception, the Articles of Confederation contained one major, structural defect, namely, the national government was too weak when compared to the strength of state governments. Problems associated with a weak national government resulted in a Constitutional Convention and the subsequent drafting, adoption and ratification of the U.S. Constitution (Worthen and Farnsworth 1996). The U.S. Constitution rectified the weaknesses of the Articles of Confederation by strengthening the powers of the national government (Carey and McClellan 1990).

During the drafting of the U.S. Constitution, the only real debate concerning Indians involved the apportionment of power between the state and federal government concerning the conduct of Indian affairs (Kronowitz et al. 1987). The framers of the U.S. Constitution perceived that a unified policy toward Indian affairs required a national policy and not a variety of differing state Indian policies (Worthen and Farnsworth 1996). In order to rectify the defects concerning Indian affairs under the articles of Confederation, James Madison recommended the provision of an Indian Commerce Clause, which was included in the U.S. Constitution.

The U.S. Constitution serves as a framework for the United States-Indian relations, and not as a source of United States power (Kronowitz et al. 1987). The U.S. Constitution embodied the prevailing view of the founders, which was in conformity with early European nations based upon Victoria's theories of international law, that no federal or state authority over Indians existed without their consent (Newton 1984; Kronowitz et al. 1987; Kalish 1996; O'Brien 1991). At the time of the drafting, adoption and ratification of the U.S. Constitution, Indian tribes were considered sovereign entities, and were considered to be capable of making and enforcing their own law outside the federalist structure in the United States. Indian tribes were considered to be outside of the "plan of the convention" when the U.S. Constitution was drafted (Kronowitz et al. 1987).

The U.S. Supreme Court, with Federalist John Marshall as Chief Justice, affirmed the concept of Indian sovereignty in three seminal opinions concerning the relationship between the federal government and Indian tribes (Kronowitz et al. 1987; Kalish 1996). The Marshall trilogy of cases, which together recognized the independent political status of Indian nations, were *Johnson v. M'Intosh*, 21 U.S. (8 Wheat.) 543 (1823); *Cherokee Nation v. Georgia*, 30 U.S. (5 Pet.) 1 (1831); and *Worcester v. Georgia*, 31 U.S. (6 Pet.) 515 (1832) (Kronowitz et al. 1987; Kalish 1996). *Johnson* involved a land title dispute. The Court held that while the Indians had an unquestioned right to occupation of their land, the Indians were not free to sell their land to whomever they desired. The Court held that only the United States could acquire the Indian's title and transfer it to a private individual. The basis of this exclusive right was the international legal doctrine of discovery. The doctrine bestowed exclusive title on the sovereign to acquire Indian lands through purchase or conquest and held that settlers could not purchase Indian lands without the consent of the discovering sovereign. Indian tribes retained possession of their land and the right to use it according to their own discretion and the power of their laws and government over their territory was unquestioned.

Cherokee Nation involved an action brought by the Cherokee Nation to prevent the State of Georgia from enforcing state laws in Cherokee territory located within Georgia. The Cherokee Nation contended that it was a foreign nation and the Court had to assume jurisdiction and resolve disputes between states and foreign nations. The Court determined that the Cherokee Nation was not a foreign nation under the U.S. Constitution and as thus, the Cherokee Nation lacked standing to invoke the original jurisdiction of the Court. Although Indian tribes were not foreign nations, the Court determined that Indian tribes had a special status within the United States.

One year alter the Court addressed and determined the issue, left unanswered in *Cherokee Nation*, of whether a state could assert authority over Indian country through state legislative enactments when it decided the *Worcester* case. In *Worcester*, the Court held that the Georgia state laws in question were unconstitutional. The Court said:

> [the] Cherokee nation, then, is a distinct community occupying its own territory, with boundaries accurately describe, in which the laws of Georgia can have no force, and which the citizens of Georgia have no right to enter, but with the assent of the Cherokees themselves, or in conformity with treaties, and with the acts of congress. The whole intercourse between the United States and this nation, is, by our constitution and laws, vested in the government of the United States.
> (31 U.S. [6 Pet.] at 561)

The Marshall trilogy of cases provided the fundamental tenants of Indian policy under the U.S. Constitution and defined the political relationship of Indian tribes under America's federal system of government. The Marshall trilogy of cases defined the status of Indian tribes as "domestic dependent nations", established the concept of a trust relationship between the federal government and Indian tribes and defined the relationship of the states and Indian tribes. The Marshall trilogy of cases also set the stage for reduced tribal sovereignty and the establishment of the plenary power doctrine over Indian affairs and policy (Kronowitz et al. 1987; Kalish 1996; Belliveau 1993; Worthen and Farnsworth 1996; O'Brien 1989).

The period of the 1840s through the 1880s represents the era of the development of the federal plenary power doctrine. In *Martin v. Lessee of Waddell*, 41 U.S. (16 Pet.) 367 (1842), the Court, under the leadership of Chief Justice Robert Taney, reinterpreted the discovery doctrine. The Court held that the discovery doctrine granted full title and ownership of Indian lands to the United States and left the Indians with only a right of occupancy. In holding that Indians possessed only a right of occupancy to Indian lands, the Court ignored the history of Indian-government relations in the United States and ignored settled precedent concerning Indian sovereignty and relations (Newton 1984; Kronowitz et al. 1987). The reinterpreted doctrine of discovery was reaffirmed and perpetuated in *United States v. Rogers*, 45 U.S. (4 How.) 567 (1846). In *Rogers*, the Court upheld a federal statute that extended federal jurisdiction over crimes involving non-Indians occurring in Indian territory. The Court's holding in *Rogers* represents the first major intrusion of federal governmental power into Indian territory and laid the foundation for the steady increase of federal intrusion upon Indian sovereignty and the establishment of the plenary power doctrine (Kronowitz et al. 1987).

Prior to 1871, the plenary power doctrine in the Indian context, held that the federal government, not the states, possessed the power under the U.S. Constitution to conduct relations with Indian tribes (Kronowitz et al. 1987). Prior to 1871, relations between the federal government and Indian tribes were conducted by treaty and Congress passed most enactments concerning Indians in order to implement the federal government's treaty obligations. As with foreign treaties, Indian treaties were negotiated by the executive branch and ratified by the U.S. Senate, and not the U.S. House, of the legislative branch (Kronowitz et al. 1987). Congress enacted the Internal Revenue Act in 1868 that provided for the imposition of federal taxes on distilled spirits and tobacco. The United States applied the Internal Revenue Act to the Cherokee Tribe, in apparent conflict with the Cherokee Tribe's 1866 treaty with the federal government. In *Cherokee Tobacco*, 78 U.S. 616 (1870), the Court held that a congressional enactment can supersede a prior treaty.

One year after the Court's decision in *Cherokee Tobacco*, the U.S. House of Representatives refused to appropriate funds for the implementation of Indian treaty obligations because of its jealousy of U.S. Senate control over the treaty process (O'Brien 1989; Kronowitz et al. 1987). The U.S. House of Representatives, desiring a greater role in formulating Indian policy, reached a compromise with the U.S. Senate. Congress enacted the Appropriation Act of March 3, 1871, which prohibited the United States from recognizing any Indian tribe as capable of executing a treaty; however the enactment provided that then existing treaties would remain in full force and effect (O'Brien 1989; Kronowitz et al. 1987). The Appropriation Act of March 3, 1871 represented a distinct, significant and permanent shift in the Indian policy making power of the federal government. The 1871 enactment provided that Congress, not the executive branch, held primary authority over the conduct of Indian policy. The plenary power doctrine has been expanded to include the allocation of power over Indian policy to Congress, in addition to the federal supremacy over the states regarding Indian policy.

The plenary power doctrine concerning Indian policy was solidified by U.S. Supreme Court decisions following the 1871 federal legislative enactment. In *United States v. Kagama*, 118 U.S. 375 (1886), the Court was asked to review the constitutionality of the Major Crimes Act of 1885 which extended federal criminal jurisdiction over crimes committed by Indians against Indians in Indian territory (Kalish 1996; Kronowitz et al. 1987; O'Brien 1989). Kagama argued that the Act was beyond the enumerated powers of Congress. The Court rejected Kagama's argument and held that Congress possessed inherent federal power over internal Indian affairs. The Court reinforced the federal plenary power doctrine in *Cherokee Nation v. Hitchcock*, 187 U.S. 294 (1902), and *Lone Wolf v. Hitchcock*, 187 U.S. 553 (1903). In these two cases the Court held that Congress possessed the power to alter or revoke any of an Indian tribe's political or property rights irrespective of applicable treaty provisions.

The articulation, development and establishment of the federal plenary power doctrine in the area of federal Indian policy are significant for three primary reasons. First, the constitutional framework for conducting relations with Indians and Indian tribes as sovereign, employed in colonial and early America in accordance with the Marshall trilogy of cases, has been politically and legally replaced (Kronowitz et al. 1987). Second, the power of Congress regarding Indian policy is characterized as one without limitation (Kronowitz et al. 1987; Kalish 1996). Third, the power of Congress regarding Indian policy is, for all practical purposes, beyond judicial review (Kronowitz et al. 1987). The U.S. Supreme Court has never invalidated a federal enactment directly regulating Indian tribes on the ground that Congress exceeded its authority to govern Indian affairs. In short, the federal plenary power doctrine has allowed for a wide-ranging and unchecked exercise of congressional power regarding Indian affairs and Indian policy.

Congress, 1 year after the *Kagama* decision and acting in accordance with the federal plenary power doctrine, enacted the General Allotment Act of 1887. This enactment is also referred to as the Dawes Act and the Land in Severalty Act. The General Allotment Act signaled the beginning of the cyclical federal Indian policy. The General Allotment Act was a federal policy of facilitating the assimilation of Indians and Indian tribes into the dominant mainstream American society and of opening Indian lands for settlement. The policy goals of the General Allotment Act were (1) to assimilate Indians into white society by teaching them farming skills, (2) to instill values of individualism, and (3) to instill values of private property ownership (O'Brien 1989). The effect of the General Allotment Act was the undermining of Indian cultural values and Indian sovereignty, although very little progress was made towards the assimilation of Indians into the dominant American culture.

In 1924 Congress enacted the Indian Citizenship Act which granted citizenship to Indians. Indians then possessed the rights and privileges of being citizens of the United States, the State of which they were residents and of their Indian tribe. Shortly after enactment of the Indian Citizenship Act, the federal government commissioned the Institute for Government Research to study Indian economic and social conditions. The Meriam Report of 1928 concluded that federal Indian policy should develop and build on Indian values rather than attempting to destroy them (O'Brien 1989). Congress, in accordance with the federal plenary power doctrine, enacted the Indian Reorganization Act of 1934. The Indian Reorganization Act represents the conclusion of the first cycle of federal Indian policy. The Indian Reorganization Act reversed the assimilationist policy of the General Allotment Act of 1887 and was a policy of self-determination for Indians and Indian tribes. The Indian Reorganization Act was an attempt to encourage economic development, political self-sufficiency, self-determination, and tribal life (Worthen and Farnsworth 1996; O'Brien 1989).

Congressional dissatisfaction with allowing Indian tribes to engage in tribal self-government, coupled with Indian resistance to self-government based upon constitutions and bylaws imposed by the Indian Reorganization Act, led to the end of the Indian reorganization era (Kronowitz et al. 1987). In 1953, Congress approved House Concurrent Resolution 108 and enacted Public Law 280, which reversed the policy of self-determination implemented by virtue of the Indian Reorganization Act of 1934 (Walsh 1983). House Concurrent Resolution 108 and Public law 280 provided the framework for the implementation of a federal Indian policy of termination. House Concurrent Resolution 108 and Public Law 280 represent an assimilationist policy and the beginning of the second cycle of federal Indian policy. House Concurrent Resolution 108 established the policy goals of the termination era, namely (1) to make Indians in the United States subject to the same laws and entitled to the same privileges and responsibilities which were applicable to other citizens, (2) to end the Indians' status as wards of the United States, and (3) to grant Indians all the rights of American citizenship (O'Brien 1989; Belliveau 1993). Public Law 280 delegated jurisdictional authority over Indian tribes directly to certain states (Belliveau 1993; O'Brien 1989). Public Law 280 also allowed other states, without regard for the preferences of Indian tribes and without their consent, to assume full criminal jurisdiction and full or partial civil jurisdiction over reservation Indians upon state popular referendum, state statutory enactment or state constitutional amendment (Belliveau 1993). Public Law 280 eliminated the jurisdictional apportionment of authority between the federal government, state government and Indian tribes in those states where Public Law 280 was applicable. Several Indian tribes were outright terminated during the termination era. Tribal government-to-government relationships with the federal government were severed, tribes were subjected to state and local laws and Indian lands were conveyed into private ownership (Wilkinson and Biggs 1977; Kronowitz et al. 1987).

In 1968, Congress enacted the Indian Civil Rights Act of 1968, which embodied the concept of continued tribal existence as opposed to a concept of termination. The Indian Civil Rights Act of 1968 extended protection under the Bill of Rights to tribal members and provided funds for the development of tribal judicial systems. This Act also amended Public Law 280 so that a state's ability to assume criminal and/or civil jurisdiction under Public Law 280 was essentially terminated. The Act required Indian tribes to hold special elections in order to determine the consent of an Indian tribe to state assumption of criminal and/or civil jurisdiction under Public Law 280. The Act also allowed states, which had previously assumed jurisdiction under Public Law 280, to return jurisdiction to the federal government (O'Brien 1989; Belliveau 1993).

    The Indian Civil Rights Act of 1968 once again represented a change in federal Indian policy. The Act reversed the policy of assimilation and represented a return to a policy of self-determination. This Act represents the conclusion of the second cycle of federal Indian policy as well as current federal Indian policy. In 1969, President Nixon delivered a speech to Congress where he denounced termination, acknowledged the failure of termination and urged Congress to repudiate termination as a federal Indian policy. President Nixon emphasized the importance of the trust relationship between the federal government and Indian tribes and advocated a policy of tribal self-management and autonomy. President Nixon declared that the then current federal Indian policy was that of self-determination (Belliveau 1993). Congress responded to President Nixon's speech through the enactment of various pieces of legislation aimed at promoting a federal Indian policy of self-determination (Belliveau 1993).

    In 1983, President Reagan made a statement concerning federal Indian policy that reaffirmed President Nixon's announcement that the federal government was committed to a policy of self-determination. President Reagan emphasized the need for Indian tribes to become self-sufficient and to reduce their dependence on federal funds by providing a greater percentage of the cost of their self-government. In order to reduce their dependence on federal funds, President Reagan emphasized that Indian tribes increase their role in the development of reservation economies. President Reagan acknowledged the distinct political status of Indian tribes and promoted the federal government's government-to-government relationship with recognized Indian tribes by transacting with Indian tribes as governments (Belliveau 1993; Worthen and Farnsworth 1996). The federal Indian policy of self-determination at present entails a necessary link between reservation economic development and self-determination. Conventional wisdom is that Indian reservations need strong economies and good business environments in order to fully achieve self-determination and political autonomy; however, another view is that Indian tribes first need true sovereignty in order to develop strong economies. Whichever comes first, self-determination or economic self-sufficiency, the linkage between self-determination and economic development on Indian reservations characterizes the present federal Indian policy of self-determination. In an environment conducive to the development of reservation economies, many Indian tribes ventured into gaming operations as a source of revenue. The modern era of federal Indian policy presents the first part of the third cycle of federal Indian policy in the United States.

Indian Country Criminal Jurisdiction

It is critical to understand the shifts in federal policy regarding Indians in order to understand Indian country criminal jurisdiction and policing Indian country in the United States. Criminal jurisdiction and policing is based upon the concept of jurisdiction. Geography constitutes an integral component of criminal jurisdiction. Indian country criminal jurisdiction is a complex maze that at a foundational level is premised upon geography, the precise location of where a criminal offense is committed and the status of the involved individuals, Indian or non-Indian. The jurisdiction maze of Indian country criminal jurisdiction is the direct result of shifts in the federal Indian policies of self-determination and assimilation. The complex maze of Indian country criminal jurisdiction creates a complex and unique environment for policing Indian country (Riley 2016).

Congress addressed crimes committed within the Indian territory when the first Indian Trade and Intercourse Act was passed in 1790. This Act included provisions punishing crimes committed within the Indian territory. From the beginning in 1790, the federal government firmly established the power of the federal government to exercise jurisdiction over Indians under the U.S. Constitution. In 1817 Congress passed the General Crimes Act. This Act provided for the federal prosecution and punishment of crimes committed in Indian country involving Indians and non-Indians. The General Crimes Act excluded crimes committed by one Indian against another Indian (Dossett 2018). In 1832 the U.S. Supreme Court decided *Worcester v. Georgia*, 31 U.S. 515 (1832). In *Worcester*, the Court held that the state of Georgia could not enforce state criminal laws upon Cherokee Nation lands because states lacked criminal jurisdiction over Indians in Indian country. In *United States v. McBratney*, 104 U.S. 621 (1881), the U.S. Supreme Court held that the state had exclusive jurisdiction over a crime committed by a non-Indian against a non-Indian in Indian county. In 1883 the U.S. Supreme Court decided *Ex Parte Crow Dog* 109 U.S. 556 (1883). In this case one Indian murdered another Indian in Indian country. The tribe internally handled the disposition of the murder. The Court held in *Ex Parte Crow Dog* that federal territorial courts did not have jurisdiction over criminal offenses committed by one Indian against another Indian in Indian country, thus allowing the tribe to determine the appropriate punishment (Wild 2019; Christensen 2019; Morrow 2019).

Ex Parte Crow Dog was decided at a time when federal Indian policy was in a state of transition from a policy of self-determination to a policy of assimilation. In response to the *Ex Parte Crow Dog* decision, Congress passed the Major Crimes Act of 1885. This Act provided for federal criminal jurisdiction over seven enumerated major crimes when committed by Indians in Indian country and over time additional major crimes have been added, bringing the total to 16 major crimes. The Major Crimes Act is applicable when the enumerated major crimes are committed by an Indian, whether the victim is Indian or non-Indian. The U.S. Supreme Court upheld the constitutionality of the Major Crimes Act in 1886 in *United States v. Kagama*, 118 U.S. 375 (1886) (Riley 2016; Wild 2019; Morrow 2019; Christensen 2019).

In accord with the federal Indian policy of assimilation, Congress passed Public Law 83–280, commonly referred to as Public Law 280. The passage of Public Law 280 provided for the first time for significant state criminal jurisdiction into Indian country. Public Law 280 transferred federal criminal jurisdiction over Indian reservations to the states of California, Minnesota, Nebraska, Oregon, Wisconsin, and Alaska, with some exceptions for specific Indian reservations. Public Law 280 provided other states with the option of assuming jurisdiction. An amendment in 1968 required a tribe's consent before states can assume jurisdiction. Thirteen of the thirty-six states with Indian reservations possess criminal jurisdiction over Indian reservations (Goldberg and Champagne 2006; Morrow 2019; Douglas 2018). In accord with the federal Indian policy of self-determination, Congress passed the Indian Civil Rights Act of 1968 (ICRA). The ICRA required that tribes base their judicial system on American notions of due process and imposed upon tribal justice systems many of the fundamental rights of the U.S. Constitution. The ICRA has had the net effect of developing tribal courts. The ICRA also limited the penalties that tribal courts could impose when Indians committed crimes on tribal lands. The ICRA limited punishments to 6 months in prison or $500 per count. Congress amended the ICRA in 1986 to expand the sentencing authority in tribal courts. The 1986 amendment expanded tribes' sentencing authority to 1 year per count and a $5000 fine; however, the ICRA did not authorize felony sentencing (Morrow 2019; Riley 2016; Wild 2019, Eid and Doyle 2010).

In 1978, the U.S. Supreme Court decided *Oliphant v. Suquamish Indian Tribe* 435 U.S. 191 (1978). In *Oliphant* the Court held that tribes did not have inherent sovereignty to prosecute non-Indians, resulting in Indian tribes not possessing criminal jurisdiction over non-Indians (Riley 2016; Christensen 2019; Douglas 2018). In 2010 Congress passed the Tribal Law and Order Act (TLOA). This Act contained many provisions addressing criminal justice in Indian country. The TLOA expanded the sentencing authority of tribal courts over defendants in cases in which the tribe would already have criminal jurisdiction. The TLOA also required the reporting of federal declination rates as well as the creation of the Indian Law and Order Commission (Morrow 2019; Riley 2016). Indian country criminal jurisdiction in the modern post-*Oliphant* era is a complex maze that at a foundational level is premised upon geography, the precise location of where a criminal offense is committed, and the status of the involved individuals, Indian or non-Indian. Criminal jurisdiction in Indian country may be divided or shared among tribal, state or federal governmental entities. The exercise of criminal jurisdiction in Indian country is dependent upon (1) the nature of the offense, (2) whether jurisdiction has been conferred on the state, and (3) whether the victim and/or the person that committed the crime is an Indian (Douglas 2018; Riley 2016; Morrow 2019).

Policing in Indian Country

Complexity characterizes the environment of policing in Indian country. The complexity of criminal jurisdiction directly impacts who polices Indian country. Federal, tribal and state governmental entities are involved in the policing functions in Indian country. The Federal Bureau of Investigation has jurisdiction to conduct investigations based upon the Major Crimes Act. Tribal law enforcement will have jurisdiction in many instances for policing in Indian country. State and local law enforcement will have jurisdiction for policing in Indian country in Public Law 280 states. Public Law 280 structures law enforcement for 23% of the reservation-based tribal population and 52% of the Indian tribes located in the lower forty-eight states (Goldberg and Champagne 2006; French 2005; Wells and Falcone 2008).

There exist five types of law enforcement arrangements for policing Indian country. The first type is Tribal or Public Law 93–638 policing. Congress passed the Indian self-Determination and Education Assistance Act of 1975. This Act, also referred to as Public Law 93–638, allowed tribes to contract with the Bureau of Indian Affairs (BIA) to assume responsibility for many programs previously administered by the federal government. Public Law 93–638 allows for police departments to be administered by tribes under a contract executed with the BIA Division of Law Enforcement. The 638 contract departments employ officers and non-sworn staff that are tribal employees. The 638 contracts delineate the administrative and organizational framework, performance standards, and provides funding for the policing operations. Tribes have used 638 contracts to assume control over the policing functions. In 1995, almost half of the Indian non Public Law 280 police departments, 88 departments, were operating under 638 contracts (Wakeling et al. 2001; French 2005).

The second type is BIA policing. BIA policing consists of BIA police departments. These departments are administered by personnel employed by the federal government and are not employed by tribal government. In 1995, approximately one-third of the non-Public Law 280 departments, 64 departments, were BIA police departments. The third type is self-governance policing. Self-governance policing receives funding from the federal government under the provisions of self-governance amendments to Public Law 93–638. Tribes with self-governance arrangements enter into a compact, similar to a contract, with the BIA to assume law enforcement responsibilities that would be provided by the BIA. The significant difference between the self-governance type and the 638 type is that financing is provided by a block grant from the federal government. The self-governance type provides the tribes with more control over government functions than operating as a 638 type. In 1995, approximately 12% of the non-Public Law 280 Indian police departments, 22 Indian police departments, were operating through self-governance (Wakeling et al. 2001; French 2005). The fourth type is tribally funded policing. Tribally funded policing is funded by the tribe. Tribally funded police departments are organized and administered by the tribe. The employees are employed by the tribe and tribes have significant control over their law enforcement agencies. In 1995, only four tribal police departments were of the tribally funded department type. The fifth type is Public Law 280 policing. Public Law 280 policing is provided by state and local law enforcement agencies. The employees of these law enforcement agencies are employed by the state and local law enforcement agencies. State and local law enforcement agency funding is derived from the revenues of the state and local governments, resulting in the larger non-Indian jurisdiction financing law enforcement services for Indian country (Wakeling et al. 2001; French 2005).

Law enforcement agencies, excluding Public Law 280 agencies, range in size from small departments to large departments. There are many more small departments than medium or large departments. There are approximately 150 small departments and these departments have 9 and fewer officers. These departments serve between 25 and 30% of the citizens served by BIA and tribally administered police departments. Medium sized police departments serve approximately 60% of the citizens living in Indian country that are served by BIA or tribally administered police departments.

Medium sized departments have between 10 and 50 officers. There are approximately 75 medium sized departments. Large departments have more than 50 officers. The two largest departments are the Navajo Nation and the Oglala Sioux Tribe. These two departments have 100 or more uniformed officers and operate under 638 contracts. These two departments combined serve approximately 15% of the nearly 1.4 million residents of Indian country (Wakeling et al. 2001).

The Future of Policing in Indian Country

A recent development provides insight as to the future of policing in Indian country. The current era is one of adherence to the federal policy of self-determination. In accordance with the policy of self-determination, Congress in 2013 passed the Violence Against Women Act Reauthorization Act of 2013 (VAWA 2013). This Act was passed to address the issue of sexual assault. Research provided insight regarding this issue. Indian women face the highest rates of sexual assault of any group in the United States. The Bureau of Justice's statistics reported that in over 80% of reported incidents of rape or sexual assault of Indian victims, the perpetrator was identified as white or black (Douglas 2018). Based upon the *Oliphant* decision, tribal governments could not criminally prosecute a non-Indian for committing a crime against an Indian victim in Indian country. Congress responded to this serious issue through passage of the VAWA 2013. Congress carved out an exception to the *Oliphant* decision rule. The VAWA 2013 expanded tribal concurrent jurisdiction over non-Indian defendants. Under the VAWA 2013 tribes may elect to prosecute non-Indian perpetrators for domestic violence, dating violence or criminal violations of protective orders. The tribal prosecution must show that the non-Indian defendant has ties to the tribe through employment, residence, and/or intimate relationship with an Indian and to the Indian victim. The VAWA 2013 represents a victory for the policy of self-determination, for tribal sovereignty and the expansion of criminal jurisdiction for tribes in Indian country (Douglas 2018; McCool 2018; Riley 2016).

References

Belliveau, J. (1993). Casino gamrbling under the Indian gaming regulatory act: Narragansett tribal sovereignty versus Rhode Island gambling laws. *Suffolk University Law Review, 27*(2), 389–423.

Carey, G. W., & McClellan, J. (Eds.). (1990). *The federalist*. Dubuque: Kendall/Hunt Publishing Company.

Christensen, G. (2019). The extraterritorial reach of tribal court criminal jurisdiction. *Hastings Constitutional Law Quarterly, 46*, 294–310.

Dossett, J. H. (2018). Indian country and the territory clause: Washington's promise at the framing. *American University Law Review, 68*, 205–280.

Douglas, M. (2018). Sufficiently criminal ties: Expanding VAWA criminal jurisdiction for Indian tribes. *University of Pennsylvania Law Review, 166*, 745–787.

Eid, T. A., & Doyle, C. C. (2010). *Separate but unequal: The federal criminal justice system in Indian country* (Vol. 81, pp. 1067–1117). Boulder: University of Colorado Law Review.

French, L. (2005). Law enforcement in Indian country. *Criminal Justice Studies, 18*(1), 69–80.

Goldberg, C., & Champagne, D. (2006). Indian law at a crossroads: Is Public Law 280 fit for the twenty-first century? Some data at last. *Connecticut Law Review, 38*, 697–729.

Kalish, J. (1996). Do the states have an ace in the hole or should the Indians call their bluff? Tribes caught in the power struggle between the federal government and the states. *Arizona Law Review, 38*(4), 1345–1371.

Kronowitz, R., Lichtman, J., McSloy, S., & Olsen, M. G. (1987). Toward consent and cooperation: Reconsidering the political status of Indian nations. *Harvard Civil Rights–Civil Liberties Law Review, 22*(2), 507–622.

Laurence, R. (1981). The Indian commerce clause. *Arizona Law Review, 23*(1), 203–261.

McCool, C. (2018). Welcome to the Mvskoke reservation: Murphy v. Royal, criminal jurisdiction, and reservation diminishment in Indian country. *American Indian Law Review, 42*, 355–389.

Morrow, K. (2019). Bridging the jurisdictional void: Cross-deputization agreements in Indian country. *North Dakota Law Review, 94*, 66–94.

Newton, N. (1984). Federal power over Indians: Its sources, scope, and limitations. *University of Pennsylvania Law Review, 132*(1), 195–288.

O'Brien, S. (1989). *American Indian tribal governments*. Norman: University of Oklahoma Press.

O'Brien, S. (1991). Tribes and Indians: With whom does the United States maintain a relationship? *Notre Dame Law Review, 66*(5), 1461–1502.

Riley, A. R. (2016). Crime and governance in Indian country. *UCLA Law Review, 63*, 1564–1637.

Smith, C. E. (1993). *Courts, politics, and the judicial process*. Chicago: Nelson-Hall, Inc.

Turner, A. (1988). Evolution, assimilation, and state control of gambling in Indian country: Is Cabazon v. California an assimilationist wolf in preemption clothing? *Idaho Law Review, 24*(2), 317–338.

Wakeling, S., Jorgensen, M., Michaelson, S., & Begay, M. (2001). *Policing on American Indian reservations (Research report)*. Washington, DC: U.S. Department of Justice.

Walsh, M. (1983). Terminating the Indian termination policy. *Stanford Law Review, 35*, 1181–1215.

Wells, L. E., & Falcone, D. N. (2008). Tribal policing on American Indian reservations. *Policing: An International Journal of Police Strategies & Management, 31*(4), 648–673.

Wild, R. J. (2019). The last judicial frontier: The fight for recognition and legitimacy of tribal courts. *Minnesota Law Review, 103*, 1603–1647.

Wilkinson, C., & Biggs, E. R. (1977). The evolution of the termination policy. *American Indian Law Review, 5*, 139–184.

Chapter 12
Law Enforcement Challenges Along the Mexican-American Border in a Time of Enhanced Migration Control

Robert Hanser and Nathan Moran

Introduction

For more than the past decade, concern over immigration issues has been at the forefront of debate among politicians. While, for some, the issue centers on whether tighter controls should be placed on immigration, especially immigration from Mexico across the southwestern border of the United States, others counter with arguments that most of these initiatives are poorly implemented, ineffective, and that there is an inherent and fundamental contradiction with such policies and the very philosophical foundation of the United States. At the present time, there is a serious backlog in visa process for potential work visas which causes challenges for many businesses in regions where documented immigrant workers are employed. Further, many undocumented immigrant workers are, in order to keep their jobs, willing to work in environments that are dangerous and/or not in compliance with many of the health and safety standards usually expected in work environments. Lastly, the emphasis on deportation tends to ignore the reality that often, families in the southwestern region may consist of legal and illegal migrants, thereby separating familial members in a manner that is detrimental to the social welfare of the family and the community around them. All of these and other issues are of importance when attempting to develop a pragmatic approach to migration control and enforcement, especially when involving local police as agents of migration enforcement.

As a result, several states have clashed with the federal presidential administrations over the use of law enforcement resources in migration policy and procedures.

R. Hanser
University of Louisiana at Monroe, Monroe, Louisiana, USA

N. Moran (✉)
Midwestern State University, Wichita Falls, Texas, USA
e-mail: nathan.moran@msutexas.edu

© Springer Nature Switzerland AG 2019
J. F. Albrecht et al. (eds.), *Policing and Minority Communities*,
https://doi.org/10.1007/978-3-030-19182-5_12

These clashes are not limited to the current administration. Consider what was observed in Arizona when Senate Bill 1070 on Immigration, Law Enforcement & Safe Neighborhoods, was called to question in 2010. This bill which eventually did become law, opened police arrest powers such that they can now make arrests solely on the grounds of probable cause that the person has entered the United States illegally, without the need for any other attendant charges or alleged crimes.

Arizona's Senate Bill 1070 legislation *required* police to stop and question potential immigrants upon a reasonable suspicion that they may be illegally in the United States. Arizona's Senate Bill 1070, mandated this for all police within the state and eliminated the discretion that agencies (and officers) had previously possessed on this complicated issue. The concern with this development and others like it had been expressed by high ranking police executives as well as those at the general patrol level. The reasons for this concern were many, but primary among them was the potential damaged agency-community relations. This was especially likely to be true in minority communities that have higher levels of newly migration (Hanser and Gomila 2015).

Regardless, in 2010, the United States Department of Justice (DOJ) filed a lawsuit against the state of Arizona in district court that declared Senate Bill 1070 invalid because it interfered with federal immigration regulations. Specifically, USDOJ attorneys noted that federal preemption existed and that a development of patchwork policies among local and state agencies was likely to be ineffective as it would likely confuse efforts in the future. At the heart of the matter, the USDOJ contended that Congress and the various federal agencies constituted a careful, deliberate, and balanced approach that included law enforcement public safety concerns, foreign relations concerns, and humanitarian concerns, simultaneously. These were concerns that were not likely as important to the state of Arizona but as to the nation as a whole. As a result, the U.S. Justice Department requested an injunction against Arizona to prevent enforcement of the law before it had a chance to go into effect.

Ultimately, in 2012, the United States Supreme Court handed down a ruling that upheld the practice of requiring immigration status checks during routine police stops in a 5–3 majority vote (Barnes 2012). However, the Court cautioned against detaining individuals for prolonged periods of time if they do not have their immigration documents and expressed concern over the potential for racial profiling to occur. This resulted in limits to the use of racial factors in arrests so that police could not use race, color, or national origin beyond what was already established as permissible (Barnes 2012).

The intense disagreement between state and federal priorities in migration control leaves local police departments in a state of uncertainty on the issue. Amidst the legal wrangling, law enforcement is left to make decisions that are tenuous and fraught with peril and uncertainty. This also creates tension between state and federal agents in areas where migration is a hotbed issue because many local agents have more of a political and cultural investment in their locations than do the federal agents assigned to their regions. Lastly, the flip-flop from democratic to republican presidential administrations further exacerbates this uncertainty; with Arizona's

Senate Bill 1070 the debate entailed a democratic presidency and a conservative republican state. More recently, California's Senate Bill 54 is exactly the opposite, involving a conservative republican presidency and a state known for being liberal and progressive.

California and Senate Bill 54

In states like California, there has been a longstanding back-and-forth tussle on the issue of involving local law enforcement in immigration policy. Consider Senate Bill 54, known as the "California Values Act," which restricts the type and amount of support that local law enforcement agencies may provide federal Immigration and Customs Enforcement (ICE) officials (Fry 2017). One key feature of SB 54 in California is the prohibition against moving inmates in local jails to immigration detention facilities (Fry 2017). While this does not prevent ICE agents from being present at the time that an offender is released from a jail facility, at which time ICE agents can take the offender into custody, it does limit the use of the jail facility as an additional conduit of migrants for ICE officials, especially if release dates and identities are not specifically sent to ICE in advance (Fry 2017).

The reasons for SB 54 have more to do with the fact that persons in migrant communities still do not contact the police near as frequently as non-migrant community members when a crime is afoot. Fear that ICE will become involved is a key reason for this lack of reporting. In many cases, because crime does tend to be intra-racial, this means that both the offending party and the victim may both be illegally within U.S. borders. In fact, in most criminal incidents, the victim and the assailant know each other, at least remotely. Thus, crime in migrant communities often goes unreported.

In response, the current presidential administration has indicated that it will challenge the new law in court. Indeed, Unites States Attorney General, Jeff Sessions, has recently filed a lawsuit against the state of California over three laws that were passed in California (Fry 2017). Collectively, these laws limit the ability of state and local agents and employers in aiding federal immigration agents (Fry 2017). These laws also give the state of California authority to inspect and review the conditions of care that are provided by federal officials to migrant detainees in facilities where they are kept. The notion that state authorities could have oversight ability over federal services is one that is quite unorthodox and has seemingly struck the ire of the federal government (Fry 2017).

Sanctuary Cities and Sanctuary Laws

The term "sanctuary city" is in informal and non-legal term that has been used during the past few years to discuss several municipalities throughout the United States that are reputed to be in non-compliance with federal immigration law. In essence, these municipal jurisdictions are thought to both fail in their support of ICE and they reputedly put social impediments in place so as to hamper and thwart the efforts of federal immigration agents (Fry 2017). It is interesting that many of these cities are those that are most affected by immigration and, presumably, would have a better idea of what should or should not be done to address the immigrant population in their areas. The current SB 54 (California Values Act) seeks to prevent disclosure of when immigrants will be released from local jails and/or state prisons and seeks to eliminate the direct transfer of migrant inmates from local or state custody to federal custody (Fry 2017). In addition, SB 54 also prevents employers from providing ICE with access to employee records without a judicial warrant and also limits the employer's ability to provide access for raids in workplace locations. Areas off-limits for such raids are those where there is a reasonable expectation of privacy, such as restrooms or inside vehicles that are on the employer's property (Fry 2017).

At issue with these legal particularities is the distinction between information that falls under civil law as opposed to criminal law. For instance, notifying ICE officials of an inmate's immigration status is mainly a civil or administrative law issue. On the other hand, notification as to when migrant inmates may be allowed early release from jail or prison programs is primarily a law enforcement and corrections issue; the two are not the same. The law enforcement issue is largely one that is owned by the local and state administration because, for the most part, the criminal infractions fall under local or state criminal laws, not federal criminal laws and not under federal jurisdiction. Further still, the issues are dissimilar because issues related to immigration are grounded in civil law whereas issues related to jail and prison sentences originate from violations of criminal law.

The Blurring of Civil Law and Criminal Law

Currently, the deportation process does not have safeguards for individual protections that are provided in our criminal system, ostensibly because it is considered a civil process. Yet, our very Supreme Court, in *Padilla v. Kentucky* (2010) acknowledged that "deportation is a particularly severe penalty…" adding that "…deportation is … intimately related to the criminal process "(p. 1486). The Court, in acknowledging both the increased blurring of distinctions between the civil proceedings of the immigration system and criminal sanctions that sometimes result, determined that noncitizen immigrants should be afforded a criminal defense attorney to provide advice prior to entering into any type of plea agreement (American Immigration Council 2013). The blurring of criminal law issues and civil law issues have also been showcased through prior lawsuits and case law from other researchers. Indeed, consider that in 2012, the United States Supreme Court handed down a ruling that upheld the practice of requiring immigration status checks during routine police stops in a 5–3 majority vote (Barnes 2012). However, this ruling was accompanied by cautionary commentary against detaining individuals for prolonged periods of time if they do not have their immigration documents and also warned against the potential for racial profiling to occur. As a result, legislation limited the use of racial factors in arrests holding that police may not consider race, color, or national origin beyond what is currently permissible by prior case law. Thus, as with this prior case law (see *United States v. Brignoni-Ponce* 1975), race (and the appearance of having Mexican ancestry) may be considered a relevant factor in enforcing immigration law, but it cannot be the sole basis for making a stop and/or an arrest.

This is an important point that can get complicated, at best, and quite confusing, at worst. While racial characteristics can be used as part of a composite rationale for a stop, it has to be articulated with other observed facts. From a legal perspective, problems quickly emerge because, unless the officer observes some other type of criminal activity, there is no reasonable suspicion (other than the appearance of the individual) to determine that an immigration violation exists. Even more to the point, this also means that there would be no probable cause for criminal activity. Thus, one must ask, why then would the officer have grounds to inquire, in the first place? In most cases, he or she would not have any reasonable grounds for questioning, particularly if the encounter was not very near to the United States and Mexico border (*United States v. Brignoni-Ponce* 1975).

The Racial Profiling Issue

According to the United States Customs and Border Protection (CBP), racial profiling is of the following:

> The invidious use of race or ethnicity as a criterion in conducting stops, searches, inspections, and other law enforcement activities based on the erroneous assumption that a person of one race or ethnicity is more likely to commit a crime than a person of another race or ethnicity (2016, p. unknown).

This definition is a bit deceptive because of the wording that persons of a race or ethnicity are erroneously assumed to be "more likely to commit a crime." This definition does not include the idea of stopping persons, based on the race or ethnicity, to check on their migration status, a civil issue. While the definition provided is certainly accurate in the case of criminal activity, this definition conveniently leaves out erroneous assumptions that a person of one race or ethnicity is more likely to be an illegal migrant than another. Thus, migration issues are not considered part-and-parcel to issues of racial profiling, only criminal ones, according to the CBP.

This distinction becomes relevant due to a legal fine-point. If racial profiling, according to the CBP, is only applicable to criminal issues, then this means that checking for legal migration into the United States (particularly within 100 miles of the U.S. border) is then a non-criminal issue. This means that police should not be engaged in migration checks. While this definition might seem to liberally free federal agents from concerns of profiling when conducting their day-to-day routines, it does not change anything for local law enforcement. This is because contemporary police experts understand that racial profiling is not an accepted practice when establishing probable cause for a crime. As noted previously, under typical circumstances throughout the United States, local police are considered crime-fighters by trade, not parties tasked with conducting migration stops. (Taylor 2014; Phelps et al. 2014).

To further drive this point home, consider that in December of 2014, the U.S. Department of Justice published a document that clarified parameters for federal law enforcement and other government officials to consider a host of demographic characteristics when engaged in their duties. Among these characteristics were race and ethnicity as a pretext consideration for stops or questioning when conducting law enforcement activities. Importantly, this document also outlined exceptions to these requirements when in the interest of national security and/or border protection. The key point is that for local police and even federal law enforcement, racial profiling is not allowed when considering suspects of criminal activity. In these cases, racial or ethnic characteristics must be attributed to a single individual suspect who is sought, not to an entire demographic group of people. On the other hand, when ICE, BCP, or other agents are conducting border security, particularly when under the auspices of national security, the same prohibition against racial profiling does not apply. Again, because local police are tasked with upholding criminal law, they do not benefit from these exceptions and, therefore, are not equivalent to federal agents who are tasked with migration control functions.

Further proof of this comes through lawsuits that have been successfully filed against local police agencies who have engaged in racial profiling. Hanser (2015) noted several cases where municipal police departments and county level sheriffs were held liable under various Section 1983 lawsuits for engaging in racial profiling within their jurisdiction. This demonstrates a long trend in the field of modern policing to refrain from this practice. Many police chiefs have incorporated changes within their organization's culture to eradicate this practice (Hanser 2015; National Institute of Justice 2013a). Racial profiling negatively affects police-community relations in communities with racial and ethnic populations which naturally makes the job of the police officer all the more difficult in that community (Hanser 2015; National Institute of Justice 2013a, b).

Civil Rights Violations in Immigration Detention Facilities

As noted previously, SB 54 proposes to give California the authority to inspect and review the conditions of care in federal immigration facilities within the state's borders. To some this may seem to be a unusual addition. Consider, however, that in late 2015, the U.S. Commission on Civil Rights conducted an investigation into the actual types of response and conditions of confinement that existed within federal detention facilities holding immigrants. They examined a variety of facilities administrated through the Office of Refugee Resettlement (ORR), which is required to maintain certain standards of care and custody of immigrant children. These standards of care include medical and mental health, education, family reunification efforts, and the provision of recreational activities.

This investigation resulted in the generation of a corrective action plan outlining the needs for providing better medical and mental health services. Further, this plan recommended that programs provide youth care workers with additional communications training when working with unaccompanied immigrant children and to foster nurturing and positive interactions. Keep in mind again, that these are youth who are held without parents, legal guardians, or other adult figures. They are also detained under civil law, not criminal law, themselves not being suspected of criminal activity and, in the United States legal system, being considered juveniles not adults, which implies that they should be provided with added protections due to their age. Children's detention centers are required to provide classroom education taught by teachers with a minimum 4 year college degree. Upon investigation, the Commission found that numerous educational workers did not meet minimal standards for hire. The Commission, in its report, pointed out that educational programming is vital to a child's development and that education for unaccompanied immigrant children gives them better odds of integrating in the American society, as a whole, and into the American job sector, specifically, should they remain in the United States. A failure to provide this essentially ensures that these youth remain in an unstable and disadvantaged status and increases the likelihood that they will not be productive within mainstream American society. This again is counterproductive to the welfare of both these youth and to the United States economy and social dignity.

Detention Facility Housing Conditions

During the past 4–5 years, there has been growing concern that the U.S. Customs and Border Protection (CBP) agency has maintained facilities that are no different than prison facilities designed for common criminals. This includes facilities that house entire families (men, women, and children) who are being detained civilly, not for criminal offenses committed in the United States. It should be emphasized that these concerns are not simply liberal or anti-establishment rhetoric. Indeed, even members of Congress have voiced concerns about the punitive nature of immigration detention facilities. In fact, 136 members of Congress signed and endorsed a letter to the Department of Homeland Security's chief administrator, indicating that:

> We are disturbed by the fact that many mothers and children remain in family detention despite serious medical needs. In the past year, we have learned of the detention of children with intellectual disabilities, a child with brain cancer, a mother with a congenital heart disorder, a 14 day-old baby, and a 12 year-old child who has not eaten solid food for 2 months, among many others. Recently, we learned of a 3 year-old child at the Berks County Residential Center who was throwing up for 3 days and was apparently offered water as a form of medical treatment. It was only after the child began throwing up blood on the fourth day

that the facility finally transferred her to a hospital. This is simply unacceptable (U.S. Commission on Civil Rights 2015, p. 105).

Naturally, the U.S. Sentencing Commission supported these Congressional concerns, adding that additional concerns included not just family detention centers, but reports of unsuitable conditions in border patrol facilities, and adult-only detention facilities. In particular, the Commission found conditions of extreme cold, overcrowding, and inadequate food to be a common problem throughout numerous CBP facilities (U.S. Commission on Civil Rights 2015). Again, this should not be interpreted as isolated incidents but was, instead, the norm throughout these facilities. Some facilities resembled the conditions of a prison rather than detention. Naturally, while some locations house immigrants convicted of serious crimes, lesser crimes, and those that have failed to appear for immigration hearings, it is important that others held on civil immigration issues not be co-mingled with the criminal population and that their treatment be substantially different. Altogether, the Commission found evidence to conclude that the Department of Homeland Security (DHS) in general and the Customs Border Protection (CBP) in particular detained undocumented immigrants in a manner more akin to prison rather than civil detention, which is a violation of the Fifth Amendment (U.S. Commission on Civil Rights 2015). Prior to this and since this time, other various levels of federal oversight, including federal district courts have had similar decisions and left similar rulings as precedent. This relates to challenges that police agencies may encounter during this period of enhanced migration control because, increasingly, these agencies are asked to house detainees in their local jails due to a lack-of-space in federal detention centers. Because these jails operate under contract with ICE and hold detainees under the authority of ICE, they are required to maintain the same standard of care. This care is different from jail inmates and is considered a different type of custody. For jails in California, this can easily result in similar deficiencies in housing requirements for detained migrants. Naturally, these police and sheriff's departments would then be held liable by the CBP, as has happened before (Hanser and Gomila 2012).

To be sure, this is no minor issue; housing detainees has become 'big business' for local jails and private facilities (Gomez 2017). This expansion in the use of detention is one of the latest developments in the current administration's efforts to increase efforts to stop illegal migration (Gomez 2017). Currently, ICE is thought to house nearly 40,000 detainees on any given day in a hodge-podge of federal, private, and local jails facilities (Gomez 2017). While certainly may help to keep illegal migrants detained, this comes at a prices that runs hundreds of millions of dollars. In addition, private companies like GEO and CoreCivic were funders of Trump when he ran for president. Since this time, both companies have seen dramatic increases in the value of their stocks, further fueling the support for increased detention. This then will likely increase the length of detentions since the facilities will have little incentive to remove detainees. Further, this will occur with less opportunities for bond (See *Jennings v. Rodriguez* 2018). For asylum seekers and migrants from dangerously violent countries, the excessive waits become a viable option due to fear of returning to their countries of origin where they might be jailed, tortured, and ultimately killed. This is especially true for migrants coming from violent areas of Central America.

Failure to Uphold Legal Requirements

Just last year, in 2017, a class action lawsuit was filed that challenged the practice of turning away asylum seekers who request United States protection at ports of entry along the border between the United States and Mexico (American Immigration Council 2017). Plaintiffs in this case allege that agents of the Customs and Border Protection (CBP) use a variety of tactics – including misrepresentation, threats and intimidation, verbal abuse and physical force, and coercion–to deny bona fide asylum seekers the opportunity to pursue their claims. Complainants in this case note that when the U.S. government refuses to allow asylum seekers to pursue their claims, it is a violation of the Immigration and Nationality Act, the Administrative Procedure Act, the Due Process Clause of the Fifth Amendment, as well as the doctrine of *non-refoulement* under international law.

The issue of *refoulement*, in particular, warrants additional attention. Refoulement refers to the expulsion of individuals who have the right to be recognized as refugees. This legal principle was first established by the United Nations Convention of 1954 which, in Article 33(1), holds the following:

> No Contracting State shall expel or return ('refouler') a refugee in any manner whatsoever to the frontiers of territories where his life or freedom would be threatened on account of his race, religion, nationality, membership of a particular social group or political opinion.

Further, it is important to clarify that this principle does not only restrict countries from sending refuges back to their nation-of-origin, it also prohibits the return of those refuges to any other country wherein it would be likely that they would be persecuted or subject to widespread victimization due to their national status, culture, race, or other demographic feature. The only exception to this is when the individual is a potential threat to national security. While the non-refoulment policy has been accepted around the globe, there have been problems with its adoption in some cases, Usually this is due to the fact that immigrants under this stipulation are required to have official refugee status. Further, not all nations around the globe are members of the United Nations Convention on the Status of Refugees and/or have failed to establish official processes to determine who does or does not have refugee status within their borders. This leads to ambiguity and a lack of consistency in these cases.

Issues with turning refugees back and failing to afford protection have been levelled at the United States and rose to a crescendo during the immigration crisis the occurred in 2014. During this time there was a noticeable increase of children from several Central American nations who sought entry into the United States. In 2014, this influx of unprotected and unchaperoned youth numbered in the tens of thousands from El Salvador, Guatemala, and Honduras. To be fair, some of these youth did have adult women who were either mothers or guardians but, for the most part, these youth migrated in droves, of their own accord.

The reason for this spike in undocumented immigration has to do with the extreme violence that erupted throughout Central America. These youth have fled poverty and excessive violence from gangs, extremist groups, and drug organizations, alike (Dart 2014). The murder rates in these countries also increased and were among the highest in the international community, with Honduras having the highest murder rate in the world (Park 2014). While it was true that these youth fled their home countries due to danger, many also fled so as to reunify with other family members who had not been deported in the United States. The perception among many Central Americans was that the United States was, as a general policy, allowing immigrant children to remain in the United States.

These perceptions developed because these youth were seldom quickly deported and, even though immigration proceedings were promptly started, they took a long period of time during which these youth would be allowed to stay with a family member or sponsor in the United States. The grounds for this were related to anti-trafficking laws that prohibited the immediate deportation of youth from Central America until a court-hearing is provided. In the meantime the Department of Health and Human Services provides health screenings and immunization shots, while assigning an average shelter stay of 35 days or more, when necessary.

The key point is that the United States, due to its own statutory requirements regarding safeguards against the potential victimization and trafficking of immigrant youth (known as the *Trafficking Victims Protection Reauthorization Act* or the TVPRA) and due to the obvious dangers that exist to these youth who are returned to their own countries (especially Honduras), has a legal obligation under international non-refoulment policies, to treat these youth as refugees. Despite this, the current Trump administration has proposed to draft policy that will deport over 150,000 of these youth who came without adult supervision, once they turn 18 years of age. Such a process would essentially dump thousands of youth into a dangerous region without the benefit of protection, essentially making the United States a culpable and contributory party to their future victimization, regardless of whether they are classified as adults, or not (Lanktree 2017). Further, such policy is considered while there is clear evidence from Senate-level investigations that many of these youth are at risk of being trafficked in the labor market in the United States and abroad (Greenberg 2016).

In a very recent case, the United States Supreme Court ruled in *Jennings v. Rodriguez* that migrant detainees, including those who have permanent legal status and even asylum seekers, can be held indefinitely within detention facilities without the benefit of bond hearings. This is largely in reaction to the various complications with the process of sorting through immigration cases, including asylum seekers. This case originated as a class-action suit that challenged lengthy immigration detentions, often averaging from 12 to 14 months, where detainees are not provided periodic review for bond. In this case, the vast majority of litigants for the plaintiff's side have either petty misdemeanor crimes or are seeking asylum. But, more to the point, is the fact that this ruling further reinforces the notion that immigration proceedings are civil in nature, not criminal. Were they based upon criminal law, a right to counsel, bond, and other features would become obligatory. Because they are not and because these proceedings are not grounded in criminal law, it would seem that law enforcement should not be compelled to be involved in these cases. It is a civil matter and law enforcement deals in criminal matters. Thus, police should be spared the burden of reporting migration status of persons leaving jail and they should also be spared the responsibility for verifying such status within the communities that they serve.

Back to the Future: How Confusing Objectives Became Today's Quagmire

Perhaps, in order to make sense of what has become a confusing system with a number of unconstitutional outcomes and consequences, we should not just understand that the criminal law and civil law are different. Rather, we must note that immigration proceedings and determinations are civil in nature due to historical etiology that can explain this development. As it turns out, the basis for these distinctions extend back to the late 1800s, when the Supreme Court held, in Fong Yue Ting v. United States (1893), that deportation was a *civil* rather than a *criminal* sanction. In other words, deportation, in and of itself is not punishment, per sè, but is instead an administrative proceeding intended to simply return immigrants to their native countries of origin. At this time, the High Court reasoned that:

> The order of deportation is not a punishment for crime. It is not a banishment, in the sense in which that word is often applied to the expulsion of a citizen from his country by way of punishment. It is but a method of enforcing the return to his own country of an alien who has not complied with the conditions upon the performance of which the government of the nation … has determined that his continuing to reside here shall depend (Fong Yue Ting v. United States 1893, p. 730).

The reasons for this ruling warrant that some context be given. During this time, Chinese laborers were immigrating into the United States in record numbers. In an effort to curtail the excessive numbers of immigrants, the Chinese Exclusion Act and the Geary Act restricted and/or delayed the immigration of additional Chinese into the United States. One of the key aspects of the Geary Act was that the burden of proof for demonstrating the right to be in the United States was placed upon the Chinese resident. During this time, Chinese immigrants were required to possess a "certificate of residence" which was proof of legal entry into the United States. Those without such a certificate, for whatever reason, was considered unlawfully in the United States and could be arrested, forced into hard labor for up to a year, and could be automatically deported thereafter.

Despite the fact that Chinese laborers could be given hard labor up to a year prior to deportation the Supreme Court continued to support the rationale that immigration proceedings were civil rather than criminal in nature. However, the true underlying reason for this has more to do with the fact that the Court also maintained that immigration policy and the enforcement of that policy were issues of the legislative and executive branches of government. Along the way, the Court upheld broad federal powers and, in recognizing that certain minimal levels of due process were required in immigration and deportation proceedings, the Court gave nearly unfettered power to Congress to define the standards, burdens of proof, and rules that applied. In the process, by making immigration proceedings civil in nature, a much lower burden of proof was required by the state (preponderance of the evidence rather than proof beyond a reasonable doubt), fewer protections were afforded the Chinese immigrants because the 'loss of liberty' standard was irrelevant since they were being removed from the United States, and (at the same time) requiring additional measures (such as forced labor) were considered payment for the cost of proceedings, not punishment for a wrong done.

Thus, by classifying deportation as a "civil" penalty, the Court held that immigrants facing removal are not entitled to the same constitutional rights provided to defendants facing criminal punishment. It is for this reason that immigrants facing deportation today are not read their rights after being arrested, are not provided an attorney if they cannot afford one, and are not permitted to challenge an order of removal for being "cruel and unusual punishment." While undocumented immigrants are not required to do forced labor (this dropped out of usage several decades ago), the requirement to provide the protections afforded to someone charged in criminal court do not exist, yet at the same time, their experience while being detained may actually be similar to that of someone who has been charged with a criminal offense. Thus again, as with the late 1800s, it would seem that the blurring of these two legal systems allow the government to vacillate between one and/or the other so as to maximize deportation goals while also maintaining a covert punitive flavor despite overt comments to the contrary. In short, it is a farce that allows the U.S. government to straddle both sides of the fence, to its advantage, and in violation of what is constitutional.

State Rights Versus Federal Rights in Responding to the Migrant Issue

At the heart of this issue is that fact that any responsibility over migration or national status begins and ends within the United States government, not state governments. Further, the United States may be in need of re-examining responses to migration, national status, and the rights of states to govern their own police resources within their borders. As it stands, states are entitled to exercise jurisdiction over criminal law and civil law within their borders as they see fit, so long as that activity ensures that no Constitutional rights are violated in doing so. Further still, states are allowed to broaden rights of individuals within their borders beyond what the Constitution permits, but they cannot restrict those rights to less than what the U.S. Constitution provides. Theoretically, this should mean that states like California are within their right to extend protections of individuals within their borders, whether citizens or not.

It is the federal government that is responsible for protecting the nation's borders and for regulating international issues that impact those borders. However, it is very unlikely that the United States will be able to effectively impact the systemic origins of the illegal migration issues. The reason is simple, citizens leaving Honduras, Guatemala, El Salvador, and Mexico are doing so because of the pervasive of these national governments. Indeed, most Central American nations experience problems with excessive political and economic corruption. It is because of this simple fact that the United States is largely powerless to provide stability. In addition, there are resentments toward the United States among many Latin nations for past military involvement into the affairs of these nations (UN News Centre 2013). It is clear that, for better or worse, many leaders of various Latin American countries have negative views of the United States.

Given this, it seems that the United States should take heed of what its neighbors are saying. This then means that Latin American nations will have to bail themselves out of the doldrums in which they find themselves. However, the nation of Bolivia has seen numerous gains by bringing people out of poverty, expanding its coverage for maternal health, boosting literacy and investing in water and sanitation (UN News Centre 2013). Indeed, President Evo Morlaes Ayma stated that "we live in sovereignty and dignity; no longer dominated by the North American empire… no longer being blackmailed by the International Monetary Fund" (UN News Centre 2013, pg. 1). This example shows both that these countries are capable of improving their condition and, just as important, they tend to resent involvement by the United States. This is an important observation when trying to actually resolve this problem at its origin rather than simply attendant symptoms of that problem.

It would therefore appear that the official governments of these countries are not aligned with the United States and prefer, instead, to go it alone without the help of the United States. While there is a possibility that these government leaders are themselves, corrupt, this only serves to further restrict the United States in responding. Indeed, aside from some act of overt or covert warfare, there is little else that the U.S. can do to counter regimes of corruption, drug cartels that paralyze entire governments, and cultures that have developed around a 'have' and 'have not' mentality. Naturally, to engage in any form of armed intervention is both desperate and counter-productive, having the potential to further victimize and harm those persons whom the United States would be liberating so as to have better access to economic and social autonomy. Thus, the issue is complicated due to the perceptions touted by Latin American governments. This means that the arguments for, or against, the use of local and state level police in migration enforcement is rooted in a problem that goes beyond the borders of that respective state and beyond the borders of the nation.

Though international issues that influence migration impacts individual states, it is primarily the state's job to regulate and respond to issues affecting its own jurisdiction. So long that this is done in a manner that does not contradict Constitutional safeguards, the state's responsibility therein begins and ends. Therefore, states have the right to adopt more liberal approaches within their own borders to the migration issue. Further, they may, ironically, have a better understanding of the complications involved with migration issues within their borders than the federal government would like to admit. This then means that, on the whole, the United States government must grapple with the international considerations that impact migrant influxes (whether legal or illegal) within its borders, as federal resources are intended for such actions. On the other hand, the business of internal governance should be left to the individual states to regulate. Should a state, as a whole, wish to engage in more vigorous expulsion of illegal migrants, then so be it. Should that state wish to not utilize their own resources for such efforts, so be that as well. In essence, part of the problem becomes a state rights versus federal rights issue. In this case, states have a right to determine their own codes, statutes, and laws on the matter, once the issue falls within their borders.

Concluding Comments

It is clear that this issue complicated due to a number of considerations that go beyond the day-to-day world of local police. Indeed, the issue is an international one that local agencies are not equipped to handle. This issue also goes beyond the scope-of-duty attributed to local and even state level law enforcement. Rather, local and state agents engage in their rightful duties of the detection and apprehension of crime and criminals because this is their actual function, regardless of the national status of the individual. Further, most law enforcement agencies discourage the personnel from becoming involved in civil matters because theirs is the criminal jurisdiction, exclusively. Generally, police do not engage in divorce law, suits related to debt between creditors and debtors, malpractice litigation, or breaches of contract, unless there is probable cause that some type of criminal issue afoot. Even in these cases, the police response is most always restricted to the elements of the criminal offense, not the civil law aspects of an incident. In fact, it is not uncommon for criminal charges to be dropped though civil litigation continues between two parties.

There is also concern that the federal government does not actually have a good track record of addressing the migration issue in the United States. Violations of Constitutional rights by federal agents have been found throughout the long and troubled history of migration enforcement. In addition, conditions within some detention facilities have been called to question. Given that the federal government exercises the right to review the operations of local law enforcement and state correctional agencies, it would seem plausible that state governments should be allowed to observe and critique the operations of federal detention facilities within their borders (as proposed under California's SB 54). Resistance to this notion by the federal government does not seem to smack of true transparency or fundamental fairness. If local and state police are to work in true partnership with federal agents, it would seem that those federal agents should not be opposed to allowing the local and statewide communities to engage in some degree of oversight of their operations within those jurisdictions. Indeed, these communities already do so with local and state agents in their region through civilian review boards and other such mechanisms. There seems to be no logical reason for excluding federal agents and federal detention centers from similar forms of oversight.

Lastly, in states where laws are favorable to communities with migrant populations (whether legal or illegal) the police response will often be aligned with those sentiments. In fact, some of the police agents themselves may be drawn from these communities. This is reflective of a culturally competent police agency, which fosters cooperation between police agencies and the community they serve. Placing mandatory requirements to become involved in deportation activities does not allow police nor state governments the ability to mitigate the social, political, and cultural concerns of populations within their jurisdiction. In some cases it will likely ruin the rapport, trust, and the sense of community that is required to engage in effective governance, in general, and effective policing, in particular, for those same communities. This is something that both state and federal agents should avoid, regardless of the political or philosophical ideologies to which they subscribe.

References

American Immigration Council. (2013). *Two systems of justice: How the immigration system falls short of American ideal of justice*. Washington, DC: Author.

American Immigration Council. (2017). *Challenging customs and border protection's unlawful practice of turning away asylum seekers*. Washington, DC: Author. Retrieved from: https://www.americanimmigrationcouncil.org/litigation/challenging-customs-and-border-protections-unlawful-practice-turning-away-asylum-seekers.

Barnes, R. (2012, June 25). Supreme court rejects much of Arizona immigration law. *The Washington Post*.

Dart, T. (2014, 09 July). Child migrants at Texas border: An immigration crisis that's hardly new. The Guardian, Houston. Retrieved 25 Sept 2017. https://www.theguardian.com/world/2014/jul/09/us-immigration-undocumented-children-Texas.

Fong Yue Ting v United States (1893). 149 U.S. 698, 730.

Fry, W. (2017, Dec. 28). How 2018 immigration law will affect local law enforcement. NBC 7, San Diego. Retrieved from https://www.nbcsandiego.com/news/local/California-Immigration-Law-SB-54-Affect-Local-Law-Enforcement-467064593.html.

Gomez, A. (2017, Oct. 17). *Trump plans massive increase in federal immigration jails*. USA Today. Retrieved from https://www.usatoday.com/story/news/world/2017/10/17/trump-plans-massive-increase-federal-immigration-jails/771414001/.

Greenberg, M. (2016). *Adequacy of the department of health and human services' efforts to protect unaccompanied alien children from human trafficking*. Washington, DC: U.S. Senate Committee on Homeland Security & Governmental Affairs.

Hanser, R. D. (2015). Using local law enforcement to enhance immigration law in the United States: A legal and social analysis. *Police Practice and Research: An International Journal, 16*(4), 303–315.

Hanser, R. D., & Gomila, M. N. (2012). Enforcement of immigration law by police: Issues and challenges. In F. Reddington & G. Bonham (Eds.), *Flawed criminal justice policy: At the intersection of the media, public fear and legislative response* (pp. 39–59). Durham: Carolina Academic Press.

Hanser, R. D. & Gomila, M. (2015). *Multiculturism and the Criminal Justice System*. Boston: Pearson.

Jennings v. Rodriguez, 15–1204, (U.S. 2018).

Lanktree, G. (2017, Sept 21). Trump administration planning law to deport thousands of unaccompanied teens from Central America: Report. Newsweek Retrieved 25 Sept 2017, from http://

www.newsweek.com/trump-administration-weighs-deporting-thousands-unaccompanied-child-migrants-668778.

National Institute of Justice. (2013a). *Racial profiling*. Washington, DC, United States Department of Justice: Retrieved from https://www.nij.gov/topics/law-enforcement/legitimacy/pages/racial-profiling.aspx.

National Institute of Justice. (2013b). *Racial profiling and traffic stops*. Washington, DC: United States Department of Justice. Retrieved from https://www.nij.gov/topics/law-enforcement/legitimacy/pages/traffic-stops.aspx.

Padilla v. Kentucky, 2010 130 S. Ct. 1473, 1481 (U.S.).

Park, H. (2014, October 21). Children at the border. New York Times, New York. Retrieved 25 Sept 2017. https://www.nytimes.com/interactive/2014/07/15/us/questions-about-the-border-kids.html?mcubz=1.

Phelps, J. R., Dailey, J., & Koenigsberg, M. (2014). *Border security* (2nd ed.). Durham: Carolina Academic Press.

Taylor, M. E. (2014). Illegal immigration and local policing. In M. D. Reisig & R. J. Kane (Eds.), *Oxford handbook of police and policing*. Oxford: Oxford University Press.

U.S. Commission on Civil Rights. (2015). *With liberty and justice for all: The state of civil rights at immigration detention facilities*. Washington, DC: United States Commission on Civil Rights.

UN News Centre. (2013). Leaders of Latin American countries urge major push to promote social justice, end inequality. Retrieved on 21 Sept 2017: http://www.un.org/apps/news/story.asp?NewsID=46022#.WdKS0cahfIU.

United States v. Brignoni-Ponce, (1975) 422 U.S. 873.

Part IV
International Perspectives

Chapter 13
The Challenges of Policing Ethnic Minority Communities in Post-Conflict Kosovo

Michael R. Sanchez and Fahredin Verbovci

Introduction

The journey from being a province without a government, steeped in seething ethnic tension, to a burgeoning modern civil society has been a rocky one. In the span of 18 years, Kosovo has gone from a post-war fractured society to a society on the road to recovery, which is no small feat. The challenges of the Kosovo Police (KP) are numerous and daunting.

In order to understand the challenges of policing ethnic minorities in Kosovo, one must first understand the history of Kosovo. The history of Kosovo reveals the origins and the ubiquitous nature of ethnic tensions in the Balkan region. Effectively policing ethnic minority communities that have built distrust, and sometimes outright-hatred of other ethnicities, over centuries is a challenge of immeasurable proportions. Post-war Kosovo was a swirling cauldron of ethnic tensions, exacerbated by old and new scores to settle between ethnicities. Bringing order to chaos, brining trust and a sense of community to a fractured society, and brining modern democratic rule of law to post-war Kosovo has been the ongoing challenge for the Kosovo Police.

Maintaining peace and public order, preventing and combating criminal activity throughout Kosovo, particularly in the North and close to the border with Serbia, has been challenge for the Kosovo Police. The numerous protests of the ethnic Serb community, road blocking in that part of Kosovo by Serbian extremists groups, supported by local Serbian politicians, has been challenge not only for Kosovo Police but also for the International police force present in Kosovo.

M. R. Sanchez (✉)
University of Texas Rio Grande Valley, Brownsville, TX, USA
e-mail: Michael.sanchez@utrgv.edu

F. Verbovci
Kosovo Police, Pristina, Kosovo

© Springer Nature Switzerland AG 2019
J. F. Albrecht et al. (eds.), *Policing and Minority Communities*,
https://doi.org/10.1007/978-3-030-19182-5_13

Brief History of Kosovo

The Republic of Kosovo is a small diamond-shaped Eastern European country. Located in the central Balkan Region of Europe in the south of the former Yugoslavia, Kosovo is landlocked by Montenegro, Serbia, Macedonia, and Albania. With an area of 4203 square miles, Kosovo is slightly smaller than Connecticut (CIA 2017). Kosovo was part of the Roman and Byzantine empires before ethnic Serbs migrated into the Kosovo region starting in the seventh century. Kosovo was formally a part of the Serbian kingdom in the thirteenth and fourteenth centuries. Serbia built several monasteries in Kosovo during this period. These monasteries would become architecturally significant symbols of the Serbian Orthodox faith.

In 1389, the Ottoman Empire defeated the Serbian army in the Battle of Kosovo, which took place just outside of modern-day Pristina, Kosovo. The hard-fought battle, which was ultimately lost by the Serbs, took on mythological significance in Serbian Culture as a heroic defeat (Baldwin 2006). The Battle of Kosovo is celebrated annually by Serbia to this day. The loss of the Battle of Kosovo was the beginning of the end of Serbian hegemony over Kosovo. In 1455, Kosovo was conquered by the Ottomans, becoming a part of the Ottoman Empire for the next five centuries.

The loss of Kosovo to the Ottomans resulted in ethnic Serbs migrating north out of the Kosovo region in what has become known as the *great migration*. Under Ottoman rule, the ethnic Albanian population flourished. Although originally Catholic, the vast majority of ethnic Albanians in Kosovo converted to Islam during Ottoman rule; however, a small number of Albanian Catholics remain in Kosovo. In 2011 the Kosovo census revealed that there were 38,438 Albanian Catholics, comprising approximately 2.2% of the Kosovo population. By the beginning of the twentieth century, ethnic Albanians supplanted ethnic Serbians as the dominant ethnicity in Kosovo (Youngblood-Coleman 2016). By 1990, the ethnic Serb minority in Kosovo had dropped from 23.6% in 1948–10% in 1990. This dramatic shift in demographics can be attributed to Albanian migration into Kosovo and the high ethnic Albanian birth rate (Dahlman and Williams 2010; Youngblood-Coleman 2016).

After the First World War, Kosovo became a province of Serbia, which became a part of the newly formed country of Yugoslavia. After World War 2, Josip Broz Tito came to power in what was then called the Socialist Federal Republic of Yugoslavia (SFRY) (Baldwin 2006). This era in Kosovo Albanian vernacular is referred to as *communism time*. Tito was quite benevolent to the ethnic Albanian province of Kosovo. Kosovo was granted increasingly more power and autonomy to run their own affairs. In 1974, the SFRY Constitution was passed, giving Kosovo almost full autonomy, although still nominally a province of Serbia. Kosovo was also denied the right to secede from Serbia as a protection against the fear of a Kosovo Albanian nationalistic movement (Dahlman and Williams 2010).

Origins of the Kosovo Conflict

Tito had been extremely successful in promoting Yugoslavian nationalism over eth-nocentrism. Tito's talent for bringing together people of different ethnic and reli-gious backgrounds ensured the strength of the SFRY (Woodward 1995). Tito died in 1980. In 1987, Slobodan Milosevic came to power on a wave of Serbian national-ism. Thus began a SFRY-wide wave of Serbian nationalism, where ethnic Serbs achieved complete hegemony over the SFRY government.

In 1981, after Tito's death, demonstrations at the University Pristina marked the beginning of a Yugoslavian governmental movement away from Tito's fair and gen-erous treatment of the Kosovo ethnic Albanians. The situation in Kosovo began to deteriorate, in particular the political, judicial, and social welfare of Kosovo Albanians were greatly reduced. This process was accelerated in 1985 when Milosevic became the president of Serbian Republic, supported by ultra-nationalist forces. Serbian nationalist slogans such as ...*where the only one Serb is living* and *autonomous provinces are two cancer in the bosom of Serbia* revived Serbian nationalist emotions.

In 1989, Milosevic stripped Kosovo of its autonomy and began a systematic repression of the ethnic Albanians living in Kosovo to include laws that restricted ethnic Albanians' ability to gain employment and education (Božić 2010). There were mass dismissals of Kosovo Albanians from positions in industry and other relevant public institutions throughout Kosovo. A new school curriculum was intro-duced in 1990 and 1991 by the Serbian authorities. Kosovo Albanian teachers, who refused to implement this curriculum, were dismissed (Mazowiecki, T. 1993).

Subsequently, a number of Laws had been adopted that set the stage for an apart-heid like society. The complete Serbian rule of Kosovo evolved into an oppressive police state that specifically targeted ethnic Albanians in Kosovo, and Albanian political movements. Ethnic Albanian freedom of movement was curtailed by checkpoints and the Serbian government purged the industries of education, health-care, and media of ethnic Albanians, replacing them with Serbs loyal to the Milosevic regime (Dahlman and Williams 2010). The Kosovo Albanian vernacular refers to this era as *Serbian time.*

In July 1990, the Serbian parliament passed the *Law on Labor relations in Special Circumstances*, which allowed the recruitment of Serbs only, excluding eth-nic Albanians, for government posts in Kosovo (Republic of Serbia, July 1990). After 1990, Serbia governed Kosovo through an expansive model of administration that relied on a large police force, creating the repression and oppression, which amounted a de-facto police state. Blatant abuses of the individual and collective human rights of Kosovo Albanians by Serbian lawmakers, political institutions, and police were recorded by various national and international Non-Governmental Organizations, which routinely sent reports of these violations to Milosevic and other Serbian and FYR politicians, officials, and government agencies (Testimony of Fredrick Abrahams 2002). Furthermore, the Serbian Government targeted the University of Pristina. All secondary and primary schools used by Kosovo Albanians were closed. Radio and television were restricted in broadcasting the news in the Albanian language.

The ever-increasingly oppression of the ethnic Albanian population in Kosovo led to a seemingly inevitable violent response against Serbian rule by the Albanian community. The Kosovo Liberation Army (KLA) was a lightly armed organic resistance movement that rose in the wake of Serbian governmental excesses. In 1998, the KLA waged a guerilla campaign against the Serbian police forces. Retaliation by Serbian police and military against suspected KLA members, who simply dissolved back into the population, caused the violence to spiral out of control (Schutte and Weidmann 2011). In many ways, the KLA represented an organic insurgency similar to Vietnam, where combatants and civilians were indistinguishable from one another (Judah 2000).

In August of 1998, the Serbian Army moved significant heavy military resources into Kosovo and unleased a brutal police and military campaign in Kosovo. The Serbian police and military began to cleanse Kosovo of ethnic Albanians. It has long been a Serbian nationalistic dream to re-establish ethnic hegemony over Kosovo, and to give Kosovo's fertile agricultural land to Serbs. Villages were burned, ethnic Albanians were expelled, and the ethnic Albanian population was terrorized (Jenne 2010).

In the wake of Serbian excesses in the Bosnian War from 1992 to 1995, the international community was not willing to stand by and allow another genocide. On March 24, 1999, the North American Treaty Organization (NATO), citing Serbian violence and excesses in Kosovo, undertook a 79 day bombing campaign of the Serbian Army in Kosovo, and eventually against Serbia proper. The bombing campaign, called *Operation Allied Force,* was halted when Serbia agreed to withdraw from Kosovo (Sanchez 2014). When Serbia withdrew from Kosovo, 180,000 ethnic Serbs, and ethic Roma and Ashkali who were suspected of collaborating with the Serbians, fled Kosovo, fearing reprisals from the ethnic Albanian community (Burema 2012; Ferreira 2003).

Having achieved total control of all governmental entities, prior to the NATO campaign, when Serbia withdrew from Kosovo in June of 1999, they took all of the components of government with them. In essence, Kosovo became a province without any functioning government (Sanchez 2014). By the time the Serbian Army and government withdrew from Kosovo, between 848,000 and 863,000 ethnic Albanians had been expelled from Kosovo and up to 590,000 had become internally displaced (Jenne 2010). Considering that the population of Kosovo at the time was less than two million, these numbers are staggering. The total number of refugees represented 90% of the entire ethnic Albanian population in Kosovo (Woehrel 2010). Kosovo was in complete shambles.

Demography of Kosovo

By 1999, Kosovo was predominantly ethnic Albanian. Ethnic Serbs represented the largest post-war minority. Brunborg (2002), estimates that the post-war demographics of Kosovo was a total population of approximately 2.1 million, of which approximately 83% were ethnic Albanian, approximately 10% were ethnic Serbs, with the remaining approximately 7% being other ethnicities, namely Roma, Bosnian, Ashkali, Gorani, and Turk. Consisting primarily of rural yeoman farmers, Kosovo has developed an enclave-based society. Kosovo is self-segregated through ethnomajoritarianism, where powerful municipal governments ultimately form ethnically based enclaves (Dahlman and Williams 2010). Centuries of ethnic tensions also contributed to the concentration of minorities into ethnically pure enclaves for common defense.

While were some integrated communities in Kosovo, the ethnic groups in Kosovo were quite separate. One metric for determining the state of inter-ethnic relations in a country or region is that of exogamous marriages, or inter-ethnic marriage. In Kosovo, the rate of inter-ethnic marriage was approximately 5%, which was the lowest rate in all of Yugoslavia (Dahlman and Williams 2010).

Historical Perspective on Policing in Kosovo

The policing philosophy of the former Yugoslavia was one of a strong state-oriented police system that was seen as a vital instrument of the state to maintain control of its republics. This philosophy was pushed to extremes by the Milosevic regime, which ultimately led to the Serbian police becoming a primary agent of oppression for the ethnic Albanian majority in Kosovo (Gippert 2015). In post-conflict recovery and democratic reform, reform of organic police forces is a paramount concern. In undemocratic or post-conflict societies, police are frequently a leading mechanism of oppression. Thus, true democratic reform cannot occur without a strong reformation of organic police forces (Bayley 2006; Durch and England 2010).

In Kosovo, the Milosevic regime used the Serbian police as a primary agent of oppression, which created a deep dis-trust of all police within the ethnic Albanian population. Due to continual ethnic tension, this distrust was exacerbated exponentially if the police officer was of a different ethnicity. The post-war situation in Kosovo was made far more complex for the fact that there *were no police* to reform. In fact, there was no government to reform.

The United Nations Mission in Kosovo

The United Nations (UN) has been conducting peacekeeping missions around the world practically since its inception in 1945. The first UN peacekeeping mission was launched in Palestine in 1948. Between 1948 and 2006, the UN has been involved in 54 separate peacekeeping missions (Bayley 2006).

In the 1960s, the UN began incorporating a police component into peacekeeping missions. Reports conducted by the World Bank, the Organization for Security and Cooperation in Europe, the European Union, and the International Monetary Fund all indicated that reforming internal security was a necessary component of democratic reform of post-conflict nations. The need for police reform was particularly crucial because police forces were frequently the agent of oppression in unstable and totalitarian countries (Bayley 2006; Durch and England 2010).

On 10 June 1999, in the wake of the forced Serbian withdrawal from Kosovo, the United Nations Security Council passed Security Council Resolution 1244. As Kosovo was a province without any governmental infrastructure, the United Nations would serve as the de-facto government until such time as the status of Kosovo could be determined. This mission would be named the United Nations Mission in Kosovo (UNMIK) (de Saint-Claire 2007). A robust police component was an integral part of the UNMIK mission. The UNMIK Police were assigned the herculean task of restoring order to Kosovo, developing, recruiting, constituting, training, mentoring, and capacity building an organic police force in Kosovo from the ashes left by Serbia's withdrawal from Kosovo. The challenges were enormous. The UNMIK Mission was the most complex, ambitious, and difficult mission the UN had undertaken (Monk 2008).

The situation in 1999 was anarchical. There was no law enforcement, courts, or governmental infrastructure. In an environment completely devoid of any law enforcement presence, crime flourishes. Inter-ethnic tensions in Kosovo were at a fever pitch. After so many years of oppression under Serbian rule, Albanian guerillas lashed out at the Serbian community that remained in Kosovo out of revenge. Serbians and Roma, who were accused of collaborating with the Serbians, left Kosovo (Burema 2012). One of UNMIK's goals was to facilitate the return of displaced Serbians. Initially, UNMIK focused more on creating conditions to encourage return, rather than facilitating the actual return of Serbians who had expatriated (United Nations Security Council 1999).

While there was a real problem with inter-ethnic violence in Kosovo, most notably between Serbs and Albanians, there were many who took advantage of these tensions. In his 2008 final report to the United Nation, UNMIK Police Commissioner Richard Monk stated that much of the criminal activity in Kosovo was merely for personal gain, but created the perception of inter-ethnic hostility (Monk 2008). By 2008, there was still strong evidence of repressed anger in the population of Kosovo, which manifested itself in robberies, assaults, street fights, and inter-family violence. Such repressed and pent-up hostility creates the potential for mindless violence and destruction (Monk 2008).

While the security situation in Kosovo in 1999 was dire, there are no statistics pertaining to inter-ethnic violence and crime, as there was no governmental infrastructure. The UNMIK Police was ramped up piecemeal as officers arrived and initial struggled to restore normalcy and order. The UNMIK Police was the first UN Police mission where the United Nations Police had executive policing responsibilities and authority. In essence, the UNMIK Police were the de-facto police in Kosovo, enforcing the law, making arrests, and conducting criminal investigations (de Saint-Claire 2007).

The State of Inter-Ethnic Relations in 1999

In 1999, post conflict Kosovo was a very dangerous place for ethnic minorities, particularly ethnic Serbs. Ethnic Albanian guerillas and partisans, as well as some citizens angered by Serbia's oppression of the Kosovo Albanian community, exacted revenge against ethnic Serbs. Many ethnic Serbs fled Kosovo. Those who stayed lived in a tense and volatile time. There were many threats, arsons, and some murders of Ethnic Serbs. During this time, the Serb and Roma minorities were particularly vulnerable to threats and violence (OSCE/UNHCR 1999).

Prior to the withdrawal of the Serbian Army the Serbian population of Pristina, the capital of Kosovo, was approximately 40–45,000. After the withdrawal, there were less than 5000 Serbs left in Pristina. Immediately following the withdrawal of the Serbian Army, there were three to four reported kidnappings of ethnic Serbs *per week* in Pristina. Many Serbs who did not want to leave Kosovo, sought safety in Serbian enclaves further segregating Kosovo. In Podujevo municipality, a primarily Albanian municipality, three Serbs were murdered in the first 2 weeks following the withdrawal (Organization for Security and Cooperation in Europe and the United Nations High Commissioner for Refugees 1999).

In Obilic municipality, in the week of the 5–10 July 1999, KFOR received reports that the Serbian community was the focus of 1 murder, 81 arsons, 36 lootings of homes, 1 kidnapping, and 4 missing persons. The security situation for ethnic minorities was precarious. During the months following the withdrawal of the Serbian Army there were many other reprisal attacks, particularly against Serbs, including Roma who were suspected of collaborating with the Serbs, throughout Kosovo. Other ethnic minorities, Croats, Muslim Slavs, Turks, Goran, and Ashkali suffered scattered violence as well (Organization for Security and Cooperation in Europe and the United Nations High Commissioner for Refugees 1999).

The security situation in Kosovo represented a uniquely complex circumstance. Ethnic Serbs located in enclaves experienced extreme difficulties with freedom of movement outside of their ethnic enclave and were vulnerable to violence if they left their enclave without NATO military escort. Conversely, in the Serb majority Mitrovica region of Kosovo, ethnic Albanians found themselves trapped in enclaves with serious threats of violence and reprisal that hampered freedom of movement (Organization for Security and Cooperation in Europe and the United Nations High Commissioner for Refugees 1999). Suffice it to say, ethnic tensions in Kosovo were at a fever pitch after the Serbian withdrawal from Kosovo. The self-segregated enclave-based society of Kosovo was further polarized along ethnic lines, and no group was completely safe. Into this breach, the UNMIK Police were tasked with creating a multicultural organic police force to restore order, trust, and civil society.

The Kosovo Police Service

Along with restoring order and developing an entire governmental infrastructure, the UNMIK mission also included the construction of an organic professional police organization.

The UNMIK mission was supported by the 1244 UNSC resolution and June 1999 military technical agreement known as *Military Technical Agreement between the International Security Force ("KFOR") and the Governments of the Federal Republic of Yugoslavia and the Republic of Serbia.* NATO troops, called Kosovo Force (K-FOR) entered Kosovo with the aim to guarantee the public security in Kosovo after the war. UNMIK structured an international police force (UNMIK police) from 47 countries of the world, to provide order and public security, protection of life, preservation of property and assets of citizens, freedom of movement, free movement of people and goods, as well as to respect and protect the human rights (United Nations Security Council 1999).

Large numbers of KFOR troops and UNMIK police were not able to guarantee public security without active participation of a local policing element. Therefore, the need to establish an organic local police force immediately was pressing. Parallel to this, UNMIK in cooperation with the Organization for Security and Cooperation in Europe (OSCE) mission, in Kosovo began preparations to establish a new Police Academy for training of a new Kosovo Police.

The duty of OSCE together with UNMIK was to create a Kosovo Police Service that was fully organized and sustainable. A police service that supports and embraces all principles of democratic policing oriented to the community in a multiethnic society. All this was a challenge in itself because at the same time there were no plans and no clear procedures to follow toward the realization of this complex task. Out of necessity, the creation and development of the KPS was done on an ad hoc basis.

There were numerous problems with the genesis of the KPS including infrastructure. One major infrastructural hurdle included upgrading the former High School of Internal Affairs, now abandoned and destroyed in Vushtrri, into a modern learning center for adults that was fully equipped and ready for training the new Kosovo Police Service. Concurrent with the training of initial KPS officers, a range of programs for capacity building, in response to the needs of a new organization and evolving police, was necessary. These basic programs should be designed in accordance with the needs of culture, language and the history of Kosovo, and should be harmonized with principles of democratic policing.

One of the most important tasks during this evolutionary period was to create a sustainable police service that could return the confidence of population in the newly police service. The Serbian regime of oppressive policing had the impact of destroying the trust and confidence of the Kosovo population in the police. The KPS would have to re-forge bonds with the community, and establish trust with the ethnic minority communities.

On 6 September 1999, the Kosovo Police Service (KPS) was formed. The first *generation* of 176 Kosovo Police officers entered the KPS academy in Vushtrri on 16 October 1999. The first generation (Class) Cadets were selected from all age groups, with a satisfactory gender representation. The most important thing about the first generation of KPS cadets was that *all* ethnicities were integrated in KPS (Albanians, Serbs, Turkish, Bosnian, Montenegrin, Roma, etc.). The integration of ethnic minorities into the KPS promised a tolerant multi-ethnic climate within the institution. The KPS expanded rapidly, being comprised of 7114 police officers and 1163 civilian staff by 31 December 2007 (Monk 2008). The development of the KPS was a complex operation. Multiple layers of leadership had to be trained and mentored simultaneously in order to provide a strong command structure. From the inception of the KPS, the UNMIK Police and the KPS held executive responsibilities in Kosovo jointly. The ultimate goal was for the UNMIK Police to slowly transition operations and responsibilities to the KPS and for the UNMIK Police to ultimately assume a monitoring and mentoring role. To that end, on 15 November 2002 the Gracanica sub-station become the first KPS controlled police station, under the monitoring of the UNMIK Police.

During the period of time the Kosovo Police was under the monitoring of the UNMIK Police, the KPS' policing activities were purely reactionary. The KPS performed regular patrols and responded to crimes or any other reported cases. The KPS would respond to the scene, but the reactionary model of policing does little to prevent crime. The KPS was initially in the role of the firefighter, arriving and putting out fires. When deluged with crime and security problems, sometimes there is no choice but to be reactionary. In this case, crime prevention was focused on very little by the KPS or the UNMIK Police.

By 2008, the challenges facing the KPS were exacerbated by the fact that successfully developing and democratizing the KPS was dependent on many factors outside of the control of the KPS. Issues such as correcting internecine political divisiveness, legislation promoting inter-ethnic communities, governmental transparency, and governmental accountability were necessary, but outside of the purview and influence of the KPS. Much of these entanglements are understandable, as Kosovo had to learn how to self-govern democratically and even-handedly after so many years of repression.

Much success in developing the KPS was achieved during the UNMIK years in Kosovo (1999–2008). With assistance from the UNMIK Police, the KPS developed an executive steering board and a Directorate of Policy analysis, along with a Professional Standards Unit, all of which helped to move the KPS incrementally toward being a modern democratic professional policing agency. In an attempt to address the problem of the reactionary nature of policing, with the assistance of UNMIK, the KPS instituted a Community Policing Program. While the Community Policing Program under UNMIK was not very effective, because the policy demonstrated a lack of understanding of the complexities of inter-ethnic relations in Kosovo, the program nevertheless moved the KPS in a positive direction.

While UNMIK achieved much in Kosovo, its efforts were not without significant problems. There were failures in UNMIK to address critical national problems because of political considerations of UN contributing countries. Every country involved in UNMIK had its own political agenda, which at times interfered with UNMIK's ability to act completely in the best interests of Kosovo, rather than the interests of international stakeholders. At times, political interference impeded the progress of effective nation building, which affected the ability of Kosovo to effect change at a meta-level. However, the UNMIK Police, to some extent, insulated the KPS from such interference (Skendaj 2014).

The State of Inter-Ethnic Relations in 2008

On 17 February 2008, after 9 years of development under the control and advice of UNMIK, Kosovo declared independence from Serbia. The Kosovo Police Service was rebranded as the Kosovo Police (KP). While the international community, first through UNMIK and then through the European Union Rule of Law Mission in Kosovo (EULEX), was still assisting the KP with development and capacity building, the KP was in control of its own strategic and operational development.

During the 9 years that UNMIK was the de-facto government of Kosovo, and the KPS was growing and developing, ethnic tensions and ethnic violence were still problematic. On 17–18 March 2004, ethnic tensions erupted in the form of riots across Kosovo. The drowning of two boys near the volatile city of Mitrovica, which was blamed on ethnic Serbs, proved to be the trigger event that sparked ethnic riots throughout Kosovo. In 2 days, approximately 30 Serbian churches and monasteries, 800 houses (displacing 4000 people), and 150 vehicles were destroyed or damaged during the riots. In addition, 19 civilians were killed and more than 900 people were injured (Woehrel and Kim 2005).

The March 2004 riots represented the worst flare-up of ethnic tension since the withdrawal of the Serbian army in 1999. The United Nations estimated that tens of thousands of people participated in violent riots and attacks throughout Kosovo (Woehrel and Kim 2005). Almost 5 years after the Serbian withdrawal, ethnic tensions were still smoldering, and subject to sudden and violent flare-ups.

An OSCE report into the prosecution of participants in the 2004 riots criticized the KPS for dragging their feet during the investigation of suspects arrested during the riots, KPS officers failing to show up in court to testify, and a failure of having department policies mandating the KPS officers cooperate and testify in criminal proceedings (OSCE 2008a). It would seem that some members of the KPS were loath to participate in the prosecution of ethnic Albanians, for acts of violence against ethnic Serbs. By 2004, the KPS was still struggling with the personal ethnic perspectives of its officers. There were difficulties as well with prosecutors and judges charging suspects with lower charges or imposing lower than minimum sentences. The OSCE determined that in response to the 2004 riots, the entire justice system in Kosovo failed to provide a strong and clear message that ethnic violence is not acceptable in Kosovo (OSCE 2008b). Clearly, by the time the Kosovo Police took full control of their own future, there was still much work to do.

In his February 2008 final report to the United Nations, UNMIK Police Commissioner Richard Monk provided an excellent analysis of the state of the Kosovo Police at the time Kosovo declared independence. Commissioner Monk spoke at length about the need for strategic vision within the KPS:

> But it is the vision for policing that determines the strategy and all other constructs that will be required to support it. Whilst structural, technical and legislative matters will require modification; it is deciding the culture of the organization and the institutions to support it that will influence its overall standing in society (Monk 2008, p. 7).

Perhaps the *guidance* of international organizations, comprised of people from many different nations, each with its own strategic vision, hampered the KPS from establishing its own strategic vision. In many ways, international assistance can only go so far. At some point, the KPS had to find *its own identity*, not an identity assigned by the international community. Commissioner Monk made the salient point that reformation of the KPS requires an intimate knowledge of the policing requirements, culture, and shifting demographics of Kosovo (Monk 2008). Such institutional and cultural knowledge must come from within the organization, not from without.

Much of the recommendations made by Commissioner Monk indicated the need for the Kosovo Police to chart its own course. As these recommendations came at the same time as Kosovo declared independence, it seems that the time was ripe for the Kosovo Police to begin to develop strategic vision, policies and procedures, accountability, and community outreach strategies on its own. It would seem that the Kosovo Police was outgrowing the role of mentee and was ready to take control of its own destiny.

One key goal for the Kosovo Police was to establish the credibility of the Kosovo Police with the community as an institution. The people of Kosovo seemed to be more responsive to leaders and people than to *institutions*. One critical goal of the Kosovo Police, particularly in dealing with ethnic minorities, was to establish the Kosovo Police as a trusted and professional *institution* (Monk 2008). When contemplating the herculean task of creating a homogenous multiethnic society, ethnic minorities *must* trust the institutions of justice to provide fair treatment to all, regardless of ethnicity. Old hatred and ethnic tensions die hard, the creation of trust in the Kosovo Police, as an institution was perhaps the key to improving the security situation of ethnic minorities in Kosovo.

The most troublesome area for the Kosovo Police was the Mitrovica Region of Kosovo. Mitrovica is the northernmost region of Kosovo, which borders Serbia. North Mitrovica is a mirror image of the rest of Kosovo in that ethnic Serbs are the majority in the North Mitrovica, with enclaves of ethnic Albanians. Mitrovica has continuously been the flashpoint of trouble in post-conflict Kosovo.

The government Serbia consistently and vehemently opposed autonomy or independence for Kosovo. Serbia created parallel governmental structures in Mitrovica. Since the withdrawal of the Serbian Army from Kosovo in 1999, Mitrovica has always been a tense and unstable region. In February 2008, the political and security situation Mitrovica deteriorated after the burning of the two border crossing points (between Kosovo and Serbia proper) by Serbian extremists groups. On March 14, 2008, the Serbian extremists also attacked and occupied the Kosovo District Court in North Mitrovica. On March 17, 2008, an ill-fated attempt by the UNMIK Police to retake the District Court Building in North Mitrovica resulted in one UNMIK Police officer dead and more than 150 people injured (BBC News 2008).

The nonfunctioning of the District Court in North, and the resistance of ethnic Serbs in the Mitrovica region to any form of Kosovo government, particularly the Kosovo Police, was another long-term challenge that perpetuated the instability of the Mitrovica Region. The Kosovo Police, working in cooperation with the UNMIK Police, found it very difficult to maintain the rule of law, prevent and fight all types of crime, and bring the potential perpetrators of criminal acts to justice. With the assistance of the UNMIK Police and KFOR, the Kosovo Police was able to re-establish public order in North Mitrovica. However, full enforcement of the rule of law proved exceedingly difficult. Policing and community outreach in the Mitrovica Region would prove to be the most daunting challenge in establishing rule of law in Kosovo.

The Kosovo Police 2008–2017

The current Kosovo Police vision is focused towards ensuring and providing security, law enforcement, and prevention of crime, to promote a safer and more peaceful environment for all of Kosovo. The Kosovo Police strategic vision aims to further develop and enhance *community oriented policing* as a primary component of the policing philosophy, already practiced and implemented in Kosovo. To implement this strategic vision, the Kosovo Police has set four main strategic objectives, which include strengthening and advancing community partnerships, increasing the level of public trust and satisfaction with the police, cooperating, coordinating, and integrating community policing activities with other strategies, as well as advancing internal reforms and mechanisms to monitor the implementation of the strategy (Kosovo Police 2017).

In charting its own course, it was critical that the Kosovo Police approach the enforcement of the law in accordance with strategies that reflect the values of the Kosovo community… the *entire* Kosovo community (Kosovo Police 2017). To this end, the strategic documents published by the Kosovo Police are remarkable in that they do not mention ethnic minorities specifically. According to Kosovo Police Director General Shpend Maxhuni, the decision not to mention ethnic minorities specifically in the Kosovo Police's strategic documents was intentional. To specifically mention ethnic minorities, and spell out their rights and treatment, would only serve to reinforce the lines that separate Kosovo's ethnic communities. Director General Maxhuni stated that the strategic plans for the Kosovo police were developed to be applicable to the *entire* Kosovo community, which includes all ethnic minorities (personal communication, May 30, 2017).

Under UNMIK, the Kosovo Police had followed a *reactive* approach to law enforcement. The only attempts at community policing were very limited, under-staffed, and lacked a firm grasp of the particular demography and nature of Kosovo society. It is difficult for the members of a multi-national support agency, such as UNMIK or the OSCE, to understand the complexities and nuances of the culture and inter-ethnic dynamics of Kosovo. Such understanding can only come from within. When the transition of competences from the UNMIK Police to the Kosovo Police occurred, the concept of policing implemented thus far, had not been suc-cessful. The outcome of this failure is that the Kosovo Police changed its concept of policing and its strategic vision, which means that the Kosovo Police considers that every member of the Kosovo Police must have the philosophy of, and function as, community police (Kosovo Police 2017).

Post-independence, one of the core strategies the Kosovo Police implemented was a robust community-policing program that adhered to the concept that "…the police are the people and the people are the police…" (Kosovo Police 2017, p. 3). After the declaration of independence by Kosovo, a brochure was drafted and printed, promoting the awareness of the entire Kosovo community, regarding the prevention and fighting of interethnic crime. These brochures and leaflets were printed in Albanian, Serbian, Turkish, and English, and were then distributed throughout all regions of Kosovo.

In conducting proactive police activities, the Kosovo Police develops, super-vises, and implements preventive projects and programs using a proactive community-policing model for solving the problems of communities. These proac-tive community-policing programs are particularly geared toward effective policing of the minorities living in Kosovo. These programs are implemented in coordination with the community to strengthen confidence in between the population and the police. In this regard, the Kosovo Police cooperates with governmental and non-governmental institutions and community security forums, to address important social problems by participating in working groups with the community in identify-ing the concerns and concerns of the minority community.

The Kosovo Police pays particular attention to potential interethnic incidents. Police officers throughout the Kosovo Police have been specially trained to deal with interethnic cases in accordance with applicable law. According to the Kosovo Criminal Code, the Court determines whether it was an ethnic motive or another motive (Kosovo Parlaiment 2012).

In addition, with the support of the OSCE Mission in Kosovo, training against hate crime was organized for police officers; not only in the community police units, but also in the operations as well as in the criminal investigation departments. Furthering the Kosovo Police commitment to address hate crime, which in Kosovo is frequently ethnically based, the Kosovo Police has also drafted a Standard Operating Procedure manual, which effectively outlines policies and procedures for the investigation of potentially interethnic cases and hate crime cases. In addition, to enhance community awareness of hate crimes further, and the Kosovo Police's commitment to addressing interethnic and hate crimes, leaflets have been printed out in almost every language in Kosovo and have been distributed by Community Policing units throughout Kosovo.

Furthermore, police officers of all ethnicities have received extensive training in interethnic communication in order to create cooperative relationships within mixed communities. This training assists Kosovo Police officers in communicating effectively with ethnic minorities. The ability to create effective partnerships with activists of different ethnicities greatly assists the Kosovo Police in creating community partnerships for identifying problems specific to particular communities and community-level problem solving.

Development of police-minority community partnerships is a critical element in the strategic planning of the Kosovo Police. Improving the trust and confidence of minority communities in the Kosovo Police is critical to the effective policing of ethnic minority communities. An excellent example of such partnerships is a current outreach program where the Kosovo Police coordinates with, and accepts the input of, minority community leaders when selecting police commanders who will serve in minority enclaves. Giving the minority enclave community leaders the opportunity to voice their concerns and be engaged in the selection of police leaders serving the enclave makes the leaders of the minority enclave stakeholders in the success of the Kosovo Police (S. Maxhuni, personal communication, May 30, 2017). Involving the minority communities in the consideration and selection of police commanders responsible for policing the minority community is a particularly insightful way of improving the minority community's trust and confidence in the police.

Post-independence, the Kosovo Police made changes to its organizational structure designed to align the command structure of the Kosovo Police with the evolving strategic vision. One example would be the creation of the Directorate of Community Policing and Crime Prevention. At the central command level of organization, the Community Policing Directorate and Crime Prevention, serves to draft the strategic policies, while at local level these strategic policies are translated into practical policy and application to move the strategic vision forward.

The year 2008 was extremely challenging, not only for the Kosovo Police, but also for the entire justice system in settlements and enclaves inhabited by mixed ethnic minorities, particularly in the northern part of Kosovo. The security problem in the Mitrovica Region of Kosovo, between the Serb community and the Albanian community, has exacerbated interethnic tensions, especially in those areas where the ethnic Serb community is the majority. The lack of functioning of the justice system (prosecution and judiciary) in North Mitrovica influenced the growth of all types of crimes. The Albanian population who lived in North Mitrovica began to feel insecure because of an increase of the interethnic incidents. The community, both Serbian and Albanian, in this part of Kosovo lost trust in the Kosovo Police due to the increase in interethnic incidents and violence.

Having seen that the situation had begun to be worsen, and as inter-ethnic incidents started to increase, in January 2009 the Kosovo Police established a community police unit in North Mitrovica. This unit's goal was to work more proactively and to be close to the community. This Community Policing Unit was created in the *Little Bosnia* community in North Mitrovica, where ethnic Serbians, ethnic

Bosnians, and ethnic Albanians are living together in an integrated community. Community policing patrols included mixed ethnicity teams comprised of Albanian, Serbian, and Bosnian Kosovo Police officers. These teams were very well received by the community due to the language abilities of mixed teams and trust. By demonstrating unity and cooperation within its ranks, the Kosovo Police was quite literally *setting the example* for community. This unit originally had 17 members containing Albanian, Serbian, and Bosnian Croats. This community policing unit's aim was to be as close as possible to communities in mixed areas, build trust among themselves (which will translate to trust in the community), to work with people who had an influence on the local population, and to gather information about incidents that have occurred with ethnic motives.

The Kosovo Police continued with community outreach programs, such as further support of local security committees and municipal security councils in the community. The organizations, in cooperation with the Kosovo Police efficiently identify and then address issues related to personal security, property rights, and the prevention and combating of all types of crime. The Kosovo Police has made several efforts to improve community security and has continued to strengthened existing safety mechanisms. Within each Kosovo Police Station, there exists a Community Unit and a Community Officer, which operates in close contact with the local population, and is appointed for each village within Kosovo.

The trust of the populace towards the Kosovo police began to return. The continuation of community outreach programs and communication was organized either through organized meetings individually or the organization of round table discussions. The population began to exchange information with police officers of the community police unit. The importance of direct contact with the community, in promoting trust and respect, cannot be overstated. This is particularly true in the case of Kosovo, where centuries of hatred and mistrust must first be overcome, before any real trust can be developed.

Another key program, that is critical in moving the Kosovo Police strategy forward, is the establishment of Local Public Safety Councils (LPSCs) in almost all municipalities throughout Kosovo. The purpose of the Local Public Safety Councils is to address the security needs of local communities and give them a voice in the law enforcement priorities in their communities. The LPSCs work closely with the local Kosovo Police Station Commander and the Kosovo Police officers assigned to the local Kosovo Police Substation.

The LPSCs have helped the Kosovo Police considerably, in particularly in ethnically mixed areas. One of the most important aspects of the LPSC program, in promoting the establishment of trust in the police, was that the representatives of population (the most influential citizens in their respective community) worked within their own neighborhoods in cooperation with and supported by community police officers. With the initiative of Kosovo Police and financial assistance from international and local organizations, there were some successful projects of the LPSC, such as playgrounds, water system renovation, etc., in mixed communities.

In ensuring effective partnerships at all levels of government, the Kosovo Police also supported the creation of Municipal Community Safety Councils (MCSC).

MCSCs essentially follow the same conceptual strategy as the LPSC, but at the municipal level. MCSCs work in cooperation with the Kosovo Police to address issues at the municipal level, where LPSCs address issues at the local community level. MCSCs focus on identifying issues of safety and security, improving community awareness as to the nature of crime, disorder, and violent behavior, and identifying concerns related to public safety and recommended action plans. MCSCs address these concerns in cooperation with municipal authorities, local communities, and the Kosovo Police.

The Kosovo Police has expanded their concept of community policing and community engagement by implementing safety forums that visited schools in mixed communities. Some of these projects include *Better Teaching in the Schools,* to Prevent Criminal Incidents and Violence near troubled schools. Kosovo Police Community Policing Officers visit schools daily, providing classroom lectures on drugs and narcotics in schools in Kosovo with reported usage of illegal drugs. Creating lasting connections and trust with *all* of the Kosovo community involved overcoming historical distrust and enmity. School outreach is an important aspect of this strategy. Allowing young Kosovars to interact with the police helps to shape the perceptions of the next generations, and promotes the concept of Kosovar national unity and community.

In addition, with the support of the OSCE Mission in Kosovo, training against hate crime was organized for police officers, not only in the community police units, but also in the operations department, as well as in the crime department. In addition, in this regard, Kosovo Police has drafted the SOP for investigation with priority of the potential interethnic cases and hate crime cases in the mixed zones. Leaflets have been printed out in almost all languages in Kosovo and have been distributed throughout Kosovo by Community policing units. Further, police officers of all ethnicities have been trained in the area of interethnic communication and creating partnerships with activists of different ethnicities for problem identification, partnership with the local police, and problem solving.

The State of Interethnic Relations and the Kosovo Police 2017

One important goal for the Kosovo Police has been the recruitment of ethnic minorities, with the goal of achieving ethnic minority representation within the Kosovo Police that is concurrent with ethnic minority concentrations within Kosovo society. In 2015, the Kosovo Police was comprised of 7635 police officers. Table 13.1 compares the 2015 Kosovo Police ethnic minority demographic as compared to the 2011 Kosovo Census.

The Kosovo Police's efforts at creating a police force that accurately reflects the community have been extremely successful. The representation of ethnic Serbians exceeds their demographic representation more than eight fold. Bosnian representation also exceeds community demographics. While there is still work to be done, with Kosovo's smaller minority groups, for a nation created in the wake of ubiquitous

Table 13.1 *Comparison of Kosovo Police and Kosovo national demographics* (Kosovo Agency of Statistics 2011; OSCE 2015)

	Number of officers	Percentage of officers	Demographic representation (2011 Census)
Albanian	6346	83.12%	92.93%
Serbian	967	12.67%	1.47%
Bosniak	181	2.37%	1.58%
Kosovo Turk	65	0.85%	1.08%
Goarni	37	0.48%	0.59%
Ashkali	17	0.22%	0.89%
Roma	13	0.17%	0.51%
Kosovo Egyptian	9	0.12%	0.66%
Total KP officers	7635		

ethnic tension, the success of the Kosovo Police's efforts to reflect Kosovo society is remarkable.

While the Kosovo Police has a coherent strategy for addressing ethnic minority communities, the police do not operate in a vacuum. There are many elements of government and society in Kosovo beyond the reach of the Kosovo Police's ability to effect change. Other governmental departments, the legislature, educational departments, and most notably the press and media can have a significant impact in shaping attitudes toward ethnic minorities in Kosovo (Organization for Security and Cooperation in Europe 2015). The resistance of the ethnic Serbian population of North Mitrovica to accept Kosovo governmental regulation, and the continued attempts at creating parallel institutions rooted in Serbia, makes the Mitrovica region particularly problematic and slow to improve. Nevertheless, there have been improvements in the policing and security situation in Mitrovica, albeit very slowly.

Freedom of movement for ethnic minorities has improved in Kosovo since independence; however, there is still work to be done. While incidents of interethnic violence have slowly declined over time, the area of North Mitrovica continues to be the most difficult area for the Kosovo Police. Fig. 13.1 shows the cumulative number to incidents with possible interethnic motives throughout 2009–2012. There were 76 such incidents reported in the Mitrovica region during the reporting period, indicating that Mitrovica is still, by far, the most troubled region in Kosovo. It is also, interesting to note that in the specified 3 year period, there were only 11 such incidents *in all other regions combined* (Organization for Security and Cooperation in Europe 2015). With the exception of Mitrovica, it would be a safe assessment that the Kosovo Police has done an excellent job in reducing interethnic violence.

Perhaps the most interesting and telling assessment of the state of the Kosovo Police pertains to comes from an assessment of ethical institutions in Kosovo. In troubled and post-conflict countries, the police and customs services tend to be the most corrupt of government department. This is particularly the case for police, since police are frequently the agent of oppression (Bayley 2006; Durch and

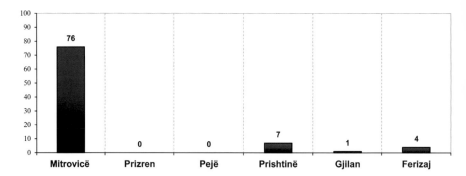

Fig. 13.1 Reported crimes with interethnic component 2009–2012, Kosovo police directorate of information 2012

England 2010). However, in Kosovo the Kosovo Police and the Kosovo Customs service are assessed as being the *least corrupt* departments in the Kosovo government (Skendaj 2014). The Kosovo Police has demonstrated considerable growth and evolution in the 18 years it has been in existence. While there is still work to be done, much has already been accomplished.

In 2017, the Kosovo Police is developing a system-wide commitment to the protection of people who may be subject to threats or acts of discrimination, hostility, or violence because of their national, ethnic, cultural, linguistic, or religious identity. Such a commitment to equal treatment under the law is paramount in developing a trusting and productive relationship with the community. In further evolution of the community policing strategy of the Kosovo Police, an officer is assigned to each sector with the explicit responsibility of maintaining contacts with the community. This permanent community contact officer knows the area, knows the community, knows the unique problems of the community, and works to address those problems.

This new strategy is particularly effective and successful in areas of mixed of minority inhabitants. Through this strategy, the Kosovo Police maintains close ties to the community, and effectively addresses their concerns. This strategy has proven to increase communities trust towards the Kosovo Police.

The Kosovo Police also endeavors to ensure that all citizens, including ethnic minorities, understand the role of the police in promoting good inter-ethnic relations. The daily engagement of the Kosovo Police, in areas inhabited by ethnic minorities, has proven the Kosovo Police's interest to providing safe communities for all, which has increased the trust of ethnic minorities towards the Kosovo Police. Having regular police patrolling, mixed units with minority officers from the community, and those who fluently speak the language, develops good and faithful relationship between the officers and the community. Citizens are increasingly more likely to approach the officers with their problems and report crimes. This burgeoning trust between the Kosovo Police and ethnic minority communities is strengthened through quick and professional police actions toward solving these problems and crimes.

Kosovo Police cooperates and is a stakeholder in every initiative of other civilian authorities and groups to promote safety and security to the community, particularly in minority areas. In the majority of cases, the Kosovo Police proposes such initiatives. It is normal that the Kosovo Police cannot solve every problem alone in the community by itself. It is essential that other specialized civilian authorities get actively involved with Kosovo Police efforts. The Kosovo Police and civilian authorities collaborate to address safety and security issues always, in close cooperation with the community.

The issues of protection of and improving the circumstances of ethnic minorities in the Republic of Kosovo are codified in Kosovo law. Besides The Kosovo Constitution, several laws directly deal with the protection of the rights of ethnic minorities in Kosovo. For example, the law on the *Protection and Promotion of the Rights of Communities and their Members in Kosovo*, the law on the Use of Languages, the Law on the Local Self- Government, the Law on Police, etc. The Kosovo Police is committed to implementing and enforcing these laws professionally and equally. In order to enforce such laws effectively, the Kosovo Police has complied comprehensive regulations, standard operating procedures, and best practices.

The Way Forward

This section was written based on interviews with Director General Shpend Maxhuni of the Kosovo Police. Director General Maxhuni was interviewed in September of 2017 and provided the synopsis of the strategic goals of the Kosovo Police moving forward. While considerable progress has been made since 2008, there is still much work to do. Director General Maxhuni is proud of the accomplishments of the Kosovo Police heretofore, and is confident that the future will bring continuing progress in the effective policing of ethnic minority communities, and the entire community that is the people of Kosovo.

Since independence, the Kosovo Police has seen many positive results in the strategic goal of providing safety and security throughout the country. The Kosovo Police have managed to build community trust slowly and has encouraged ethnic minorities to be properly represented in the ranks of the Kosovo Police. Many cases of suspected interethnic crime reported by minority communities are professionally investigated as speedily as possible. The Kosovo Police has continuously worked to develop good relationships with all communities throughout the country, and continues to maintain that relationship. The assessment of the Kosovo Police as being one of the most trusted institutions in Kosovo is supported by many local and international reports. Being one of the most trusted institutions in Kosovo speaks volumes to the progress made in providing a professional impartial police force to the people of Kosovo.

Kosovo Police will continue to stress the importance of effectively policing of minority communities. Establishing productive and cooperative relationships with minority communities will be maintained and advanced in every way possible. Current initiatives will be continues and new methods of improvement of relations with minority communities will continue to be sought. The Kosovo Police will continue to engage actively in problem solving, crime prevention, and response to criminal acts. The goals of crime prevention cannot inhibit the Kosovo Police's ability to respond to crimes, investigate crimes, and submit criminals to the justice system for persecution. The Kosovo Police will continue to seek initiatives designed to improve safety and security with all security stakeholders, civil and institutional, in order to keep the Republic of Kosovo a safe and secure place to move and live for every citizen.

The Kosovo Police's commitment to professional growth and development, along with continued improvements in building decision-making policies in the security sector, proving to be a crucial factor not only for the security of the country, but it is increasingly playing an active role in the region and beyond. As the Kosovo Police continues development into a professional police force, cooperation with regional police forces will continue to expand. The rapid global development in crime, primarily through technology, communication, and other innovations, lead to perpetrators using increasingly more sophisticated methods. The globalization of crime affects every police organization with growing challenges. In order to become a regional and world partner in fighting international crime, the Kosovo Police must invest in education, ongoing training, and investments in infrastructure and technology.

The Kosovo Police has thus far maintained the positive trajectory of its development and is continually working hard to maintain a quiet and safe environment. The ultimate goal of the Kosovo Police is for citizens of the country to be able to enjoy a peaceful life, and conduct their daily activities in all areas of life without concern for their personal safety or the safety of their property. The Kosovo Police plans to continue to promote its overarching philosophy that the …the police are the people and the people are the police.

Kosovo police, in accordance with the *Strategic Development Plan 2016–2020*, and other national strategic plans, is currently drafting the annual report for 2017. It is anticipated that in addition to daily accomplishments, some of the critical strategic priorities and objectives set forth in the *Strategic Development Plan* will be achieved in 2017. The process of strategic planning, supplemented with annual reports, has been instrumental in providing structure and clear articulation to the guiding strategies on the Kosovo Police.

The objectives the Kosovo Police has set for the next annual period, include providing ever-improving security to the population, and strengthening cooperation with citizens. The prevention and combating of organized crime and corruption, terrorism, radicalism and violent extremism are important strategic goals that will improve the quality of life not only for the people of Kosovo, but for the region as well. Investigation of serious crimes, control and supervision of the state border, the advancement of human resources management, and the standardization of physical and technical infrastructure and information technology must continue to develop.

   The tasks and challenges still facing the Kosovo Police, have not taken the Kosovo Police away from the guiding principles and values of the Kosovo Police. The realization of the set objectives established by the strategic planning that guides the Kosovo Police shall be based on the strategy of the Kosovo Police being a credible and professional police organization. The Kosovo Police is committed to ever-increasing quality of service, continued commitment to the improvement of the performance of police officers, and the transparency of the Kosovo Police, while maintaining the highest regard for human and democratic values. The continuing challenges makes every officer in the Kosovo Police work harder and continue to be committed to creating a much safer environment for all citizens. These goals, which challenging, can be accomplished through professionalism, equal treatment of citizens, respect of human rights, impartiality, integrity, transparency, and legitimacy.

A Portion of the Information in this Chapter is a Result of the Authors' Personal Experiences

Dr. Michael R. Sanchez served as the Director of Personnel and Administration for the United Nations Mission in Kosovo (UNMIK) International Police from 2005 through 2008. In this position, Dr. Sanchez was a member of the UNMIK Police Commissioner's Senior Staff. Dr. Sanchez also served as a Regional Commander for the UN Police in Haiti from 2009–2010.

   Colonel Fahredin Verbovci has served in the Kosovo Police since January 8, 2001. Colonel Verbovci currently serves in the position of Project Manager with the European Union with the Kosovo Police. Colonel Verbovci earned a Master's Degree in Economics Sciences in Entrepreneurship and Local development, State University of Pristina 2010, Master Class on Law, Politics and Terrorism, Inter-university center Dubrovnik, Croatia 2017.

References

Baldwin, C. (2006). *Minority rights in Kosovo under international rule*. London: Minority Rights Group International.

Bayley, D. (2006). *Changing of the guard: Developing democratic police abroad*. New York: Oxford University Press.

Božić, G. (2010). The ethnic division of education and the relations among non-serb minorities in Kosovo. *Canadian Slavonic Papers, 52*(3–4), 273–298.

Brunborg, H. (2002). *Report on the size and ethnic composition of the population of Kosovo*. The Hague: ICTY.

Burema, L. (2012). Reconciliation in Kosovo: A few steps taken, a long road ahead. *Journal on Ethnopolitics and Minority Issues in Europe, 11*(4), 7–27.

Central Intelligence Agency. (2017). *The world fact book: Kosovo*. Retrieved from Central Intelligence Agency: https://www.cia.gov/library/publications/the-world-factbook/geos/kv.html.

234 M. R. Sanchez and F. Verbovci

Dahlman, C., & Williams, T. (2010). Ethnic enclavisation and state formation in Kosovo. *Geopolitics, 15*, 406–430. https://doi.org/10.1080/14650040903500890.

de Saint-Claire, S. (2007). *The significance, role and impact of UN Police in peace operation: Regarding transnational crime, peacebuilding and normalization.* The Saint-Claire Group.

Durch, W., & England, M. (2010). *Enhancing United Nations capacity to support post-conflict policing and rule of law (revised).* Washington, DC: The Stimson Center.

Ferreira, M. (2003). *Following the returns process of serb minorities to Kosovo: A new beginning.* State University of New York Empire State College.

Gippert, B. (2015). Exploring local compliance with peacebuilding reforms: Legitimacy, coercion and reward-seeking in police reform in Kosovo. *International Peacekeeping, 23*(1), 52–78.

Jenne, E. (2010). Barriers to reintegration after ethnic civil wars: Lessons from minority returns and resitution in the balkans. *Civil Wars, 12*(4), 370–394. https://doi.org/10.1080/13698249.2010.534622.

Judah, T. (2000). *Kosovo: War and revenge.* New Haven: Yale University Press.

Kosovo Agency of Statistics. (2011). *Kosovo population and housing census 2011, final results.* Pristina: Kosovo Agency of Statistics.

Kosovo Police. (2017). *Strategy and action plan 2017–2021.* Pristina: Republic of Kosovo.

Mazowiecki, T. (1993). *Situation of human rights in the territory of the former Yugoslavia.* New York: United Nations.

Monk, R. (2008). *End of mission report of the seventh police commissioner of the United Nations international police in Kosovo.* Pristina: This is an unpublished report and was obtained from the author.

BBC News. (2008, March 18). UN Officer dies after Kosovo riot. *BBC News.*

Organization for Security and Cooperation in Europe. (2015). *Community rights assessment report* (4th ed.). Pristina: Organization for Security and Cooperation in Europe.

Organization for Security and Cooperation in Europe and the United Nations High Commissioner for Refugees. (1999). *Preliminary assessment of the situation of ethnic minorities in Kosovo.* Vienna: Organization for Security and Cooperation in Europe.

Organization for Security and Co-operation in Europe Mission in Kosovo. (2008a). *Follow up of march 2004 riots cases before the Kosovo criminal justice system.* Pristina: Organization for Security and Co-operation in Europe Mission in Kosovo.

Organization for Security and Co-operation in Europe Mission in Kosovo. (2008b). *Human rights, ethnic relations and democracy in Kosovo.* Pristina: Organization for Security and Co-operation in Europe Mission in Kosovo.

Kosovo Parlaiment. (2012). *Criminal procdure code.* Pristina: Republic of Kosovo.

Republic of Serbia. (1990, July). *Official gazette of the republic of Serbia number 40/90.* Belgrade: Republic of Serbia.

Sanchez, M. (2014). Coordinating police responses to critical events in United Nations mission areas. In J. Albrecht, M. Dow, D. Plecas, & D. Das (Eds.), *Policing major events* (pp. 152–177). Boca Raton: CRC Press.

Schutte, S., & Weidmann, N. (2011). Diffusion patterns of violence in civil wars. *Political Geography, 30*(3), 143–152.

Skendaj, E. (2014). *Creating Kosovo: International oversight and the making of ethical institutions.* Ithaca: Corness University Press.

Testimony of Fredrick Abrahams. (2002).

United Nations Security Council. (1999). *Report of the security council mission on the implementation of security council resolution 1244.* New York: United Nations.

Woehrel, S. (2010). *Kosovo: Current issues and U.S. policy.* Washington, DC: Congressional Research Service.

Woehrel, S., & Kim, J. (2005). *Kosovo and U.S. policy.* Washington, DC: Congressional Research Service.

Woodward, S. (1995). *Balkan tragedy: Chaos and dissolution after the cold war.* Washington, DC: Brookings Institution.

Youngblood-Coleman, D. (2016). *Kosovo review 2016.* Houston: Country Review.

Chapter 14
New Zealand Police Cultural Liaison Officers: Their Role in Crime Prevention and Community Policing

Garth den Heyer

Introduction

Relationships between the police, and indigenous and ethnic minorities have a long history of being tense, often involving violent encounters and accusations of police violence, bias or victimization (Pearson et al. 1989). The relationship between the New Zealand Police and the country's ethnic minorities, especially Maori, is no exception (Hill 1989; Newbold 2000).

The implementation of community policing through the establishment and development of community relationships and partnerships and the criminality of ethnic minorities are a topic of discussion and concern around the world. Of particular concern, is the countering of terrorism and the investigation of sexual crimes and domestic violence (Collins 2005; Goodman and Ruggiero 2008, Hunter and Dantzker 2005; Rasche 1988), and the maintenance of policing legitimacy and policing by consent in minority and ethnic communities. Police legitimacy and community relationships have become even more important as a result of the tragedies experienced in Ferguson, Missouri and New York in 2014. However, although research has been undertaken in the United Kingdom that examined the role of Police Community Support Officers, there has been no research that examined Police Cultural Liaison Officers that work specifically with minority and ethnic communities.

Police Community Support Officers (PSCOs) were introduced in England and Wales to increase visible police patrols (Loveday and Smith 2015) and to reposition community safety as a government priority (Brown 2017). According to Johnston (2005) however, the use of PSCOs by the police was to also 'extend' the police family and to increase the diversity of police employees. PSCO's were identified as having a vital role in neighbourhood policing, building social capital and, as a result,

G. den Heyer (✉)
School of Criminology and Criminal Justice, Arizona State University, Tempe, AZ, USA

© Springer Nature Switzerland AG 2019
J. F. Albrecht et al. (eds.), *Policing and Minority Communities*,
https://doi.org/10.1007/978-3-030-19182-5_14

police legitimacy in high-crime areas (O'Neill 2014a). The establishment of PSCOs has led to the police being more 'outward-focused', open to collaboration and a change in organizational culture (O'Neill 2014b).

An alternative to PSCOs, is one approach adopted in the mid-1990s by the New Zealand Police. As a part of their community policing model, the New Zealand Police established a specialist unit of indigenous and ethnic officers to assist with building relationships with the indigenous and ethnic communities. Since its inception, this unit has increased in size and has changed its emphasis from focusing solely on New Zealand's indigenous population, Maori, to also establishing relationships with other ethnic and religious minority communities from the South Pacific, South East Asia, China and India.

Ethnic Liaison Officers are a part of the Police Maori, Pacific and Ethnic Services, which has staff in each police district,[1] but is managed and coordinated from New Zealand Police National Headquarters. The role of this unit, the advice it gives, and the performance of its Liaison Officers has not been evaluated or examined. This article examines the role of Maori, Pacific and Ethnic Services Liaison Officers, the reasons why these officers choose to enter this specialized area of policing and their understanding of their role. In particular, the research seeks to answer the following three questions:

- What is the role of New Zealand Police Maori, Pacific and Ethnic Liaison Officers?
- How do New Zealand Police Maori, Pacific and Ethnic Liaison Officers contribute to developing relationships with the community?
- How do New Zealand Police Maori, Pacific and Ethnic Liaison Officers perceive that they contribute to the New Zealand Police Prevention First Operating Strategy goals of reducing the level of reported crime and to reducing the number of cases referred to the justice pipeline.

The article discusses these three areas primarily within the context of Maori, with minor reference to other ethnic minorities. This approach has been adopted because of the unique position that Maori hold in New Zealand, the relationship of the New Zealand Police with Maori and the development by the police of The Turning of the Tide, a specific strategy for Maori, which is more mature in comparison to other strategies that relate to ethnic minorities.

The article begins by describing criminal offending by Maori and then discusses the strategic response of the New Zealand Police to this major social issue. The main strategies used as a response by the police are examined, and the findings of a survey of Maori, Pacific and Ethnic Service officers, which was conducted in early 2016, are presented and discussed.

---

[1] The New Zealand Police are a national police and are structured into 12 geographical districts.

The Issue of Maori Offending/Crime in New Zealand

According to O'Reilly (2014), the policing of Maori accounts for a large amount of police time. This is because Maori are at a greater risk of involvement in violent behaviors, are more likely to be victims of crime, and experience repeat victimization (particularly for domestic or family violence and child abuse) (Fergusson 2003; Statistics New Zealand 2010).

While Maori make up only 14.9% of the total population of New Zealand, they comprise of 45% of police arrests, 38% of court convictions and over 50% of sentenced prison inmates (New Zealand Police 2016; Statistics New Zealand 2010, 2013). Speirs' (2002), research revealed that Maori are significantly more likely to be re-convicted and re-imprisoned[2] than non-Maori.

The over-representation of Maori in the criminal justice system can clearly be seen in Fig. 14.1. The figure shows Maori as a proportion of the total population and the proportion of Maori in progressive stages of the criminal justice system: apprehension, convictions and imprisonments. Maori, as a proportion of the total population and in the criminal justice system, is compared with that of New Zealand European (who, as a group commit a similar numbers of offences), who are also in the criminal justice system. Maori are disproportionally represented across all stages of the criminal justice system, and particularly in the case of imprisonment (Department of Corrections 2008). One in every 47 Maori males, aged between 15 and 40, is currently in prison (among Maori prisoners, 80% were first imprisoned at age 24, and 57% were imprisoned before the age of 19 years). According to the Ministry of Justice, these figures are exacerbated when they are adjusted for age. The age-adjusted imprisonment rate for Maori men is approximately seven times that of New Zealand European men, and for Maori women, it is approximately nine times the rate (Ministry of Justice 2009).

The high rate of Maori offending is also prevalent in youth apprehensions. Nearly two-thirds (63%) of arrests of people under 18 years are Maori (O'Reilly 2014). One reason for the high percentage rate of Maori youth apprehensions, according to O'Reilly (2014), is the high rate of repeat apprehensions among Maori youth. A further reason is that Maori have a youthful population, with a median age of 23.9 years (Statistics New Zealand 2013).

In recent years, Maori and the New Zealand Government have expressed concerns at the high rate of Maori offending and as a consequence, entering the criminal justice system. According to one researcher, one of the reasons for the high number of Maori entering the criminal justice system is institutional bias (Morrison 2009). According to Morrison (2009), this bias can take the form of direct discrimination and/or indirect discrimination, for example, through policies which appear

---

[2] Over three-quarters (78%) of Maori are reconvicted within 2 years of their release from prison, a rate around 10% points higher than that for New Zealand European (68%) or Pacific Peoples inmates (66%). At 2 years from release, the reimprisonment rate for Maori is 43%, around 10% higher than New Zealand European (31%) or Pacific Peoples inmates (32%) (Speirs 2002; Nadesu 2009).

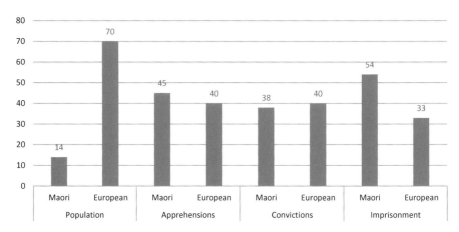

Fig. 14.1 A Comparison between the percentage of Maori with European and different stages of the criminal justice system. (Source: Statistics New Zealand 2013)

neutral but actually create a non-intended bias, such as not granting bail to people who are unemployed.

The possibility of institutional bias within the criminal justice sector is compounded by other social ills experienced by the majority of Maori. Researchers have, for example, identified a number of adverse social outcomes that are experienced by Maori, including mental and physical ill-health (Statistics New Zealand 2013), unsatisfactory progress in housing and health intervention measures (Flynn et al. 2010), lower educational achievement (Ford 2013), and Maori receiving lower salaries (Pack et al. 2016).

The social variables or influences that contribute to conviction rates for crimes and other anti-social activities in New Zealand are poorly understood. To understand the variables that adversely impact on Maori, it is crucial to understand the relationship between the law and the criminal justice sector and the community and the character and the situation of those who break the law (Hook 2009a, b, c).

The Police Response to Maori Offending

As a response to the increasing awareness of the inequitable involvement of Maori in the criminal justice system, an increase in the number of minority immigrant communities and the importance of relationships and partnerships, the police have developed and implemented a number of actions to increase the community's confidence in its procedures and service delivery. Police acknowledge that it is important for the community to have confidence in their ability to work with other government agencies and to achieve the social outcomes set by the government.

A 'commitment to Maori and the Treaty,[3]' was a core institutional value of the New Zealand Police in the mid-1990s, which recognized that one of its most critical community relationships of the police was that with iwi[4]/Maori (O'Reilly 2014). Comprehensive strategies, procedures to improve the recruiting of Maori and minority police officers, the establishment of advisory boards, and the establishment of the Maori, Pacific and Ethnic Services within the police were all introduced to improve the organization's commitment to the Treaty.

In 1996, the Police Commissioner expressed his concern that the response of the police to the over-representation of Maori in the criminal justice system could be perceived as the police not being committed to the principles of the Treaty of Waitangi (New Zealand Police 2014a; O'Reilly 2014). To ensure that the police would succeed in accomplishing its vision of 'Safer Communities Together', the police would establish, maintain and develop problem-solving partnerships with Maori (O'Reilly 2014). This reasoning led to the development of the strategy 'Responsiveness to Maori', which became the overarching document for the development of strategies relating to the ethnic minority community and Maori.

In late 1996, the police developed Te Urupare Whitiki, a foundational document, which was designed to build strategic relationships and partnerships with Maori. The document outlined three key objectives for establishing effective partnerships with Maori:

1. the police were to gain a greater understanding and acceptance of the significance of the Treaty of Waitangi to Maori and to New Zealand;
2. the police were to learn how to bring the voice of Maori into policing decisions and operational procedures; and
3. the police were to implement strategies that were designed to reduce the incidence of and the impact of offending by Maori (O'Reilly 2014).

The vision was to consult and share the development of policy, and leadership with Maori, and to recognize cultural perspectives in police practice. To develop this vision, two research projects were commissioned in 1998: 'Maori Perceptions of Police' (Te Whaiti and Roguski 1998) and 'Police Perceptions of Maori' (Maxwell and Smith 1998). As a result of the implementation of the projects and the commissioning of the research, the police were one of the first government agencies to develop a formal strategy for engaging with ethnic and minority groups, including Maori and Pacific peoples (New Zealand Police 2004). The strategy was documented in 'Working Together with Ethnic Communities – Police Ethnic Strategy Towards 2010', which created the platform for police actions to be taken in relation to its responsiveness to ethnic communities.

---

[3] The Treaty of Waitangi is a treaty between the Government (originally British and now the New Zealand) and Maori signed in 1840 that established a British Governor of New Zealand, recognized Māori ownership of their lands, forests and other properties, and gave Māori the rights of British subjects
[4] Iwi is an identifiable Maori community and is often a tribe or part of a tribe.

The strategy, which was to be achieved by 2010, outlined the procedures to be followed and the objectives to be achieved in conjunction with ethnic communities (New Zealand Police 2004). The initial strategy suggested that proactive community policing for ethnic communities should be introduced to reduce the ethnic communities' fear of being a target of crime and to increase their confidence in the police. It recommended a specific direction, key priority areas for action, and two policing outcomes:

- Outcome 1 – Police have the capability and capacity to engage with ethnic communities
- Outcome 2 – Culturally appropriate strategies are implemented with ethnic communities that increase community safety, prevent and reduce crime, road trauma and victimization (New Zealand Police 2004).

The document also provided practical steps as to how these strategies and areas would be implemented nationally and in relation to frontline policing (New Zealand Police 2004). In 2011, this strategy was replaced by a more targeted strategic document that concentrated specifically on Maori, called 'The Turning of the Tide'.

The Turning of the Tide was developed by the Commissioner's Maori Focus Forum and the Maori, Pacific and Ethnic Service set specific targets for reducing the disproportionate representation of Maori in offending, victimization and crash statistics.[5] The strategy consolidated the earlier work on iwi-led, crime-and-crash reduction community developments, programs and plans. A key feature of The Turning the Tide was the recognition of the role that iwi and Maori agencies, groups, whanau[6] and communities had in achieving these objectives and outcomes (O'Reilly 2014).

According to the police, a 20% reduction in repeat offending among Māori between the introduction of The Turning the Tide in 2011–2025, could translate into:

- savings of up to $800 million for the criminal justice system;
- earnings of up to $300 million for Māori households and a tax revenue of up to $40 million for the government; and
- a $3.6 million saving in social costs for every fatal crash prevented (New Zealand Police 2016).

To ensure that the voice of Maori was being included in the development of police policy, the police in 1998 established the Commissioner's Maori Focus Forum. In 2000, this forum was replicated in the 12 police districts with the

---

[5]The Turning the Tide targets to be achieved by June 2014 were: 15 percent reduction in prosecutions of Maori, 10 percent reduction in Maori repeat offending, a 5 percent reduction in Maori first time offenders, 10 percent reduction in Maori repeat victims and a 10 percent reduction in Maori victims of fatal and serious vehicle crashes. Similar targets are in place for Turning the Tide phase 2, which are to be achieved by June 2018 (New Zealand Police, 2011a, 2011b).

[6]Whanau is an extended family or community of related families who live together in the same geographical area.

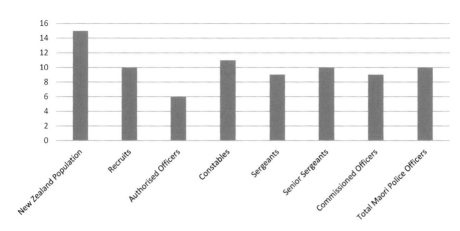

Fig. 14.2 Percentage of Maori at each Police rank in 2013. (Source: New Zealand Police People Group (2015))

establishment of Maori Advisory Boards. These Advisory Boards mirrored and complimented the work of the Commissioner's Maori Focus Forum and comprised of Maori community representatives, academics and cultural advisors. The forums provided a Maori perspective on policing issues and provided an avenue for the police to receive feedback on the service it delivered (O'Reilly 2014).

The third political strategy that was adopted by the police was increasing the number of minorities and Maori recruited to become police officers. This was not only to ensure that the ethnic population of the police reflected the make-up of the wider population, but to secure and maintain the public's trust and confidence, and ensure police legitimacy. Targeted advertising and the development of relationships with education providers has led to an increase in the number of Maori police (an increase of 31% since 2004) and Maori police officers now constitute more than 10% of the total constabulary (New Zealand Police 2015).

Figure 14.2 shows Maori as a proportion of the general population and of the New Zealand Police in rank, and in total. While 9% of commissioned officers (Inspector and above) are Maori, two of the 42 Area Commanders are Maori, but there are no Maori District Commanders. At the executive level, the Deputy Chief Executive: Maori and one of the Deputy Commissioners are Maori (O'Reilly 2014).

New Zealand Police Maori, Pacific and Ethnic Services

The final strategy developed in 1996 as a response to the over-representation of Maori in the criminal justice system was the establishment of a network of Iwi Liaison Officers throughout the 12 policing districts. The intention was that Liaison

Officers would support the relationship of the police with iwi/Maori and other minority communities in an effort to reduce offending and victimization among Maori and minority communities.

Despite the initial negative reaction to the selection and appointment of Iwi Liaison officers, demands have been made for increasing the number of appointments made to this role. This has come from, not only the Maori community, but also from minority communities and from within police (Haumaha 2003). As a result of the increase in immigration since 2000, the number of the Liaison Officers has increased to 50 officers and now includes a number of different Asian, Indian and Pacific ethnicities.

The Response to Maori and the Link to Prevention First

The Policing Excellence and the Prevention First strategies commenced in August 2010 and were a series of operational initiatives that were designed to enable the police to perform preventative policing activities, which were specifically directed toward reducing victimization and offending, and improving public safety (New Zealand Police 2014b). Prevention First focused on five areas of risk: families, youth, alcohol, organized crime and drugs, and road policing (New Zealand Police 2014b). Maori, unfortunately, are disproportionately represented across all five areas.

Methodology

This is a qualitative study, based on a survey of the New Zealand Police Cultural Liaison Officers. To answer the three research questions, the study surveyed police members who were currently performing the role of Maori, Pacific and Ethnic Services Liaison Officers. The survey consisted of 31 questions which explored the reasons as to why the respondents had become a Liaison Officer, what type of training they had received, what they thought the role entailed, how they undertook their role, what the main strengths and weaknesses of the role were, and how the role could be improved. The survey questions are presented in Appendix A.

The questionnaire was emailed to 50 officers who were performing the role of Liaison Officer in November 2015, and a reminder was emailed to those officers who had not replied to the initial email in late January 2016. Fourteen officers (28%) returned completed survey questionnaires by 28 February 2016.

The methodology adopted for undertaking this research was partly informed by Parker's (1992), critical discourse analytic approach. This approach focuses on a greater analysis of macro-level influencing factors such as relationships, discourses and structural or systemic racism. Parker's micro-level approach was used to examine the role of the survey respondents and their reasons for becoming Liaison

Officers. The method of analysis used by Parker was based on the respondent's discourse, and repeatedly used themes and phrases, which were compared to texts and comments to find emerging premises and theses. As a result of the analysis, the discourse was interpreted and analyzed, along with each of the respondents' explanations, accounts and attributions.

How the respondents undertook their role and developed relationships with minority communities was the focus of this research. The information received from the survey respondents was divided into broad thematic areas using preliminary coding. Discrete coding was then conducted; the texts examined, read and reread, and compared and contrasted and grouped according to codes that defined a single idea (Potter and Wetherell 1987). The procedure used to define and discuss the role of Liaison Officers was to lay out, in separate, but at times, overlapping themes, which were identified by the participants. These themes pertained to relationships, culture, support and community are discussed in the following section.

Survey Results

The results of the survey are summarized and discussed below using the three main survey headings.

The Organizational Profile of a Maori, Pacific and Ethnic Liaison Survey Respondents

Approximately 28% or 14 Maori, Pacific and Ethnic Liaison Officers, responded to the survey. The demographics of the 14 survey respondents are summarized in Table 14.1. One respondent was of Samoan ethnicity and thirteen were of Maori ethnicity. While the Maori, Pacific and Ethnic Services includes members of Indian (2), Chinese (3), Korean (2) and Vietnamese (2) ethnicities, no members of these ethnicities responded to the survey.

All of the survey participants were long serving and widely experienced police officers when they became a Maori, Pacific or Ethnic Liaison Officer. The least amount of service of a survey participant was 9 years of service and the longest was more than 36 years. Three of the participants had more than 30 years of service and a further three had more than 25 years. The majority of the participants had between 10 and 20 years of service. In relation to the participants' service as a Maori, Pacific or Ethnic Liaison Officer, this ranged from between 1–13 years, with more than 70% of the participants having more than 5 year's experience as a Liaison Officer.

Two of the participants were non-sworn (civilian) members of the police and the remaining 12 were sworn members. Both of the non-sworn members were retired sworn officers. Of the sworn participants, eight were Constables, two were

Table 14.1 Survey participant information

Participant	Ethnicity	Rank	Years of police service	Years as a cultural liaison officer
1	Maori	Constable	12	8
2	Maori	Sergeant	36	8
3	Maori	Sergeant	34	13
4	Maori	Constable	15	7
5	Maori	Non-sworn[a]	9	9
6	Maori	Senior sergeant	16	8
7	Maori	Non-sworn[a]	11	5
8	Maori	Senior Constable[b]	35	2
9	Maori	Senior Constable[b]	25	6
10	Maori	Non-sworn	17	13
11	Maori	Inspector	27	1
12	Maori	Senior Constable[b]	25	10
13	Maori	Constable	10	7
14	Samoan	Senior Sergeant[c]	11	2

[a]Retired police officers prior to being Cultural Liaison Officers
[b]Automatic rank after 14 years' service
[c]Promotional rank

Detectives, one a Sergeant and one an Inspector. The least amount of police service for both groups prior to becoming a Liaison Officer was 3 years. One sworn member had 4 years of service prior to becoming a Liaison Officer, while three of the participants had more than 20 years of service, with another having more than 33 years of service.

Research by Wehipeihana et al. (2010), examined the strategies that were used to increase the recruitment of Maori into the police. They found that one of the main factors for Maori to join the police was that a recruit, upon graduating from the Royal New Zealand Police College, would be able to return to the district or the geographical area of their iwi or whanau. Only three of the respondents had to transfer to another police district to become a Liaison Officer, while the other eleven had either completed all of their police service in the district where they became a Liaison Officer or had transferred to the district prior to taking up the role.

All 14 respondents gave similar reasons as to why they had become Liaison Officers. Only one of the reasons given was not for altruistic reasons, being for promotion. The other reasons given included "to give back to Maori", "to make a difference", "to intervene and prevent issues from arising in the community", and "to improve the police relationship with the community".

Training to Become a Liaison Officer

To develop the skills of Maori, Pacific and Ethnic Liaison Officers, the police delivered a 2 week theoretical in-class course. Ten survey respondents had completed this course, but this was some time after they had become a Liaison Officer. Only one respondent had completed this course prior to becoming a Liaison Officer, while two respondents were given some training in culture and language prior to taking up their roles. In defence of this situation, one respondent stated:

> *"I knew what the role was and the expectations of an iwi liaison officer and knew at the time of taking the job that I was facing a huge battle to reduce Maori offending and victimisation"* (Respondent 2).

The respondent appears to have an understanding of the fact that they would have problems in reducing Maori offending and victimization. Liaison Officers were not provided with the skills that would enable them to develop police relationships with Maori, nor were they provided with the skills that would enable them to identify a specific problem, develop a response or implement a chosen response. In other words, they were not given any training in how to analyze and solve problems. One respondent commented:

> *"The introductory course was extremely valuable, but it left many questions unanswered about the iwi liaison officers role"* (Respondent 10).

The Role of a Liaison Officer

The respondents were asked what they perceived the principle elements of their role as a Liaison Officer were. The majority of the respondents thought that their role was to liaise with minority communities in general, attend events and celebrations, gather and share intelligence, and undertake community and preventative policing. One respondent considered their role to be "a conduit between the cultures" (Respondent 3). Another respondent summarised their role in detail:

> *"The main role or purpose as an iwi liaison officer was to reduce Mäori offending and victimisation. The role was about working with the Maori community, working alongside government departments and non-government departments, working with the sub tribes, iwi, Mäori wardens and families within the community. Handling land disputes, handling deaths and to make sure police staff were trained to work with the families who had a mother, father, grandparent, uncle or aunty or grandchildren or children die as a result of an un-natural death and where a PM [post mortem] was required as a result of the death"* (Respondent 2).

Another respondent had a more police-centric perspective:

> *"You need to be across all matters Maori and know your business. Building partnerships with not only Iwi but Police staff and that trust and confidence. I have to be across any structural or logistical changes in Policing and again that I know that side of the business and can explain to Iwi if needed. There has been a fear within Police regarding tikanga*

(customs) and Marae[7] *protocols. The reverse being explaining to the staff to gain their trust and confidence. I'm mindful that it can be a balancing act between dos and don'ts both on Police and Iwi space"* (Respondent 7).

As liaison and relationship building were perceived to be large components of the work of Liaison Officers, survey participants were asked as to how, or what methods they utilized to expand their relationship networks. All 14 respondents revealed similar relationship building methods, including using face-to-face meetings with minority community groups and leaders; building trust with the community by providing communication, presence and through attending events; holding and establishing public forums and regular meetings; and through working with Maori and other community service providers. One respondent commented that the best way to build relationships was:

"By getting to know who was in my community and who the key contacts were, making contact and from there establishing trust, confidence and a relationship. You could say 'it's the cup of tea' of community policing, where it starts out very informal just meet and greet and then this grows. A lot of hard work to establish some of the harder to reach communities i.e gangs, at risk whanau etc." (Respondent 12).

The most significant difference in the responses from the survey participants was from the question pertaining to how much time in an average week they spent on seven specific activities. The seven activities and the percentage of time spent on each is presented in Table 14.2. While there may be a problem with defining of each of these activities, or that the respondents "bundled up" all of their time into one activity, the responses clearly identify a difference in how the Liaison Officer role is delivered or perceived to be delivered by an individual Liaison Officer. The second point of interest from this question is that all of the respondents stated that they would work between 45 and 50 h in an average week, and working more than 50 h per week was a common occurrence. One respondent noted in relation to the workload:

Table 14.2 Average time liaison officers spend on specific activities

Specific liaison officer activity	Percentage of time devoted to activity	Mean	Standard deviation
Liaison with minority community	0–75	14.0	7.7
Crime and investigation issues	0–5	9.4	6.3
Events and celebrations	0–25	10.5	5.2
Intelligence related	0–15	13.3	6.1
Relationship building	0–60	25.8	13.9
Community policing	0–5	12.2	6.1
Preventative policing	0–100	20.8	21.3

[7] A marae is a communal or sacred place that serves religious and social purposes in Polynesian societies

"The role is very diverse and covering a number of streams, 1 ILO [Iwi Liaison Officer] *for a community of 25,000 Maori would be maximum. Frequently the role requires to work outside of hours and to be oncall 24/7, there is no toil or oncall available, only the reliance on the member's passion and commitment to the job"* (Respondent 6).

Personal Expectations of Liaison Officers and Possible Improvements for the Role

The final section of the survey included questions as to whether the participant's expectations of the role had been met and what could improve the Liaison Officer's role. The majority of respondents stated that their expectations were met and, in most cases, they were exceeded. One respondent, for example, stated:

"Absolutely! Probably above and beyond, as I've seen it evolve and improve over the past 10 years. The organisation is always assessing and analysing to see how things can be done better and creating new policies and strategies, which includes the Turning of the Tide, which I believe has been one of the most important documents!" (Respondent 12).

However, one respondent claimed that their expectations were not met, saying:

"No it was sadly lacking across the board as far as engagement/implementation and sustainment. Our own organisation has and still has a long way to go to change the mindset of meeting the treaty commitments and looking to a preventative model through Turning of the Tide" (Respondent 4).

The second question participants were asked was whether they found the role rewarding. It was presumed that owing to most Liaison Officers remaining in the role for a long period of time and that all of the participants had become Liaison Officers for specific cultural altruistic reasons, the majority of officers would find the role rewarding. The question generated a variety of responses. All respondents found the role extremely rewarding, especially because they were able to work with Maori, and because, as more than half of the respondents noted, they were able to establish leadership roles within their communities and that they were able to solve the issues that the community presented to them. The level of value and reward is clearly demonstrated in the following comment made by one of the respondents:

"Yes. Personally/for the organization – How have you found it rewarding? Just job satisfaction, the fact that you are called upon to do jobs others can't or haven't been able to. The fact my behaviour and attitude have made it a pleasant job. It has its issues with the fact you are challenged by police staff as opposed to iwi as to what and why you do what I do." (Respondent 9).

Participants were also asked as to what could be done to improve the role of Liaison Officers. This question also generated extensive comment, and while two respondents commented that the police needed to increase their commitment to partnerships with minority communities, all of the respondents commented on the need to improve the training given to Liaison Officers. Concerns were also raised about the lack of a career structure. The absence of a career structure means that officers with experience and skills are not retained and that Liaison Officers need to apply to other areas of the organization if they are seeking promotion.

Discussion

The comments from the participants of this research demonstrate that in their view they are making progress in establishing relationships with Maori and other ethnic communities, and that they are influencing the participation of Maori in criminal offending. As a result of their perception of establishing these relations, the participants also felt that they were contributing to the New Zealand Police Prevention First Operating Strategy goals of reducing the level of reported crime that involved Maori offenders. There may be some justification in the participants perception as the number of arrests of Maori for a criminal offence has decreased from 230 per 10,000 in 2009 to 159 per 10,000 in 2014 (Statistics New Zealand 2018). This trend is presented in Fig. 14.3.

The survey participants' comments also support the earlier research undertaken on behalf of the police by Wehipeihana et al. (2010). This research examined the factors as to why Maori join the police and found that Maori join the police because of a passionate desire to serve Maori, and a desire to create positive change in their communities and with police interactions with Maori, particularly Maori youth (Wehipeihana et al. 2010).

The Wehipeihana et al. (2010) research determined that while the establishment of the Maori, Pacific and Ethnic Services had been reasonably successful in creating and maintaining relationships with Maori, and in some cases, the establishment of partnerships with Maori, there is a need to extend the same to other ethnic minority

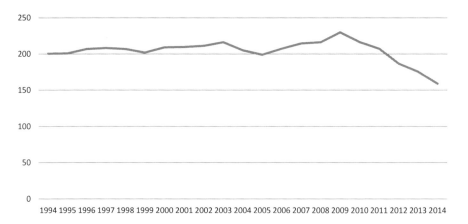

Fig. 14.3 Apprehension of Maori for a criminal offence (per 10,000 population) from 1994 to 2014. (Source: Statistics New Zealand 2018)

communities. This gap in police service to ethnic communities also applies to the role of Liaison Officers, in that while all of the research participants enjoyed their position, there is little formal training or on-going training provided to assist Liaison Officers with identifying methods for developing relationships with communities.

The organizational identity of Liaison Officers and their management and the clash between being of a specific ethnicity and the police culture is an institutional weakness of the current structure of the Maori, Pacific and Ethnic Services. Increasing the number of Maori or officers of a different ethnicity, for example, will not lead to a change if the culture of the organization does not allow officers to be 'Maori' or of another ethnicity, for example, for officers from a minority culture to use their native language. Such officers are recruited by police because of their ethnicity, but if these officers are not able to make use of their specific skills in ethnic areas, their recruitment will add little to legitimizing the police or adding to the community's confidence, especially the confidence of minority communities.

One group of researchers do not agree with recruiting individuals of specific ethnicities to become police officers. According to Bartkowiak-Theron and Asquith (2014), assuming cultural competency from an individual's cultural identity "devalues the significant skills required to operate successfully in multicultural and cross-cultural encounters" and using such officers to develop and strengthen the police-community relationship "compromises them in the eyes of both their communities and their police peers" (p. 95). This perspective however, was based on an analysis of recruitment quotas introduced following the Macpherson (1999) report that examined the murder of a Western Indian youth in London and was an examination of police liaison roles that have been designed to work with minority communities.

The results of the research discussed above does not support the view posed by Bartkowiak-Theron and Asquith (2014). As a number of long serving Liaison Officers argue, other police officers were initially skeptical when the roles were created in the mid-1990s. However, over time, the role has become accepted and its specialist skills are called upon by generalist police officers. Furthermore, the Liaison Officers stated that they are capable of maintaining and building on existing police-community relations and with providing an avenue for undertaking other policing roles within indigenous and minority communities.

Conclusion

There are three limitations in this research. The first is that there is very little research undertaken in New Zealand relating to the police relationship with Maori and other ethnic minorities, which means a context for analyzing this research is hard to develop. The second limitation relates to the limited number of participants involved in this research and as a result, the generalizability of the research result. The third limitation follows on from the second limitation in that all of the survey participants were of either Pacific Island or Maori descend and none of the other minority ethnicity officers answered the survey. This means that the results of the survey may only apply within the context of officers of Maori or Pacific Island descent not to the perceptions of officers of other ethnic minority descent. These limitations could provide a basis for future research pertaining to the policing of minorities in New Zealand and Australia.

The majority of the survey participants identified their role as developing the police relationship with the Maori community, principally through attending events and celebrations, and as implementing community and preventative policing initiatives. All of the participants identified the importance of attending public forums and regular meetings to build trust and communication.

The strategic approach and the practical experience discussed in this research illustrates the need for a balanced, holistic and coordinated approach to combating and preventing Maori crime, and for **improving police-community relationships**. While some progress has been made in recent years towards this goal with public having 78% of full or substantial trust in the New Zealand Police in 2009 and 2014[8] (Gravitas Research and Strategy 2009, 2014), there is still significant fragmentation of approach, effort and resources within the police and across the government departments in relation to the over-representation of Maori in the criminal justice system. The principle problem for the police in relation to Maori is how to increase the profile of its Liaison Officers and ensure that these officers are able to undertake their role with the support of police management. In parallel to this problem is the need to increase the number of ethnic liaison officers. Currently, the ratio is one staff member with a specialized focus on Maori to approximately 14,000 resident Maori population (O'Reilly 2014). This figure does not take into account other minority communities and the need for further Liaison Officers in these communities.

This article has presented one model of community policing that is capable of building relationships with indigenous and minority communities. The role of a Maori, Pacific and Ethnic Service Liaison Officer is part of a comprehensive and multi-level strategy for increasing the legitimacy of the police in indigenous and minority communities, and further research is required to identify its suitability for adaption by other police agencies to use to improve their relationships with their communities.

New Zealand Police Cultural Liaison Officers – Survey Questions

1. Respondent Current Rank (or retired)
2. First Name of Respondent (to contact for clarification, if required)
3. Current Position Title (or retired)

---

[8]This figure has remained at 77 percent in 2015/16 and 2016/17, but went from 65 percent to 67 percent for Maori over the same period (see New Zealand Police, 2017, p. 36).

4. Total Length of Service as a member of New Zealand Police (or Length of Service at Retirement)
5. Length of Service as a Maori, Pacific or Ethnic Liaison Officer
6. Email Address (to contact for clarification, if required)
7. Phone Number (to contact for clarification, if required)
8. Position Title and Rank prior to taking up your role as a Maori, Pacific or Ethnic Liaison Officer
9. Length of Service at the time of your appointment to your first Maori, Pacific or Ethnic Liaison Officer position
10. Location as a Maori, Pacific or Ethnic Liaison Officer
11. Did you transfer to take up your appointment as a Maori, Pacific or Ethnic Liaison Officer? Yes or no
12. What was/were the reason(s) for applying for the role

    (a) Promotion/advancement, end of career, interested in role, cultural, give back to your specific culture

13. Were you given any training/briefings prior to taking up the role
14. If so, what did the training entail? Culture, language, other
15. If so, was this training adequate?
16. Were you advised/told as to what the role would entail prior to taking up the role – yes or no
17. If yes, what were you advised as to the main purpose(s) of the role – liaison, crime, events/celebrations, Intelligence gathering/sharing, relationship building, community policing, preventative policing
18. During your term as Maori, Pacific or Ethnic Liaison Officer – what did you perceive the principle elements of your role - liaison, crime, events/celebrations, Intelligence gathering/sharing, relationship building, community policing, preventative policing
19. When you needed assistance from PHNQ, did you receive support? Did this support meet your needs?
20. When you needed assistance from District, did you receive support? Did this support meet your needs?
21. Did you supply information/intelligence to PNHQ? Was this CT, Drugs, Immigration, Other Crime, events/celebrations, community policing, preventative policing
22. On an average week, what percentage would you have spent on - - liaison, crime, events/celebrations, Intelligence gathering/sharing, relationship building, community policing, preventative policing
23. On reflection. Did the role meet your expectations – How or why not
24. When you took up your posting did the NZP have relationships with local Maori, Pacific or other ethnic groups? Yes or no
25. If no to Q25, have you since established this relationship?
26. If yes to Q25, were these relationships adequate for you to undertake/complete your role? If not, why were they not adequate?

27. Did you see your role as building and/or improving the NZP relationship with local Maori, Pacific or other ethnic groups? Yes or no?
28. How did you expand your relationship network?
29. Did you find the experience as a Maori, Pacific or Ethnic Liaison Officer rewarding? Personally/for the organization – How have you found it rewarding? why or why not
30. What could be changed to improve the Maori, Pacific or Ethnic Liaison Officer role in the future? For the individual/for the organization
31. Is there any further comment that you would like to make in regard to your Maori, Pacific or Ethnic Liaison Officer role or in regard to the role of Maori, Pacific or Ethnic Liaison Officer?

References

Bartkowiak-Theron, I., & Asquith, N. (2014). Policing diversity and vulnerability in the post-Macpherson era: Unintended consequences and missed opportunities. *Policing, 9*(1), 89–100.

Brown, D. (2017). Beyond the thin blue line? A critical analysis of Scotland' community warden scheme. *Policing and Society: An International Journal of Research and Policy, 27*(1), 6–20.

Collins, J. (2005). *Ethnic minorities and crime in Australia: Moral panic or meaningful policy responses.* Paper presented to a public seminar organized by the Office of Multicultural Interest, Perth, Western Australia.

Department of Corrections. (2008). *Maori Strategic Plan 2008–2013.* Department of Corrections: Wellington.

Fergusson, D. (2003). Ethnicity and interpersonal violence in a New Zealand birth cohort. In D. Hawkins (Ed.), *Violent crime: Assessing race and ethnic differences* (pp. 138–153). Cambridge: Cambridge University Press.

Flynn, M., Crane, S., & Soa-Lafoa'I, M. (2010). *Maori housing trends 2010.* Housing New Zealand report 2010. Retrieved from Housing New Zealand website: http://www.hnzc.co.nz.

Ford, T. (2013). My research journey: Contributing to a new education story for Maori. In N. Berryman, S. Soohoo, & A. Nevin (Eds.), *Culturally responsive methodologies* (pp. 87–106). Bingley: Emerald Publishing Group.

Goodman, A., & Ruggiero, V. (2008). Crime, punishment, and ethnic minorities in England and Wales. *Race/ethnicity: Multidisciplinary Global Perspectives, 2*(1), 53–68.

Gravitas Research and Strategy Limited. (2009). *New Zealand Police – Citizens' satisfaction survey: Final report for year two results (July 2008 – June 2009).* Retrieved from the World Wide Web on February 17, 2014 from: http://www.police.govt.nz/sites/default/files/publications/citizen-satisfaction-survey-2009-full.pdf.

Gravitas Research and Strategy Limited. (2014). *New Zealand Police – Citizens' satisfaction survey: Final report for 2013/14 fiscal year (July 2013 – June 2014).* Retrieved from the World Wide Web on September 24, 2014 from: http://www.police.govt.nz/sites/default/files/publications/citizen-satisfaction-survey-2014-full.pdf.

Haumaha, W. (2003). *Leadership and community partnerships in the 21st century: Rhetoric or reality?* Unpublished master's thesis. University of Waikato, Hamilton.

Hill, R. (1989). *The colonial frontier tamed: New Zealand policing in transition 1867–1886.* Wellington: Government Print.

Hook, G. (2009a). The criminalization of Maori and Pacific Islanders under the domestic violence act 1995. *MAI Review, 3.* Retrieved from http://www.review.mai.ac.nz/index.php/MR/article/view/228/310.

Hook, G. (2009b). The potential influence of legislation on the criminality of Maori and Pacific Islanders in New Zealand. *MAI Review*, 3. Retrieved from http://www.review.mai.ac.nz/index.php/MR/article/view/227/311.

Hook, G. (2009c). 'Warrior genes' and the disease of being Maori. *MAI Review*, 2. Retrieved from http://www.review.mai.ac.nz/index.php/MR/article/view/222/243.

Hunter, R., & Dantzker, M. (2005). *Crime and criminality: Causes and consequences*. New York: Willow Tree Publishers.

Johnston, L. (2005). From 'community' to 'neighbourhood' policing: Police community support officers and the 'police extended family' in London. *Journal of Community & Applied Social Psychology, 15*, 241–254.

Loveday, B., & Smith, R. (2015). A critical evaluation of current and future roles of police community support officers and neighbourhood wardens within the Metropolitan Police Service and London boroughs: Utilising 'low-cost high-value' support services in a period of financial austerity. *Police Science & Management, 17*(2), 74–80.

Maxwell, G., & Smith, C. (1998). *Police perceptions of Maori: A report to the New Zealand Police and the Ministry of Maori Development*. Wellington: Te Puni Kokiri.

Macpherson, W. (1999). *The Stephen Lawrence inquiry – report*. London: The Stationery Office Limited.

Ministry of Justice. (2009). *Maori overrepresentation in the criminal justice system*. Strategic Policy Brief. Wellington: Ministry of Justice.

Morrison, B. (2009). *Identifying and responding to bias in the criminal justice system: A review of the international and New Zealand research*. Wellington: Ministry of Justice.

Nadesu, A. (2009). Reconviction patterns of released prisoners: A 60-month follow-up analysis. In *Wellington*. New Zealand: Department of Corrections.

Newbold, G. (2000). *Crime in New Zealand*. Palmerston North: Dunmore Press Limited.

New Zealand Police. (2004). *Working together with ethnic communities: Police ethnic strategy towards 2010*. Wellington: New Zealand Police.

New Zealand Police. (2011a). *The turning of the tide: A whanau ora crime and crash prevention strategy 2012/13 to 2017/18*. Wellington: New Zealand Police.

New Zealand Police. (2011b). *The turning of the tide: Phase one 2012/13 to 2014/15*. Wellington: New Zealand Police.

New Zealand Police. (2014a). *Establishing Maori advisory boards manual chapter*. Police Executive Meeting, 24 March 2014.

New Zealand Police. (2014b). *Policing Excellence: The transformation of New Zealand Police 2009–2014*. Wellington: New Zealand Police.

New Zealand Police. (2015). *Annual report 2014/15*. Wellington: New Zealand Police.

New Zealand Police. (2016). *The turning of the tide strategy 2012/13–2017/18*. Wellington: New Zealand Police.

New Zealand Police. (2017). *Annual report 2016/2017*. Wellington: New Zealand Police.

O'Neill, M. (2014a). Ripe for the chop or the public face of policing? PCSOs and neighbourhood policing in austerity. *Policing, 8*(3), 265–273.

O'Neill, M. (2014b). The case for the acceptable 'other': The impact of partnerships, PCSOs, and neighbourhood policing on diversity in policing. *Policing, 9*(1), 77–88.

O'Reilly, J. (2014). *A review of Police and iwi/Maori relationships: Working together to reduce offending and victimization among Maori*. Wellington: New Zealand Police.

Pack, S., Tuffin, K., & Lyons, A. (2016). Accounting for racism against Maori in Aotearoa/New Zealand: A discourse analytic study of the views of Maori adults. *Journal of Community Applied Social Psychology, 26*(2), 95–109.

Parker, I. (1992). *Discourse dynamics: Critical analysis for social and individual psychology*. London: Routledge.

Pearson, G., Sampson, A., Blagg, H., Stubbs, P., & Smith, D. (1989). Police racism. In R. Morgan & D. Smith (Eds.), *Coming to terms with policing* (pp. 118–137). London: Routledge.

Potter, J., & Wetherell, M. (1987). *Discourse and social psychology: Beyond attitudes and behavior*. London: Sage.

Rasche, C. (1988). Minority woman and domestic violence: The unique dilemmas of battered women of color. *Journal of Contemporary Criminal Justice, 4*(3), 150–171.

Speirs, P. (2002). *Reconviction and imprisonment rates for released prisoners*. Wellington: Ministry of Justice.

Statistics New Zealand. (2010). *Crime victimization patterns in New Zealand: New Zealand General Social Survey 2008 and New Zealand Crime and Safety Survey 2006 compared*. Wellington: Statistics New Zealand.

Statistics New Zealand. (2013). Quick stats about Maori. Retrieved from Statistics New Zealand website http://www.stats.govt.nz/Census/2013-census/profile-and-summary-reports.

Statistics New Zealand. (2018). New Zealand crime data, 1975–2014. Retrieved from Statistics New Zealand website: http://archive.stats.govt.nz/tools_and_services/nzdotstat/tables-by-subject/new-zealand-recorded-crime-tables/apprehensions.aspx.

Te Whaiti, P., & Roguski, M. (1998). *Maori perceptions of the police*. Wellington: Victoria Link Limited.

Wehipeihana, N., Fisher, E., Spee, K., & Pipi, K. (2010). *Building diversity: Understanding the factors that influence Maori to join Police*. Wellington: New Zealand Police.

Chapter 15
The 2016 Failed Coup Attempt and its Influence on Policing the Kurdish and Other Ethnic Minorities Across Turkey

Hasan Arslan

Introduction

The history witnessed that the Turks as a civilization, which consist of not one group but groups of peoples, established sixteen empires in more than 2000 years of history. In every aspect of the Turkish state, the concept of organization has been the crucial essential element since the beginning of institutionalism and socialization process of societies. Therefore, the pre-Islamic Turk Empire was both an administrative organization and a tribal confederation, which combined Turkish tribes and clans in Central Asia. There is not much information about the types of security and crime in the literature during either at the tribal level or government level, but to protect and serve was always at the center of a Turkish organizational ideology. Public safety was the primary task for the military corps. In other words, a Turkish state would protect their citizens including minority groups from any kinds of internal or external enemies and would establish the confidence and peace among its people. In the very early Turkish history, the Kagan (a title referring to the ruler of all rulers)'s possible "success depended critically on his ability to mobilize and redistribute resources, whether through tribute or trade" (Findley 2005). In the Tribal era, public security had some militaristic characters; people who were in charge of this task were called "Subaşı," which refers to the commander of soldiers. The first known Subasi was InalKagan, whose name mentioned in the Bain Tsokto inscriptions (emniyet.gov.tr). During war times, Subaşı was leading and commanding his army; in peacetime, he was providing the public safety of his region, which he was also obligated to manage.

Throughout Turkish history, during the governments of different Turkish nations, public order and public security have been provided by the State along with the

H. Arslan (✉)
Western Connecticut State University, Danbury, CT, USA
e-mail: arslanh@wcsu.edu

© Springer Nature Switzerland AG 2019   255
J. F. Albrecht et al. (eds.), *Policing and Minority Communities*,
https://doi.org/10.1007/978-3-030-19182-5_15

national defense. Thus, this chapter examines the evolution of Turkish policing through the different historical eras. It also discusses the emerging problems of the policing in Turkey, particularly after the July 15, 2016, the failed coup.

Policing During the Ottomans

There is more information about the public safety during the reign of the Ottomans which lasted for more than six centuries (1299–1923). The Ottomans was a world state and able to create a continental super-state that controlled hundreds of ethnic groups with various religious beliefs. It was a multi-national society; within its dominion lived hundreds of millions of people, of different creeds and ethnic origins. "Enforcement was highly complex and varied from location to location and among the multitude of ethnoreligious groups of the Ottoman Empire" (Piran 2011: 31). The Ottoman Rulers were usually called Padishah and Hunkar or Sultan. "The Muslim Ottoman elite, headed by a sultan who was also (after 1517) caliph (spiritual leader of Sunni Islam) incorporated a variety of subject peoples" (Cam 2014: 317). The Ottomans inherited rich political traditions from entirely different ethnic groups: Turks, Arabs, Persians, and Mongols. In the classical period of the Ottomans, Padishah was officially the government; was the ruler, leader and the commander in chief of the state.

> "From the earliest period, the Ottoman sultans had always appointed two authorities to administer a district- the *bey* (military commander), who came from the military class and represented the sultan's executive authority, and the *Qadi* (Judge), who came from the *ulema* (a name for a group of respected Islamic scholars) and represented the sultan's legal authority. The bey could not inflict any punishment without first obtaining the Qadi's judgment, but the Qadi could not personally execute any of his sentences. In his decisions and his application of the Sharia (Islamic law) and kanun (traditional law and customs), the Qadi was independent of the bey" (Inalcik 1973: 104).

The Ottoman military was also made up of people of many nationalities. At the early stages of the State, the security and public safety were very similar to the applications of the old Turkish states. However, "following the conquest of İstanbul in 1453, Sultan Mehmet II organized his nonMuslim subjects into millets, or separate religious communities, under their own ecclesiastical chiefs to whom he gave absolute authority in civil and religious matters and over criminal offenses that did not come under Islamic law" (Guclu 2017). By the fifteenth century, the state began to compartmentalize the bureaucracy, and public security was still a part of the national defense in the hands of the Ottoman military. Under the jurisdiction of the Qadi, the Turkish cavalry called Sipahis and the foot soldiers called Kapikulu, consist of Christian youths from the Balkan region, were in charge of the security in the countryside (emniyet.gov.tr). More specifically, the members of the Kapikulu unit represented the elite in the society and formed the core of famous Janissary (Yeniceri-new soldier) infantry, which was renowned for its military skills. Nevertheless, in the capital city of Istanbul, the public safety was maintained by a unit, similar to the modern law enforcement patrolmen, called Yasakcilar (Prohibitors), led by the Subasi under the direct authority of the Grand vizier. However, outside the capital, in the country region, Subasi was working under the influence of Qadi. Subasi's were protecting the public against any criminals and rebellions. After the conquest of Istanbul (1453), the bureaucratic and military structure expanded and became more organized. In the countryside, three different groups: kollukcular (patrolmen), yasakcilar (prohibitors), and bekciler (night-watchmen) maintained the public order.

After three centuries of success and expansion, the Ottoman State has reached the apex of its time. By the eighteenth-century confusion and the corruption started to show up all administration level. Janissary corps, once the core and the dynamic of the Ottoman power, had ceased to function as the best-selected and trained unit of the Ottomans. In 1826, Sultan Mahmud II abolished the Janissary corps, which this incident later was called Auspicious Incident (in Turkish: Vaka-i Hayriye). The new Ottoman army had a particular unit formed, "Asakir-i Redife Mansure" (Victorious Reserve Soldiers) that was specifically assigned to maintain the public order. The commander of this new military police, Serasker (Captain), had the same authority as the commander of the Janissary units (Yeniceri Agasi) in Istanbul. This new military police were attached to the Ministry of Finance. Therefore, there were two different police units at the time: one for the capital (Istanbul), affiliated with the Ministry of Finance; one for the countryside (the Sipahi's) under the command of "bey's" (military commanders). This double structure continued until the establishment of the first police organization assigned to maintain the public safety in 1845.

It should also be noted that, during the years between 1839 and 1879, Ottoman society had experienced a certain degree of cultural transformation regarding minority rights in the country. "The Ottoman bureaucrats sought to save the empire from further demise and advance of European imperialism by borrowing and implementing European methods of governance" (Piran 2011: 30). Indeed, the Ottoman intelligentsia, civil servants, bureaucrats, journalists, writers, and military officers, were "pushing for a huge transformation, a rapid adaptation to modernity, and smooth incorporation into the world system" (Hanioglu 2008). This dynamic alteration was also an attempt to ease the European pressure over the politics of the state. It began with the declaration of Tanzimat Fermani, (Edict of Gulhane), in 1839, which aimed to transform the Empire into a new modern state. "As a matter of fact, the imperial edicts which constituted the core of formal and political attempts are manuscripts produced to enforce laws to ensure the security and intactness of life, property, and honor" (Kozleme 2018). Thus, within this political atmosphere, on March 20, 1845, the first police organization regulation (Polis Nizami) formed of 17 codes (emniyet.gov.tr) was made by Sultan Abdulmecid administration. This day marked the birthdate of the modern day police force in Turkish history.

The primary duties of the police were defined in the Polis Nizami as protecting the lives and the properties of all people; preventing the probable criminal events against Muslim and non-Muslim citizens, and foreigners; regulating the traffic (Gulcicek 2004). Moreover, "the word 'police' was used in the official language for the first time. The source for the regulation of new police institution was based on

French law (Birinci 1999). A year later, a second regulation required the separation of the entire police forces from the general commandership of Serasker (Captain). The new public security administration called Zaptiye Mudurlugu with the legislative assembly and a policing administrative board (Zaptiye Meclisi) technically separated the police from the military. According to Turkish police scholar Ferdan Ergut, the reformers attempted to transform police from a military bureaucracy to a civilian one during the Tanzimat era (Piran 2011). In 1879, Zaptiye Mudurlugu and Zaptiye Meclisi were finally united under the new Ministry of Security (Zaptiye Nezareti). Centralization became a vital point in the modern era of policing. The new ministry was doing the same job as the Turkish National Police organization in contemporary time. It was followed by the first police officer training school in 1891 and the first jurisprudence document regarding police management where the duties and responsibilities of the police organization were defined explicitly in 1896 (emniyet.gov.tr). Nevertheless, the first Police Regulation with 167 codes, published on April 19, 1907, was the first document that is deemed to be a Turkish style policing code written without the influence of or citation of any foreign western policies or systems (Birinci 1999).

In 1908, a second constitutional period (II. Mesrutiyet) with a new parliament started in the Ottoman Empire. The Ottoman constitutionalism movement was "a consequence of the conflict between Sublime Porte (Bab-ı Ali) ruling elite and conservatives which had been continuing since Reforms Period" (Akin 2009: 52). During this era, the new German and French police systems became a model for the Turkish police organization (Cam 2014). Hence, by 1909, a General Directorate of Police (Emniyet-i Umumiye Müdürlüğü) and a Police Directorate under the İstanbul Governorship replaced the older Ministry of Police (Zaptiye Nezareti) (Alyot 1947). The units were attached to the newly established Ministry of Interior (Dahiliye Vekaleti).

During the Turkish Independence War (1919–1922) three organizations were providing internal security in the country:

1. Gendarmerie, a military branch of the army, was in charge of rural areas.
2. Istanbul Police did have the jurisdiction within the city of Istanbul.
3. The National Police Organization in charge of the towns and the provinces.

In 1923, the Police Organization Act (Emniyet Teşkilatı Kanunu) unified the Police force and centralized the police command. In the early years of the Turkish republic, Mustafa Kemal Ataturk started revolutionary changes that have altered the foundation of the modern state. "In building a modern system of police training and education, the new Republic of Turkey established three different types of police training institutions. These were police schools, a Police Institution, and a Police College" (Cam 2014: 324). Police schools train police cadets to serve as patrolmen level; while the graduates of police colleges, which are high school level institutions, continue their university-level education at the Police Academy to become the administrators of the Turkish National Police. The Police Regulation Act of 1934, along with procedural guidelines, and 145 different auxiliary acts defined the jurisdictional and procedural authority of the police work (Nalla and Boke 2011). The centralized organization is hierarchically structured with a quasi-military rank and command system. Each province has a police department that is directly controlled by the General Directorate headquarter in the capital city, Ankara.

The politicization of the institutions is a sad but true reality of Turkish politics since the late Ottoman era. Throughout the years, different cliques emerge to control the Turkish police whether in the form of ultra-nationalism, Islamism or socialism. The police force has always been found itself in the middle of ideological wars from left to right movements. This has been the case during the Single Party regime (1923–1950) under the Republican People's Party (in Turkish: Cumhuriyet Halk Partisi – CHP) to Adnan Menderes administrations in the 1950s. However, one of the worst examples of the political polarization took place during the 1970s, where at a time the Turkish public was divided along the lines of political ideologies. Many college campuses became battlegrounds between the leftist and rightist student factions in major cities. Along with political and social fragmentation, the intensity of ideological conflicts also polarized the members of the TNP. At the time, under the 1961 constitution, they were allowed to establish two unions: "Pol-Bir (Police Unity), which was the extreme and central rightist police officers and Pol-Der (Police Union), which was the leftist and social democratic-oriented police officers association. This division led to further tension and rivalry in the police rank and file" (Piran 2011: 45). During the 1980 military coup, which was carried out by the Kemalist military officers. The National Security Council showed more sympathy for the members of the nationalists than the leftists when they were dismissing police personnel from the national police force. It is also alleged that the national police have been more hostile toward the leftist movements than their counterpart, right-wing movements (Patterson 2013, June 7). It is a chronic ailment of Turkish politics that the policing in Turkey has been shaped and dictated by the policies of ruling parties in power. The modern Turkish Republic later adopted the Western models of policing and established police schools and training program for police officers. In her dissertation, Leila Piran from the Catholic University of America asserted the idea that "it was not until the 1980s, specifically under Prime Minister Turgut Ozal"s leadership, when the police began to emerge as a professional civilian force" (2011: 4). During many coalition governments in the 1990s, political parties were fighting to seize the control over the national police through the Ministry of Interior. Because:

> "The police are under the full control of the party led government...All policing matters are the responsibility of the Minister of the Interior in Turkey. The minister has a great role and power in policy making; he is the only police authority" (Aydin, 1996:78–79).

Also, the modernization effort started after the mid-1990s, which included the study abroad programs. Hundreds of first-line supervisors have been sent to Europe and the United States for training, masters and doctoral programs. New policing methods like community policing have been adopted through the members of the TNP who studied in the western nations.

The Police Image and Criticism

Police work does not only consist of crime-fighting efforts; studies indicate that a significant portion deals with minor disturbances service calls and administrative duties (Siegel and Worrall 2015). Research also suggests that the public generally holds positive attitudes toward the police (Ren et al. 2005; Cao et al. 1998; Dean 1980; Huang and Vaughn 1996; Schafer et al. 2003). Indeed, the 2017 results of the Survey on Social and Political Trends in Turkey, conducted every year by Kadir Has University's Center for Turkish Studies, revealed that police (62.3%) and gendarmerie (60.8%) were seen to be the most trusted institutions by Turkish public. Despite all political fear and retribution, the public confidant on two internal security agencies has increased significantly for the first time. However, more specifically since the failed coup of July 15, 2016, the members of Turkish National Police have been subjected to fear of retribution, loss of employment and imprisonment by political reasons as well as are under the strain of pursuing terror suspects for mostly political reasons. Frankly, "there may be differences in attitudes toward the police based on ethnic variation as well as variation in attitudes toward the degree of secularism and religion in society" (Karakus et al. 2011). Therefore, whether it is police brutality or excessive police response to civil unrest or peaceful demonstrations, Turkish police have been under constant scrutiny by many significant actors: political leadership, citizens, and international media. All of these factors define the public image of police in Turkey. It is noted that "the legitimacy of the police is linked to public judgments about the fairness of the processes through which the police make decisions and exercise authority" (Sunshine and Tyler 2003: 514). Reports of police brutality news damage the level of trust between the police and the Turkish public. Below describes some of the cases in recent years:

- In the spring of the new millennium, a six-volume report by a parliamentary human-rights panel "documented cases of torture in police stations across Turkey, contradicting government assertions that abuse is not systematic."
- In 2008, Human Rights Watch was concerned about the police abuse in Turkey after the release of an 80-page report, which had cited 28 cases of police abuse against civilians dating back to the start of 2007 (Report cites alleged Turkish police abuse 2008, December 5).
- In 2012, the son of AKP parliamentarian from Hatay province had exchanged words with a police officer from district police station. A video leaked to the media showed some officers of the station were lined up before the son for putative identification of the officer who had insulted him previously during the day. Two years later, a Turkish court sentenced the officer to 6 months prison for insulting and intimidation whereas the son of the AKP representative received fine (Benli 2015, January 30).
- In Spring 2013, a wave of demonstrations and civil unrest started initially to protest the urban development plan for Gezi Park at Taksim Square in Istanbul. Smaller than the Central Park in Manhattan, Gezi Park protests have underlined

divisions in an already polarized society in the recent years of the Justice and Development Party (Adalet ve Kalkinma Partisi – AKP) administrations. "But tensions between these protesters and the Justice and Development Party, AKP, has made the wider Turkish population acutely aware of the sort of police and military mistreatment that has long been experienced by Kurds, Alevis and other minority groups" (Sevi 2013, May 11).

- The corruption scandal that was exposed by two different police operations on December 17 and 25, 2013, shows how politics impacted both the legitimacy and image of the police in Turkey. The first police raid resulted in the arrest of 52 people, including the sons of three cabinet ministers, and the head of the state-owned Halkbank; suspects either were considered to be Erdogan's inner circle or connected in various ways with the ruling AKP. The second operation was interrupted by Erdogan before even conducted. Like in the case of July 15, 2016, failed coup, "the AKP and Erdogan were quite clear in deciding whom to blame for these problems: a U.S.-based Islamic cleric who held deep sway in Turkey" (Taylor 2014, December 30). They even further contended that members of the Hizmet movement (in English: Service) are "traitors and terrorists allied with foreign interests" (Sterling 2014, December 10). Within 2 weeks after the police operations, the 350 police officers including the officers in the financial crimes, anti-smuggling, and organized crime units were dismissed and replaced with police officials from other parts of the country (Bilefsky and Arsu 2014, January 7). More than 5000 police officers have been dismissed or transferred within a year after the corruption scandal in Turkey (Butler and Toksabay 2014, January 31).

- According to the UN Human Rights Office, more than 160,000 people have been arrested, and 50,000 remain in jail awaiting trial during an 18 month state of emergency (Turkey: UN report details extensive human rights violations during protracted state of emergency 2018, March 20). In another report, 'In Custody Police Torture and Abductions in Turkey' by Human Rights Watch (2017): "There has been a spate of reported cases of men being abducted, some of whom were held in secret detention places, with evidence pointing to the involvement of state authorities."

July 15, 2016, Failed Coup and the Government's Purge

Fear of coups has a substantive background in Turkey because Turkish history frequently repeated in regards to coups and plots. There seems to be a specific chronic crisis in Turkish political history that need to be understood. There are individual elements and dynamic factors that could be observed almost in every coup that has occurred in the following timeline: 1960, 1971, 1980 and 1998 along with several attempts and plots in between. The post-2000 era also witnessed some unusual and non-traditional forms of coup plots in Turkey. While the Email Memorandum (E-Memo) in 2007 and Judiciary Coup (J-Coup) in 2008 are the perfect examples of the unorthodox coups whereas the recent failed military plot on July 15, 2016, stands as the enigmatic coup with a polysemous nature, since it was characterized as "operatta" rather than an actual military intervention attempt by most of the Western media (Terzides 2016, August 12). Indeed, the July 15 attempt seemed like a precipitous and disorganized action that was engineered by some of the estranged and disgruntled hardliners of the Turkish military, who thought they were about to be purged by upcoming National Council Meeting in late August 2016. "Turkey's government and courts say the Gulen movement masterminded the coup attempt, and deem it as a terrorist organization" (Human Rights Watch 2018). Fethullah Gulen, a self-exile Turkish-Sunni Scholar, has been living in the Poconos Mountains in Pennsylvania for 20 years denied accusations and condemned the coup plotters. However, "Mr. Gulen also acknowledged that he could not rule out involvement by his followers, saying he is unsure who his followers are in Turkey" (Saul 2016, July 16). Following the coup attempt on July 15th, Turkey declared the state of emergency on July 20, 2016, and the government crackdown continues to this day on a grand scale. Just a week after the coup, "the first decree signed by Erdogan authorized the closure of 1043 private schools, 1229 charities and foundations, 19 trade unions, 15 universities and 35 medical institutions over suspected links to the Gulen movement" (Jones and Gurses 2016, July 23). As of August 2018, the Turkish government has issued a total of 31 decrees since July 20, 2016. More than 125,000 people have been removed from public sector jobs including military, police, judiciary, and education and 30% of them were law enforcement personnel (turkey-purge.com n.d.).

When it comes to politicization and indoctrination of the police force, the recent AKP policies made it worse than the past experiences. Following the failed coup, the AKP promoted officers who are close to the party goals and gave them vast punitive powers to conduct investigations under the state emergency law. Once again, their policies ensured the fact that the Turkish National Police has "a broad reputation for religiously conservative and right-wing nationalist tendencies."

Conclusion

It is evident that the policing has been shown significant progress since the old Turkish states. Every historical period has a characteristics transformation of the concepts of nation and security in the history of Turkish policing. The Ottomans paved the path with bricks of pre-Islamic management principles and Turkish customs along with harmony of modern-day applications for today's Turkish police force. "Before the professional police force was founded in 1845, military forces and the Janissaries carried out enforcement of public order and policing as part of their military duties" (Nalla and Boke 2011: 289). The Turkish policing system still displays the characteristics of the military (Aydin 1997). Today, the national police are the mirror of the Turkish society, which reflects the security, moreover, the trust of the Turkish public in its government. "There are undeniable indications of interference by politicians in the Turkish police" (Ozcan and Gultekin 2000: 3). Margaret

Levi points out, "the major sources of distrust in government are promise breaking, incompetence, and the antagonism of government actors toward those they are supposed to serve" (1998: 88). Since July 15, 2016, failed coup, severe deviations from the constitution and the laws indicate the fragile structure of the Turkish democracy once more.

Moreover, the increasingly authoritarian nature of the current leadership also forces police to deviate out of its legitimate work. Besides the current intensity of constant fear of losing employment and imprisonment with almost no due process generate low morale and incapability. "Low morale is a real problem, as it negatively impacts the mission and efficacy of a department and the emotional and physical wellness of officers" (Wasilewskia 2010, October 6). In addition to the fearful working atmosphere and low morale, the loss of the invested experience of officer knowledge and training in critical units like intelligence, organized crime, and financial crimes divisions will hurt the efficiency and operational capability of the national police in the long term. Turkey should able to develop an active recruitment program that should be purely based on merit by evaluating the officer's qualification and knowledge rather than seeking ideological loyalty to the political parties and religious movements.

Finally, both the police working conditions and hours should not be forgotten. "Research shows long hours and off-duty work can negatively impact officers' performance" (Maciag 2017). Indeed, long hours has been one of the ongoing problems within the TNP. Police officers whether as patrolmen or first-line supervisors, work 12 h daily shifts and they only have one off day of the week, which can be canceled anytime during an emergency situation. Therefore, in addition to low-morale working conditions with being influenced by the party politics in recent years, the police work shifts also impact the performance of the members of the Turkish National Police. New regulations must be created to adjust both the conditions and the hours of the police officers.

References

Akin, R. (2009). Ottoman parliament and its political legacy to modern Turkey. *International Journal of Turcologia, 4*(8), 51–67.

Alyot, H. (1947). *Türkiye'de Zabıta Gelişimi ve Bugünkü Durumu (In English: Police improvement and current situation in Turkey)*. Ankara: Kanaat Basimevi.

Aydin, A. H. (1996). Policy making structures of the Turkish National Police Organization. *Policing and Society, 6*, 73–86.

Aydin, A. H. (1997). A comparative study of military involvement in policing in England & Wales, Turkey. *The Police Journal: Theory, Practice and Principles, 70*(3), 203–219.

Benli, M. H. (2015, January 31). Vekil oğluna para, polise hapis cezası. Hurriyet Daily News. Retrieved 6 Aug 2018, from http://www.hurriyet.com.tr/gundem/vekil-ogluna-para-polise-hapis-cezasi-28082696.

Bilefsky, D. & Arsu, S. (2014, January 7). Purge of police said to be move by Turkey to disrupt graft inquiry. The New York Times. Retrieved 5 Aug 2018, from https://www.nytimes.com/2014/01/08/world/europe/turkey-corruption-inquiry.html.

Birinci, A. (1999). The "Firsts" in Turkish National Police. *Turkish Journal of Police Studies, 1*(3), 9–16.

Butler, D. & Toksabay, E. (2014, January 31). Turkey purges hundreds more police over graft probe, media reports. Reuters News Agency. Retrieved 4 Aug 2018, from https://www.reuters.com/article/us-turkey-corruption/turkey-purges-hundreds-more-police-over-graft-probe-media-reports-idUSBREA0U0OL20140131.

Cam, T. (2014). Turkish police schools and their roles in the modernization process of the new state during the early Turkish republic period, 1923–1938. *Turkish Studies, 9*(8), 315–326.

Cao, L., Stack, S., & Sun, Y. (1998). Public confidence in the police: A comparative study between Japan and America. *Journal of Criminal Justice, 26*(4), 279–289.

Dean, D. (1980). Citizen ratings of the police. *Law & Police Quarterly, 2*(4), 445–471.

Findley, C. V. (2005). *The Turks in world history.* Oxford: Oxford University Press.

Guclu, Y. (2017). Turkish-Armenian relations: The past, present, and future. *International Journal of Turkish Studies, 23*(1/2), 59–76.

Gulcicek, H. (2004). 159). Kuruluş Yılında Dünden Bu Güne Polis Teşkilati (in English: Police organization from yesterday to today in the 159th establishment year). *Çağın Polisi Dergisi. Journal of the Police of the Current Era, 3*(29), 38–42.

Hanioglu, S. (2008). *A brief history of the late ottoman empire.* Princeton: Princeton University Press.

Huang, W. W. S., & Vaughn, M. S. (1996). Support and confidence: favorable attitudes toward the police correlates of attitudes toward the police. In T. J. Flanagan & D. R. Longmire (Eds.), *Americans view crime and justice: A national public opinion survey.* Thousand Oaks: Sage Publications.

Human Rights Watch. (2017). In custody police Torture and abductions in Turkey. Retrieved on 4 Aug 2018, from https://www.hrw.org/report/2017/10/12/custody/police-torture-and-abductions-turkey.

Human Rights Watch. (2018). Turkey Events of 2017. Retrieved on 4 Aug 2018, from https://www.hrw.org/world-report/2018/country-chapters/turkey.

Inalcik, H. (1973). *The ottoman empire; the classical age* (pp. 1300–1600). New York: Praeger Publishers.

Jones, G. & Gurses, E. (2016, July 23). Turkey's Erdogan shuts schools, charities in first state of emergency decree. Reuters News Agency. Retrieved 5 Aug 2018 from https://www.reuters.com/article/us-turkey-security-emergency-idUSKCN1030BC.

Karakus, O., McGarrell, E. F., & Basibuyuk, O. (2011). Public satisfaction with law enforcement in Turkey. *Policing: An International Journal of Police Strategies & Management, 34*(2), 304–325.

Kozleme, A. O. (2018). Turk Modernlesmesinin Proto-Tipi ve Batililasma Tanzimi olarak Tanzimat. (Tanzimat: A Prototype of Turkish Modernization and a Westernization Movement). *Turkish Studies, 13*(10), 515–539.

Maciag, M. (2017). The alarming consequences of police working overtime. Retrieved 24 Aug 2018 from http://www.governing.com/topics/public-justice-safety/gov-police-officers-over-worked-cops.html.

Nalla, M. K., & Boke, K. (2011). What's in a name? Organizational, environmental, and cultural factors on support for community policing in Turkey and the U.S. *European Journal on Criminal Policy and Research, 17*, 285–303.

Ozcan, Y. Z. & Gultekin, R. (2000). Police and politics in Turkey. British Society of Criminology, (3). Retrieved 6 Aug 2018, from http://www.britsoccrim.org/volume3/011.pdf.

Patterson, R. (2013, June 7). The Turkish police force: Where violence meets impunity. Retrieved 6 Aug 2018 from http://muftah.org/the-turkish-police-force-violence-meets-impunity/#.VVgR9ut8Pww.

Piran, L. (2011). *Turkey and the European Union Reforms: Institutional Change in the Turkish National Police.* (Unpublished doctoral dissertation). The Catholic University of America. Washington, D.C.

Ren, R., Cao, L., Lovrich, N., & Gaffney, M. (2005). Linking confidence in the police with the performance of the police: Community policing can make a difference. *Journal of Criminal Justice, 33*, 55–66.

Report cites alleged Turkish police abuse. (2008, December 5). UPI NewsTrack. Available from NewsBank: https://infoweb-newsbank-com.ezproxy.shsu.edu/apps/news/document-view?p=WORLDNEWS&docref=news/124E903163128FB8.

Saul, S. (2016, July 16). An exiled Cleric Denies playing a leading role in coup attempt. The New York Times. Retrieved 4 Aug 2018 from https://www.nytimes.com/2016/07/17/us/fethul-lah-gulen-turkey-coup-attempt.html.

Schafer, J. A., Huebner, B. M., & Bynum, T. S. (2003). Citizen perception of police services: Race, neighborhood context, and community policing. *Police Quarterly, 6*(4), 440–468.

Sevi, S. (2013, May 11). Istanbul's police violence is no surprise to Turkey's minority groups. *The Globe and Mail*. Retrieved 4 Aug 2018, from https://www.theglobeandmail.com/opinion/istanbuls-police-violence-is-no-surprise-to-turkeys-minority-groups/article12986317/.

Siegel, L., & Worrall, J. L. (2015). *Essentials of criminal justice*. Boston: Cengage Learning.

Sterling, H. (2014, December 10). Turkish leader's words disclose his darker side; Erdogan's extremism a clear danger, writes Harry Sterling. The Calgary Herald. Retrieved 4 Aug 2018, from https://www.pressreader.com/canada/calgary-herald/20141210/281891591609627.

Sunshine, J., & Tyler, T. R. (2003). The role of procedural justice and legitimacy in shaping public support for policing. *Law & Society Review, 37*(3), 513–548.

Taylor, A. (2014, December 30). This single tweet got a Turkish journalist detained. *The Washington post*. Retrieved 30 Nov 2015 from http://www.washingtonpost.com/blogs/worldviews/wp/2014/12/30/this-single-tweet-got-a-turkish-journalist-detained/

Terzides, C. (2016, August 12). The Caliphate of Sultan Erdogan. *The Huffington Post (New York City)*. Retrieved on August 16, 2016 from http://www.huffingtonpost.com/christos-terzides/the-caliphate-of-sultan_b_11430874.html.

Turkey: UN report details extensive human rights violations during protracted state of emergency. (2018, March 20). *UN Humans Right Office*. Retrieved 06 Aug 2018 from https://www.ohchr.org/EN/NewsEvents/Pages/DisplayNews.aspx?NewsID=22853.

Turkeypurge.com. (n.d.) *Turkey's post-coup crackdown*. Retrieved 31 July 2018 from https://turkeypurge.com/purge-in-numbers-2.

Wasilewskia, M. (2010, October 6). Current threats to police morale. Retrieved 6 Aug 2018, from https://www.officer.com/training-careers/article/10232318/current-threats-to-police-morale.

Chapter 16
Police Strategies for Dealing with Tribal Conflicts in Nigeria

Amos Oyesoji Aremu and Perry Stanislas

Introduction

The question of insecurity globally is receiving much more attention given its increasing occurrence and the challenges it presents. More often, the affects of insecurity are not only grievous, harrowing and tragic, they are also multifarious and not uncommonly adversely impacts on some of the most vulnerable groups, who are often marginalized. These groups of people and the problems they experience are usually historical and geographical in character. The conflict of ethnic and other minority groups and their agitation for political and social inclusion is pronounced in many countries, and receive international attention; especially from the United States, the European Union, Britain and Russia inter alia. Many of the ethnic and tribal tensions in Nigeria have experienced similar exposure.

In this chapter, the agitation of tribal groups in Nigeria and policing strategies are interrogated with a view to reappraising Nigerian police effectiveness in providing security generally for society and specific groups within it. The chapter will first appraise the insecurity challenges confronting the country, especially in the last few years. Secondly, the chapter details the emergence of a policing framework that could be used to improve policing, particularly for ethnic/tribal groups and help to reduce tensions in Nigeria. The framework elucidates some of the fundamental problems facing the Nigerian police with serious ramifications for the quality of democracy in the country.

A. O. Aremu
University of Ibadan, Ibadan, Nigeria

P. Stanislas (✉)
Assistant Professor of Policing and Security, Rabdan Academy, Abu Dabi, UAE
e-mail: pstanislas@dmu.ac.uk

© Springer Nature Switzerland AG 2019
J. F. Albrecht et al. (eds.), *Policing and Minority Communities*,
https://doi.org/10.1007/978-3-030-19182-5_16

Nigeria and Contemporary Insecurity Challenges

Other than the economic challenges confronting Nigeria as a sovereign nation, the problems around insecurity has undoubtedly impacted negatively on the entire fabric of the country. This has brought untold hardships. The insecurity which initially aggravated in 2009 and later blossomed into a full blown terrorism motivated by *Boko Haram*, a Jihadist fundamental group in the North East, Nigeria has practically affected the entire North East and by extension, the entire country (Aremu 2015). At the root of this problem is the perceived regional and religious inequality, which intersects with ethnic and tribal identities around the impact of western education among Muslim communities in North Western Nigeria, and hostility towards the corrupt Federal Government (Ford 2014, Stanislas and Iyah 2016). *Boko Haram*-motivated terrorism more than any insecurity prior to 2009 in Nigeria was the most serious security challenge that almost brought the entire security apparatus to an operational halt. The Nigerian Police have been the worst hit of the security agencies given the ferocious *Boko Haram*'s terrorism which has been directed at them. The Nigerian Police not only lost its personnel, the institution also suffered losses in terms of arms, ammunition and stations. While it is difficult to estimate losses suffered by the Nigerian Police due to lack of records, it is believed that between 2009 and 2015 when *Boko Haram* is said to have been 'technically incapacitated' by the Nigerian Federal Government, the Police has lost about 525 personnel excluding civilians who were estimated to be 30,000 (see Azard et al. 2018). This also excluded the economic loss estimated to be millions of dollars.

The casualty figure is also put about 2.1 million people in internally displaced camps as of December, 2015 from 207 local government areas covering 13 states in Northern Nigeria including Abuja Adamawa, Bauchi, Benue, Borno, Gombe, Kaduna, Kano, Nasarawa, Plateau, Taraba, Yobe and Zamfara (Internal Displacement Monitoring Centre 2016). Although the Database of Terrorism in Nigeria from 2009 to the present is unavailable, the Global Terrorism Index (2015) ranks Nigeria with a score of 9. 213 as the third most terrorism ridden country after Iraq and Afghanistan out of 125 globally. The GTI data underscores the seriousness of terrorism in Nigeria.

The fight against Boko Haram has been hampered by the fundamental institutional weaknesses of the security services (primarily the police and army) which is characterized by poor salaries, endemic corruption, poor motivation, lack of appropriate equipment, nepotism and weak leadership (Ahmed and Eckel 2014). This is compounded by inappropriate tactics which rely on brutal methods and serious human rights abuse which alienates communities and replicates similar matters elsewhere, such as in Kenya. Walker (2014) citing a British military adviser attached to the Nigerian security services critically describes the government's approach of desperately searching for the 'big red button' rather than carrying out the hard and serious work of modernizing the police and military (see Mkutu and Stanislas ibid). At the heart of this reluctance is the inescapable observation that the Federal Government and politicians' self interests are rooted in the established order, regardless of how poorly this serves the majority of citizens, regardless of ethnic and tribal affiliations.

In spite of the Federal Government of Nigeria's position that *Boko Haram*'s sect has been 'technically' defeated, concerns from security stakeholders on the seeming rejuvenation of *Boko Haram* indicates the contrary. Although, the sect given intelligence report is said to be split into two with the emergence of Sheikh Abu Musab Al-Barnawi, competing leadership with Sheikh Abubakar Shekau, it is still extremely dangerous going by the fact that it still operates albeit minimally (Aremu 2015). Up until the current time, the sect is still holding hostage, most of the Chibok girls who were captured more than 3 years ago. Boko Haram's renewed 'strength' is still a major concern in Nigerian security circles.

Another security concern in Nigeria is the *Fulani* cattle-motivated killings that sprang up in Benue and Nasarawa states between the *Agatu* in Nasarawa and Benue; and nomadic *Fulanis* over land resource control. Of particular concerns is the strongly held beliefs among the affected ethnic and geographic communities that the slow if not sluggish response to this crisis, which has seen significant amount of loss of life and serious injuries, by the Federal Government and the police (who are centrally controlled) has been shaped by the tribal affiliation of the President and many of his inner circle who are from the Fulani ethnic/tribal group. This type of ethnic support network helps explains the arming of these herdsmen (with apparent heavy weaponry) and what could be perceived impunity which structures the environment in which they operate (Ochab 2018). Moreover, these suspicions can be understood in a cultural context of 'big' and powerful men sponsoring communal violence and individual assassinations to instrumentally maximize and protect their self interests (Stanislas and Iyah 2016).

These two insecurity challenges (*Boko Haram*-motivated terrorism and *Fulani/* farmers predatory violence) not only brought Nigeria to the spotlight of insecurity globally, kidnapping and hostage-taking are equally prolific simultaneously across the country; especially in states like in North Central (especially Kogi State), South West and chiefly in the South. The latter's philosophy is quite different as it is motivated by pecuniary gains mainly as a result of widespread unemployment and poverty within the country that has driven many forms of crime such as violence caused by religious extremism (Stanislas and Iyah 2016, p.330–331).

The fourth in the scheme of insecurity challenges confronting Nigeria is the militancy in the South East and Niger Delta. While the philosophy of the two-pronged insecurity is toward self-determination, the significant loss of life and especially of oil installations in the most southern parts of the South has made it assume a more fearsome dimension because of its link to the poor economy. Conservatively, the militancy orchestrated by the Niger Delta Avengers (NDA) from January 2016 to the current time has cost the country enormous amounts of barrels of oil in terms of its production. The NDA purportedly consists of individuals drawn from many ethnic/tribal groups who have been adversely affected by the ruthless oil producers, and its corrupt state agents. The plight of the Oguni people has acted as a rallying call for these militants and highlighted in the state killing of Oguni environmental activists Ken Saro Wira and his eight colleagues which received international condemnation (Stanislas 2014, p. 209) This challenge of insecurity, especially involving the NDA is infiltrating the coastal areas of the South West states like Lagos and Ogunand thereby making life and property no longer safe in the region.

The totality of economic, social and psychological costs of insecurity in Nigeria as experienced during the administration of President Goodluck Jonathan, and currently in the administration of President Muhammadu Buhari, has not only overstretched the security agencies (especially the police), it has also made the Nigerian society distraught. Nigeria is therefore, security-wearied and her people psychologically frayed particularly in the North Eastern and South Eastern parts of the country; and by extension, other parts of the country. The increasing insecurity of life and property has made Nigeria according to the Global Terrorism Index (2016) as the third most insecure country in the world after Iran and Iraq. Nigeria is probably the most unsafe country in South Saharan Africa, given the spate of tribal conflicts (many of which have religious overtones) and security issues in parts of the country (Stanislas and Iyah ibid). The import of this as it affects the Nigerian nation is discussed in the latter part of this chapter. However, it is instructive to note early in this chapter that insecurity being discussed so far is internal security which is the operational responsibility and constitutional jurisdiction of the Nigerian Police.

Tribal Group's Agitation in Nigeria

Nigeria is the most populous black Africa country with over 200 languages and multiple ethnic groups. These ethnic groups include: the Yoruba predominantly in the Southwest, the Hausa/Fulani in the North, the Igbo in the South East, and the Ijaw in the most southern parts of the South. Others are the Tiv, Idoma, Nupe, Urobo, Birom, Anang, Ebira, and a host of others. Expectedly, where such a diverse ethnic groups exist, conflicts of various types is a feature of life. Nigeria is no exception to inter and intra tribal conflicts. These conflicts, largely over resources and opportunities or territorial claims predated the independence struggles in Nigeria. According to Ebegbulem (2011), the history of ethnicity and ethnic conflicts in Nigeria is traced back to the colonial transgressions that forced the ethnic groups of the northern and southern provinces to become an entity called Nigeria in 1914. Ajayi and Owumi (2013) buttress this by noting that Nigerian nation is sharply divided along ethnic, religious and regional lines. Ajayi and Owumi's observations reflect the deep seated animosity that exists among different ethnic groups in Nigeria, it also underscores the yearning for self-determination; especially in the Southeastern part of the country since 1967 when Nigeria fought the civil war in response to the violence against the Igbo of the Eastern Region living in the northern part of the country (Stanislas and Iyah 2016, p. 328. The agitation for self-autonomy was championed by the former military Eastern Governor, Emeka Odumegwu Ojukwu. The struggle for the agitation of the same cause continues under NnamdiKanu using the outlawed Indigenous People of Biafra (IPOB). IPOB has also been labeled a terrorist group in the mould of Boko Haram by the Federal Government of Nigeria using the pronouncement of the High Court.

From this background, it can presumed to aver that tribal issues in Nigeria will always engender conflict given the fact that Nigeria is a mere geographical expression of a forced marriage with diverse cultures, social background, religious affiliation and psychology of the people that make up each tribal groups. These tribal conflicts have always threatened internal cohesion which most often heat up the polity of the country. This, often, stretches the human capacity of the Nigerian police. The intervention of the police, is also, often questioned by many of the tribal groups and leaders; especially when the police extra judicially respond to the security challenges posed by the tribes that are on the 'war path.'

The Nigerian Police and Security of a Distraught Society

Police and policing are two intertwined concepts in criminal justice that scholars have extensively and continuously discussed, not only because of the place of importance that the concepts enjoy in literature, but also because of the attention that they draw in contemporary discussion in security globally. Right from the Peelian's years till now, policing as a concept and as a subset of criminal justice system has remained very significant part of discourse in literature and contemporary discussion. Although much if not all the literature in this respect is from Europe and America and perhaps from Asia in recent times, African perspectives of criminal justice and security with emphasis on police and policing are limited, albeit growing. Earlier scholars on police literature have focused on historical documentation of police and policing activities (Emsley 2009). While these cannot be said to address criminal justice and insecurity in true sense, the works of the likes of Tekena Tamuno (1970) have given the next generation of African police scholars like Alemika a solid foundation to develop their unique contribution. It was not until early 2000s that serious empirical investigations started emerging on the Nigerian Police and policing structure in Nigeria. The works of Aremu (2000, 2006, inter alia) Aremu et al. (2009), Aremu and Tejumola (2008), Aremu and Jones (2011) are instructive here. From thence, serious scientific analysis of the Nigerian police, the structure of the organization and performance of the rank and file takes the centre stage in the literature.

The Nigerian Police, from 1930's to the current era still possess critical features of its colonial past (Aremu 2014). The constitutional responsibilities of the Nigerian Police as contained in Part Two and Section 4 of the Police Act and Regulations are as follows:

- The prevention and detection of crime,
- Apprehension of offenders,
- Preservation of law and order,
- Protection of life and property,

- The due enforcement of all laws and regulations with which they are directly charged
- Performance of military duties within or without Nigeria as may be required by law.

These provisions as clearly as they are, bestow huge security responsibilities of Nigerian Police personnel (Aremu 2014). This also comes with greater responsibilities on the internal governance of the Nigerian Police authorities. Doing so, would improve policing effectiveness and could engender public trust which is lacking. Aremu (ibid) argues that public trust is not earned flippantly given the history of police ineffectiveness. However, in what appears like a way out, Purdy (2013) admonishes that public trust could be earned if the police would embrace what he refers to as the "three spirits". These are: the police personnel, the government and the public. Essentially, policing effectiveness of the society should rest on this tripod.

From 2009 onwards Nigeria has witnessed a geometric decline in peace. According to Global Peace Index (GPI 2016), of the nine countries (excluding Syria) with the most internal conflict deaths in the world, Nigeria is ranked number four after Mexico, Iraq and Afghanistan. These figures underscore the level of criminality in Nigeria. As observed above, Nigeria has become an unsafe country. The degree of insecurity has reached an all-time high and has caused economic, social and psychological distress in the country.

Globally, the economic impact of violence in 2015 was estimated to be $13.6 trillion in purchasing power parity (PPP) terms (GPI 2016). A fraction of these expenditures was for peacekeeping and peace building. This perhaps account for the rise of insecurity profile in 2016 in countries like Turkey, Germany, France, Sudan, Iraq, Libya, the US, Pakistan, and Nigeria. Specifically, Nigeria is getting more attention with the increasing insecurity in some parts of the country. Recently, the Government of the US declared 20 states in Nigeria unsafe and warned its citizens against visiting these places. These and other related factors undermine the wellness of a society. The outcome of this environment is both physical and psychological and has also impacted negatively on the image of the country globally given the rating of the country on both Global Terrorism and Peace Indexes.

The insecurity facing the country is classified as internal and therefore under the watch of the Nigerian Police. Nigeria has a weak police both in very fundamental terms: numbers of personnel, resourcing, its basic leadership and institutional ethos and intelligence capabilities. In this regard, Nigerian Police organizations exhibit many of the classic symptoms of former colonial police in South Saharan Africa and elsewhere (see Mkutu et al. 2017). Alluding to this, the former Nigerian Chief of Army Staff and the current Interior Minister, Gen. Bello Dambazau in a lecture delivered in November 2013 described the intervention of the military in counterinsurgency operations as an aberration and clear indication that the police are unable to carry out their basic legal and constitutional mandate as outlined in the Police Act of 1990 (Stanislas and Iyah 2016, see Jatto and Stanislas 2017). The Nigerian Police are incapacitated in terms of personnel, logistical capacity and motivation to be able to deliver on their security mandate. This explains the potential usefulness of particular approaches to community policing.

The Nigerian Police Strategies and Responses

According to Aremu (2013), the Nigerian Police embraced the philosophy of community policing at the intervention of President Olusegun Obasanjo following his state visit to Houston in America. This led to the beginning of community-oriented policing in Enugu State in February 2004 (Aremu et al. 2009). From thenceforward, the Nigerian Police has accepted the reality of community policing in its operations, albeit largely symbolically. The Nigerian Police has a Community Policing Unit at its headquarters in Abuja. While the Unit has been working hard at encouraging community policing principles at the police state commands through the Commissioners of Police, much in terms of its operational reality has been further undermined, on top of the many institutional problems faced which have already been elucidated above (see Alemiko 2010) and has been exacerbated by the increase in crime. Community policing should be designed to be peculiar to each society's fundamentals, culture and psychology. However, this can only be achieved under the basic conditions of: lack of political interference by the government and politicians, compliance with the constitution and law by police leaders and the ability to generate sufficient legitimacy among civil society in the police as an institution and the community approach to policing (Alemiko 2010, p. 19).

Writing on the concept, Purdy (2013), describes community policing as a natural extension of the process of reform and modernization of the police institution. Purdy's contention is premised on the notion that the idea of community policing itself is not entirely novel in the police in advanced liberal democratic societies and in some developing countries (see Stanislas 2019)[1]; it was a reaction to the increasing challenges of insecurity. The principle of community policing is therefore, to make it specific to the need of a particular society or neighborhood. It is not straight-jacketed given the fact that policing challenges vary according to the culture, psychology and needs of each society.

Purdy (2013) defines community policing as a partnership between the citizens and the police working towards safety and an enhanced quality of life for all. Cox and Wade (1998) describe community policing as collaboration between the police and members of the public, focusing on solving community problems and improving the quality of life in the community. Such a relationship between the public and the police is to make both responsive to the security needs of the society. Greene and Decker (1989) maintain that citizens who are less satisfied with police are less likely

---

[1] Contrary to prevailing belief colonial police were often unable to entirely police colonised territories and relied on indigenous structures in the co-production of policing or as in the case of St Lucia in the Eastern Caribbean relied on autonomous community stakeholders.

to be cooperative with police officers and less willing to share information critical to making police work more efficient.

The philosophy of community policing places responsibility on the police and the public. Robert Peel (1829) averred the police are the public and the public are the police; the police being only members of the public who are paid to give full time attention to duties which are incumbent on every citizen in the interests of community welfare. By the same token citizens can carry out most of the functions seen by many as being monopolized by the state police. This synergy is the hallmark of policing philosophy in liberal democratic societies. This has however, being eroded over the years given the fact in some societies; the police institution has 'alienated' itself from the public due to their prioritization of government and politicians needs over citizens. In Yoruba land in Nigeria, the police are referred to as 'agbefoba' (those who do the bidding of only the authorities). In effect, as long as policing work is the sole preserve of the state police and not participatory with the willing involvement of members of the public, the philosophy of community policing is defeated.

Generally in literature, community policing has been variously described as neighborhood policing or police and the public working together in different ways. Beyond this, the most important principle of the philosophy of community policing is bringing the police and the public together with the sole aim of partnership in crime reduction or prevention. Some models of community policing restricts the role of citizens to a very limited and passive role, while others view citizens as co-producers of policing in terms of their active utilization and deployment of resources (Friedman 1992). In the approach advanced by Jatto and Stanislas (2017) for Edo State, Nigeria they recommend the establishment of very disciplined and well led voluntary auxiliary policing system that significantly reduces its reliance on state police at the local level, given its highly problematic and crimogenic nature. This policing approach gives control to communities and increases their capacity to prevent crime and protect themselves from external violent attacks. In Kenya, the Sungusungu tribal police system proved far more effective in reducing crime and corruption than the state police, and led to their redeployment and a more rational use of resources in communities who needed more police (Heald 2007).

What drives community policing is the need to proactively reduce crime in society. Effective crime reduction is therefore, a function of effective community policing. While effective community policing is a function of the willing public and police officers to cooperate to achieve a desired outcome. As part of the continued search for police effectiveness that the proposition of the 'Trinity Model' serves in the quest for police reform in Nigeria.

The 'Trinity' Policing Model: A Model for the Future

All over the world, scholars and stakeholders have always theorized on the best policing approaches. It was an answer to this that led to the conceptualization of community policing in the US. This chapter has discussed community policing and its relevance to policing effectiveness. Arguably and given its wide acceptance in America and Europe and in some parts of Asia (especially in India), it has been found to be very effective in limited contexts (Skolnick 1988; Sommerville' 2009). For example despite community policing having its origins in efforts to reduce the problems experienced by black minority communities in the US during the 1960s, which includes aggressive and violent policing, poor interactions with citizens and low legitimacy. Over 50 years later many of these problems remain a feature of policing black communities in parts of the country which led to formation of the campaign group Black Lives Matter. Both Berlin (2013) and Chappell (2015) highlight the resistance and countervailing trends within US police thinking and training against community policing in favor of militarized approaches to police work, with the tragic results that has contributed to the current crisis described by Camp and Heatherton (ibid).

The Nigerian Police has uncritically accepted community policing as an effective policing principle. Fundamentally, policing basics in Nigeria was associated with community approaches given the fact it was people that well-known in the community who were recruited into the native police. This was later adopted by the regional governments in the first republic. Eventually, the Nigerian Police was again unified (the first reunification was in April 1930 when the Northern Nigerian Police Force was unified with the Lagos Police Force and the Niger Coast Constabulary) with the absorption of the regional police under one body (Tamuno 1970). The major criticism against the regional police in the first republic was that the regional administration used the police to oppress the opposition.

Nigeria's flirtation with community policing should not mask the intrinsic commitment of the political class and police leadership and a significant number of rank and file officers to its dysfunctional police institution, which while ineffective in meeting the needs of citizens and most ethnic/tribal communities and regions, is instrumental in protecting their interests. Ikuteyo (2009) and Ordu et al. (2017) detail the experience of community policing in Nigeria and its predictable failings. Among the plethora of problems cited are interference of powerful individuals in using their influence in traditional ways to shape policing outcomes, inertia and resistance of police leaders and officers to change, financial constraints, and finally the deep public distrust of the police and its fundamental lack of legitimacy.

These feelings are not difficult to understand. In the recent 2019 general elections citizens informed the media how the police guarding voting stations suddenly 'disappeared' minutes before they were bombed, or set on fire or attacked by violent mobs (and by soldiers in some instances), and could not be found.[2] It is these features of Nigerian policing which contributed to Jatto and Stanislas' (2017) thinking in advancing a model of community policing that significantly reduces the involvement of the state police as the only feasible way to meet local people needs.

As an outcome of the continuous search for effective policing in Nigeria, the "Trinity' Policing framework was evolved with a view to capturing basic fundamentals that studies have found to have impeded policing effectiveness. There are three

---

[2] https://www.youtube.com/watch?v=w96iaNgg9yA&t=1457s 28 February 2019

core mutually-related conceptual strands in police literature globally: the police personnel, the governance of policing activities and the consumers of policing product. Purdy (2013) refers to this as the "three spirits" (the government, the police and the public). This I consider as a tripod of policing effectiveness. Aremu (2014) notes that it is instructive to conclude that effective and result-oriented policing rests squarely on the 'Trinity' (the government, the police and the public). The need for an effective, lawful and people-oriented police organization cannot be overemphasized (Aremu 2013).

As a consequence of these observations the idea of the 'Trinity' Model of policing was developed. It is important to explain the model using each component that forms the 'Trinity' and its function and inputs for effective policing. The first leg of the model is driven by police governance. Police effectiveness is determined by the quality of its internal inputs and processes and external governance (see Alemiko 2010: 11–17). This explains why governance constitutes the first intervention of the 'Trinity' Model of policing. More often than not, the quality of the police personnel and their productivity are dictated by the government in terms of funding the institution receives and the integrity and professionalism of its selection systems (Stanislas 2013a, b, p. 213–214). Purdy (2013) attests to this by stressing that without resources the police cannot be productive. However, without having good honest and robust selection processes money invested in recruiting and training more police officers is wasted when incompetence, nepotism and corruption is tolerated and rewarded, particularly among police supervisors, managers, and leaders who shape institutional culture (Mkutu et al. 2017, p. 185–186).

In Nigeria, the police institution has a special status under the constitution. The police institution until the administration of President Muhammadu Buhari had its own ministry, Ministry of Police Affairs. The police is now under the supervision of Interior Ministry although with a supervisory commission, the Police Service Commission. One of the challenges in this respect is the incessant changes of the leadership of the police which makes internal governance of the institution unstable. Over a 50 year period the Nigerian Police has been headed by 18 Inspectors General of Police (IGPs). This is an average of 2.7 years for each of the police IG.

Evidence from other former colonial police organizations suggest the high turnover of leaders illustrates institutional cultures of political expediency, both in how appointments are made and discarded, the lack of professional competence of postholders which became glaringly apparent and or the absence of professional autonomy (Adebayo 2005; Hills 2007; Wayne 2010). This practice of expediently firing police leaders constitutes a danger and threatens internal security by weakening the police institution and partly explains the failure to curb Boko Haram's activities (Aremu 2014). In effect, the first intervention of the model could hamper police effectiveness given the associated challenges. Aremu (2014) concludes that too much political interference may disorganize police commitment and organizational behaviour.

The second leg of the intervention of the 'Trinity' Model of Policing is the workforce. The quality of the personnel that constitute a police institution is a direct reflection of the operational working of the institution and its various systems. The quality of personnel is contingent on police recruitment policy, selection processes, training content, and delivery and evaluation procedures (Stanislas ibid). Writing on this, Purdy (2013) argues that the hiring process should support the recruitment efforts and focus on individuals who meet the established criteria of ethics, intelligence, interpersonal skills, logical thinking, decision-making, psychological suitability and maturity (see Stanislas 2013a, 2014).

Writing in the same vein, Aremu (2014) contends that twenty-first century policing requires thinking outside the conventional box. He notes further that the police and its personnel, more than ever before, should be more proactive, intelligence-driven, solution-focused and develop problem-solving abilities. Recruiting higher caliber police officers to enact smarter policing strategies and tactics should be viewed as part of the broader process of professionalization and modernization, which includes improving the pay and conditions and general status of the police occupation to make it more attractive (Stanislas ibid). Eliminating nepotism and corruption is an essential dimension of this process of change (Mkutu et al. ibid) and reflected in the views of Aremu et al. (2009) who has called for a major paradigm shift in how Nigerian policing is seen.

Police effectiveness is determined by the quality of both its internal and external governance. This explains why governance constitutes the second effect of the 'Trinity' Model of policing. Related to the second tripod in the model is too much government interference in the police's internal governance. All over the world, police governance is heavily influenced by the powerful, which in many cases can be abused.

The last leg of the model is the public which Aremu (2014) refers to as the consumers of policing products. Police work is a function of the support base of members of the public. Unarguably, the public is the determinant of the quality of policing work in the society. The nature of the interaction between the police and public is critical. Robert Peel (1829) maintained that the effective carrying out of police functions and duties are dependent on public approval. However, it is important to underline the legitimacy of the police is not derived directly from their actions but by the behavior of government, which in turn shapes how the former operates (Bennett and Morabito 2006). With these three interventions- the police personnel, police governance and the public, 'Trinity' Policing Model could engender effective policing in the society if the interventions work optimally. The model is diagrammatically illustrated in Fig. 16.1:

In the model above, the three interventions are mutually inclusive and could through the intervening variables in the boxes (policies, funding, leadership inter alia) determine policing effectiveness. The feedback systems as shown in the model are also crucial to the outcome measure (police effectiveness) in the model.

Rethinking Policing Work for Effectiveness in Nigeria

Nigeria as a country is going through a significant security challenges which have impacted negatively on many strata of its national life. Given these challenges and evident ineffectiveness of the Nigerian Police, there is a need to rethink policing

The 'Trinity' Policing Model

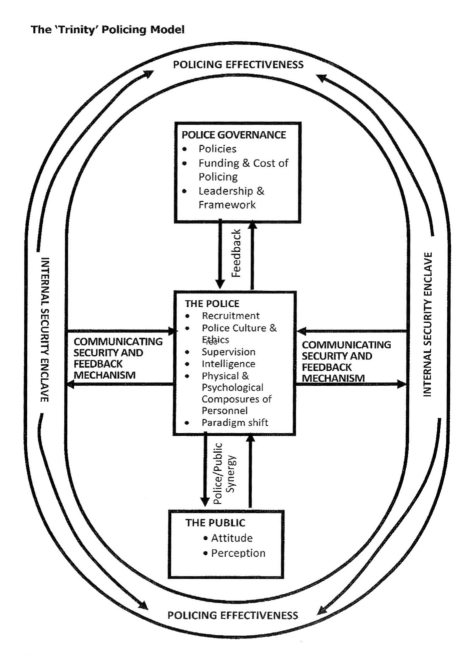

Fig. 16.1 The 'Trinity' policing model

work as operationalize by the Nigerian Police. The clarity is expedient in that other security agencies like the army, navy, air force, civil defense, Department of State Security Service, and others also engage in policing work. The Nigerian Police is arguably the only constitutionally empowered security institution in charge primarily of internal security. It also has a special role in contributing to ethnic and tribal harmony or helping to reduce tensions at bare minimum. In spite of this constitutional role of the police, all is not well with the institution. Policing work in Nigeria is daunting and burdensome as a result of challenges confronting the institution. With about 365,000 police personnel and a population of more than 175 million people, the population size of police to civilian ratio is 1: 480. This indicates that the country is under-policed and a far cry from the United Nations recommended standard. With the population projected to be 186.9 million people in 2016 (United Nations, Department of Economic and Social Affairs 2016) and no corresponding increase in the number of police personnel in Nigeria, it is worrisome to suggest that police effectiveness could be very difficult to achieve.

Nigerian policing like in other former colonial jurisdictions and in South Sahra Africa in particular is reliant on relatively out of date ways of viewing law enforcement, particularly given the range of technologies and strategies which are available. Intelligence Led Policing as a policing concept and practice is solution-driven geared towards public safety using information and dissemination (Aremu 2014). ILP is also potentially useful in the context of s police and community collaboration for effective security interventions, however this comes with much caution as one of the major criticisms of CP is that is used primarily for intelligence gathering and not meeting the needs of communities and citizens. This illustrates the need for a fundamental organizational change and a much needed paradigm shift in how public safety is conceived and perceived in Nigeria in order for these techniques to be used in legitimate ways (Aremu 2015).

ILP, within a context of the types of broader organizational changes already highlighted, would help the Nigerian Police to reposition itself to engage in policing by brain and less policing by force. The Nigerian Police realize this by removing the word, 'Force' from its name some years, although this has been more symbolic than real. Policing in other climes especially in Western Europe, the US and former developing nations such as Dubai is by brain, third-eye (Close Circuit Television) and public engagement. Emphasis on ILP can be again be inferred from Ratcliffe's (2008) definition as a conceptual model that uses crime analysis and criminal intelligence in a strategic manner to determine offenders for targeting and or preventative measures. The Nigerian Police need to add more value to its operations. This requires paradigm shift from the former colonial policing model to value-added policing (see Mkutu et al. 2017).

Value-added policing is a potential outcome of the 'Trinity' Policing Model. To add value to policing work in Nigeria, the three core elements of the personnel, police governance and the public would have to be reengineered for desired results and significantly improve community relations, especially where ethnic and tribal matters are concerned. This model contributes to policing effectiveness especially in Nigeria where the three elements are at variance with one another – the police are suspicious of the public, while the public dislikes the police; and the state's interference and underfunding and mismanagement of the police institution does either party any favours. A fundamental inference from the philosophy of the model is to harness the three interventions to promote police effectiveness and legitimacy. The model is therefore, a seamless and strategic determinant of police effectiveness.

Conclusion

This chapter encapsulates the need for criminal justice reform with emphasis on the Nigerian Police's approach to internal security as it relates to tribal conflict. The chapter is motivated to interrogate this matter with a view to addressing insecurity posed by tribal conflicts and Nigerian police's responses and contribution to many of these problems. In doing so, the chapter gleans from a policing philosophy, community policing and explores, the 'Trinity' Policing Model. The crucial preconditions of wholesale institutional change required to make the model realizable is also critically explored.

Obviously the security challenges that are often cause by tribal conflict in Nigeria should be reappraised with a view to addressing the institutional deficiencies and operational laxities of the Nigerian police's and its contribution to these problems. These are best addressed by the police who are constitutionally empowered to ensure internal security. There is no doubt that Nigeria needs to address the challenges confronting the police for the institution to be repositioned for paradigm shift which can assist crime reduction. To address the problem of police ineffectiveness given the rising profile of insecurity in Nigeria, especially where tribal and ethnic and regional issues are concerned, and the general poor quality of service received by the public. The second intervention in the 'Trinity' Policing Model, police governance will have to be well addressed. This is not exclusive of the other two interventions (the police and the public). The challenges here are police culture, governance and public attitude as addressed in the chapter.

With the above still on the burner, security stakeholders will continue to address the problem of police effectiveness and responses. This challenge will continue to exercise the minds of both police practitioners and researchers beyond the political will to drive the needed policies for the expected paradigm shift in Nigerian policing. Ordinarily, police are expected to provide safety to citizens by proactively fighting crime and maintaining public order. This cardinal security responsibility of the police can only be achieved when the personnel are well-motivated and properly supervised and managed. Until then police effectiveness and responses would continue to be a mirage in Nigeria given the range of problems highlighted in the chapter.

References

Adebayo, D. (2005). Perceived workplace fairness: Transformational leadership and motivation in the Nigerian police: Implications for change. *International Journal of Police Sciences & Management, 7*(2), 110–121.

Ahmed, I. & Eckel, M. (2014). Vox exclusive: Nigerian officers says corruption hampers fight against Boko Haram. www.voanews.com. 30 May. Retrieved 14 March 2019.

Ajayi, J. O., & Owumi, B. (2013). Ethnic pluralism and internal cohesion in Nigeria. *International Journal of Development and Sustainability, 2*(2), 926–940.

Alemiko, O. E. (2010). *Enhancing police accountability systems in Nigeria: The missing link, enhancing accountability systems in the Nigerian police*, Cleen Foundation.

Aremu, A. O. (2000). Psychological assessment of the problem-solving skills of Nigeian police officers. *Ife Journal of Psychology, 2*(1), 1–8.

Aremu, A. O. (2006). The effect of two psychological intervention Programmes on the improvement of interpersonal relationships of police officers in Osogbo, Nigeria. *Criminal Justice Studies, 19*(2), 139–152.

Aremu, A. O. (2013). The impact of emotional intelligence on community policing in democratic Nigeria: Agenda setting for National development. In A. Verma, D. K. Das, & M. Abraham (Eds.), *Global community policing: Problems and challenges* (pp. 25–40). Boca Raton: CRC Press, Taylor & Francis Group.

Aremu, A. O. (2014). *Policing and terrorism in Nigeria: Challenges and issues in intelligence.* Ibadan: Stirling-Horden Publishers Ltd.

Aremu, A. O. (2015). Police planning to curb insurgency in Nigeria: The need for a strong and effective police-public partnership. In J. F. Albrecht, M. C. Dow, D. Plecas, & D. K. Das (Eds.), *Policing Majo events: Perspectives from around the world* (pp. 115–124). Boca Raton: CRC Press, Taylor & Francis Group.

Aremu, A. O., & Jones, A. A. (2011). Improving commitment and productivity within the Nigerian police. In J. F. Albrecht & D. K. Das (Eds.), *Effective crime reduction strategies: International perspectives* (pp. 261–280). Boca Raton: CRC Press, Taylor & Francis Group.

Aremu, A. O., & Tejumola, T. O. (2008). Assessment of emotional intelligence among Nigerian police. *Journal of Social Sciences, 16*(3), 221–226.

Aremu, A. O., Pakes, F., & Les, J. (2009). Locus of control and self-efficacy as means of tackling corruption in Nigeria. *Policing: An International Journal of Police Science & Management, 11*, 1–19.

Azard, K., Crawford, E, & Kaila, K. (2018). *Conflict and violence in Nigeria: Results from the north east, North Central, and South Central zones, The World Bank.*

Bennett, R., & Morabito, M. (2006). Determinants of constables perceptions of community support in three developing Nations. *Police Quarterly, 9*(2), 234–265.

Berlin, M. (2013). An overview of police training in the United States, historical development, current trends and critical issues. In P. Stanislas (Ed.), *International perspectives on police education and training*. London: Routledge.

Chappell, A. (2015). Police training in America. In P. Stanislas (Ed.), *International perspectives on policing education and training* (pp. 274–288). London: Routledge.

Cox, S. M., & Wade, J. E. (1998). *The criminal justice network: An introduction.* Boston: McGrwa-Hill.

Ebegbulem, J. (2011). Ethnic politics and conflicts in Nigeria: Theoretical perspective. *Khazar Journal of Humanities and Social Sciences., 14*, 76–91.

Emsley, C. (2009). *The great British Bobby.* London: Quercus.

Ford, J. (2014). *The origins of Boko haram.* www.nationalinterest.org.

Friedman, R. (1992). *Community policing: Comparative perspectives and prospects.* London: Macmillan.

Global Peace Index. (2016). The global peace index records a historically less peaceful and more unequal world. Institute for Economic and Peace.

Global Terrorism Index. (2015). *Institute for Economics and Peace*. www.economicsandpeace.org.

Global Terrorism Index. (2016). *Institute for Economics and Peace*. www.eceonomicsandpeace. org.

Greene, J. R., & Decker, S. H. (1989). Police and community perceptions of the community role in policing. The Philadelphia experience. *Howard Journal of Criminal Justice, 28*(2), 105–123.

Heald, S. (2007). Controlling crime and corruption from below: Sungusungu in Kenya. *International Relations, 21*(2), 183–199.

Hills, A. (2007). Police commissioners, presidents and the governance of security. *Journal of African Studies, 45*(3), 409–423.

Ikuteyo, L. (2009). Challenges of community policing in Nigeria. *International Journal of Police Sciences, 11*(3), 285–293.

Internal Displacement Monitoring Centre Annual Report. Quarterly Update, July, 2016.

Jatto, A., & Stanislas, P. (2017). Contemporary territorial, economic, and political security in Edo state, Nigeria. *Geopolitics, History and International Relations, 9*(2), 118–140.

Mkutu, K., Stanislas, P. & Mogire, E. (2017). Book conclusion: State and non state policing: The challenge of postcolonial political and social leadership: Building inclusive citizenship, safety and security in East Africa, in Mkutu, K. (ed.) Security Governance in East Africa.

Ochab, E. (2018). Trump may not be wrong on the Fulani herdsmen crisis in Nigeria, www.forbes. com. 4 May. Retrieved 12 March 2019.

Ordu Enyidah-Okey, G. & Nnamu, M. (2017). Community policing in Nigeria: A critical analysis of current development, International Journal of Criminal Justice Sciences 12(1) January 1-June.

Purdy, D. W. (2013). Community policing: Theoretical problems and operational issues. In A. Verma, D. K. Das, & M. Abraham (Eds.), *Global; community policing: Problems and challenges* (pp. 1–24). Boca Raton: CRC Press Taylor & Francis Group.

Ratcliffe, J.H. (2008). Intelligence-led Policing: Trends and issues in crime and criminal justice, 248, 1–6.

Robert, P. (1829). The metropolitan police act.

Skolnick, J. (1988). Community policing: Issue and practices around the world, University of Michigan Library.

Sommersville, P. (2009). Understanding community policing. *Policing: An International Journal of Police Strategies and Management, 32*(2), 261–277.

Stanislas, P. (Ed.). (2013a). *International perspectives on police education and training*. New York: Routledge.

Stanislas, P. (2014) Transforming St Lucian policing through recrcuit training in a   context   of high crime. In: Stanislas, P. (ed.) International perspectives on police   education and training. Abingdon: Routledge, pp. 209–234.

Stanislas, P. (2019).The changing perceptions of St Lucian policing: How St Lucian police officers view contemporary policing. Submitted October 2018 to Police, Research, and Practice. Accepted.

Stanislas, P., & Iyah, I. (2016). Changing religious influences, young people, crime and extremism in Nigeria. In K. Sadique & P. Stanislas (Eds.), *Religion, faith and crime*. Palgrave.

Tamuno, T. N. (1970). *Police in modern Nigeria*. Ibadan: University of Ibadan Press.

United Nations, Department of Economic and Social Affairs. (2016). *Population division*.

Walker, A. (2014). *Why Nigeria has not defeated Boko Haram*. www.bbc.co.uk 14 May. Retrieved 14 March 2019.

Wayne, R. (2010). *Lapses and infelicities: An Insider's perspective of politics in the Caribbean*. St Lucia: Star Publishing Co Ltd Lucia.

Chapter 17
Whakatupato: Community Policing or the Police Response to a Social Problem in New Zealand?

Garth den Heyer

Introduction

The first form of control over firearms in New Zealand was the Arms Importation Ordinance of 1845. The ordinance codified controls over the importation of firearms and the changes of their ownership, but only with the objective of preventing the indigenous population, Maori, from obtaining and owning firearms, "rather than to regulate the ownership or possession of firearms by European settlers" (Thorp 1997, p. 9). The basis for the ordinance was a dispute about the acquisition and the ownership of land between the colonial powers in the United Kingdom and Maori.

The ordinance was the beginning of the different approach to managing and controlling the ownership of firearms in New Zealand. More significant controls were not introduced until 1920, when all rifles and shotguns were required to be registered, and the importation and use of pistols was almost totally banned. A more fundamental governance change to the administration of firearms did not take place until 1983. These changes were a response to the increase in the occurrence of criminal violence, especially gun crime, and the deterioration of the decentralized gun register system managed by the New Zealand Police (Thorp 1997).

The introduction of new legislation in 1983 and 1992 has had an impact on the use of firearms in relation to crime and socially, especially in regard to Maori living in rural areas. The inclusion of rural Maori within the formal firearms licensing system was non-existent until 2009 (New Zealand Police 2009). Anecdotal evidence provided the view that a large number of rural Maori owned firearms, but little was known about the Maori approach to firearm safety, their possession of firearms, and the state of repair of the weapons they used.

G. den Heyer (✉)
School of Criminology and Criminal Justice, Arizona State University, Tempe, AZ, USA

© Springer Nature Switzerland AG 2019
J. F. Albrecht et al. (eds.), *Policing and Minority Communities*,
https://doi.org/10.1007/978-3-030-19182-5_17

This article examines a program called Whakatupato[1] which was introduced by the New Zealand Police in conjunction with the New Zealand Mountain Safety Council and iwi.[2] The program provides comprehensive firearms safety training for Maori, and for firearms users in rural communities who may not be able to access firearms and hunter safety training (Spray et al. 2010). The uniqueness of the program is that it is culturally based and delivered within Maori tribal and iwi areas, usually on a marae.[3]

The article discusses the program within the context of the community policing strategies of the New Zealand Police: 'Prevention First' and 'The Turning of the Tide' and explores the wider impact of the delivery of the program and the possibility of it being a catalyst for improving other social problems in rural Maori communities. The first section of the article examines the literature relating to the public's attitude toward police (ATP) within the context of community policing. The second section presents the major social issues facing Maori and this is followed by a discussion of the two strategies; The Turning of the Tide and Prevention First, which have been introduced to improve the relationship between the police and the community and to improve the delivery of policing services to the community. These sections are followed by a discussion of the Whakatupato firearms safety program and the reasons that led to its development and implementation. The article concludes with an assessment of the firearms safety program within the framework of community policing and the relationship of the police with the community.

Police-Community Relationships and Attitudes

The approaches and processes involved in the delivery of police services to the community is extremely complex and multifaceted (Thurman and Zhao 2004; den Heyer 2013). Since the 1980s, the majority of western nations have adopted community policing approaches to re-establish or to improve the police-community relationship (Cao 2001; Eck and Rosenbaum 1994; Zhao et al. 1999). Changing to a community approach to service delivery has increased the need to understand what determines the public's attitudes to the police (Ren et al. 2005).

The implementation of community policing is associated with three fundamental assumptions. The first assumption is based on the assertion that the effectiveness of current police strategies in controlling crime can be improved if the police increase the quantity and quality of their contact with, and collaboration with the community (McElroy et al. 1993; Moore et al. 1988). The second assumption maintains that different communities have differing policing priorities and needs, and therefore, if policing is to be successful, it must be able to be adapted to those local needs and

---

[1] 'Whakatupato' means 'take care'.
[2] Iwi is an identifiable Maori community and is often a tribe or part of a tribe.
[3] A marae is a communal or sacred place, usually a community building or hall, which serves religious and social purposes in Polynesian societies.

priorities (Kusow et al. 1997). The third assumption relates to both the first and the second assumptions and proposes that an increase in police community collaboration together with an awareness of the different needs and priorities of communities will improve the image of police, resulting in a stronger relationship with the community (Grinc 1994).

The proviso in relation to community policing is that it is not known whether programs established as part of a community policing strategy improve the community's confidence in the police or promote the image of the police within a community (Kusow et al. 1997). According to Kusow et al. (1997), realizing community trust and confidence must be seen as the cornerstone upon which community policing programs can be implemented.

The literature relating to the relationship between the police and the community, especially in minority communities, is based primarily on research conducted in the United States of America and the United Kingdom. This narrow base of research applies generally to issues pertaining to race or ethnicity or aspects of community policing and indicates that the most significant determinant of attitude towards the police is the individual's perception of how the police related to that person in previous encounters (Scaglion and Condon 1980). Although the majority of the earlier studies show that ethnicity had an impact on attitudes to police, a study by Fultz in 1959 suggested that contact with the police was the most important determinant of an individual's attitude towards the police (cited in Webb and Marshall 1995). The perception of a previous encounter has been identified as being more significant in the individual's attitude towards the police than all other socioeconomic variables, including the individual's ethnicity or income (Scaglion and Condon 1980). The significance of the previous encounter in personal attitudes towards the police suggests that one of the most important variables in the police-community relationship is the style of policing. Furthermore, the variable highlights that policing programs that stress respectful officer-community interactions will reinforce positive police-community relationships (Scaglion and Condon 1980).

Historically however, research on the public's attitudes toward the police has been in two areas. The first area focused on identifying the determinants of the public's attitudes towards the police and the second focused on the fundamental and complex structure of the public's attitudes towards the police (Webb and Marshall 1995). The research into police-community relationships highlighted that the nature of citizen attitudes toward the police and the police attitude towards the community or towards a group within the community is an important determinant of whether the two groups can work together in a community policing context, especially in response to community safety or security (Greene and Decker 1989). The effect of attitude towards the police was taken a step further by Murty et al. (1990), who suggested that the police needed to portray a positive image towards the community in order to be able to function effectively and efficiently.

A more direct perspective was taken by Decker (1981), in relation to the effectiveness of the police. Decker emphasized that the police, because they are a public sector organization, needed community support to meet its goals. However, this research was based on individual-level and contextual variables and maintained that the most important predictors of attitudes towards the police are four individual-level variables – race, socioeconomic status, age, and gender (Decker 1981). Decker also identified that contextual variables such as neighbourhood culture, experiences with police, victimization, and experience with police programs could influence attitudes.

The one variable that can influence the public's attitude towards the police is the perception of police practices or the delivery of police services (Dunham and Alpert 1988). According to Dunham and Alpert (1988), the appropriateness of different police practices in some neighborhoods can influence the public's attitude, espe-cially in neighborhoods that reflect distinct cultures or that have different values from what are identified as mainstream values. Perception of the delivery of police services by a specific group in the community could affect their attitude towards the police to such a level that the police service in that area could be totally ineffective (Dunham and Alpert 1988; Murty et al. 1990; Webb and Marshall 1995). Durham and Alpert (1988), concluded that the linkage between police practices and cultural appropriateness was fundamental and justified the use of different police practices in different neighborhoods or different communities.

In summary, the research revealed that a community policing program that has been designed to improve the interaction between the police and the community may not specifically reduce crime, nor improve the community's attitude or confi-dence in the police, but the program may still need to be implemented as part of a wider community policing strategy to enhance the objectives of the police. An alter-native method to increase the probability of achieving an improvement in police-community relations from the introduction of a specific program is to ensure that strategies that improve the community's satisfaction with the police are imple-mented prior to implementing the community policing program (Kusow et al. 1997).

Firearms in New Zealand

The statutory basis for the licensing of firearms and their use in New Zealand is presented in the Arms Act 1983. The legislation creates the environment where pos-session of a firearm in New Zealand is considered a privilege, rather than a right (New Zealand Police 2013).

The Arms Act 1983, replaced the earlier dysfunctional firearms registration sys-tem that required a firearms user or owner to be licensed and introduced an intensive screening procedure for firearms applicants and lifetime firearms licenses. The intention of the Act was "to consolidate and amend the law relating to firearms and to promote both the safe use and the control of firearms and other weapons" (Arms Act 1983). The Act is a "licensing/no registration" system and does not restrict the number of firearms that a licence holder may acquire or own. The Act provided legislation in relation to the following areas:

- The licensing of firearms dealers;
- The importation of firearms;

- Restrictions on possession of specific firearms;
- The issuance of firearms licenses; and
- The procurement of pistols and restricted weapons (Arms Act 1983).

The Act sought to control firearms users rather than the actual firearm and marked a new era in the control of firearms in New Zealand. This approach added to the concept that it was the firearms user and not the firearm which posed a potential danger and hinged on the assumption that a preliminary vetting/check of firearms licence applicants would eliminate or minimize the prospect of unsuitable or possible high risk people from using or owning firearms (Thorp 1997).

To comply with the Act, the police were to develop and implement a firearms licence test that would ensure that licence applicants had a basic knowledge of firearm safety and their legal obligations (Forsyth 2011). The test was designed with the assistance of firearms and hunting groups and the delivery of the test was outsourced to the New Zealand Mountain Safety Council (Forsyth 2011).

This liberal approach to the control of firearms changed following the shooting of 13 people on 13 November 1990, in a small town in New Zealand's South Island by a young man using two semi-automatic rifles. The tragedy raised questions about the adequacy of the Arms Act, as the offender had been issued with a new licence in 1984, and the tragedy increased the call from the public for the introduction of tighter controls on the ownership of firearms (Thorp 1997). In response to the tragedy, the government introduced the 1992 Arms Amendment Act.

The Amendment Act legislated that all Military Styled Semi-Automatic weapons were to be registered, changed the lifetime firearms licence to a 10 year licence and introduced a number of firearms security storage prerequisites. These changes also saw the police investigating the suitability of a person to hold a licence, which included interviews with the applicant and referees and visits to their residence to evaluate the security in place for the storage of firearms and ammunition.

In 1997, there were approximately 210,000 firearms licence holders and between 700,000 to 1 million firearms in New Zealand (Thorp 1997). However, these figures increased to more than 250,000 firearms licence holders and between 1.5 and 2.2 million firearms by 2016 (Gatland 2016). The actual number of firearms in New Zealand is not known owing to the emphasis of the firearms licensing system being on the licence holder rather than on the registration of firearms.

In relation to the number of firearms licence holders and weapons, New Zealand experiences a low rate of casualties from the unintentional discharge of a weapon, but a high ratio of deaths to casualties. From 2000 to 2015, there were 97 casualties from an unintentional weapon discharge, but 27 deaths (27.2%) (Forsyth 2015). The high ratio is caused by the large number of hunting rifles in New Zealand in comparison to other firearms. Hunting rifles have greater power, which reduces the chance of survival (Forsyth 2015), especially when the incident takes place in a remote hunting location. The number of casualties and the number of deaths from unintentional firearms shootings for the period 2000–2015 is presented in Table 17.1.

Table 17.1 Unintentional firearms casualties and deaths 2000–2015

Year	Total casualties	Deaths	Year	Total casualties	Deaths
2000	17	4	2008	10	3
2001	14	4	2009	12	4
2002	4	0	2010	12	1
2003	18	6	2011	11	4
2004	6	1	2012	9	3
2005	9	1	2013	5	1
2006	11	1	2014	5	1
2007	7	1	2015[a]	N/K	6

Source: Forsyth 2011; 2015;
[a]*McQullan 2015.*

The Challenge for Maori

Maori are the indigenous people of New Zealand and make up 14.9% of the total population (Statistics New Zealand 2016). They are the most victimized social group in New Zealand society and according to police, generate more resolved crime and prosecutions than any other social group (New Zealand Police 2012). Maori comprise of 45% of police arrests, 38% of court convictions and over 50% of sentenced prison inmates (New Zealand Police 2016; Statistics New Zealand 2010, 2013). According to Speirs (2002), Maori are also significantly more likely than non-Maori to be reconvicted and re-imprisoned.[4]

The over-representation of Maori within the criminal justice sector is compounded by other social ills experienced by the majority of Maori. Researchers have, for example, identified a number of other adverse social problems experienced by Maori, including mental and physical ill-health (Statistics New Zealand 2013), unsatisfactory progress in housing and health intervention measures (Flynn et al. 2010), low educational achievement (Ford 2013), and low salaries (Pack et al. 2016).

In 2012, just under 40% of Maori youth left school without any qualifications and approximately 25% of Maori youth were unemployed (Marriott and Sim 2014). In 2015, 12.1% of adult Maori were unemployed (Statistics New Zealand 2016).

---

[4] Over three-quarters (78%) of Maori are reconvicted within 2 years of their release from prison, a rate around 10 percentage points higher than that for New Zealand European (68%) or Pacific Peoples inmates (66%). At 2 years from release, the reimprisonment rate for Maori is 43%, around 10% higher than New Zealand European (31%) or Pacific Peoples inmates (32%) (Speirs 2002; Nadesu 2009).

The Turning of the Tide

In response to the over-representation of Maori in the criminal justice system and the increasing importance of relationships and partnerships in community policing, the police developed and implemented a number of specific programs and strategies that would build the community's confidence in its procedures and its service delivery. It was hoped that the programmes and strategies would build a relationship with Maori and this would ensure that the police met their obligations under the Treaty of Waitangi.[5]

In 1996, the then Commissioner of the Police expressed his concern that the response of the police to the over-representation of Maori in the criminal justice system could be perceived as the police not being committed to the principles of the Treaty of Waitangi (New Zealand Police 2014; O'Reilly 2014). To ensure that the police were able to succeed in accomplishing its vision of 'Safer Communities Together', the police needed to establish, maintain and develop problem-solving partnerships with Maori (O'Reilly 2014). This reasoning led to the development of the strategy 'Responsiveness to Maori' in the early 2000s, which became the overarching document for the basis for the development of strategies to address ethnic minority and Maori criminal offending.

The Turning of the Tide strategy was developed in 2011 and set specific targets for reducing the disproportionate representation of Maori in offending, victimization and crash statistics.[6] The targets that police are to achieve by 2014/15 and 2017/18 are presented in Table 17.2. The strategy consolidated the earlier crime reduction programs developed by iwi groups. A key feature of The Turning of the Tide was the recognition of the role that iwi and Maori agencies, groups, whanau[7] and communities play in achieving these specific police objectives and outcomes (O' Reilly 2014).

The vision of the strategy was that "all Maori will live full and prosperous lives, free from crime and road trauma" and was presented within four specific values:

1. Aroha – we all make mistakes. We stand by our people who accept responsibility for their mistakes and try to put things right. We do not turn our backs on them, or judge them. But we don't make excuses for them either.
2. Whakarira – each generation strives to better themselves, for their own sakes and for the sake of their children.

---

[5] The Treaty of Waitangi is a Treaty between the Government (originally British and now New Zealand) and Maori signed in 1840 that established a British Governor of New Zealand, recognized Māori ownership of their lands, forests and other properties, and gave Māori the rights of British subjects

[6] The Turning the of Tide targets to be achieved by June 2014 were: 15% reduction in prosecutions of Maori, 10% reduction in Maori repeat offending, a 5% reduction in Maori first time offenders, 10% reduction in Maori repeat victims and a 10% reduction in Maori victims of fatal and serious vehicle crashes. Similar targets are in place for Turning the of Tide phase 2, which are to be achieved by June 2018 (New Zealand Police 2011b).

[7] Whanau is an extended family or community of related families who lived together in the same geographical area.

Table 17.2 Measuring success of the turning the tide strategy

Phase 1 – Comparing 2010/11 to 2014/15	Phase 2 – Comparing 2014/15 to 2017/18
A 5% decrease in the proportion of first-time youth and adult offenders who are Maori	A 5% decrease in the proportion of first-time youth and adult offenders who are Maori
A 10% decrease in the proportion of repeat youth and adult offenders who are Maori	A 10% decrease in the proportion of repeat youth and adult offenders who are Maori
A 10% decrease in the proportion of repeat victims who are Maori	A 10% decrease in the proportion of repeat victims who are Maori
A 15% reduction in Police (non-traffic) apprehensions of Maori resolved by prosecution	A 10% reduction in Police (non-traffic) apprehensions of Maori resolved by prosecution
A 10% decrease in the proportion of causalities in fatal and serious crashes who are Maori	A 10% decrease in the proportion of causalities in fatal and serious crashes who are Maori

Source: New Zealand Police (2011b)

3. Manaakitanga – we are hospitable, fair and respectful – to ourselves and others (New Zealand Police 2011b, p. 2).

The police implemented and delivered the strategy through a three-part operating model consisting of:

1. Mahi Tahi – everyone working together to prevent crime and crashes;
2. Whanau Ora – extended families preventing crime and crashes among themselves; and
3. Korerorero – talking crime and crash prevention in our homes and schools and on our marae (New Zealand Police 2011b)

The preferred method for reducing the disproportionate representation of Maori within the criminal justice system was to include actions that would bring about change. These actions included working with iwi and establishing support frameworks to reduce Maori male absenteeism from their families, improving the supervision of Maori children, keeping Maori children in school and improving Maori parenting skills (New Zealand Police 2011b).

To coordinate the national implementation of The Turning of the Tide, the strategy included a two phase action plan, with phase one covering the period 2012–2015. Both The Turning of the Tide and the action plan drew heavily on the philosophy and infrastructure that underpinned the all of government strategy Whanau Ora[8]; to work more closely with extended families to bring about change in individuals and in the community (New Zealand Police 2012).

---

[8] Whānau Ora (*family health*) is a major contemporary indigenous health initiative by Māori cultural values. Its core goal is to empower communities and extended families (*whānau*) to provide support within the community context rather than to individuals within an institutional context (Controller and Auditor General 2015).

Prevention First

Prevention First: The National New Zealand Police 2011a was launched in December 2011 and was the central element of the police service delivery model, which placed crime and prevention and the needs of victims at the front of policing (New Zealand Police 2011a). It was developed to provide the police with a platform to develop stronger partnerships with the community and to provide an opportunity to strengthen their responsiveness to Maori. Strengthening their response programs was to be achieved by working in partnership with iwi and local service providers to address the over-representation of Maori in the criminal justice system and as victims (New Zealand Police 2011a).

Prevention First sought a 13% reduction in recorded crime and as a result, had similar reduction targets as The Turning of the Tide (New Zealand Police 2012). The implementation of both Prevention First and The Turning of the Tide jointly in late 2011 provided a number of organizational synergies. Firstly, the strategies complemented each other through the provision of a similar prevention ethos to victimization, offending, and crashes among Maori, and secondly, both strategies committed the police and Maori to working together to achieve common goals (New Zealand Police 2012).

The Beginning of Whakatupato

In the late 2000s, there were four firearm-related events that took place in the Central North Island that led to the implementation of the Whakatupato program: the findings from research that found that a large number of rural Maori in the Bay of Plenty did not have firearms licenses; the response by the police in 2008 to a security intelligence operation that identified that a number of young Maori were undertaking guerrilla-type weapons training in an isolated area of the Bay of Plenty; recommendations made in a Rotorua firearms safety training development workshop held in early 2009; and research conducted in 2005 by a Rotorua Police Firearms Officer that examined the increasing trend in the number of hunting accidents that involved firearms in the Bay of Plenty district. The research found that:

- approximately 25% of rural Maori who use a firearm receive formal firearms safety training, the remainder rely on casual training from parents, relatives and friends;
- approximately 60% of rural Maori firearms users considered that they did not need a firearms licence to hunt on tribal or privately owned property;
- approximately 50% of rural Maori in the Northern Te Urewera area who possess a firearm are unlicensed;
- the main barrier to rural Maori receiving formal firearms training and testing is the cost and the travel (often multiple trips) required from remote rural communities to towns for such services;

- approximately 90% of firearms used by rural Maori is for harvesting food; and
- approximately 30% of rural Maori women use a firearm for shooting opossums and/or in the process of generating income (New Zealand Police 2009).

In the final summary of the research, the Firearms Officer made three observations: that the research findings indicated that there was a need for a comprehensive firearms training program which is tailored to the culture and interests of rural Maori communities; that such a program be delivered locally by the community for the community; and that the program is self-supporting for the long term (New Zealand Police 2009).

The second event that led to the development and the implementation of the Whakatupato program was, what has been colloquially referred to as, the Te Urewera raids, in 2008. The raids were the result of the monitoring by the New Zealand Security Intelligence Service of a group of young Maori training in the use of guerrilla-type weapons at paramilitary camps in isolated areas of the Te Urewera region. The intelligence gathered during the monitoring of the group led to the consideration of charges being laid under the Terrorism Suppression Act 2002. During the execution of the arrest warrants, police cordoned large areas of the district, including towns and communities, restricting the freedom of movement for the residents. The charges against the group were eventually dropped or re-laid as minor firearms offences.

The raids resulted in a number of complaints by the community and in allegations of a heavy-handed police response and the Police Commissioner subsequently apologized to Maori, especially the Tuhoe tribe, upon whose land and tribal area the raids took place.

The final event which led to the development of the Whakatupato program was a workshop hosted by the police and the New Zealand Mountain Safety Council in Rotorua in February 2009, which sought input into the development of a firearms safety training program specifically for rural Maori communities. Attendees of the workshop included local police officers and Firearms Officers, police management from national headquarters, local Maori Kaumatua,[9] and New Zealand Mountain Council Safety firearms instructors and administrators. Also in attendance was the mayor of one of the largest cities in the district and the Police National Manager of Maori, Pacific and Ethic Services, as well as a number of Police Maori Liaison Officers (New Zealand Police 2009). The workshop concluded with the development of three recommendations:

1. Local people that are suitably qualified and supported should be selected to deliver the firearms safety training to their communities;
2. Any specifically designed firearms safety training program should initially be delivered in the Northern and Central Te Urewera, Northland and Maniapoto regions; and

---

[9] Kaumatua is a local or iwi leader or elder. It is a title of respect.

3. All firearms safety training material should be specifically designed to ensure that it is suitable for delivery to rural Maori, especially in relation to cultural awareness (New Zealand Police 2009).

The Design of the Whakatupato Program

The information gathered from the research completed by the Rotorua Police Firearms Officer in 2005 and the three recommendations made by the workshop held in Rotorua in February 2009 formed the foundation for the development of the program. The intent of the program was founded on three overarching principles. The first principle was that the program must be delivered in a way that was culturally appropriate for Maori. The second was that the program was to be accessible to rural Maori and other rural community members, not only Maori, but members of other ethnicities and finally, that the program addressed the reasons for Maori possessing and using firearms (Spray et al. 2010, p. 4).

The design of the program included factors that would enable an understanding of firearms to be embedded and the skills and knowledge to not only ensure safe firearms practices but to also provide the opportunity for those in isolated communities to obtain a firearms licence (Spray et al. 2010). The program also recognised a number of Maori cultural factors, including the importance of firearms to Maori in supporting their traditional practices of food collection and the eradication of pests and the program was to be delivered as a cooperative program using the resources of police, the New Zealand Mountain Safety Council and iwi (Spray et al. 2010).

The police viewed the development of the program as a critical initiative for improving their relationship with Maori, and as a part of the apology process to the Tuhoe tribe in the Te Urewera region (New Zealand Police 2009; Spray et al. 2010). The view that the program would assist in improving relationships with Maori was also shared by the Mountain Safety Council (Spray et al. 2010). Both institutions identified the program as a vehicle to further integrate the needs of Maori into their policies and service delivery procedures and as a method for developing an improved understanding of the outdoor safety needs of Maori, especially in relation to hunting (Spray et al. 2010).

The initial aims of the program were to promote the safe use of firearms in rural communities and to encourage people to gain their firearms licence to comply with New Zealand law (Wakefield n.d.). The intention was that the program would be extended over the 5 years following its introduction to eventually being offered throughout the country and it was for this reason that it was believed that it was important that support for Maori be established and their input included in the program development. Maori support was essential in order to ensure that the program would be integrated into a range of iwi settings and communities (Spray et al. 2010).

The First Whakatupato Course

To identify the locations that would receive the delivery of the first series of Whakatupato courses, the police conducted a number of consultation sessions in mid-2010 with local Maori leaders and elders and those who had an interest in Maori firearms safety in the Bay of Plenty region (Spray et al. 2010). These meetings led to the first Whakatupato courses being delivered in early 2011 in the Te Urewera and in the East Cape region, both of which are extremely isolated and suffer from a number of social deprivation and poverty issues. The courses were based on the Arms Code, firearms safety, firearms legislation, types and uses of firearms, firearms handling, transporting, care and maintenance, safe hunting practices and guidance with applying for a firearms licence (Wakefield n.d.).

In the program's first year, six one-day courses, each having a budget of $50,000 were delivered to between 40 and 50 participants (Spray et al. 2010). During the period 2010/2011 to 2014/2015, the same delivery model and budget remained in place with the program delivering between six and eight courses a year to 15–25 course participants in rural communities in the Bay of Plenty, Northland and the East Cape.

The importance of the program was finally recognized in mid-2014, when one of the largest Maori tribes in the North Island, Tuwharetoa, approached the Mountain Safety Council to deliver the program across its 26 maraes. Tuwharetoa were primarily interested in improving the safety of the people in their tribe and in improving firearms safety in all of its rural areas and proposed that the tribe would pay the firearms licence fee for 20 iwi members from each of its marae over the following 3 years (Pyatt 2015). From April 2015 to January 2016, the program was delivered to an approximately 20 participants at three different maraes.

View of Whakatupato Participants

The quality of the content and the delivery of the program has been measured since the first course was delivered in 2011 by surveying the participants at the conclusion of the course. The survey included six Likert-type questions pertaining to the level of quality of the course, whether the safety information was delivered in a way that the participants understood and whether the course would make a difference as to how the participants would use a firearm in the future.

The return rate of the surveys varied between 85–100%, while the overall satisfaction with the course ranged from 90 to 100% (McKee 2016a, b). The lowest overall satisfaction score was recorded for the first course delivered in Te Urewera in 2011 at 75% (Pyatt 2015).

Since the introduction of the program, another area that has improved is the delivery of the content to suit the participants. 60% of participants in the first course claimed that the course was very easy to understand and 25% maintained that the course was easy to understand (Pyatt 2015). These results improved to 75% and 25% respectfully by 2015 (McKee 2016a, b).

Discussion

The past 40 years have seen numerous efforts by police around the world to implement specific community oriented service delivery programs to regain public trust.
Programs have been introduced to address specific vulnerabilities within communities, particularly when the vulnerability is relevant to the policing process (Williams
1982; Tyler 2005). In this case study, the term 'vulnerability' pertains to the possibility that the police have ignored the issue that a large percentage of the rural community have access to firearms and that a large percentage of the users of these
firearms are unlicensed or have not received any firearms safety training. This perception was substantiated by a number of commentators when this information was
linked anecdotally to the number of unintentional firearms discharges that resulted
in deaths to hunters (New Zealand Police 2009; Wakefield n.d.).

The design and the implementation of Whakatupato were in response to the
perceived risk in vulnerability and in response to the three firearm events that
occurred in the central North Island in the late 2000s. Central to the development of
the program was the result of the research examining firearms related deaths in the
Bay of Plenty. The findings of the research indicated a need for a comprehensive
firearms training program that was specifically tailored to the culture and the interests of rural communities, especially Maori (Wakefield n.d.).

Although the Whakatupato program has been operating since 2010, police have
been reticent in realizing its full benefit and potential. However, this approach may
be changing. In November 2015, a report was prepared for the Deputy Chief
Executive of the Maori, Pacific and Ethnic Services outlining the benefits of the
program. The report identified that the program could provide some assistance in
the implementation of the three police strategies: Prevention First, The Turning of
the Tide and Iwi Partnerships (Taikato 2015).

In relation to Prevention First, in the wake of an increasing number of unintentional firearms incidents by recreational firearms users in 2015, the Whakatupato
program enhanced the expansion of the firearms safety message and increased the
awareness within the rural and Maori community of the need to provide adequate
security storage for firearms (Taikato 2015). These safety messages would also have
an impact on the operationalization of the Turning of the Tide strategy through the
program's heavily reliance on productive partnerships with iwi and the rural community. This could mean that there maybe a factor of efficiency with the implementation of both the strategy and the program.

The efficiency of implementing both the strategy and the program together could
be realized through the strategy's key operationalized component; iwi ownership
and delivery of the program. In this sense, efficiency would be increased through
iwi taking responsibility for ensuring their members attend the Whakatupato
program, which would result in an increase in firearms safety awareness and the
participants of the program obtaining a firearms licence (Taikato 2015).

Delivering the Whakatupato program in partnership with iwi could provide a
number of benefits to the police. These benefits could be achieved through the
Police Firearms Safety Officers and Iwi Liaison Officers working with iwi to deliver

the program on maraes. This would ensure that the firearm safety message is disseminated widely within the rural community (Taikato 2015). A joint approach to the delivery of the program should improve iwi-police relationships (Taikato 2015).

The relationship between police and Maori, or individual iwi is the crux to improving Maori confidence in the police, increasing firearms safety in rural Maori communities and reducing the occurrence of crime in rural communities. However, to start building a relationship with Maori, any police crime prevention program must be based on Maori cultural values (Doone 2000). According to Doone (2000), using Maori cultural values in crime prevention programs is successful in reducing offending by Maori because the approach:

1. builds cultural knowledge, self-image and pride in being Maori;
2. creates a sense of identity, belonging and confidence;
3. improves retention in programs;
4. breaks down barriers to learning and gives a sense of achievement;
5. enhances willingness to learn other skills; and
6. builds positive attitudes towards program providers, whanau and wider society.

The use of Maori cultural values in crime prevention is supported by earlier research by Maxwell and Stephens (1991), who claim that given the right type of police contact with Maori, it is possible that the police will increase their understanding of Maori and promote positive responses that are more widely accepted by the Maori community. However, O'Reilly (2014), noted that such an approach by the police will take time to produce a tangible result because establishing a relationship takes time and needs to be in place before a relationship can be developed into a partnership.

The development of a partnership with Maori is not only important in the current context of Maori being the most victimized social group in New Zealand, but is important because indications are that the Maori population will increase which will result in larger numbers of Maori offenders and victims. This creates a pressing need for a better response by government agencies to address offending and victimization among Maori, especially young Maori. Maori have a youthful population, and the number of Maori in the 15 to 29-year-old age group is projected to increase by 28% by 2021 (Statistics New Zealand 2013, 2016). This means that a reduction in demand from Maori for police services will have more of an impact on the performance of the police and the achievement of their strategic goals than if there were a similar reduction in the level of offending in any other social group.

Conclusion

The Whakatupato firearms safety program is different from other programs because it is culturally based and includes a specific venue, presentation style and course content that has been adapted to suit the audience. As a result of the community focus of the program, its delivery is bringing a sense of awareness, safety, education, pride and legality in the handling and use of firearms to rural communities (McKee 2016b). According to the program's participants, the cultural approach has also been the basis for its success (McKee 2016a, b).

The police need to build on the success of the program. This is something that the police are not currently doing, but should strongly consider. The program should be expanded to other tribal areas in the North and the South Islands which will strengthen their relationship with Maori and will allow other crime prevention programs for Maori and rural communities to be developed. What is not associated with the program, is the level of associated social capital. In the reports prepared by McKee (2015, 2016a) and Pyatt (2015), it is noted that the completion of the course by the participants and the obtaining of their firearms licence is regarded highly as a personal achievement, and for some participants, the first educationally-based achievement in their lives. This achievement, for some participants, is a catalyst to seek legal employment (McKee 2016a,b). It is the economic and capability components that are missing from any discussion of the benefits of the program.

This article has discussed one crime prevention program that has been designed to address a specific problem affecting an indigenous community but is capable of being adapted as a response to other crime problems in indigenous or ethnic communities. The Whakatupato firearms safety program provides an avenue for the police to improve community trust and to further develop their relationship with Maori. However, a more in-depth evaluation of the program is required in order to determine its suitability as a crime prevention model for use by other police agencies to improve their relationships with their ethnic or minority communities.

References

Arms Act. (1983).

Arms Regulations (1992) (SR 1992/346).

Cao, L. (2001). *Origins of community policing in the US and its implications for Chinese policing.* Paper presented at the International Symposium on Community Policing, Nanjing, China.

Controller and Auditor General. (2015). *Whanau Ora: The first four years.* Wellington: The Officer of the Auditor General.

Decker, S. (1981). Citizen attitudes toward the police. *Journal of Police Science and Administration, 9*(1), 81–87.

den Heyer, G. (2013). Shape or adapt? The future of policing. *Salus Journal, 1*(1), 41–54.

Doone, P. (2000). *Report on combating and preventing Maori crime.* Wellington: Crime Prevention Unit, Department of Prime Minister and Cabinet.

Dunham, R., & Alpert, G. (1988). Neighborhood differences in attitudes toward policing: Evidence for a mixed-strategy model of policing in a multi-ethnic setting. *The Journal of Criminal Law and Criminology, 79*(2), 504–521.

Eck, J., & Rosenbaum, D. (1994). The new police order: Effectiveness, equity and efficiency in community policing. In D. Rosenbaum (Ed.), *The challenge of community policing* (pp. 3–23). Thousand Oaks: Sage.

Flynn, M., Crane, S. & Soa-Lafoa'I, M. (2010). *Maori housing trends 2010.* Housing New Zealand Report 2010. Retrieved from Housing New Zealand website http://www.hnzc.co.nz.

Ford, T. (2013). My research journey: Contributing to a new education story for Maori. In N. Berryman, S. Soohoo, & A. Nevin (Eds.), *Culturally responsive methodologies* (pp. 87–106). Bingley: Emerald Publishing Group.

Forsyth, C. (2011). *New Zealand firearms: An exploration into firearm possession, use and misuse in New Zealand*. Wellington: New Zealand Deerstalkers' Association.

Forsyth, C. (2015). Analysis of mountain safety council and New Zealand police data on unintentional shootings 2004–2014. Retrieved from Spring Shooters New Zealand website http://sportingshooters.nz/wp-content/uploads/2015/12/Analysis-of-MSC-unintentional-shootings-mk-2.pdf.

Gatland, E. (2016). Personal correspondence. National Firearms Coordinator, New Zealand Police.

Greene, J., & Decker, S. (1989). Police and community perceptions of the community role in policing: The Philadelphia experience. *The Howard Journal, 28*(2), 105–121.

Grinc, R. (1994). Angels in marble: Problems in stimulating community involvement in community policing. *Crime and Delinquency, 40*(July), 437–468.

Kusow, A., Wilson, L., & Martin, D. (1997). Determinants of citizen satisfaction with the police: The effects of residential location. *Policing: An International Journal of Police Strategy and Management, 20*(4), 655–664.

Marriott, L., & Sim, D. (2014). *Indicators of inequality for Maori and Pacific People.*. Working papers in public finance 09/2014, August. Wellington: Victoria University Business School.

Maxwell, G. & Stephens, D. (1991). *Police perceptions of Maori: A report to the New Zealand Police and the Ministry of Maori Development*. Wellington, New Zealand: Te Puni Kokiri.

McElroy, J., Casgrove, C., & Sadd, S. (1993). Community policing: The CPOP in New York. In *Newbury Park*. California: Sage.

McKee, M. (2015). Report on Whakatupato firearms safety delivery at Otukou Marae, *Turangi 28/29 November 2015*. Wellington: Firearms Safety Specialists New Zealand Limited.

McKee, M. (2016a). *Report on Whakatupato firearms safety delivery at Tokaanu Marae,*. Turangi 30/31 January 2016. Wellington: Firearms Safety Specialists New Zealand Limited.

McKee, N. (2016b). *Whakatupato programme for firearm safety in isolated areas* (pp. 37–38). Autumn: New Zealand Hunting and Wildlife.

McQullan, L. (2015). Shooting deaths spark calls for gun laws shake-up. *Stuff.* Retrieved from http://www.stuff.co.nz/national/73030491/shooting-deaths-spark-calls-for-a-gun-laws-shakeup.

Moore, M., Trojanowcz, R., & Kelling, G. (1988). *Crime and policing. Washington DC. Perspectives on policing, monograph number 3*. Washington, DC: National Institute of Justice, US Department of Justice.

Murty, K., Roebuck, J., & Smith, J. (1990). Image of the police in black Atlanta communities. *Journal of Police Science and Administration, 17*(4), 250–257.

Nadesu, A. (2009). *Reconviction patterns of released prisoners: A 60-month follow-up analysis*. Wellington: Department of Corrections.

New Zealand Police. (2009). *Proposal: Firearms safety training programme for rural Maori communities*. Wellington: New Zealand Police.

New Zealand Police. (2011a). *Prevention first: National operating strategy 2011–2015*. Wellington: New Zealand Police.

New Zealand Police. (2011b). *The turning of the tide*. Wellington: New Zealand Police.

New Zealand Police. (2012). *The turning of the tide: Action plan – Phase one 2012/13 to 2014/15*. Wellington: New Zealand Police.

New Zealand Police. (2013). *Arms code: Firearms safety manual*. Wellington: New Zealand Police.

New Zealand Police. (2014). *Establishing Maori advisory boards manual chapter*. Police Executive Meeting, 24 March 2014. Wellington: New Zealand Police.

New Zealand Police. (2016). *The turning of the tide strategy 2012/13–2017/18*. Wellington: New Zealand Police.

O'Reilly, J. (2014). *A review of Police and iwi/Maori relationships: Working together to reduce offending and victimization among Maori*. Wellington: New Zealand Police.

Pack, S., Tuffin, K., & Lyons, A. (2016). Accounting for racism against Maori in Aotearoa/New Zealand: A discourse analytic study of the views of Maori adults. *Journal of Community Applied Social Psychology, 26*(2), 95–109.

Pyatt, M. (2015). *Report on Whakatupato programme at Pakira Marae*. Wellington: New Zealand Mountain Safety Council.

Ren, L., Cao, L., Lovrich, N., & Gaffney, M. (2005). Linking confidence in the police with the performance of the police: Community policing can make a difference. *Journal of Criminal Justice, 33*(1), 55–66.

Scaglion, R., & Condon, R. (1980). Determinants of attitudes toward city police. *Criminology, 17*(4), 485–494.

Speirs, P. (2002). *Reconviction and imprisonment rates for released prisoners*. Wellington, New Zealand: Ministry of Justice.

Spray, M., Carpenter, D., & Brodie, R. (2010). Rural Maori communities – Firearms safety training programme: Stage 1 – Pilot (Bay of Plenty). In *Wellington*. New Zealand: New Zealand Mountain Safety Council.

Statistics New Zealand. (2010). *Crime victimization patterns in New Zealand: New Zealand General Social Survey 2008 and New Zealand Crime and Safety Survey 2006 Compared*. Wellington: Statistics New Zealand.

Statistics New Zealand (2013). Quick stats about Maori. Retrieved from Statistics New Zealand website: http://www.stats.govt.nz/Census/2013-census-profile-and-summary-reports.

Statistics New Zealand (2016). Maori social indicators. Retrieved from Statistics New Zealand website: http://www.stats.govt.nz/browse_for_stats/snapshots-of-nz/nz-social-indicators/Home/Labour%20market/unemployment.aspx.

Taikato, P. (2015). *Revised Whakatupato 'rural community firearms safety' programme*. Wellington: New Zealand Police.

Terrorism Suppression Act (2002) (No 34).

Thorp, T. (1997). *Review of firearms control in New Zealand: Summary and conclusions of the report of an independent inquiry commissioned by the Minister of Police*. Wellington: GP Print.

Thurman, Q., & Zhao, J. (2004). *Contemporary policing: Controversies, challenges and solutions: An anthology*. Los Angeles: Roxbury Publishing Company.

Tyler, T. (2005). Policing in black and white: Ethnic group difference in trust and confidence in the police. *Police Quarterly, 8*(3), 322–342.

Wakefield, T. (n.d..). Whakatupato: A firearms safety training programme for rural communities. Press release by Mountain Safety Council.

Webb, V., & Marshall, C. (1995). The relative importance of race and ethnicity on citizen attitudes toward the police. *American Journal of Police., XIV, 14*(2), 45–66.

Williams, D. (1982). The Brixton disorders: Case and comment. *Cambridge Law Journal, 41*(1), 1–6.

Zhao, J., Lovrich, N., & Thurman, Q. (1999). The status of community policing in American cities: Facilitators and impediments revisited. *Policing: An International Journal of Police Strategies and Management, 22*(1), 74–92.

Chapter 18
Policing in the Multi-Cultural and Multi-Ethnic Environment of South Africa

Christiaan Bezuidenhout

Introduction

The first Europeans to discover "the Cape" in South Africa and to write about it were the Portuguese. The Southern tip of Africa or Cape Town as it is known today has no written history before it was first mentioned by Portuguese explorer Bartholomeu Dias in 1488. Bartholomeu Dias arrived in 1488 after journeying south along the west coast of Africa. The next recorded European sighting of the Cape was by Vasco da Gama in 1497 while he was searching for a route that would lead directly from Europe to Asia. The Dutch was next to write about Cape Town and to settle or inhabit the Southern tip of Africa in 1652. Before 1652, when the Dutch Commander Jan van Riebeeck and his 90-man crew settled in South Africa, the earliest representatives of South Africa's diversity, at least the earliest that is identifiable, were the San and Khoekhoe people (otherwise known as the Bushmen and Hottentots or Khoikhoi). They were residents of the Southern tip of the continent for thousands of years before its written history began with the arrival of European seafarers. Other long-term inhabitants of the Southern tip of Africa were the Bantu-speaking or Black people who had gradually moved into the Southern tip of the continent from the far north (Congo) many years before the arrival of the Europeans. Several different ethnic groups developed over time and settled in different geographical rural areas in South Africa. Over time they developed their own unique languages and informal indigenous legal as well as cultural practices. In 1652 Jan van Riebeeck was send by the Dutch East India Company to build a fort and develop a vegetable garden in South Africa (Cape of Good Hope / Cape Town) for the benefit of ships on the Eastern trade route. He brought with him European legal practices. By the end of the eighteenth century, the Dutch interest in the Cape

C. Bezuidenhout (✉)
University of Pretoria, Pretoria, South Africa
e-mail: christiaan.bezuidenhout@up.ac.za

© Springer Nature Switzerland AG 2019
J. F. Albrecht et al. (eds.), *Policing and Minority Communities*,
https://doi.org/10.1007/978-3-030-19182-5_18

of Good Hope faded, and the British used this opportunity to seize the Cape in 1795. The British also implemented some of their legal practices. This imply that South Africa have a mixture of indigenous, Dutch-Roman, English, Apartheid as well as democratic legal initiatives merged into the current legal and policing system (Bezuidenhout 2015, p. 196; Bezuidenhout 2017, p. 143; Bezuidenhout and Little 2012, p. 369; Dippenaar 1988, pp. 322–323, 421, 480–481, 486–487, 497, 539, 557, 634, 637; Official South Africa Yearbook 1993, pp. 9–20; South Africa Yearbook 1995, pp. 27–35).

British sovereignty of the area was recognized at the Congress of Vienna in 1815. The British introduced British law into the Cape after the seizure of the Cape Colony from the Dutch. The Union of South Africa is the historic predecessor to the present-day republic of South Africa. It came into effect on 31 May 1910 with the unification of four previously separate British colonies. A centralised police was needed because it was believed that the, police was too local and decentralized in each of the separate British colonies and the territories formerly recognised as part of the Boer (White European citizens opposed to the British rule) republics. The different police forces had diverse missions and functions which were problematic (Brewer 1994, p. 29–30). In this vein during 1911 it was decided to reorganize the police forces of the newly formed Union of South Africa similar to the structures that were used in the former Cape Colony. This implied that from 1 April 1913, two police forces were formed within the Union of South Africa, namely the:

- South African Police (SAP) who was deemed the regular police force of the Union. The policemen could also be called up in time of war.
- South African Mounted Rifles (SAMR) who was deemed the first permanent force of military constabulary. These police men could, in a time of peace undertake policing duties in areas traditionally occupied by the majority Black population of South Africa (South African Police Services (SAPS) 2012).

These two forces therefore worked together with the SAP basically having policing jurisdiction in urban areas mostly frequented by the White minority and the SAMR having jurisdiction over rural areas mainly populated by Black people (Brewer 1994, p. 38). While the SAP was promulgated under the Police Act and was developed to maintain law and order and manage crime, the SAMR was promulgated under the Defence Act and had a para-militaristic style of law enforcement. Race relations, political unrest, strikes in the mining industry and the looming World War II (WWII) at the time also had an influence on the policing style of SAP and the SAMR (Brewer 1994, p. 38). In 1926, the SAMR was absorbed into the SAP and the SAP and the SAMR became one force (Brewer 1994, p. 74). However with the outbreak of the WWII the SAMR members were called to war duty and the SAP assumed their policing responsibilities in the rural areas. In addition some SAP members were also called for military duty in the war.

The SAP was therefore eventually officially created after the Union of South Africa was established in 1913. The SAP was the successor to the police forces of the Cape Colony, the Natal Colony, the Orange River Colony, and the Transvaal Colony. The entire force had to be restructured, and for a short period, the South

African Defence Force's (SADF) military police assisted the SAP when necessary. The SAP and the military maintained their close relationship even after the SAP assumed permanent responsibility for domestic law and order in 1926. Police officials often called on the army for support in emergencies. In WWII, one SAP brigade served with the 2nd Infantry Division of the South African Army in North Africa (Potgieter 1974, p. 632). The police of the time saw their duty of providing security to the country as a type of rivalry and the citizens of the country were viewed as enemies [us and them] (Hornberger 2013, p.598). By 1948 there was growing irritation from the White population with wartime restrictions that were still in place as set by the British rule of the time, and in addition living costs had increased sharply. These factors as well as continued pressure, domestic wars and resistance paved the way for a parliamentary election in South Africa on 26 May 1948.

When the Reunited National Party (later changed to the National Party [NP]) edged out its more liberal opponents in nationwide elections in 1948, the new government enacted legislation strengthening the relationship between the police and the military. Although racial segregation in South Africa began in colonial times under Dutch and British rule, apartheid as an official policy was introduced following the general election of 1948. New legislation classified inhabitants into four racial groups ("Native," [Black] "White," "Coloured," and "Asian"), and residential areas were segregated, sometimes by means of forced removals. This system of racial segregation and the enforcement thereof through legislation by the NP government (the ruling party from 1948 to 1994) caused many frustrations and grievances. In line with the segregation between White and Black the SAP maintained its military character. The police were given more power during this time period with the scope of their duties being extended, police brutality being allowed and specified legislation allowing the police to search people and their premises without a warrant (Brewer 1994, p. 207). After the 1948 election The National Party also removed remaining symbols of the historic British control. The elected government greatly strengthened minority White control of the country.

Under this system, the rights of the majority Black inhabitants of South Africa were curtailed, and White supremacy and Afrikaner minority rule was maintained. The police also focused their intentions predominantly on the protection of the White minority. Apartheid was therefore cultivated after WWII by the White Afrikaner-dominated NP and "Broederbond" (brotherhood) organizations. The minority White police force were heavily armed after that, especially when facing unruly or hostile majority Black crowds. During the apartheid regime, the police were used mainly for the protection of the White minority and the furtherance of the unequal political climate. This was a paradox in policing at that time as the majority usually dictates the political and policing structures and dogma in a country. The police were tasked with the function of guaranteeing the success of segregation in South Africa, which resulted in general crime prevention mainly being allocated to the White minority (apparently a 70%:30% distribution). At that stage, political unrest was rife, and the majority Black population regularly staged different uprisings. The government used announcements to declare a state of emergency whenever uprisings threatened the stability of the country. They used this tactic to crack down against their Black political opponents at times of heightened resistance. Police could detain anyone for reasons of public safety. Also, meetings and gatherings could be banned by the police. The first state of emergency was declared in 1960 after the Sharpeville Massacre when the African National Congress (ANC) and Pan Africanist Congress (PAC) also were declared illegal political parties (Bezuidenhout 2015, p. 196; Bezuidenhout 2017, p. 143; Bezuidenhout and Little 2012, p. 369; Brewer 1994, p.76).

During the National Parties reign (1948–1994), several political liberation struggles by different "illegal" political parties forced the White minority government to use the police as their pawns. This led to the SAP being used as a tool of repression by the minority White population against the Black majority population. No special strategies were known to accommodate different Black ethnic groups, the Coloured or Indian groups. All were treated as the enemy of the state. The police were the gatekeepers of the apartheid government. The police was used to protect the White minority against the actions of the Black majority to attain sovereign political power. The pinnacle was the 1976 uprising by school-going children who protested against the Afrikaans Medium Decree of 1974, which forced all Black schools to use Afrikaans and English in a 50:50 mix as languages of instruction ("Afrikaans" was the first language of most of the White Afrikaner group, the Coloured group and some other minority groupings in South Africa [e.g. Riemlanders] – the language was developed from Dutch, French, German and other languages). This Decree introduced a wave of uprisings and strikes against the White minority government as many Blacks have their own unique indigenous language and refused to be educated in a second language. Also, by the 1990's the police had received a reputation of being brutal and ill-equipped to deal with ordinary crime and specific groups who needed special policing strategies and interventions. Special crime strategies to work with minority groups or sensitive groups in society did not exist. The police were highly militarized and hierarchical. Change was needed if a democratic policy was to be pursued. After extended international pressure, sanctions and increasing pressure from the majority Black populace in South Africa did the minority White group decided to hand over their political control to a Black majority coalition in 1994. It was the work since 1990 of the then leader of the National Party President F.W. de Klerk who began negotiations to end Apartheid. His decision to negotiate for the end of the segregation period led to the Democratic elections that were held in 1994. The African National Congress (ANC) won the elections by a large majority and Nelson Mandela was elected as the first Black president of South Africa. The immediate focus was on the abolition of the death penalty, the improvement of rehabilitation services, the reduction of oppressive control mechanisms, and the recognition of the rights of every SA citizen including suspects and prisoners. The objective was to criminalize less, to minimize the use of custody, to humanize prisons, and to reintegrate prisoners into the community. A restorative justice approach was adopted at the same time that crime rates increased dramatically after democratization.

Already In 1991 the South African Police began a series of internal restructurings which included elements such as the de-politicization of the police, greater levels of accountability, more visible policing, changes in service delivery objectives and the restructuring of the police force (Rauch 2001, p. 1–12). The role of most of the specialised units was also integrated into general policing functions. The challenge to policing now became even more demanding as the Black majority coalition consisted of several different Black ethnic groups. Each ethnic group came with their own identity, language, policing needs and requirements. Some of the Black ethnic groups were now minorities (e.g. The Venda group) and some Black ethnic groups were more dominant than others (e.g. The Zulu and the Xhosa ethnic groups). They (Zulu and Xhosa) represented a majority representation compared to many other Black ethnic groupings in South Africa. The previously dominant White political grouping became a small minority grouping in South Africa. The diversity in race, ethnicity and language posed many challenges in the ideal of implementing a fair democratic police. Thus policing practices faced very complex challenges in South Africa as many members come from different ethnic backgrounds and the different groupings needed to be policed fairly. South Africa adopted eleven official languages in its Constitution. Mr. Mandela wanted everyone in South Africa to be equal before the law. He envisaged the police in South Africa to change their character from operating in a militarised manner to a demilitarised style. In 1995, the introduction of the South African Police Service Act (Act 68 of 1995), implemented the changes envisaged into a legal framework. The restructuring of the police was now in full progress and the "force" had to make way for a "service" and a more accountable and civilian based police service was envisaged. The emphasis on creating better relations between the police and the community and adopting a new mind set within policing was inevitable. With the appointment of the national commissioner of the SAPS in January 1995, the process of changing from a police force to a police service formally started. The idea of the early 1990s of a police service accountable to the community through its democratically elected institutions had to be given practical manifestation (De Vries 2008, p. 129). The plethora of legislative and policy changes which South Africa has undergone since 1994 has had a significant impact on the approaches and philosophy informing the transformation of policing services. Aimed at improving the effectiveness and efficiency of policing services, these changes have emphasised two important elements, namely community involvement and a human-rights based approach to policing. The vision of the South African Police Service (SAPS) envisaged endeavours to create a safe and secure environment for all the different groupings in South Africa. Its mission is to create this by participating in activities to deal with the root causes of crime in all communities, as well as working to prevent any action which may threaten the safety and security of any community or person and finally, to investigate incidents of crime in order to bring the perpetrators of such action to justice (Govender 2010, p. 69). Many service delivery changes and initiatives were introduced and the police were renamed to the SAPS. Demilitarization occurred and different police strategies and philosophies were introduced such as community policing (CP) and sector policing (SP). Mass recruitment drives were initiated to change the police profile from a dominant White organization to a dominant Black organization to ensure that the police represented the race profile of the country. The last two decades has seen many challenges for policing in South Africa, caused by aspects influencing the internal and external environment of the police service. It was believed that community and sector policing were adequately solving the country's widely documented crime problem. However the changes after 1994 did not produce the envisaged results. In fact, many practitioners and academics question the impact and value of the new types of police philosophies in South Africa and highlight that SAPS have unofficially reverted back to a shoot first and ask later approach (militarisation). Violent crimes are soaring and the police service in South Africa is buckling under the pressure to police according to a client friendly human rights ethos in an extraordinary violent country. Every citizen in South Africa as well as special needs and minority groups are all dealt with in a similar way. No special permissions or grants exist for minority groups in South Africa.

Overview: Changes from Militaristic to a Service-Oriented Policing and Back Again

The South African Police Service (SAPS) has undergone a paradigm shift since the abolishment of the apartheid regime in 1994. Before 1994, the South African Police (SAP) employed a militaristic approach to policing, which was based on limited community involvement in policing matters. Since then, the 'force' has changed into a 'service' with the emphasis on community policing, a philosophy of policing that emphasises a co-operative approach between the police and citizens focusing on solving community problems and improving the quality of life in the community in general (Wilson et al. 2001: 30). Specific policing strategies for minorities were not introduced as everyone in South Africa was promised equal treatment by the new Constitution. In Chap. 2: Bill of Rights (South African Constitution) the following is pledged:

Equality means the following in Section 9:

1. Everyone is equal before the law and has the right to equal protection and benefit of the law.
2. Equality includes the full and equal enjoyment of all rights and freedoms. To promote the achievement of equality, legislative and other measures designed to protect or advance persons, or categories of persons, disadvantaged by unfair discrimination may be taken.
3. The state may not unfairly discriminate directly or indirectly against anyone on one or more grounds, including race, gender, sex, pregnancy, marital status, ethnic or social origin, colour, sexual orientation, age, disability, religion, conscience, belief, culture, language and birth.
4. No person may unfairly discriminate directly or indirectly against anyone on one or more grounds in terms of subsection (3). National legislation must be enacted to prevent or prohibit unfair discrimination.

5. Discrimination on one or more of the grounds listed in subsection (3) is unfair unless it is established that the discrimination is fair.

In addition the South African Police Service Act, 1995 (Act No. 68 of 1995) was promulgated after the Constitution was finalized. Lesese (2018) state that in the preamble of this act it requires for the establishment, organisation, regulation and control of the South African Police Service to provide a police service throughout the national territory to inter alia:

– ensure the safety and security of all persons and property in the national territory;
– uphold and safeguard the fundamental rights of every person as guaranteed by the Constitution;
– ensure co-operation between the Service and the communities it serves in the combating of crime;
– reflect respect for victims of crime and an understanding of their needs; and
– ensure effective civilian supervision over the Service.

Lasese (2018) indicates that SAPS makes no distinction between persons on the basis of race, gender, sex, pregnancy, marital status, ethnic or social origin, colour, sexual orientation, age, disability, religion, conscience, belief, culture, language and birth. Although no specifically trained minority policing squad exist SAPS are sensitive to the needs of the community and victims of crime. There are broad legislative frameworks that can be hazily interpreted that the police are considerate to some minority groups such as the victims of crime. This "sensitivity" is illustrated in some official police documents such as:

– National Instruction 2 of 2012: Victim Empowerment;
– National Instruction 3 of 2013: Sector Policing;
– Sections 18 to 23 of the South African Police Service Act, 1995 (Act No. 68 of 1995) dealing with Community Police Forums and Boards;
– The Rural Safety Strategy;
– Crime Prevention Partnership Guidelines;
– The Manual for Community Based Crime Prevention;
– National Instruction 5 of 2014: Reporting the detention, death or complaint of a foreign national and Standard Operating Procedure 1 of 2016 Detention, death and victim of crime of a Foreign National.

Some new policing initiatives were therefore introduced to provide momentum with this "equality" before the law approach. With regard to the aforementioned a few initiatives will now be unpacked to determine their value to policing in general and more specifically on minority policing. When South Africa became a democracy in 1994 CP was introduced but, has until now, not adequately solved the country's widely documented crime problem. Against the background of a struggling community policing philosophy in South-Africa many police managers and politicians became desperate to nullify criticisms. After much deliberation and non-consensus since 1998 between senior managers in the police was SP officially accepted as an additional tool to community policing to ensure "equality" before the law. A national instruction about SP was promulgated in this regard on 13 July 2009. After 2009, a fresh emphasis was placed on the sector policing initiative, which was aimed at preserving the social order by encouraging police involvement in smaller, more manageable geographical sectors contained in a particular police precinct (Bezuidenhout 2011, p. 11; Van Niekerk 2016, p.3).

Although SP was officially implemented much later (2009) than CP (1994), it can essentially be described as a tool or strategy to implement community policing more effectively. As a strategy or method, sector policing implies a co-operative and symbiotic relationship between law enforcement and the community. In 2003, before proper endorsement and implementation of sector policing in 2009, sector policing was not only regarded as a practical manifestation of community policing, but also as "… a step towards the development of a modern, democratic policing style for the present century and thus to address the safety and security need of every inhabitant of South Africa" (SAPS Training Division 2004, p. 4).

After the official instruction that sector policing was an additional official instrument of policing in South Africa, clear guidelines for the implementation of sector policing were given in a national instruction in 2009. This five-page document gave instructions to all station commanders on how to implement the strategy and how the community should get involved in sector policing. However, shortly after the 'official' implementation of sector policing in 2009, the SAPS national commissioner instructed the divisional commissioner, Visible Policing, in 2010 to review the status and implementation of sector policing as a policing approach. Not all police stations, especially police stations situated in rural areas, were able to implement sector policing to its full extent and in accordance with the standards set out in the former national instruction on sector policing, National Instruction 3/2009. In addition, it was further determined that a common understanding in respect of sector policing as a policing approach did not exist internally in the SAPS, as well as externally in the broader community. The review by the divisional commissioner, Visible Policing, regarding sector policing as a newly implemented policing approach dealt with the following:

> *identification of all implementation challenges;*
> *proposals on how to solve the identified challenges;*
> *identification of good practices and lessons learnt; and*
> *the roll-out to all police stations which have not yet*
> *implemented sector policing (Van Niekerk 2016, p. 23).*

Following the review process of the divisional commissioner, Visible Policing, the SAPS top management realised that Sector Policing National Instruction 3/2009 had to be amended. The amendment was made accordingly and was approved to enhance the operationalisation of sector policing in the SAPS. The amended version of the 2009 national instruction was absorbed in Sector Policing National Instruction 3/2013. This new instruction was approved on 8 July 2013. The aim was to enable all police stations to implement sector policing as a policing approach. An implementation plan was drafted in consultation with the provincial commissioners to guide the implementation and roll-out of the minimum criteria for sector policing implementation standards at police station level. On 13 January 2014, National Instruction 3/2013 on Sector Policing was rolled out to 1138 police stations for implementation. Minimum implementation criteria were determined in an effort to assist all police stations to implement sector policing successfully.

With these two approaches in mind [CP & SP] the concept of policing can be deemed as a social function in the community. The major aims are to "maintain law and order in society" (Berning and Masiloane 2011, p. 60). In accordance with the Constitution the police need to respect the rights of all people in the community in which they serve. The paramilitary style of policing is not compatible with a democratic South Africa as it is authoritative and repressive (Berning and Masiloane 2011, p. 60).

The community and sector policing initiatives were imported from the United Kingdom to South Africa after 1994. This was justified as part of the on-going modernisation and internationalisation of the SAPS and the re-entry of the problem oriented community based policing into the international market of police ideas. Initial documents by the SAPS abound with references to the UK-based "problem-oriented policing" (Dixon and Rauch 2004, p. 57).

As early as 1994, the then Minister of Safety and Security's draft policy document on change in the police mentioned community police officers with an intimate knowledge of a particular area and its problems as the main operational units of a lean and efficient police organisation. 2 years later, in 1996, the term sector policing made an appearance in the National Crime Prevention Strategy (NCPS) as an operational strategy aimed at maximising police deployment in areas affected by "intergroup conflicts". During the finalization stages of the Constitution, the National Crime Prevention Strategy (NCPS) was launched in May 1996. It was hailed as a holistic national strategy for reducing crime in South Africa and keeping South Africa safe. A team of multidisciplinary experts from government and civil society were tasked to develop a long-term strategy to assist government on addressing the root causes of crime in South Africa. The crime prevention strategy is a multidimensional approach that accommodated different important role-players and aimed to reduce crime (Bezuidenhout and Little 2012; Newham 2005). The NCPS subsequently defined sector policing as the rendering of police services as close as possible to the community. It entailed the division of geographical areas into smaller, more manageable sectors and the assignment of police members to these sectors on a full-time basis (Mahuntse 2007, p. 20; Maroga 2004, p. 1). It did not refer to minority groups and special policing strategies for minority groups. The community is the populace of South Africa in general. The new service-oriented approach adopted by the SAPS aligned itself rather with a vision-driven and not a rule-driven approach (Rauch and van der Spuy 2006, p. 55). Community cooperation (community policing and sector policing) was seen as a vital part of policing the country and all the different cultural and ethnic groups in South Africa (Roelofse 2007). It is the belief that by being more readily involved in the community, the problems faced by any community grouping could be recognized instantly and could be prioritized by the police. It is believed that closer ties with the community increase the level of accountability of the police because they are not only accountable to the individuals who are in command, but they are accountable to the community in which they work (Berning and Masiolane, 2011, p. 66). Greater interaction with the community as well as higher levels of accountability in the police was envisaged as an expected outcome of this democratisation process. Minority groups within smaller community groupings did not feature in the service approach agenda.

In addition to all the changes, the police, although being demilitarized after 1994, have recently been remilitarized in some ways. Specific reference to the reintroduction of the military ranking system is applicable. The former military ranking system was reintroduced in an effort to garner respect and discipline. Many feel that this reversion to the old ranks simply instils fear and not respect (National Planning Commission 2011, p. 355; Burger 2012). It is understood that the police have been reverting to a paramilitary type of force since the year 2000, but the official changing of ranks back to a militarised style only occurred in 2010. However, there is still the belief that the SAPS has continued to view itself more as a "force" than as a "service" (Police revert to military ranks in April 2010). The changing of the ranks was done in order to create more respect for the police and within the policing ranks. This argument has, however, been questioned as police brutality rates have increased since the military ranks have been reintroduced. A general understanding is that effective and efficient policing will harness more public respect than military ranks (National Planning Commission 2011, p. 355).

A general consensus has been gained in that, although the remilitarization was supposed to decrease crime rates, it has, in effect, increased police violence toward the public. The sentiment is shared by the National Planning Commission as well as Berning and Masiolane (2011). A report conducted by the Independent Complaints Directorate in 2011 found an increase of 800% in the torture rate committed by police against civilians since the remilitarization (National Planning Commission 2011, p. 356). Berning and Masiolane (2011) indicate that the rise in police shootings, police brutality, use of excess force, and a culture of questioning senior superior orders shows how South Africa once again now faces a militarized police. The brutality and "absence" of the police in the community has tarnished relationships with the community even more. Also many police officials are guilty of corrupt actions. Different factors contribute to this breakdown in the relationship between the community and the police and the intolerance communities show toward police officials. Factors that compound the poor relationships and probably contribute to the high number of police killings in SA include poor management, poor training, and incorrect application of police procedure during police patrols. But as South Africa has learned, race, ethnicity or status is hardly the only obstacles to good relations between the police and the people. Corruption, poverty and the continued use of deadly force, especially in the townships and informal settlements are fuelling distrust and division as well (Onishiaug 2016).

In addition the culture of intolerance and violence in SA has a significant effect on current community–police relationships. Soon the hope of a new way of engaging with crime and the community dissipated which resulted in governments' primary focus and resources being directed to the different bodies of the criminal

Table 18.1 Mid-year population estimates for South Africa by population group and sex (2017)

Population group	Male		Female		Total	
	Number	% Distribution of males	Number	% Distribution of females	Number	% distribution of total
African	22,311,400	80.8	2,334,500	80.8	45,656,400	80.8
Coloured	2,403,400	8.7	2,559,500	8.9	4,962,900	8.8
Indian/ Asian	719,300	2.6	689,800	2.4	1,409,100	2.5
White	2,186,500	7.9	2,307,100	8.0	4,493,500	8.0
Total	27,620,600	100.0	28,901,400	100.0	56,521,900	100.0

Source: Statistics South Africa (http://www.statssa.gov.za/)

justice system, and the term crime prevention has now become synonymous with policing (Newham 2005).

To understand the challenges with the implementing specialised crime prevention, crime control and specific policing strategies and philosophies in a diverse country like South Africa one needs to understand its geographical and racial profile (Table 18.1).

Policing Minorities in South Africa

The transformation of South Africa's police force, from the enforcer of white-minority rule to an institution controlled by the Black majority, has been troublesome and increasingly violent. Black policemen make up 76% of the SAPS, with White policemen account for about 11% of the police population. In the 2017 census, Blacks totalled 80.8% of South Africa's population and whites 8.0%. Police in South Africa are known for their violent hard handed approach. However, international news often refers to the United States as a racist society where White police officers treat Black Americans differently and with more impunity. Be it as it may, members of SAPS also act with impunity. The difference however is that SAPS tend to treat everyone in society with impunity should they need to act against someone. Black on Black violence is very common in South Africa especially with regard to illegal immigrants. Xenophobia is rife in South Africa and in some instances police do not attend to matters pertaining to a Black immigrant on the same level as a Black local SA citizen. In addition some police turn a blind eye when immigrants are harassed (Bekker 2015, p. 233; http://www.statssa.gov.za/).

Currently the SAPS staff profile mirrors a population that is 80.8% Black. With this in mind one should think that police-community relationships will be improved. However, relations remain particularly fraught between the police and Black communities in different areas of South Africa. Black on Black violence is very common and Black police officers are regularly killed by Black perpetrators. This peculiar situation and the fact that violent crimes are increasing leave no room for fancy "sensitive" policing strategies for minorities. During the Apartheid era one could argue that the White minority police protected the minority White population. However I find it difficult to explain why Black on Black, especially Black police officers on Black community members is so rife in the country (Onishiaug 2016). It is also believed that the police use more force in the poor traditionally Black areas toward Black citizens compared to affluent Black and White community members (Onishiaug 2016). Reports like this stands against Section 9(1) of the Constitution of the Republic of South Africa, 1996 which declares that everyone is equal before the law and has the right to equal protection and benefit of the law.

Challenges to Minority Groups in South Africa

Currently the police deem everyone equal before the law. Therefore no clear "minority policing guidelines" and only broad hazy policies regarding this matter are available. The Constitution of our country guarantees every person the right to life and the right to security, which includes among other things, the right to be free from all forms of violence from either public or private sources. The Constitution further guarantees that adequate protection of such rights is fundamental to the well-being, social and economic development of every person. South Africa accommodates a population of more than 56 million people and it harbours 11 official languages and a myriad of different cultures, ethnic groups (each with a preconceived perception of each other) and customs that demand special attention in the policing task. However the "holistic blanket" policing approach in South Africa does not accommodate for these needs.

Nevertheless certain minority groups need to be identified as they are in need of special policing initiatives. Racist and xenophobic violence and sentiment are rising across the world. Cutting across religious and cultural divides, racism and xenophobia threaten communities of ethnic (e.g. Venda) or national minorities (e.g. White Afrikaner people), including immigrants (e.g. Individuals seen derogatively referred to as "Shangaan"), general citizens (e.g. Farmers), long-time residents (e.g. Black local person) mistakenly regarded as a "makwerekwere" (derogative term to refer to an illegal immigrants) and newcomers (e.g. individuals from across our borders). Immigrants, Farmers, White Afrikaans speaking citizens and refugees are currently among the most vulnerable groups in South Africa regarding Xenophobia and therefore need specialised policing strategies.

Since the replacement of the Apartheid regime by a democratic government in South Africa, the dominant economic power on the continent has become an attractive destination for millions of (un)documented migrants from the continent. The downfall of neighbouring Zimbabwe especially increased (un)documented migration to South Africa. Countless assaults against foreign Africans show that a climate of Xenophobia has been penetrating the South African society since the end of Apartheid. Instead of protecting illegal immigrants many South African politicians, police members and Black communities as well as the media rather intensify the atmosphere of Xenophobia and Black on Black violence. Foreign Africans are also used as scapegoats for the problems of the South African society (e.g. crime, scarce job opportunities etc.). Thus African migrants are often generally associated with criminal activities, and not infrequently politicians underline that migrants are a drain on scarce public resources. Often during xenophobic attacks the police stand neutral between opposing parties (Bekker 2015, p. 231). So instead of special minority policing strategies the minority is victimised and sometimes brutalised by the police. One example to illustrate this non care attitude is the case of Mido Macia. On 12 November 2015 the world saw the sentencing of eight former police officers as they were convicted of the murder of 27-year-old Mido Macia, a Mozambican taxi driver, and sentenced to 15 years imprisonment. Macia had been arrested for an alleged traffic violation and had died 3 h after being detained in February 2013. This was after being handcuffed to and dragged behind a police vehicle for 200 meters in Daveyton, East of Johannesburg and assaulted within the holding cell. Macia had suffered severe head injuries and internal bleeding. The entire incident was recorded on a cell phone and went viral. During the hearing, the eight police officials showed little to no remorse for their brutal actions against the foreign national (Hartleb 2015).

To conclude, the once dominant White minority group and especially White farmers are now deemed a very sensitive minority group with very special policing needs. Farmers are being killed with impunity in South Africa. Murders on farms or farm killings have come to haunt the rural communities of South Africa. They arouse strong emotions in White South Africans, regardless of what they believe to be the causes of this type of violence. According to Geldenhuys (2010, p. 9), most people know what is meant by a farm attack and that several crimes that belong to the different serious crime categories (assault, robbery, rape and murder) are usually committed during a farm attack.

According to the South African Police Service National Operational Coordinating Committee (NOCOC):

"Attacks on farms and smallholdings refer to acts aimed at the person of residents, workers and visitors to farms and smallholdings, whether with the intent to murder, rape, rob or inflict bodily harm. All actions aimed at disrupting farming activities as a commercial concern, whether for motives related to ideology, labour disputes, land issues, revenge, grievances, racist concerns or intimidation, should be included" (Criminal Justice Monitor 2003).

Farm attacks and especially the ruthless murdering of farmers, their family members and farm labourers, are somewhat unique to South Africa (Bezuidenhout 2011, p. 204). Although these attacks occur globally, farm attacks on South African soil are estimated to be 700% higher than in any other country in the world (Bezuidenhout 2011, p. 204; Mistry 2003, p. 7). In the same vein, Jacobs (2008) reports that although farmers from different racial groups fall victim to farm attacks, White farmers stand a substantially higher risk to become a victim of an attack. In addition, the chances of a farmer being murdered on a farm in South Africa are anything between four to eight times higher than the average murder rate risk for the general population. It is believed that it is more dangerous to be a farmer in South Africa than a policeman.

Most farm attacks leave a trail of blood, death and destruction. Very often these attacks are accompanied by extreme violence and torture (gratuitous violence), similar to home invasions. It seems as if perpetrators not only focus on killing the victim, but also on inflicting pain and bringing about suffering. Most farm attacks are precisely executed and thoroughly planned (Bezuidenhout 2011, p. 204; Bezuidenhout 2013; Geldenhuys 2010, p. 10; Strydom and Schutte 2005, p. 117–123). The difference with regards to home invasions in a city is that often during attacks on farms, criminals have more time to commit the crime. Since farms are usually more isolated, the perpetrators have time and know no one will hear the agony during the torture and brutality. In addition, many farmers hunt on their farms so a gunshot usually does not attract attention. There are no reliable data on farm attacks in South Africa but several reasons have been put forward for farm murders and farm attacks, such as revenge, retaliation, hatred, negative working relationships, poor wages, poverty, unemployment, hardship and easy access to a "big" score (Bezuidenhout 2011, p. 204). On most farms the perpetrators will get money, vehicles, food, alcohol and high-tech electronic equipment as well as firearms. A farm is therefore a profitable target for robbery. Illegal immigrants who are flocking to South Africa for a better life have also been implicated in several farm attacks. In addition, racism and xenophobia have also been put forward as reasons for farm attack (Bezuidenhout 2011, p. 204; Geldenhuys 2010, p. 11; Mistry 2003, p. 7; Strydom and Schutte 2005, p. 117–123; Vena 2010). According to the Institute for Contemporary History (1998, p. 4), land claims and racism are regarded to be the main motives for farm attacks. The actual figures of farm attacks in South Africa are far from clear or complete (Vena 2010) since the SAPS stopped releasing figures on farm attacks and murders in 2007. Surely this group should be deemed a minority with very special policing needs. Only with the necessary political will could farmers and illegal immigrants see specialised policing priorities for these minority groups? Smaller Black Ethnic groups like the Venda group also need specialised policing. The Venda group is mainly situated to the far Northern area in South Africa; very close to Zimbabwe. They are often referred to as "Shangaans" and regularly bear the brunt of scapegoating and victimisation by other South African Black ethnic groups. Homeless street dwellers and street children surely also qualify as a minority group that needs specialised policing intervention.

Another vulnerable minority group who needs specialised policing is the LGBTQI-community in society otherwise known as the lesbian, gay, bisexual, transgender, queer and inter-gender community. This minority is also currently not privy to specialised policing in South Africa. Many members of this minority grouping are regularly the victims of hate crimes which justify special policing. Although special legislation is in place in SA to protect members of this population special policing units with specific training are not in place to attend to policing matters related to this group. During the writing of this chapter the author requested the police to comment on this matter. Lasese (2018) informed the author that

> "The Division Visible Policing in the South African Police Service is currently developing a Standard Operating Procedure dealing with the arrest and detention of members of the LGBTQI community involved in crime, which will be read with Standing Order (General) 341 (Arrest and the treatment of an arrested person until such person is handed over to the

community service centre commander) and Standing Order (General) 361 (Handling of persons in the custody of the Service from their arrival at the police station). As far as illegal immigrants are concerned they are currently dealt with in terms of Standard Operating Procedure 2 of 2018 (Arrest and detention of illegal foreigners) and the Immigration Act, 2002 (Act No. 13 of 2002)".

From this the author deduced that no specific policing plan and dedicated policing team will be introduced to exclusively police minority groups in general and specifically the more vulnerable groups such as the LGBTQI community.

The challenge regarding the policing of minority groups are compounded by prejudice and stereotypes which often leads to hate crimes. These crimes are committed by persons that are motivated by that person's prejudice, bias or intolerance towards a victim because of one or more of the following characteristics or perceived characteristics of the victim: race, gender, sex (including intersex), ethnic or social origin, colour, sexual orientation, religion, belief, culture, language, birth, disability, HIV status, nationality, gender identity, albinism as well as occupation or trade (Booyens and Bezuidenhout 2018, p. 65). Police officers are also human and many hold the same prejudices as the general community. This calls for dedicated, specialised police teams with very specific training and guidelines to police minority groups in South Africa.

Conclusion

The majority of citizens can concur that South Africa is a violent high-risk country where crime flourishes. The murder rate in South Africa is of grave concern, as it is five times higher than the global average. The country has been in the global top 10 for its high homicide rate for all but 2 years since 2000. In addition to the challenges to police the soaring violent crime rate certain groups need special policing strategies in South Africa. Unfortunately the SAPS deem everyone equal before the law and police everyone in the same manner. In some cases certain groups are even discriminated against by the police. In addition Black on Black violence is rife and in some instances police participate or turn a blind eye when Black citizens attack Black illegal immigrants from neighbouring countries. The "neutral" policing attitude that is guided by the Constitution and the Police Act needs to be revisited as several minority groups in South Africa are in need of exclusive and dedicated police teams, special prioritised policing methods, guidelines and training to address this void in the current policing system in South Africa.

References

Bekker, S. (2015). Violent xenophobic episodes in South Africa, 2008 and 2015. AHMR, Vol.1 No3, September-December, Special Issue.
Berning, J., & Masiloane, D. (2011). Police militarisation: Is South Africa disproving or failing to learn from police history? *Acta Criminologica, 24*(3), 60–69.

Bezuidenhout, C. (2011). Sector policing in South Africa—Case closed—Or not? Pakistan Journal of Criminology, 3(2) & (3), April–July, 11–25.

Bezuidenhout, C. (2013). Oorsig van plaasaanvalle in Suid Afrika en die potensiële uitwerking daarvan op die samelewing. [Overview of farm attacks in South Africa and the potential influence thereof on society] Part 3: Studies regarding farm attacks, pp. 437–459. In D. Hermann, C. van Zyl, & I. Nieuwoudt (Eds.), Treurgrond: Die realiteit van plaasaanvalle, 1990–2012. Pretoria: Kraal Publishers.

Bezuidenhout, C. (2015). Intriguing paradox: The inability to keep South Africa safe and the successful hosting of mega global sporting events. In J. F. Albrecht, M. C. Dow, D. Plecas, & D. K. Das (Eds.), Policing major events: Perspectives from around the world. Boca Raton: USA Taylor and Francis Group (CRC Press).

Bezuidenhout, C. (2017). Using police reserves to support the South African Police Service. In J. F. Albrecht (Ed.), Police reserves and volunteers: Enhancing organizational effectiveness and public trust. Boca Raton: USA Taylor and Francis Group (CRC Press).

Bezuidenhout, C., & Little, K. (2012). Juvenile justice in South Africa: Challenges and existing processes. In P. C. Kratcoski (Ed.), Juvenile justice administration. Boca Raton: CRC Press (Taylor & Francis Group).

Booyens, K., & Bezuidenhout, C. (2018). The nature and extent of child and youth misbehaviour in South Africa (4th). (Chapter 3, pp. 37–79). In C. Bezuidenhout (Ed.), Child and youth misbehaviour in South Africa: A holistic approach. Pretoria: Van Schaik.

Brewer, J. D. (1994). Black and blue. New York: Oxford University Press.

Burger, J. (2012). To what extent has the South African police service become militarised? Available: https://www.issafrica.org/iss-today/to-what-extent-has-the-south-african-police-service-become-militarised. Accessed 29 March 2018.

Criminal Justice Monitor. (2003, 31 July). Report of the Committee of Inquiry into farm attacks. SAPS.

De Vries, I. D. (2008). Strategic issues in the South African Police Service (SAPS) in the first decade of democracy. Acta Criminologica, 21(2), 125–138.

Dippenaar, M. D. (1988). SA police commemorative album 1913–1988 (1st ed.). South Africa: Promedia Publications.

Dixon, B., & Rauch, J. (2004). Sector policing: Origins and prospects. Pretoria: Institute for Security Studies.

Geldenhuys, K. (2010). SA farms = War zones? (Part 1). Servamus Safety and Security magazine, 103(4), 8–13.

Govender, D. (2010). Policing a changing society in South Africa: Challenges for the police officer. Acta Criminologica, 2(1), 69–83.

Hartleb, T. (2015). Mido Macia's killers to be sentenced – News24. Available: https://www.news24.com/SouthAfrica/News/Mido-Macias-killers-to-be-sentenced-20150922. Accessed 29 March 2018).

Hornberger, J. (2013). From general to commissioner to general – On the popular state of policing in South Africa. Law & Social Enquiry, 38(3), 598–614.

Institute for Contemporary History. (1998). Violent attacks on farmers in South Africa 3/98. Bloemfontein: University of the Free State.

Lasese, P.R. (2018). Electronic mail communication with major General P.R. Lesese, 9 July 2018. [Head: Governance, Policy and Legislation Management; Legal and Policy Services; South African Police Service].

Mahuntse, N.N. (2007). Sector policing in the Johannesburg central Police Station area. Pretoria: Tshwane University of Technology. (MA Dissertation).

Maroga, M. (2004). Sector Policing: What are the challenges? Research report written for the Centre for the Study of Violence and Reconciliation.

Mistry, D. (2003). Ploughing in resources. Investigation of farm attacks. SA Crime Quarterly ISS No 6 December 2003 pp. 7–12.

National Planning Commission. (2011). National development plan vision for 2030. Available: http://www.npconline.co.za. Accessed 29 March 2018.

Newham, G. (2005). A decade of crime prevention in South Africa: From a national strategy to a local challenge. Research report written for the Centre for the Study of Violence and Reconciliation. www.csvr.org.za.

Official South Africa Yearbook. (1993). Cape Town: CTP book printers (on behalf of the Government Printer).

Onishiaug, N. 2016. Police in South Africa struggle to gain trust after apartheid. 13 (August 2016 – The New York Times). Available.

Police revert to military ranks from April. (2010). defenceWeb, 26 February. Available: http://www.defenceweb.co.za/index.php?option=com_content&view=article&id=6889:222&catid=3:Civil%20Security&Itemid=113. Accessed 29 March 2018.

Potgieter, D. J. (Ed.). (1974). *Standard encyclopaedia of Southern Africa* (Vol. 8). Cape Town: Nasou.

Rauch, J. (2001). *Police reform and South Africa's transition*. Available: http://www.csvr.org.za. Accessed 29 March 2018.

Rauch, J. & van der Spuy, E. (2006). Police reform in post-conflict Africa: A review. Available: http://www.idasa.org. Accessed 29 March 2018.

Roelofse, C. J. (2007). *The challenges of community policing: A management perspective*. Durban: LexisNexis.

SAPS Training Division. (2004). *Manage the implementation of sector policing*. Pretoria: SAPS.

South Africa Yearbook. (1995). Cape Town: CTP Book Printers (on behalf of the Government Printer).

South African Police Services (SAPS). (2012). Available: http://www.sahistory.org.za/organisations/south-african-police-sap. Accessed 29 March 2018.

Strydom, H., & Schutte, S. C. (2005). A theoretical perspective on farm attacks in the South African farming community. *Acta Criminologica: Southern African Journal of Criminology, 18*(1), 115–125.

Van Niekerk. (2016). An investigation into the perceptions of police officials regarding the implementation of sector policing in Limpopo province. Pretoria: University of Pretoria. (MA Dissertation).

Vena, V. (2010). Anatomy of a farm murder JOHANNESBURG, SOUTH AFRICA – 8 April 2010. Source: Mail & Guardian Online. Web Address: http://www.mg.co.za/article/2010-04-08-anatomy-of-a-farm-murder.

Wilson, D., Ashton, J., & Sharp, D. (2001). *What everyone in Britain should know about the police*. London: Blackstone Press.

Part V
Final Thoughts/Epilogue

Chapter 19
Final Thoughts – Examining Policing Options to Enhance Transparency and Community Trust

James F. Albrecht

Epilogue and Discussion

As the epilogue for this insightful and thought-provoking work, I would like to discuss my observations as both a former police practitioner and an open-minded criminal justice researcher as it relates to police and community, specifically minority group, relations and interactions. As a police administrator who has worked both locally, in New York City, and internationally, for the United Nations and European Union as an international police official, I am saddened at the negative criticism that appears to overwhelm law enforcement practitioners. As a whole, we sincerely view ourselves as committed to the rule of law in search of a safer and more comfortable environment for our constituents and the public-at-large. Most police officers select this challenging profession as a means to help others and are truly altruistically oriented. Yet, there has been consistent criticism, particularly from under-represented groups, that extol that police officers are inherently bad individuals, often acting with racist or discriminatory intentions, that are mere pawns of the controlling and self-serving elite.

The condemnation of police professionals over the last few decades, most recently fueled by rather over-sensationalized and often inaccurate social media accounts, has left many law enforcement officers to question their innate benevolent nature, with many opting to unfortunately strive more for career survival over public service. This is obviously unfortunate, as this movement has caused many to alter their personal ideologies in contradiction to their intrinsic beliefs.

On the other hand, my perspective as a criminal justice researcher, and sociologist at heart, has caused me to concede that there is a major disconnect in today's society that critically needs to be acknowledged and effectively addressed. Certain sections of society, both in western cultures and globally, convey such a distrust and

J. F. Albrecht (✉)
Department of Criminal Justice and Homeland Security, Pace University,
New York, NY, USA

© Springer Nature Switzerland AG 2019
J. F. Albrecht et al. (eds.), *Policing and Minority Communities*,
https://doi.org/10.1007/978-3-030-19182-5_19

dismay for the police that are clearly unacceptable in the contemporary world. Unfortunately, this mistrust commonly appears to afflict under-represented groups. In the United States, these complaints often originate in the African-American, Black, Hispanic, Native American and Muslim communities. In Europe, these voices come from immigrant and other minority groups. In the Middle East, religious sects, in Africa, tribal groups, and in Asia, ethnic minorities, routinely coincide with the discontent conveyed in government and the criminal justice system. There is also a common overlap between these accusations and socio-economic disadvantage that appears to fuel the stance that local governance has been designed as a means to hamper accomplishment, personal success and general contentment of those in minority groups.

Even with the most impressive crime reduction and counter-terrorism accomplishments, these achievements can be said to be for naught if they do not coincide with high, if not total, public trust and confidence. As Gary Cordner has noted in the book *Preface*, a totalitarian state can be blessed with low crime rates, but this may coincide with diminished trust and satisfaction in regional authorities and local government officials. In reality, without public support and acclaim, can anyone truly assert to be an effective and successful leader? When one describes a police officer, one can paint many roles, but the most relevant is one as a public servant. But what measures can be taken to ensure that police officers actually do serve the public, and actually make certain that all factions of the communities are properly heard and acknowledged? This appears to be the paramount challenge and, one could say, quagmire that plagues police administrators in the contemporary era. The many authors of this book have outlined many options for enhancing organizational transparency and improving public confidence in the law enforcement profession. Let's now examine some of these proposals.

The book is divided into sections that highlight the multi-faceted issues inherent in policing minority communities, including the many sensitive and controversial factors, and contrasts the North American and global perspectives. The first section starts with Chap. 1 by Albrecht, which underscores the foundations of the law enforcement profession as proposed by the esteemed Sir Robert Peel and contrasts the goal of direct public involvement in police practice and prioritization with public perceptions of the police from a global perspective. Generally speaking, the more corrupt and abusive the police are perceived, the less trust and confidence the community will convey in them. Chapter 2 by Stanislas and Sadique critically examine the role that faith and religion issues play in police training. They have discovered that these issues play limited roles in most law enforcement jurisdictions, particularly those in English speaking nations, which is not surprising given the secular nature of many democratic societies. However, there has been considerable effort in raising religious considerations within police cultural sensitivity training. Aarset and Glomseth in Chap. 3 examine the overwhelming challenges faced by today's police administrators, analyze leadership concepts in policing, and conclude with recommendations to enhance organizational efficacy and efficiency. Albrecht in Chap. 4 continues with an overview of critical criminology, the proposed theory that an isolated elitist class devises law, policy and criminal justice practices that are designed to hinder under-represented groups across society. The 'left realism' ideology, a sub-theory of critical criminology, which advocates enhanced involvement of the public and the crime victim in law enforcement and criminal justice policies and practices, is proposed as an option to re-engage all facets of the population into prioritizing government and police actions.

The second section of the book examines sensitive and controversial aspects of the dynamic between police and community. Chapter 5 by Tobin examines the challenges posed by the all-too-common interaction of the police with the mentally ill in the United States and outlines the measures that the New York City Police Department, in collaboration with other public and non-governmental organizations, have implemented in order to more effectively direct the mentally ill to the appropriate services and to better de-escalate the interaction between the two parties. Can in Chap. 6 examines public perceptions of police fairness and legality based on race, ethnicity and other democratic variables by examining these interactions in two American jurisdictions. Arslan in Chap. 7 moves on to an even more controversial topic in posing the need for more thorough analyses of police-involved shootings and outlining preliminary findings of the evaluation of the available American data from 2000 through 2017. Chapter 8, by Can and Frantzen, continues with an insightful study on public perceptions of police actions related to search and seizure in the United States by examining racial and regional differences.

North American perspectives are further examined in the next section, with Chap. 9 by Parent and Parent, comprehensively evaluating the measures that the police in Canada have undertaken to better serve all factions of the population, with specific attention paid to the LGBT and First Nations (i.e. indigenous or Native American) communities. Chapter 10, by Jacobs, Seidler, Middleton, Mullen and Whitaker, outlines the highly regarded *Project Illumination*, that impressively swayed public opinion in Charleston, in the American state of South Carolina, to dramatically increase public perceptions of the police and which permitted direct community input into the development of agency policies and priorities. Specific attention was made to ensure that every facet of the population was heard and permitted to provide critical input and insight. Morin and Morin, in Chap. 11, outline the measures that are taken to address the concerns of Native Americans (i.e. indigenous populations) in the United States, a sector that has traditionally been plagued by socio-economical challenges throughout American history. In Chap. 12, Hanser and Moran address the sensational issue of migration control along the United States and Mexican border. Border and migration control are both a federal and a local issue in America, but initiatives are often complicated as these resources do not necessarily act in unison and are often accompanied by jurisdictional conflicts, particularly as it relates to the prioritization of strategies. The lessons learned from the American experience may provide guidance to other global leaders who face similar circumstances and criticism.

The final section of the book moves from North America to provide a more global perspective of the challenges involved in providing professional and respected police services to all aspects of the population. Chapter 13, by Sanchez and Fahredin, outline the efforts made by the international community and local actors to create a harmonious environment and develop a functional criminal justice sector following inter-ethnic conflict and violence in the Kosovo region of Serbia in the southern area of former Yugoslavia. In Chap. 14, den Heyer moves to the other end of the planet to describe the successful efforts made to deploy cultural liaison officers within the New Zealand Police. Arslan in Chap. 15 notes the challenges in maintaining an effective and respected policing mechanism in Turkey following a coup attempt in 2016, particularly as the government alleges that many police officials took part or supported the attempt to overthrow the still existent political hierarchy. The Ottoman Empire in Turkey was the true crossroads between west and east, and the many ethnic and religious groups present, particularly the Kurds in eastern Turkey, continue to be plagued by negatively perceived governmental actions. Aremu and Stanislas in Chap. 16 evaluate the policing strategies in Nigeria within the context of tribal differences and political gerrymandering. Chapter 17 by den Heyer takes a close look at community policing attempts within New Zealand as it relates to the indigenous population, which statistically appears to be disproportionally targeted by police action and which is more likely to convey distrust in local law enforcement officials. Finally, Bezuidenhout in Chap. 18 examines policing policy and practice within the multi-cultural and multi-tribal environment in South Africa.

Overall, common themes do appear throughout this book. It should be obvious that all regions of the globe have generally been affected by mistrust in the police, and this dissatisfaction appears to be concentrated within minority and under-represented groups. Conflict, violence and allegations of over-policing targeting minority communities appear to be common sources of complaint and result in repeat calls for reform and action. There is a broad call for transparency across government agencies and this book has attempted to analyze and propose recommendations to address these concerns within the criminal justice and policing sectors. Extensive efforts must be made to enhance the perceived legitimacy of the police and to increase public confidence and trust in this critical aspect of the democratic process. Without true rule of law, there is no true democracy. And social equality across all sectors of the population is a key factor in this regard.

The goal of this book has been to provide insight and recommendation to those interested in the critical fields of criminal justice, criminology and sociology, particularly as it relates to providing policing services to minority communities across the globe. It is hoped that this objective has been achieved through this enlightening collection of research, reflection and introspection.

Index

© Springer Nature Switzerland AG 2019   325
J. F. Albrecht et al. (eds.), *Policing and Minority Communities*,
https://doi.org/10.1007/978-3-030-19182-5

Printed in Great Britain
by Amazon